RUSSIA
AFTER THE GLOBAL
ECONOMIC CRISIS

RUSSIA
AFTER THE GLOBAL
ECONOMIC CRISIS

Anders Åslund, Sergei Guriev, and Andrew C. Kuchins, editors

PETERSON INSTITUTE FOR INTERNATIONAL ECONOMICS
CENTER FOR STRATEGIC AND INTERNATIONAL STUDIES
NEW ECONOMIC SCHOOL
Washington, DC
June 2010

PETER G. PETERSON INSTITUTE
FOR INTERNATIONAL ECONOMICS
1750 Massachusetts Avenue, NW
Washington, DC 20036-1903
(202) 328-9000   FAX: (202) 659-3225
www.piie.com

C. Fred Bergsten, *Director*
Edward A. Tureen, *Director of Publications,*
  Marketing, and Web Development

CENTER FOR STRATEGIC
AND INTERNATIONAL STUDIES
1800 K Street, NW
Washington, DC 20006
(202) 887-0200   FAX: (202) 775-3199
www.csis.org

John J. Hamre, *President and CEO*
James Dunton, *Director of Publications*

NEW ECONOMIC SCHOOL
Suite 1721
Nakhimovskii Prospekt 47
117418, Moscow, Russia
+7 (495) 956-95-08   FAX: +7 (499) 129-3722
www.nes.ru

Sergei Guriev, *Rector*

Typesetting by Susann Luetjen
Printing by Edwards Brothers, Inc.
Cover photos: © Marek Slusarczyk and
Savvamor—Fotolia

For reprints/permission to photocopy please
contact the APS customer service department
at Copyright Clearance Center, Inc., 222
Rosewood Drive, Danvers, MA 01923; or
email requests to: info@copyright.com

Printed in the United States of America

12 11 10   5 4 3 2

Library of Congress Cataloging-in-
Publication Data

Russia after the global economic crisis /
Anders Åslund, Sergei Guriev, and Andrew
Kuchins, editors.
   p. cm.
   Includes index.
   ISBN 978-0-88132-497-6
   1.   Russia   (Federation)—Economic
conditions—21st   century.   2.   Russia
(Federation)—Economic   policy—21st
century.   3.   Financial   crises—Russia
(Federation)   4.   Corruption—Russia
(Federation)   5.   Russia   (Federation)—
Economic policy—21st century. 6. Russia
(Federation)—Foreign economic relations.
I. Åslund, Anders, 1952- II. Guriev, S. M.
III. Kuchins, Andrew. IV. Peterson Institute
for International Economics. V. Center
for Strategic and International Studies
(Washington, D.C.)
   HC340.12.R8277 2010
   330.947—dc22

                                    2010014253

Contents

Preface

The Russian roller coaster continues. After a decade of 7 percent annual growth, Russia suddenly faced a plunge of 8 percent of its economic output in 2009. This was quite a blow for a proud emerging economic power. Some commentators even suggested that the "R" was falling out of BRIC (Brazil, Russia, India, and China), the group of largest emerging economies with high economic growth. Russia is unlikely to face significant financial problems in the foreseeable future, but in the long term a large number of structural problems have accumulated, from corruption to demographic changes, many of which this volume discusses.

When Barack Obama became president in January 2009, he launched a policy of "resetting" US-Russia relations. It is still early to pass a judgment on the success of this new policy, but US-Russia relations have certainly improved and intensified. A bilateral commission has been established with 16 working groups, and bilateral relations have once again widened and deepened. Presidents Obama and Dmitri Medvedev have established a close personal relationship. Signing the new START treaty on April 8 in Prague is the most tangible success, but important cooperation has also developed in transit of supplies to US forces in Afghanistan and in dealing with Iran's nuclear program. Less discussed in public, but of perhaps greater importance for the bilateral relationship, is the maintenance of peace in Georgia. The key question in foreign economic policy is whether Russia will finally join the World Trade Organization. The conclusion of this volume is that it should and that it could gain very substantially from accession.

The statement has been made many times before, but after the global economic crisis Russia once again stands at a crossroads. One trajectory is the current "inertia scenario" with a severe "energy curse" leading to continued pervasive corruption, little diversification or innovation, and low economic growth. The alternative is renewed market reform and much higher economic growth. Obviously, this is a key political choice, but to a considerable extent it may be determined by the world oil price: The higher the oil price, the less the incentive for the Russian leadership to carry out reforms, and ironically the lower Russia's long-term economic growth is likely to be.

Four years ago, the Center for Strategic and International Studies (CSIS) and the Peterson Institute for International Economics (PIIE) teamed up on the China Balance Sheet project to provide a basis for sound and sensible judgments about China. Two years ago, we did the same for Russia in the Russia Balance Sheet project. We believe that US policies toward Russia must rest, first and foremost, on a firm and factual analytical footing. The Russia Balance Sheet project's primary purpose is to provide comprehensive, balanced, and accurate information on all key aspects of Russia's developments and their implications for the United States and other nations. The first book in this project, *The Russia Balance Sheet*, coauthored by Anders Åslund and Andrew C. Kuchins with input from many contributing authors, was published in April 2009. It tried to provide an overview of Russia's current dilemma as a new administration entered the White House, offering a clear Washington outlook and concluding what Washington could and should do.

This second volume has been written in the aftermath of the global economic and financial crisis and has been a full-fledged US-Russian cooperative project, as the eminent New Economic School (NES) in Moscow has become a partner with PIIE and CSIS. This book includes contributions from leading American and Russian experts on their topics of investigation. Unlike the first book, this is an edited volume providing more insights into Russia's current economic and foreign policy dilemma.

The book is only part of the activities of the Russia Balance Sheet project. The pinnacle was President Obama's speech at the NES in Moscow on July 7, 2009. In Washington, PIIE and CSIS have had the honor of cohosting Minister of Finance and Deputy Prime Minister Alexei Kudrin and First Deputy Prime Minister Igor Shuvalov. The book will be discussed at the Russia Balance Sheet session at the St. Petersburg International Economic Forum in June 2010. The NES organized a workshop for the book in Moscow in November 2009, and CSIS and PIIE cohosted a large number of seminars during 2009 primarily devoted to discussing the chapters in the book.

This project has been codirected by Anders Åslund, senior fellow at PIIE, Andrew C. Kuchins, director and senior fellow of the Russia and Eurasia Program at CSIS, and Sergei Guriev, Morgan Stanley Professor of Economics at and rector of NES.

At CSIS, thanks go to Amy Beavin and Heidi Hoogerbeets for their organizational and research assistance. At PIIE, gratitude is due to Anna Borshchevskaya for research assistance, to Edward Tureen as director of publications, in particular to Madona Devasahayam for excellent copy-editing, and to Susann Luetjen for production coordination.

We are especially grateful to the supporters of the Russia Balance Sheet Project: Caterpillar, Chevron, Coca-Cola, ExxonMobil, Microsoft, PepsiCo, and Procter & Gamble. We also thank Peter Aven, who has supported the participation of the NES in the project.

John J. Hamre, President and CEO
Center for Strategic and
International Studies

C. Fred Bergsten, Director
Peterson Institute for
International Economics

April 2010

Foreword

The global economic and financial crisis of 2007–09 caused more damage to the Russian economy than to any other G-20 country. Russia's GDP shrank by 8 percent in 2009, while the stock index fell 80 percent from its peak. Until 2008, Russia was hailed as an economic miracle, enjoying rapid GDP growth, macroeconomic stability, and an unprecedented rise in real disposable income (more than 10 percent per annum on average over eight years). Huge oil revenues and capital inflows drove Russia's impressive growth. The oil and gas sector's share of the country's GDP, budget revenues, and exports grew with the rise in oil and gas prices.

Since the global crisis hit, however, Russia has seen some of its largest companies go bankrupt, has wasted one-third of its foreign currency reserves, and is suffering from a surge in unemployment. The Russian economy crumbled in 2008–09 for obvious reasons: A sharp decline in the price of oil and other commodities as well as capital outflows ($131 billion in the fourth quarter of 2008 alone) put the economy in a tailspin. Corporate debt equaled more than 25 percent of GDP by the time the global crisis broke, while the share of foreign borrowing in banks' liabilities reached 20 percent.

The crisis not only hurt Russia's economy but also uncovered some acute problems facing the country, which, if left unresolved, will hinder sustainable growth in the future. Even without a global crisis, these problems would have inevitably led to an economic collapse (or at least a significant slowdown) by the end of the decade. Many Russian economists note that a slowdown in some important sectors began well before the crisis, and the causes were purely domestic, having nothing to do with the global environment. In particular, growth in the construction sector com-

pletely ceased by the end of 2007, and manufacturing growth also deceler-
ated. Capital investments began to decline rapidly in 2008. The existence
of a bubble in sectors such as construction and retail (which account for
25 percent of the labor force) is proved by the high share of borrowed
funds in these sectors, which had reached 80 percent by 2008. Most of this
borrowing was foreign.

The Russian economy has been facing acute problems for the past decade. The spectacular growth of 1999–2007 masked but did not eliminate
them. These concerns include:

- Russia's energy efficiency is the lowest in the world, lagging far behind
developed countries. One of the main reasons is cross-subsidization
within and between sectors, which has declined from 5 to 3 percent of
GDP but is still unjustifiably high.

- Labor productivity is low, amounting to 36 percent of the US level and
roughly 72 percent of China's.

- The official share of small and medium-sized enterprises in GDP has
remained flat in recent years, at 17 percent, demonstrating the illiberal
character of the Russian economy. Corruption is largely a natural consequence of a lack of economic freedom and the state's excessive influence on business.

- The burden of social spending, especially pensions, on the budget is
excessive, and consolidated budget spending is exceptionally high.
Public spending, after declining in 2004–06, started to grow again in
2007 and reached 41 percent of GDP in 2009. Given Russia's level of
development, sustainable growth is hardly possible with such high
spending. Russia still does not have a private pension system: Only
2 percent of Russians have transferred part of their pensions to non-
state funds.

- The incompetency of the bureaucracy has been "compensated for" by
an increase in the number of government officials, by at least 25 percent since 2000. Overall, 16 percent of Russia's population is employed
in the public sector.

Some steps taken by the government undoubtedly contributed to the
economic success of 2000–2007. They included the tax reform of 2001 and
various measures aimed at strengthening the banking system, which was
rebuilt virtually from scratch after the financial crisis of 1998. The corporate
loan portfolio grew by an average rate of 37 percent per annum between
2000 and 2009, while the average growth rate of the retail loan portfolio
was 63 percent per annum. Along with banks, many private companies
have also undergone fundamental changes, improving their transparency,
corporate culture, and efficiency.

These new types of businesses, along with a functioning banking system and macroeconomic stability, give some hope for sustained economic growth. But the country's unresolved economic problems could jeopardize these hopes. Moreover, these are not problems that can be tackled individually; the entire paradigm must be changed from "survival" (in times of crisis) to growth and not "precrisis stability and consumption."

The steady, high growth of real disposable income gave rise to inflated expectations that it would continue for a long time, which was bolstered by official statements and social welfare policy with frequent increases in pensions and wages of public-sector employees. The cult of consumption resulted in twofold decline in savings as a share of an average household's annual income from 2000 to 2008. Wage growth overtook productivity growth. Whereas the gap in productivity between the United States and Russia remained stable, the latter's wage and real disposable income growth was among the highest in the world. The share of consumption in Russia's GDP (66 percent) approximates that in developed countries (67 percent in the United Kingdom and 71 percent in the United States) but far exceeds that in countries that successfully pursue policies aimed at high economic growth (51 percent in China).

At the same time, the share of investment in Russia's GDP (about 20 percent) is well below that of China, India, and Kazakhstan. The Russian economy badly needs investment, especially in infrastructure. Rapid growth after 1998 was achieved largely by resuming use of capacity constructed before the fall of the Soviet Union. In 1998 capacity utilization stood at 55 percent, while in 2006 it was over 80 percent. This number fell during the crisis, but by the beginning of 2010 it had recovered to its previous level. Russia's production capacity is in need of expansion and modernization, which requires huge additional investment. The obstacles to investment remain the same: illiberal economy, corruption, weak legal system, inflation, and lack of long-term resources in the banking system (particularly owing to the absence of private pension funds). The generally opaque business climate scares off not only foreign investors (Russia's level of FDI has traditionally been low) but also Russian corporations: Since 2007, corporate deposits have been growing rapidly because companies put their profits and foreign loans in Russian banks rather than investing them in the economy.

Meanwhile, the state is playing a larger role in investment: Between 2003 and 2007, personal savings as a share of total savings fell by one-third (to 20.8 percent), corporate savings fell from 53 to 42.8 percent, but state savings grew from 22.5 to 43.4 percent. Unfortunately, state investments in Russia are not very efficient.

In essence, Russian authorities have to choose between short-term stability (which can be elusive) and long-term growth. Contraction of budget spending and sterilization of money supply will help lower inflation and increase vital investment. However, the strengthening of the ruble will stymie the growth of an economy mainly driven by commodity exports. Pension reform is needed for a number of obvious reasons, but it will inevitably lead to a temporary rise in social tensions. The problems of the pension system are aggravated by demographics: 12 percent of Russians are above the age of 65, much more than in Brazil, India, or China. Moreover, the population will continue to age in the coming years, and pension spending has already grown by 33 percent per annum for the last three years.

Russia needs serious economic reforms comparable in scale to those of the early 1990s. Is the government ready? What must be done for these reforms to be successfully carried out? The last Russian leader to face such momentous questions was Mikhail Gorbachev. The fall in oil prices in the autumn of 1985 resembles what happened in Russia in 2008. And Gorbachev was no less popular at the time of that fall than Dmitri Medvedev and Vladimir Putin are today. Unfortunately, he had not yet committed to radical reform and quickly lost his popularity. Reform went ahead without him.

What will the current Russian government do? How long will Russian society be willing to live with low growth, which is inevitable without serious reforms (unless oil prices hit new records)? Will the government remain popular if real disposable income rises at 1 to 2 percent per year rather than 9 to 10 percent? What can and must be done?

This book answers these questions to a considerable extent. It presents a comprehensive analysis of Russia's current state in a comparative context. A similar project of the Center for Strategic and International Studies and the Peterson Institute for International Economics is the China Balance Sheet, which has produced thoughtful analyses on China's rise as a global superpower. The two collaborated once again on the Russia Balance Sheet, releasing their first book of the same name in 2009. Analyzing different countries (or the same countries at different periods) using the "balance sheet" methodology allows us to gain new, more profound understanding of a country's economic and social situation. This second book, in partnership also with the Moscow-based New Economic School, covers a vast range of topics on Russia's economy and society, from army reform to relations within the former Soviet space. Top experts with thorough knowledge of these issues have contributed to the book.

Peter Aven
President
Alfa Bank

April 2010

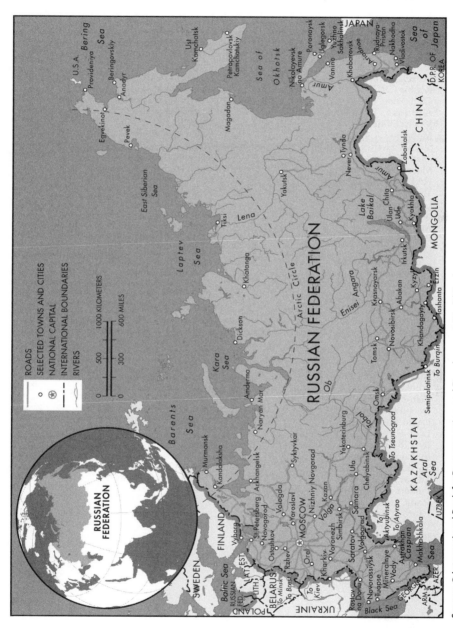

Source: © International Bank for Reconstruction and Development, World Bank.

Introduction

The economic and financial crisis that swept through the world in 2008–09 shook us all hard. Until the fall of 2008, Russia appeared to be a safe haven with its steady, high growth rate of 7 percent a year and its massive international currency reserves, which peaked at $598 billion in August 2008, the third largest in the world after China and Japan.

But by October 2008, it was clear that Russia had been hit hard. The Russian stock market plunged by no less than 80 percent from May to October 2008. In 2009 Russia's GDP fell by 8 percent, more than in any other economy of the Group of Twenty (G-20) largest economies in the world, though admittedly less than in Ukraine and the Baltic states.

Yet Russia's public finances and international financial balances have been very strong. We therefore prefer to speak of an economic crisis in Russia and not a financial crisis. Unlike many other countries, Russia is suffering not from major foreign debt or public debt but from too low economic growth. Will the precrisis high economic growth return, or has Russia hit a serious roadblock?

This second book from the Russia Balance Sheet project examines Russia's current dilemma. Why did Russia suffer so badly? What are the critical problems and bottlenecks and what opportunities are at hand? Did Russia just have bad luck, or has the global crisis revealed profound shortcomings that need be fixed?

To penetrate this conundrum, we the editors have chosen twelve major issues of importance for Russia's social and economic development: the current economic dilemma, impact of the economy on Russian politics, functioning of federalism, corruption and rule of law, role of high technology, climate change and energy efficiency, Gazprom, military reform, foreign policy, foreign economic policy, the post-Soviet space, and US-Russia relations. In order to illuminate these issues, we chose the best Russian and American specialists on these topics that we could find. We conclude with our outlook for Russia.

In our first book, *The Russia Balance Sheet*, published in 2009, we selected eight themes: Russia's historical roots, political development after the end of the Soviet Union, Russia's economic revival, policy on oil and gas, international economic integration, challenges of demography and health, Russian attitudes toward the West, and Russia as a postimperial power. That book concluded with what a "reset" of US-Russia relations should amount to, while this book focuses on Russia's current challenges. We have followed up on some themes, such as economic policy, foreign economic policy, and foreign policy, but have largely selected different themes or angles.

The Arguments

Our basic question is, How serious has the global crisis been for Russia? Why did Russia see such a large decline in GDP in 2009? How profound is the impact of the crisis? Did it have such an effect that Russia may change its course?

In chapter 1, Sergei Guriev and Aleh Tsyvinski illustrate how strong the Russian economy looked before the crisis. Their main explanation for the sudden drop in GDP is the sharp fall in the oil price. They argue that economic policy during the peak of the crisis was adequate. Their main concern is the challenges that Russia faces after the economic crisis. Global growth is and will continue to be lower, and Russia suffers from its resource curse, which has constrained desired economic reforms. They argue for a renewal of structural economic reforms to improve economic efficiency and governance. Russia faces a choice between Brezhnev-era stagnation and difficult economic reforms that will build the foundation for faster economic growth.

Daniel Treisman presents his original view of Russian politics in chapter 2. He argues that Russian politics has been far more dependent on public opinion than is commonly understood. The Kremlin has persistently been a great consumer of opinion polls, which shows that the politicians care. The popularity of the presidents in power was determined by economic performance, over which they had little control. The ability of the president to enact and implement policies depended on the president's popularity. By contrast, changes in Russia's formal political institutions explain little about the varying ability of presidents to pursue their policies. The ideas of the president were effective only when the president was popular. The conclusion for the future is that worse economic performance should reduce the popularity of the president and thus render him less effective as a policymaker. Yet, if the economy recovers quickly, political backlash might be limited.

In chapter 3, Ekaterina Zhuravskaya reviews federalism in Russia in light of global experiences and theory. Her exercise is remarkably fruitful. A large and complex country such as Russia needs a federal structure of government for its successful development. However, President Vladimir Putin's creation of a "strong political vertical" with the appointment of governors has created major problems, including inadequate provision of public goods, because of the absence of accountability of both regional and federal officials. Without a strong opposition and free media, the federal center cannot pursue efficient policies. Federalism without local elections can potentially work if the policy aims at economic growth and not provision of public goods, such as good education and health care, but Russia is too advanced for such a single-minded approach. The alternative to the political vertical is the building of strong national political parties, which can exercise accountability.

Timothy Frye studies corruption and rule of law in chapter 4 on the basis of his own enterprise surveys in 2000 and 2008. He identifies reducing corruption and strengthening the rule of law as the greatest modernization challenge that Russia faces. His results are rather depressing. He finds that businesspeople perceive that corruption has increased since 2000 and that the security of property rights has become more contingent on political connections. President Dmitri Medvedev has repeatedly exposed these conditions and called for improvements, but to date his record on reform is not very impressive, although he has initiated large personnel changes in the main villain, the Ministry of Interior. Frye concludes that strengthening the rule of law requires a leveling of the political playing field between the powerful and the powerless.

In chapter 5, Keith Crane and Artur Usanov analyze the role of high technology in the Russian economy. They establish that Russian high-technology products pertain to five major areas: software, nanotechnology, nuclear energy, aerospace, and armaments. They review the size, companies, and relative strength of these five industries. They give Russian software the highest rating; it is the only high-technology industry that consists of start-ups and is dominated by private enterprises. The other four industries are built around state-holding companies, with the last two belonging to the military industry, which is not in great shape. The general impression is that Russia is doing quite a lot in high technology, but overall this industry is strikingly limited, and its future prospects are not great since it is both poorly financed and stifled by state power.

Climate change and energy efficiency have become two major international themes in recent years, which Samuel Charap and Georgi Safonov discuss in chapter 6. Even though Russia has high energy intensity and is the third largest emitter of carbon dioxide in the world after the United States and China, the Kremlin paid little attention to these issues until recently. Modernization of Russian industry has led to a sharp reduction in Russia's energy intensity, but much remains to be done. In 2010, President Medvedev has taken up this theme and given it new prominence in Russian policy. Russia still has unique opportunities to save energy, and the question is whether President Medvedev's recent statement really indicates a new beginning.

For the last two decades, Gazprom has been Russia's dominant corporation. In chapter 7, Anders Åslund reckons that Gazprom has entered a serious structural crisis. It has thrived on piping gas to the growing European gas market, but Europe is experiencing a large gas glut, which will last for several years. Expanded production of shale gas in the United States has suddenly made that country a larger gas producer than Russia and eliminated its need for liquefied natural gas, which instead is flooding the European market. The gas price is likely to decouple from the oil price and stay much lower. Europe is also likely to produce shale gas in multiple places. In addition, energy saving will reduce the demand for gas. So far, Gazprom has neglected both other markets and technologies. It was forced to cut production sharply in 2009 because of falling demand and also reduced its purchases from Central Asia and postponed the development of new fields. These challenges are severe and call for a new, more market-oriented, and diversified gas policy.

In one area, however, Russia has been pursuing radical reform, namely in the military, which Pavel K. Baev deals with in chapter 8. This reform is considered the greatest since the reforms after the Crimean War in the 1860s. The aim is to transform the Russian military from a mass tank army to well-equipped rapid deployment forces. The reform was initiated by Minister of Defense Anatoly Serdyukov in October 2008, who keeps it in his tight reins. The ideas of the reform are in line with modern military thinking, but the reformers are accidental and maintain great secrecy, while the officer corps offers solid resistance. The reform proposes to reduce the number of units, officers, and tanks of the army. Out of the current 22,000 tanks, only 2,000 will remain. Baev is skeptical that the reform will be successful because it is underfinanced, not very consistent, and encounters extraordinary opposition from the officers. In any case, the Russian military has already changed considerably.

Dmitri Trenin discusses the dilemma of Russian foreign policy—modernization or marginalization—in chapter 9. He emphasizes the importance of Russia's relative economic size for its foreign policy. Russia does not have sufficient resources to play the role of a superpower, but it still remains a significant power. A major policy of President Putin's second term (2004–08) was to abandon Russia's aspirations to join the West and instead build up an alternative center of power with former Soviet republics. However, Russia's economic resources are not sufficient for such a policy. Instead, Moscow's priority should be to strengthen Russia's own economic, intellectual, and social potential and to develop its soft power. Russia's conventional forces, even if they are successfully reformed, will have only limited capacity, and the Russian defense industry has to be restructured. As Trenin concludes: "For Russia, the age of empire is definitely over, but postimperial adjustment continues."

In chapter 10, David Tarr and Natalya Volchkova deal with trade and foreign direct investment policy. They strongly argue why Russia needs to join the World Trade Organization (WTO). Their estimates for Russia's benefits are substantial: Russia would gain annually no less than 3.3 percent of its GDP in the medium term. The benefits to the global community, by contrast, would be small. The authors also contradict the common view that Russia is facing excessive demands from the WTO, showing that the demands are somewhat more lenient than has otherwise been the case. They see no particular advantage for Russia in establishing a customs union with Belarus and Kazakhstan. In the end, Tarr and Volchkova see Russia's choice of the WTO as the choice of an open economy and integration into the global economy.

One sphere of Russia's foreign policy has been the post-Soviet space, which Anders Åslund considers in chapter 11. His view is that Russia is largely contradicting its own interests in its policy toward these countries. It is attempting to develop closer relations with these countries than they desire and is therefore being perceived as a potential threat. In four areas, Russia has left its neighbors dissatisfied, namely territorial integrity, gas policy, trade policy, and financial assistance. Russian private foreign direct investment, however, has been remarkably large and noncontroversial. China has been expanding its role in Central Asia and Eastern Europe. Russia is no longer unchallenged, but it has no viable policy. Åslund suggests that Russia may as well dissolve the Commonwealth of Independent States and its suborganizations, since they apparently do not benefit but rather contradict Russia's national interests. Instead, Russia needs to convince its neighbors of its good intentions.

So what does all this mean for US-Russia relations? Andrew Kuchins concludes in chapter 12 that while US-Russia relations have undoubtedly improved in the first year of the Barack Obama administration, the relationship is constrained by an enduring mismatch in strategic outlooks in Washington and Moscow. More than 20 years after the Cold War, Russia still persists in arguing that the United States represents the greatest risk to its security. This deeply anachronistic assumption not only naturally places significant constraints on the bilateral relationship but also leads Moscow to pursue many foreign policies that seem at odds with its stated goals of economic modernization and prevent it from addressing the security challenges it actually faces.

The Russia Balance Sheet

This book is the second in a series from the three-year Russia Balance Sheet, a collaborative project of the Peterson Institute for International Economics (PIIE), the Center for Strategic and International Studies (CSIS), and the New Economic School in Moscow. In it we seek to address key questions about Russia's political and economic development and its foreign policy through a rigorous, multidisciplinary, and comprehensive approach. Our goal is to be factual, objective, and balanced, looking at Russia beyond the stereotypes.

The timing is right for such an effort. President Medvedev assumed office in Russia in May 2008 and President Obama did so in Washington in January 2009. The two countries have embarked on a third epoch in post-Soviet US-Russia relations, following the Yeltsin-Clinton and Putin-Bush periods. They have called this new phase a "reset," indicating both their dissatisfaction with the prior relations and the aspiration to achieve something better.

In 2008, the United States appeared to be in the doldrums and Russia on a new peak with all its oil wealth, but 2009 was equally cruel to both of them. This is a time of reconsideration and rethinking. Our conviction is that the United States and Russia need to understand each other, have substantial common interests, and had better handle their differences. But a big question is whether both governments will agree on that and actually move forward.

The US business community views Russia as one of the large emerging markets. It presents many challenges for trade and investment, but so do other large emerging markets such as Brazil, China, and India (with Russia, the so-called BRICs or the trillion-dollar club). It may be an exaggeration to call Russia a "normal country,"[1] but the American and international business communities do not view Russia as so different: They recognize it as both an important supplier and market, where all major global companies have to be present.

The US policy community remains preoccupied with the Russian nuclear arsenal. Their views were reinforced during the Putin years, when Russia became a centralized, authoritarian state as well as more aggressive in its foreign policy, but it does not necessarily mean that Russia has the economic or military muscle to pursue its old role of a great power.

We chose the title *The Russia Balance Sheet* for the first, overview book and the larger project to build on the brand name established by the very successful collaboration between CSIS and PIIE for the China Balance Sheet, launched in 2005 and broadly supported by the business and policy communities. The motivation for entitling this book *Russia after the Global*

---

1. Andrei Shleifer and Daniel Treisman, "A Normal Country," *Foreign Affairs* 83, no. 2 (2004): 20–38.

Economic Crisis stems from our view that economic drivers are crucial for Russia's future growth, and neither Russia's political system nor its foreign policy can be well understood without a firm grounding in its current economic realities, its goals, and the global economic system within which Russia operates. Russians not only are more prosperous than ever but are also more integrated into the global economy than ever before.

1

Challenges Facing the Russian Economy after the Crisis

SERGEI GURIEV AND ALEH TSYVINSKI

In 1999–2008, Russia was one of the fastest growing economies in the world. In 2009, it was one of the worst affected by the global economic crisis. Its GDP fell by 8 percent, more than any other economy in the Group of Twenty (G-20)—the group of the world's largest economies. Does this mean that Vladimir Putin's "growth decade" of 1999–2008 was just an aberration? That Russia failed to respond to the crisis in a smart and resolute way? That Russia is facing a serious crisis in the near future?

The growth in the precrisis decade was not a fluke. The benefits of this growth have trickled down to all parts of Russian society. At the same time, however, the growth decade failed to address several major problems in the Russian economy—most importantly, corruption and dependence on commodity exports. Given these challenges, we argue that (1) Russia's response to the first wave of the crisis in 2008 was mostly adequate; (2) the dramatic fall was largely to be expected but was exacerbated by poor economic policies in 2009; and (3) the Russian economy is not facing major difficulties in the immediate future. However, our long-term perspective of the Russian economy is not optimistic. We believe that as long as world oil prices remain high, Russia may suffer from the "resource curse" and follow what we call a "70–80 scenario." Given high oil prices, Russian elites may prefer to delay the restructuring of the economy and building of pro-growth political and economic institutions. This will in turn slow economic growth and make it very unlikely for Russia to catch up with advanced economies in the next 10 to 15 years. In other words, if oil prices remain at $70 to $80 per

Sergei Guriev is rector of and Morgan Stanley Professor of Economics at the New Economic School. Aleh Tsyvinski is professor of economics at Yale University and the New Economic School. Certain parts of this chapter are based on articles they have written for Russian and international media.

barrel, Russia will revert to Brezhnev-era conditions of the 1970s–1980s—a stagnating economy and 70 to 80 percent approval ratings.

In the first part of this chapter we provide a snapshot of the Russian economy before the crisis. We summarize the benefits of the growth decade and the problems economic policy failed to solve. We discuss why Russia did not foresee the crisis. We then analyze Russia's anticrisis policy—both the swift and mostly adequate response to the first wave of the crisis in 2008 and the "preserving the status-quo" policies of 2009. We pay special attention to the level of decline in 2009 and argue that the poor performance of the Russian economy was due to both its dependence on oil and capital inflows and the burden of the previous lack of reforms and poor economic policies in 2009.

Finally, we discuss lessons the Russian government learned from the crisis—and the lessons it should have learned. We argue that Russia is under a "resource curse"—a situation in which resource rents reduce elite's incentives to reform and where nonresource sectors are unlikely to grow unless reforms are undertaken.[1] We then draft a reform agenda that Russia needs to carry out and analyze the likelihood of its implementation and alternative scenarios.

Before the Crisis

In June 2008 the 12th St. Petersburg International Economic Forum gathered the who's who of Russian business and government elite and leaders of major world corporations. The Russian economy was at its peak. Long forgotten were the days of the Soviet collapse and the turbulent nineties. Putin's administration appeared to have left Russia's economy in an admirable state. Economic growth averaged more than 7 percent per year between 1999 and 2008. The stock market had increased twentyfold. Foreign investors were enamored by Russia being a part of the fashionable BRIC group of the world's fastest-growing emerging markets (the others being Brazil, India, and China).

This economic growth record was impressive by any measure (figure 1.1). Russia was closing the gap with the advanced and newly industrialized economies, overtaking such successful emerging markets as Chile and its oil-rich counterpart Venezuela. Russia was doing better than other large transition countries such as Kazakhstan, Poland, and Ukraine. Within the BRIC quartet, it was second only to China, which was natural given that China had a lower starting point. Economists explain the faster growth of poorer economies through a "conditional convergence" law that states that, other things equal, richer countries should have a lower rate of growth.

---

1. Richard M. Auty introduced the term in 1993. See Richard M. Auty, *Sustaining Development in Mineral Economies: The Resource Curse Thesis* (London: Routledge, 1993).

Figure 1.1   GDP per capita (in purchasing power parity) in selected countries, 1992–2009

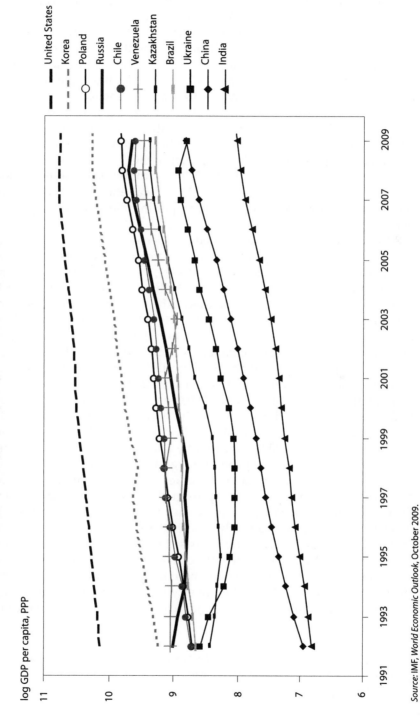

Source: IMF, *World Economic Outlook*, October 2009.

Russia was awash with cash. The government's reserve fund, created to cushion the economy from a fall in oil prices, stood at $140 billion, and the National Welfare Fund (NWF), intended mainly to solve the looming pension crisis, held another $30 billion. The NWF, though not yet officially a "sovereign wealth fund," was already among the 10 largest such funds, rivaling the Brunei Investment Agency. A combined Russian sovereign wealth fund would rival Singapore's Temasek Holdings (the sixth largest in the world) and lag just behind the China Investment Corporation.

The Russian stock market was doing well. According to the World Bank's *World Development Indicators*, the ratio of market capitalization to GDP in Russia was 117 percent, just slightly below the Organization for Economic Cooperation and Development (OECD) average (120 percent) and above France and Korea (both 107 percent). While it was below India and China (both above 150 percent), Russia was ahead of Brazil (103 percent), the eurozone (85 percent), and upper middle income countries (86 percent on average).

Russian private and state-owned companies were expanding abroad extensively, often buying stakes in large foreign companies. A survey of Russian multinational enterprises (MNEs) showed a dramatic internationalization of Russian firms.[2] The top 25 Russian companies held $59 billion in assets abroad, which made Russia the third largest investor among emerging markets in 2006 in terms of foreign direct investment (FDI) outflows, following Hong Kong and Brazil, and the second largest in terms of outward FDI stock. Russian companies had nearly $200 billion in foreign sales and employed 130,000 people abroad. Foreign assets, sales, and employment each had more than doubled since 2004.

Did the growth decade of 1999–2008 benefit the average Russian? Contrary to widespread opinion, growth did trickle down to both the middle class and the poor, not just benefiting the rich or very rich parts of society. Real incomes in 1999–2008 increased by a factor of 2.5. Real wages more than tripled. Mobile phone penetration grew from virtually zero to more than 100 percent. The Russian car market became the largest in Europe. Moscow real estate prices went up from about $700 per square meter at the end of 1999 to $6,000 per square meter in the summer of 2008.[3] The financial system grew manifestly in terms of size and sophistication. For example, the credit to GDP ratio increased from about 10 percent to about 40 percent reflecting a boom in both retail and corporate lending.

Unemployment went down by more than half—from 12.9 percent in 1999 to 6.3 percent in 2008. The poverty rate (percent of population below the official minimum living standard) went down from 29 percent in

---

2. This survey was conducted by SKOLKOVO Moscow School of Management and the Columbia Program on International Investment.

3. Data are from Real Estate Market Indicators, www.irn.ru.

1999 to 13 percent in 2008. The poverty gap (the income that would suffice to bring all the poor to the minimum living standards) decreased from 4.9 percent of total households' income in 1999 to 1.2 percent in 2008. Moreover, self-assessed life satisfaction rose significantly. Sergei Guriev and Ekaterina Zhuravskaya (2009) use data from a panel of Russian households (Russian Longitudinal Monitoring Survey, RLMS) that under-represents the rich and upper middle class, thus reflecting a poorer part of the society, and show that both incomes and life satisfaction in this panel have increased substantially.[4]

Even inequality had *not* increased. Using the same RLMS dataset, economists Yuriy Gorodnichenko, Dmitriy Stolyarov, and Klara Sabiriano-va-Peter show that inequality might have even slightly decreased (from the Gini coefficient of 0.42 in 1999 to 0.38 in 2005).[5] The official data on Gini coefficients show an increase from 0.40 in 2000 to 0.42 in 2008. Given the quality of Russian inequality data, it is safe to say that inequality in Russia has not changed during the decade.

Yet, despite its real achievements, "Putinomics" failed to resolve several very important issues. First, inflation was still very high (in 2007 and 2008 it remained above 10 percent a year, the highest among G-20 countries). Second, no significant results were achieved in the war on corruption. Figure 1.2 shows that whatever successes in fighting corruption were achieved in the early 2000s were then wiped out so corruption returned to pre-Putin years. Third, even though inequality had not increased, it remained unacceptably high. Fourth, economic policies failed to diversify the economy away from it heavy dependence on production and exports of commodities.

We argue that it was difficult to foresee the crisis in 2008. The reasoning of the government officials and many independent economists at the time was based on three arguments: (1) the oil price was high and rising; (2) Putin's government did undertake certain significant reforms and carried out reasonable macroeconomic policy; and (3) the "decoupling" theory seemed to be consistent with data. We go through these arguments one by one as they are important for understanding the postcrisis developments in the Russian economy.

The first reasoning was that the economy was fundamentally strong, especially because of the skyrocketing oil prices. On January 2, 2008, the oil price rose to $100 per barrel. Oil broke through $110 on March 12, $125 on May 9, $130 on May 21, $135 on May 22, $140 on June 26, and $145 on July 3, 2008. On July 11, 2008, oil prices rose to a new record of $147.27. The

4. Sergei Guriev and Ekaterina Zhuravskaya, "(Un)Happiness in Transition," *Journal of Economic Perspectives* 23, no. 2 (2009): 143–68.

5. Yuriy Gorodnichenko, Dmitriy Stolyarov, and Klara Sabirianova-Peter, "Inequality and Volatility Moderation in Russia: Evidence from Micro-Level Panel Data on Consumption and Income," *Review of Economic Dynamics* 13, no. 1 (2010): 209–37.

Figure 1.2   Control of corruption in Russia

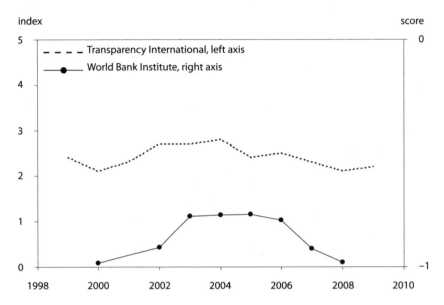

Sources: Transparency International, Corruption Perceptions Index, www.transparency.org; World Bank Institute's Governance Indicators Project, data for 2000, 2002–08 (world average is normalized to 0, world standard deviation is normalized to 1).

economic turmoil in the United States did not seem to slow the growth of oil prices, which seemed unstoppable, and the optimism of Russian officials and the business elite reflected the rosy future. The CEO of the Russian gas giant Gazprom, Alexei Miller, made headlines on June 16, 2008 in a briefing to European energy executives, predicting that world oil prices could reach $250 per barrel by 2010.

Second, Russia's economic success could not be solely attributed to high oil and commodities prices. At most, half of Russian growth during 1999–2008 can be attributed to the growth in oil prices. It is essential to recognize the contribution of economic reforms undertaken during Putin's first term.

Three important reforms stand out in their contribution to growth. First, the tax reform of 2001 improved incentives to work and decreased tax evasion. Second, liberalizing the procedures for corporate registration and licensing and limiting inspections improved the climate for small businesses and entrepreneurs. Third, conservative macroeconomic policy and financial-sector reform lowered interest rates and fueled an investment and consumption boom. These claims are supported by quantitative and empirical evidence.

In a 2009 study Yuriy Gorodnichenko, Jorge Martinez-Vazquez, and Klara Sabirianova-Peter provided microeconomic evidence on the real benefits of introducing the flat income tax.[6] They studied a representative panel of Russian households (RLMS) and showed that the tax reform increased labor supply and lowered tax evasion. In January 2001 Russia introduced a reform of its personal income tax, becoming the first large economy to adopt a flat tax. The Tax Code of 2001 replaced a progressive rate structure with a flat tax rate of 13 percent. The study found that the flat tax reform was instrumental in decreasing tax evasion in Russia and that a part of greater fiscal revenues in 2001 and several years beyond can be linked to increased voluntary tax compliance and reporting. The study also found that the productivity effect on the real side of the economy was positive, although smaller than the tax evasion effect.

In a 2007 study, Evgeny Yakovlev and Ekaterina Zhuravskaya followed a representative panel of 1,600 small businesses in 20 regions of Russia over five years—before and after the major deregulation reforms.[7] Between 2001 and 2004, Russia simplified procedures and reduced red tape associated with entry regulation (registration and licensing) and regulation of existing businesses (inspections). The laws introduced clear measurable limits to the regulatory burden. In particular, the new laws required that registering a business should involve a visit to just one government agency ("one-stop shop") and take at most one week; each inspecting agency inspects a business no more than once in two years; licenses are valid for at least five years. In addition, about 90 percent of business activities that previously had required licenses became exempt. The authors found that this elimination of administrative barriers resulted in the growth of small businesses—in terms of both number and employment. They also found that the impact of the reform varied greatly across regions. The deregulation was more successful in regions with transparent government, low corruption, independent media, powerful industrial lobby, and stronger fiscal autonomy.

Erik Berglof and Alexander Lehmann provide evidence on the contribution of the financial sector to economic growth in Russia.[8] They argue that there is strong evidence of strengthening of the links between finance and the real sector in Russia. Russian data show that financial development had a beneficial impact on corporate finance, corporate growth, and broader economic growth. Early reforms had lasting impact, but it took until 2001 for bank credit to the private sector to show strong and sustained growth.

---

6. Yuriy Gorodnichenko, Jorge Martinez-Vazquez, and Klara Sabirianova-Peter, "Myth and Reality of Flat Tax Reform: Micro Estimates of Tax Evasion and Productivity Response in Russia," *Journal of Political Economy* 117, no. 3 (2009): 504–54.

7. Evgeny Yakovlev and Ekaterina V. Zhuravskaya, "Deregulation of Business," CEPR Discussion Paper DP6610 (Washington: Center for Economic and Policy Research, 2007).

8. Erik Berglof and Alexander Lehmann, "Sustaining Russia's Growth: The Role of Financial Reform," *Journal of Comparative Economics* 37, no. 2 (2008): 198–206.

The third reason for complacency was a then fashionable economic concept of "decoupling," which stated that emerging markets such as China, Brazil, Russia, or India had entered a phase of development in which economic crisis in the developed world would not significantly affect their economies. This idea was widespread in media and policy circles worldwide. An article in the *Economist* published in March 2008, "Decoupling Is Not a Myth," argued the importance of this concept.

> Decoupling does not mean that an American recession will have no impact on developing countries. That would be daft.... The point is that their GDP-growth rates will slow by much less than in previous American downturns.... The four biggest emerging economies, which accounted for two-fifths of global GDP growth last year, are the least dependent on the United States: exports to America account for just...1% of Russia's [GDP]. The benefits of the reserves of foreign currencies built up during years of current account surplus are yet to be fully appreciated.... But for perhaps the first time ever, developing countries would be able to make full use of monetary and fiscal policy to cushion their economies.

This was the optimistic picture that the Russian government and businesses were expecting just three months before perhaps the largest economic turmoil that the modern Russian economic and political system built during Putin's rule had ever experienced.

The Crisis

The Shock of the Fall of 2008

Now fast forward to the fall of 2008. By September, the Russian Trading System (RTS) stock index had plunged almost 54 percent, making it one of the worst performing markets in the world. On September 16, trading in Russia's most liquid stock exchange, the Moscow Interbank Currency Exchange (MICEX), and the dollar-denominated RTS was suspended. Trading was suspended again the next day and on September 18 for the third day. On October 6, the Russian stock market fell by more than 18 percent in a single day. Bank failures worsened the stock market collapse. On September 15, KIT Finance, a large financial institution, failed to pay off its debt.

The price of oil also foreshadowed problems for Russia. On September 15, the oil price fell below $100 for the first time in seven months. On October 11, it fell to $78. On December 21, 2008, oil was trading at $33.87 a barrel, less than one-fourth the peak price reached four months earlier. Prices did not rebound once 2009 started. Instead, after initially climbing above $48, prices descended by mid-February to below $34. Russia's other major export, metals, experienced a similar price decline (figure 1.3).

Even Russia's oligarchs were pawning their yachts and selling their private jets. Signs of political instability were mounting. Approval ratings

Figure 1.3   Oil, metal, and stock market prices during the 2008–09 crisis

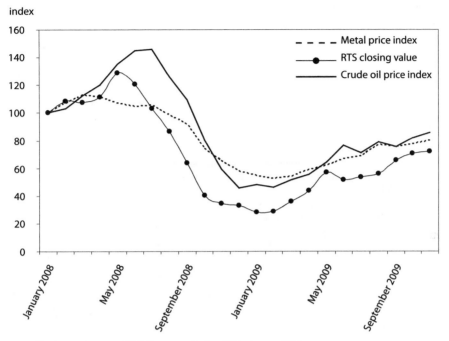

Note: All prices are in current US dollars normalized to 100 for January 2008.

Sources: Russian Trading System (RTS) for the RTS stock market index closing value; International Monetary Fund; www.indexmundi.com for oil and metal price indices.

for Russia's president and prime minister were heading south. Mass street protests started—not led by opposition political parties but by workers and middle-class families facing job losses and declining wages. More importantly, protesters were demanding that the government resign, unthinkable just a year before.

Why the Crisis Hit Russia So Hard: Role of Oil Prices

The impact of the economic crisis on the Russian economy was stronger than on any other G-20 economy. Not only was the 8 percent Russian GDP contraction for 2009 the largest among G-20 countries but also the *change* in the growth rate between 2008 and 2009 by far exceeded that in other G-20 members. Figure 1.4 plots growth rates in the G-20 countries before and during the crisis (2008 and 2009, respectively)[9] based on the Inter-

---

9. While the acute phase of the financial crisis started in September 2008, the effect on the real economy was somewhat delayed, so it is safe to take 2008 as the last precrisis year.

Figure 1.4   GDP growth in selected G-20 countries, 2008 and 2009

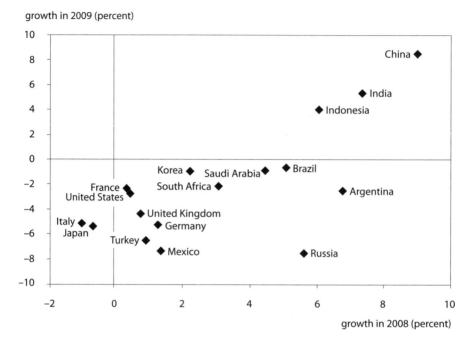

Source: IMF, *World Economic Outlook*, October 2009.

national Monetary Fund's October 2009 data. It shows that all countries performed worse in 2009 than in 2008. Yet, the difference was largest for Russia—more than 13 percentage points! The next worst change was experienced by Argentina at 9 percentage points. The average change in growth rate between 2008 and 2009 for other countries was just 4 percentage points. Why has Russia switched from being one of the fastest growing countries to one that is faltering the most?

The main suspect is the dramatic fall in oil prices from the peak of $140 per barrel in summer 2008 to the trough of below $40 per barrel just half a year later. Can we calibrate this effect? There are two approaches to answering this question based on precrisis data. One can estimate the total rent that Russia generates in oil and gas and then determine the direct effect of the oil price changes. Or one can estimate the covariation of Russian GDP and oil price (controlling for other factors) in recent years.

These two approaches may err on both sides. The first, "accounting," approach has a number of drawbacks: (1) it is very hard to measure the total oil and gas rent precisely; (2) it does not take into account the indirect effects of oil prices—effects through changes in oil and gas output driven by oil prices, changes in markets for other commodities, and effects on cross-border capital flows; and (3) it neglects the policy responses such as sterilization of petrodollars through building up the reserve fund and sovereign wealth fund. The alternative, "econometric," approach captures the actual observed correlation. But it is also problematic as it is not clear whether precrisis data can easily be extrapolated to crisis and postcrisis periods. Indeed, at the very least, reactions of policymakers and investors may change. More likely, the economy that has undergone structural changes during the crisis would respond differently to the change in oil price. Finally, neither approach can help mitigate the nonlinearity of the effect of oil price on GDP. Nonetheless, we discuss the results from both approaches to obtain ballpark estimates.

We start with the estimate of the oil and gas rent. Cliff Gaddy and Barry Ickes argue that official data on the value added in the oil and gas sector (around 10 percent of GDP) are misleading.[10] Using data and assumptions on excess costs and price subsidies they arrive at a much larger number: Total oil and gas rent in 2005 constituted about 25 percent of GDP. This number is similar to the estimate obtained by the World Bank,[11] which used 2000 input-output tables for Russia, the United Kingdom, and the Netherlands to offset the effect of transfer pricing. The World Bank's estimate of Russia's value added in oil and gas was 20 percent of GDP in 2000 (the official figure for 2000 was 8 percent of GDP). The difference is not surprising given that the average oil price in 2000 was only $27 per barrel—much lower than $50 per barrel in 2005.

Using the Gaddy-Ickes methodology, we estimated the total oil and gas rent for 2008 (when the oil price peaked) at about 30 percent of GDP. Moreover, their methodology implies that a decrease in oil price by $10 per barrel costs Russia about 3 percentage points of GDP. Using this benchmark, the fall in Urals oil price from the average of $95 per barrel in 2008 to $60 per barrel in 2009 should have resulted in a drop in GDP by about 11 percentage points. The alternative, econometric, approach was used by a number of authors, most importantly Jouko Rautava, who estimated the long-run elasticity of GDP to oil at 0.24.[12] In other words, a permanent 10 percent change in the oil price has a long-run effect of 2.4 percentage points of GDP. Roland Beck, Annette Kamps, and Elitza Mileva extend Rautava's dataset and methodology and obtain similar results: The long-run effect of a 10 percent change in oil price is 2 percentage points of

---

10. Cliff Gaddy and Barry Ickes, "Resource Rents and the Russian Economy," *Eurasian Geography and Economics* 46, no. 8 (2005): 559–83.

11. World Bank, *From Transition to Development: A Country Economic Memorandum for the Russian Federation* (Washington, 2005).

12. Jouko Rautava, "The Role of the Oil Prices and the Real Exchange Rate in Russia's Economy—A Cointegration Approach," *Journal of Comparative Economics* 32, no. 2 (2004): 315–27.

GDP.[13,14] This effect is reached, however, only six years after the shock. The short-run effect is smaller: In the first quarter after the shock, the change in GDP is only 0.5 percentage points, and after the first year, the change is 1 percentage point. Beck, Kamps, and Mileva also deliver an important caveat: As even their extended data series are rather short, the margins of error are large. For example, the 95 percent confidence interval extends from 0.6 to 1.6 percentage points one year after the shock.

Similar to the econometric approach, Bruno Merlevede, Bas Van Aarle, and Koen J. L. Schoors build and calibrate a small macroeconomic model for the Russian economy.[15] They then subject the model to a $25 per barrel permanent shock to the oil price (considering scenarios with $20, $45, and $70 per barrel from 2005 onward). Even though the model includes two mitigating mechanisms, the "Dutch disease" effect and the Stabilization Fund, the shock still results in a long-term change in GDP of 12 percentage points. Interestingly enough, most of this change (9 to 10 percentage points) takes place within one year of the oil price shock. The results from the two approaches are therefore not very different. The change in the oil price from $95 per barrel in 2008 to $60 in 2009 should have resulted in a decline in GDP of 9 to 16 percentage points. For the short run, if we consider the fall from 2008Q2's $118 per barrel to Q3's $56 per barrel, it should have resulted in the loss of at least 7.5 percentage points of GDP.

Note that these losses should be subtracted from the "counterfactual" Russian GDP—what would have happened if there were no crisis? Assuming the long-run average growth rate of 7 percent per year, the effect of oil price alone would move Russia from growing at 7 percent a year to falling at 2 to 9 percent a year. While the precision of these estimates is very low, they do imply that it is at least plausible to ascribe the dramatic fall of the Russian economy at the end of 2008 and in the first three quarters of 2009 to the effect of oil prices alone (assuming that change in oil prices also affects capital flows, exchange rate, etc.).

Why the Crisis Hit Russia So Hard: Role of Economic Policy

In the fall of 2008, the Russian government responded to the crisis in a resolute and effective way. The fall in the oil price and related capital out-

---

13. Roland Beck, Annette Kamps, and Elitza Mileva, "Long-Term Growth Prospects for the Russian Economy," ECB Occasional Paper 58 (Frankfurt: European Central Bank, 2007).

14. The long-run elasticity estimates also allow understanding of the contribution of the oil price to the 1999–2008 economic growth. The elasticity of 0.2 implies that if the world price of Urals oil goes up from $17 (in 1998, constant 2008 dollars) to $97 per barrel (in 2008), then GDP should go up by a factor of 1.4 or grow at 3.5 percent a year for 10 years. Therefore, the growth in oil explains about one-half of Russia's total growth.

15. Bruno Merlevede, Bas Van Aarle, and Koen J. L. Schoors, "Russia from Bust to Boom: Oil, Politics or the Ruble?" Working Paper 722 (William Davidson Institute, 2004).

flows posed a very tangible threat of financial collapse. The government could rely on its reserves but was forced to do so quickly to stop the panic. Fortunately, it did it reasonably well. The Russian financial system came out of the acute financial crisis virtually unscathed, and unemployment remained under control; the Russian government managed to stick to most of its fiscal commitments.

The government prevented the collapse of the banking system. Many Russian banks were heavily exposed in foreign markets and faced severe financial problems once the crisis hit. A massive liquidity injection by the government ensured that no major bank collapsed, and minor bank failures were administered in an orderly fashion.

Moreover, the crisis did not result in major nationalizations of private companies. The government could have nationalized all banks and companies in financial distress under the banner of fighting the crisis, but it did not, despite its large foreign reserves, which gave it the means to acquire a significant portion of the economy at fire-sale prices. Instead, the government mostly provided (high-interest) loans rather than engaging in massive equity buyouts. Contrary to popular opinion, even the oligarchs were not bailed out free of charge. Of $50 billion that the Russian government gave to the large state-owned bank VEB to refinance the external debt owed by Russian banks and firms in 2008, the government refinanced only $11 billion. Apparently, the terms offered by the government (reportedly, at least LIBOR+5 percent) turned out to be right on target and expensive—most companies and banks decided not to borrow from VEB. Finally, the government postponed the increase in social taxes (taxes on labor), which was planned for 2010 to finance an increase in pensions. Such an increase would have had a devastating effect on employment.

The government, however, made several mistakes in fighting the crisis. The first important mistake was that it was too slow in depreciating the ruble. While one can argue that a one-off devaluation was risky—as it could have triggered a panic—gradual depreciation should have been faster and should have started earlier than it did. In October 2008 the government insisted on maintaining the exchange rate above the market rate. In the last two months of 2008, the central bank allowed the ruble to weaken at a rate of 1 percent per week, then at 2 to 3 percent per week. In the meantime, the central bank hemorrhaged reserves defending this slow correction, while commercial banks held on to dollars in anticipation of the ruble's further decline. The total decrease of reserves was around $200 billion, or a third of the precrisis amount.

Not all of the $200 billion was "wasted." Only a fraction of it—proportional to the difference between the equilibrium exchange rate and the rate maintained by the government—was lost by the central bank, i.e., it was transferred to the pockets of the private sector (mostly banks and foreign investors). In that sense, gradual depreciation was an implicit bailout of banks and investors. This bailout resulted in substantial collateral damage. One of the universal laws of economics is that indirect transfers are always inferior to direct transfers. If the government wanted to bail out banks, it should have done so directly rather than through an inefficient depreciation. Apart from distorting decisions by economic agents (including destroying all lending in rubles) during the whole period of gradual depreciation, this policy also undermined the government's credibility. One cannot announce a gradual depreciation—if a government official says that the ruble will fall by 30 percent within a month, the market will bring it down by 30 percent immediately. Therefore, economic policymakers had to make confusing and contradictory announcements for several months in a row. This undermined their credibility to such an extent that when the depreciation really stopped, the market did not believe the new monetary policy. The central bank had to prop up the ruble with high ruble interest rates, which further hurt the Russian economy.

The second important mistake was to raise import duties, especially for imported cars. This was not just economically foolish—as with many other import-competing sectors, the automotive industry would certainly be protected by the weakened ruble—but also politically dangerous. Car owners are an affluent, socially active, and easily organized group. Street protests against the import duties became the first serious popular uprising that Russia had seen in many years. Additionally, higher import duties—especially on food—imposed a tax on labor in all other (unprotected) sectors. As import duties raised the cost of basic consumer necessities, firms in other sectors could not react by lowering wages.

The third major mistake was continuing subsidies to inefficient companies. Part of the reason was political, as many such large companies employ a significant part of the population of the cities in which they are located, and their bankruptcy could cause popular protests. Most notably, the notoriously inefficient and unprofitable auto manufacturer AvtoVAZ received more than a billion dollars of subsidies during the height of the crisis. The government was persisting in its desire to keep afloat this behemoth of inefficiency. Japan's "lost decade"—and its main culprit, "zombie companies"—is an important example of how much damage to economic growth a policy of supporting inefficient companies such as AvtoVAZ can do (see box 1.1).

Instead of supporting zombies, the economic policies should have protected the unemployed directly (again, direct transfers are better than indirect ones). The government did start to support the unemployed, their retraining, and relocation. But the support to inefficient enterprises was an order of magnitude higher. Consider the government's Anti-Crisis Plan for 2009.[16] Direct support to the unemployed (increase in unem-

---

16. Government of the Russian Federation, Prime Minister of the Russian Federation, "Anti-Crisis Measures Program of the Government of the Russian Federation for the Year 2009," June 19, 2009, first published in April 2009 on the prime minister's website and then revised in June 2009, available at http://premier.gov.ru.

Box 1.1   Japanese zombies and the lost decade of growth

What happens to an economy in which the cleansing mechanisms of bankruptcy are turned off and inefficient companies supported? One of the most revealing examples is the experience of Japan in the 1990s. Ricardo Caballero, Takeo Hoshi, and Anil Kashyap show how Japan's policy to support companies that should have gone bankrupt resulted in a lost decade of growth.[1]

Recall the history of the Japanese economic crisis. The economy had steadily grown for three decades. During the real estate bubble in the 1980s, land under the Emperor's Palace in Tokyo cost more than all of the land in the state of California. The bubble burst, and 10 years of stagnation followed. The main question is, Why was the growth slowdown in Japan in the 1990s so lengthy? And why did banks continue to lend to companies that economists aptly called "zombies"?

One reason is almost obvious. Banks did not want to admit their mistakes. If the insolvent lenders stopped paying, banks would have been forced to recognize losses, which could have led to bankruptcy of the banks themselves. Instead, lenders chose to place the half-dead, inefficient companies on life support. For example, banks gave new loans so that those companies could pay interest on the old loans! The second reason is government pressure on banks, as one of the goals of Japanese anticrisis policy was to avoid bankruptcies and support small and medium-sized businesses through bank loans.

Japan achieved the goal of supporting the zombies. But at what price? By the beginning of 2000, a stunning 30 percent of all Japanese companies (15 percent of the country's assets) were zombies. The number of zombies grew especially rapidly in sectors that lacked significant international competition—construction, retail, and services. Employment in these sectors did not significantly decrease, but very few jobs were created.

A significant negative effect of the Japanese government policy of supporting zombies was slowdown of productivity. In sectors where the number of zombies grew by only 5 percentage points, productivity growth averaged 2 percent per year. But in sectors where the number of zombies jumped by 20 percentage points, productivity growth fell on average by 5 percent.

It is essential to note that zombies, by the mere fact of their existence, created significant obstacles to the growth of healthy companies. Not surprisingly, in sectors where employment was artificially supported, growth and the number of new jobs were significantly lower. Zombies attracted not only banks' and

(continued on next page)

---

1. Ricardo J. Caballero, Takeo Hoshi, and Anil K. Kashyap, "Zombie Lending and Depressed Restructuring in Japan," *American Economic Review* 98, no. 5 (2008): 1943–77.

Box 1.1   Japanese zombies and the lost decade of growth
    (continued)

taxpayers' financial resources but also skilled workers by inefficiently keeping
wages too high. For example, a typical healthy real estate developer would
have hired 30 percent more workers if zombies had not created additional
demand for jobs. If Japan had allowed zombies to go bankrupt, the level of
investment in various sectors would have been higher by 4 to 36 percent per
year. Not surprisingly, the Japanese economy in the 1990s grew at an anemic
0.5 percent per year (compared with 2.6 percent in the United States during
the same period).

---

ployment benefits and support of regional active labor market policies)
constituted 74 billion rubles (about $3 billion, or 0.25 percent GDP). The
support to the "real sector" was an order of magnitude higher: 675 billion
rubles ($20 billion). This sum was about equally divided between "tar-
geted" and "general" support (373 billion rubles and 302 billion rubles,
respectively). The former was to provide assistance to specific industries
and, in most cases, to specific enterprises. The bulk (282 billion rubles
out of 302 billion rubles) of the "general support" was the reduction in
the corporate profit tax rate. While it seems to be general, this support
certainly disproportionately benefited a few specific enterprises—mostly
Gazprom and other raw material exporters—that remained profitable
even during the crisis.

Many critics argued that Russia's political system was too centralized
and would choose very bad economic policies. They said that the regime's
ideology, after all, places the state and loyalty to the rulers ahead of private property and merit. When the crisis hit with full force, such a government would have nationalized major banks and companies, with the
resulting inefficiency then burying the Russian economy, just as it doomed
the Soviet Union.

How did reasonable economic policies prevail in this crisis? The key
factor is that, for the first time in many years, the political and economic
system faced a genuine threat. The survival of the system depended on
preventing economic collapse. The crisis energized the government and
shifted more decision-making power to those who knew about and could
do something for the economy. The relatively promarket members of the
government were listened to and their advice was implemented to some
extent. The global economic crisis finally forced the government to adopt
sensible policies, thereby fending off disaster.

Unlike the fall of 2008, however, economic policy actions in 2009, when the most acute phase of the crisis was over, were quite different. As the oil prices started to recover, the government regained confidence and returned to preserving the precrisis status quo. There was no immediate danger to the economic system, and the urgency of correct economic policies subsided. Why did the government not use the crisis as the opportunity to restructure the economy and create a foundation for new businesses, diversification, and faster growth?

On the one hand, designing an anticrisis policy in a country like Russia would be easy. Given the massive lack of infrastructure, one might argue that the Russian government should have reacted to the crisis with a sizable fiscal stimulus directed at building much-needed and growth-enhancing infrastructure.

Why would such a stimulus have a significant effect on the Russian economy? There is an ongoing debate on the effectiveness of fiscal stimulus in the United States and other OECD countries. The most recent evidence points out that a fiscal stimulus has small effects in a developed economy. The main reason is the so-called Barro-Ricardian equivalence: In response to increased government expenditures, households would expect higher taxes in the future to pay for this extra spending and increase their savings, thus negating the potential impact on current consumption and GDP. Most recent detailed studies put the size of the multiplier at 1, i.e., GDP increases only by a dollar in response to a dollar increase in government expenditures. Economists such as Robert Barro argue that the multiplier is even lower and ranges between 0.7 and 0.8.

On the other hand, in Russia the fiscal multiplier on building roads, airports, electricity transmission lines, and broadband internet would certainly be large. This investment will have to be undertaken at some point in the future anyway, so Barro-Ricardian equivalence does not undermine the effectiveness of the stimulus. The problem with this argument is that the Russian government is ineffective and corrupt. The government's infrastructure spending may be misplaced—thus resulting in no desired long-term effect for the economy. Moreover, it may even lack the Keynesian property of supporting aggregate demand. If much of the stimulus is stolen and taken out of the country, the Russian economy does not receive it. Another issue is that the government did not make sufficient inroads in the fight against corruption, which in addition to the usual effects also complicates support of the unemployed. As we argued earlier, it is better to withdraw subsidies from inefficient enterprises and spend these funds for direct support of Russians suffering from the crisis. However, the government's ineffectiveness and corruption may make such targeted social assistance impossible or prohibitively costly. High inequality further aggravates this problem. If the government opts for restructuring the economy and prefers supporting the unemployed but fails, the increase in unemployment undermines social cohesion further and results in political upheaval.

The disappointing performance of the Russian economy can be contrasted with Brazil's much better weathering of the economic crisis, which was also heavily dependent on the prices of commodities. A recent article in the *Wall Street Journal* argues that the better performance in Brazil was largely due to good economic policies.[17]

> While most economies were battered by the global economic crisis last year, Brazil emerged largely unscathed and, by some measures, set record highs.... Latin America's biggest economy shrank only around 0.2 percent last year. Market and government forecasts now see Brazil's 2010 gross domestic product growth returning to pre-crisis levels of 5 percent to 6.5 percent. The center-left administration of President Luiz Inacio Lula da Silva proved sure-footed during the dark days of the global economic downturn. Government measures maintained employment and domestic demand, while inflation was comfortably kept in check below its 4.5 percent annual target. Thanks to tax cuts, improved credit conditions amid an aggressive easing in monetary policy and the stability of spending power for middle- and low-income households, demand for consumer durables continued through the worst of the crisis.

Another comparison is Chile, which significantly depends on the price of a natural resource (copper). Like Russia during the precrisis years, it maintained prudent fiscal policy, instituted sovereign wealth funds, and accumulated reserves. Chile is also similar to Russia in terms of per capita income (see figure 1.1). Yet, in 2009 Chile's GDP went down only by 1.6 percent and is expected to grow by more than 4 percent in 2010. Why has Chile weathered the crisis so much better than Russia? Chile was better prepared for the crisis as it had a competent and effective government, a flexible, liberal economy, and progressive social spending.[18] The government budget does not have the burden of supporting the pension system (which is privatized) and inefficient enterprises. Thus it can focus on alleviating the shock of the crisis via massive antipoverty programs and on investing in the future through building the education system.

Lessons Learned and Lessons that Should Have Been Learned

What lessons have Russian economic policymakers learned from the crisis? Seemingly, the government has all the evidence for the following:

The government is sufficiently competent to withstand the crisis. We agree only partially. While the government did implement mostly correct economic policies to fight the crisis, it made a few serious mistakes. Yet, the government's resolute response to the crisis shows that even within the current system there are reserves of efficiency that can be tapped.

---

17. "Brazil Ends 2009 Largely Unscathed by Global Economic Crisis," *Wall Street Journal*, January 5, 2010, http://online.wsj.com.

18. Philip Stephens, "Tables Turned: A Lesson from Latin America for the West," *Financial Times*, February 6, 2009.

Accumulation of reserves is good. We agree. Economic literature provides two strong arguments to support the idea. The first is the textbook argument related to the permanent income hypothesis. A country, like an individual, prefers to stabilize the level of consumption and avoid fluctuations. In times of boom (such as a commodity boom) it is optimal to stash away the extra funds for the rainy day of a recession. The second mechanism is described by Ricardo Caballero, Emmanuel Farhi, and Pierre-Olivier Gourinchas, who argue that the existence of so-called global imbalances is normal.[19] Global imbalances are a situation in which major emerging-market investors (China, Russia) are the net savers investing in the Anglo-Saxon financial system. The reason for such a pattern of investment flows is that these countries have higher risks and relatively less developed financial systems, especially in terms of credible long-term instruments (no developing country has instruments that match the liquidity and trustworthiness of, say, 30-year US bonds). In other words, the optimal policy for emerging markets is to accumulate reserves and invest them in (relatively) safer and long-term assets in developed countries. Before the crisis, the quality of Anglo-Saxon assets was exaggerated, but even after the crisis the quality is still above that of the assets in the rest of the world. An important issue to note is that, while the crisis supported accumulation of reserves, the Russian government was still very inefficient at using the reserves during the crisis. For example, almost a third of the reserves were spent in the ill-fated attempt to support the ruble.

Oil prices cannot stay low forever. Given Russia's reserves, policymakers can hope for luck. We disagree. If the global crisis lasted longer (remember all the discussion about the crisis being the second Great Depression?), oil prices would not have recovered so fast. It is also quite likely that global growth will slow down in the future—which will in turn result in significantly lower oil prices.

State ownership of banks is good. The government's fiscal stimulus has been slow and ineffective, but state-owned banks did relatively well in supporting the economy. However, we believe that it is dangerous to rely on state banks for financing long-term growth. At least outside of a crisis, private banks do a better job. They are free from political pressure in their lending decisions and manage risks more responsibly than state banks. Indeed, while state banks can hope for a complete bailout, private banks—via the deposit insurance system—can rely on only a partial bailout.

19. Ricardo J. Caballero, Emmanuel Farhi, and Pierre-Olivier Gourinchas, "An Equilibrium Model of 'Global Imbalances' and Low Interest Rates," *American Economic Review* 98, no. 1 (2008): 358–93.

In addition, two important lessons *should* have been learned from the crisis. First, the problems inherited from Putin's growth decade, corruption and inequality, are very serious and almost brought the economy to the brink of collapse during the crisis. Most importantly, these problems undermined the government's ability to respond to the crisis. Second, the government—as it acknowledged itself—has failed to use the crisis as an opportunity to restructure the economy.

Russia After the Crisis: The Challenges

Now fast forward to June 2009, the 13th Annual St. Petersburg International Economic Forum. While the receptions were less lavish than those of the previous year and the mood was not very festive, it was far from the panic of the fall of 2008. The topics of the sessions were vague, and they duplicated what almost every other large global conference discussed: the crisis, globalization, and the new financial architecture.

Usually, the interesting part of these forums is the plenary speeches by the main speakers. Of course, the most anticipated speech was by President Dmitri Medvedev. First, he said that the anticrisis economic decisions of 2008 were successful. Second, Russia continues lobbying for reform of the international financial architecture, improving the system of global financial regulation, empowering the international financial institutions, and creating reserve currencies as an alternative to the dollar. Finally, Medvedev rebuked protectionism and supported lowering taxes as part of the growth stimulus.

However, the main message of the forum lay in Deputy Prime Minister Igor Sechin's session, "What Is the Price of Oil?" During the session, participants were asked to answer the question using individual electronic devices. Most people voted for a range of $70 to $80 per barrel. Perhaps the "70-80" scenario is what Russian officials are hoping for. And indeed, the price of oil soon climbed back to $70 per barrel and stayed in the $70 to $80 range for the rest of 2009.

The return of high oil prices had important implications for the Russian economy: The markets believed that the global crisis was over and demand for oil was higher, and growth in Russia resumed. The experience in 2009 shows that the Russian economy has not decoupled from the world economy. Russia won the bet that oil prices would rise—and it is now on its way out of the economic crisis. The IMF forecasts Russia's growth (as of October 2009) at 3.5 percent per year until 2014. And the government itself acknowledged in its Anti-Crisis Program 2010 adopted on December 30, 2009 that so far its policies have not resulted in the restructuring of the economy.[20]

---

20. Ministry of Economic Development of the Russian Federation, "Anti-Crisis Measures

The postcrisis period for Russia will be very difficult. Russian economic growth will slow down because of both external and—most importantly—internal reasons. Lower worldwide economic growth will almost certainly result in lower oil prices than in the precrisis decade. It is reasonable to expect such slower growth as the world's largest economies will have to increase taxes to pay for the expenditures to support their economies during the crisis and as there is an unprecedented increase worldwide in antimarket sentiment and policies. In the less likely scenario where advanced economies inflate away the debt, Russia—as a reserve holder—will also suffer. Thus, even if oil prices remained high, they are very unlikely to continue to grow at precrisis rates—which will be a significant factor in Russia's growth slowdown. Moreover, tighter regulation of financial markets worldwide will increase risk aversion of investors and therefore decrease capital flows to emerging markets in general and to Russia in particular.

Russia's internal problems relate to the "resource curse." If oil prices remain high, Russia will probably delay much-needed economic reforms. The "low hanging fruit" of basic economic reform and prudent macroeconomic policies has already been picked. Future economic growth requires building political and economic institutions—such as constraints on the executive branch, improving the rule of law, lowering corruption, improving protection of property rights, contract enforcement, and competition. Such institutions are difficult to build in every society.

But in Russia it is especially problematic as the ruling elite is not interested in building such institutions. The "resource curse" provides an explanation: All other things equal, resource-rich economies tend to grow at slower rates. Jeffrey Sachs and Andrew Warner have provided cross-country evidence that resource-exporting countries have lower rates of economic growth.[21] Initially, the slower growth of resource-abundant economies was ascribed to macroeconomic effects of "Dutch disease," but later a consensus emerged that the resource curse mostly works through the institutional channel.[22] In particular, if a resource-rich economy has bad institutions to start with, it is less likely to improve its institutions than a similar resource-poor economy. This, in turn, has an adverse effect on growth. Interestingly, if a resource-rich economy already has good institutions, it does not suffer from the resource curse.

Program of the Government of the Russian Federation," June 19, 2009, available at www. economy.gov.ru.

21. Jeffrey Sachs and Andrew M. Warner, "Fundamental Sources of Long-Run Growth," *American Economic Review* 87, no. 2 (1997): 184–88.

22. See a survey of literature in Sergei M. Guriev, Alexander Plekhanov, and Konstantin Sonin, "Development Based on Commodity Revenues," EBRD Working Paper 108 (European Bank for Reconstruction and Development, 2009); and *Transition Report 2009: Transition in Crisis?* European Bank for Reconstruction and Development, 2009, chapter 4.

How can this pattern be explained? Consider the incentives of the ruling elite in a country with bad institutions. Such an elite trades off the returns from building good institutions against its costs. Good institutions result in higher economic growth and increase the "size of the pie." However, good institutions also constrain rent seeking by the ruling elite and increase political competition, raising the chances of the elite being replaced. How does resource abundance affect this tradeoff? The answer is straightforward: Resource rents weaken incentives to improve institutions. Indeed, the higher the resource rents, the greater the stakes of staying in power. Also, since growth in resource sectors is less sensitive to institutions, returns to good institutions in resource-rich economies are lower.

Weaker incentives for institutional reforms are only one part of the "resource curse" trap. Unfortunately, the fact that resource sectors are less sensitive to bad institutions creates a vicious circle. Indeed, if institutions are bad in a resource-rich economy, they are unlikely to improve, hence the nonresource sectors do not develop. Therefore, the economy remains resource-dependent with bad institutions. Moreover, the higher the oil price, the lower the incentives to develop institutions.

Figure 1.5 plots the dynamics of six key governance indicators during Boris Yeltsin's second presidential term and Putin's first and second presidential terms. The figure shows a clear downward trend in the quality of institutions during Putin's second term (2004–08), when oil prices rose to historically high levels.

In postcrisis Russia, two specific factors reinforce the resource curse. First, due to a massive renationalization since 2004, state-owned companies are once again controlling the commanding heights of the economy. State companies have no interest in developing modern institutions that protect private property and promote rule of law. Second, high inequality results in the majority preferring redistribution rather than private entrepreneurship.

The Russian elite fully understand these challenges.[23] Yet, the incentives to get out of the resource trap are weakened by the very importance of resource rents.

Inequality and corruption are also crucial obstacles to sustainable economic growth. Despite Russia's recent economic achievements, both remain at alarmingly high levels. Russians perceive inequality of opportunity to be very high; this undermines their trust in the capitalist economy and their support for private property rights. The majority of Russians believe that to acquire wealth one needs to be involved in criminal activity and have political connections; only 20 percent believe that

---

23. Sergei M. Guriev and Igor Fedyukin, "Challenges 2020: The View from Russian Business" (Moscow: New Economic School, 2008).

Figure 1.5   Dynamics of six key governance indicators during Boris Yeltsin's second (1996–2000) and Vladimir Putin's first (2000–2004) and second (2004–08) presidential terms

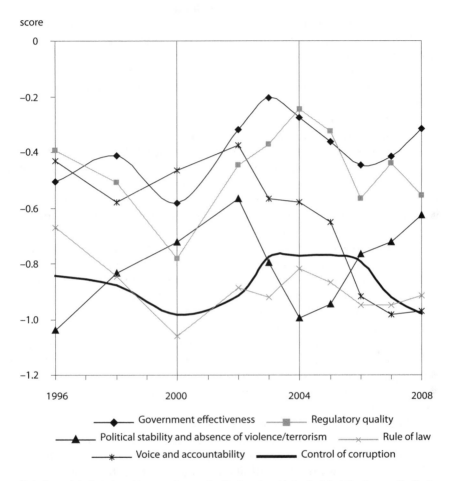

Note: For each indicator, world average is normalized to 0, and world standard deviation is normalized to 1.

Source: World Bank Institute's Governance Indicators Project.

talent matters.[24] These beliefs are self-fulfilling prophecies. Aside from the relatively small middle class and the even smaller business and intellectual elite, most Russians neither take risks to become entrepreneurs nor favor economic and political liberalization. According to the same survey, only 36 percent of Russians support democracy and a mere 28 percent

24. According to EBRD's Life in Transition Survey, quoted in Irina Denisova, Markus Eller, and Ekaterina Zhuravskaya, "What Do Russians Think about Transition?" *Economics of Transition* (forthcoming 2010).

support market reform, by far the lowest among all transition countries on both counts. The other major barrier to growth is corruption. Forty percent of firms in Russia reported making frequent unofficial payments, and roughly the same percentage indicated that corruption is a serious problem in doing business.[25] Unlike in other emerging markets, corruption has not declined with economic growth; it remains as high as in countries with one-quarter the per capita income of Russia. One reason for sustained corruption is that Russia's powerful bureaucracy stands to lose too much from economic liberalization. Perhaps more importantly, it is difficult to fight corruption without political reform, media freedom, and a vibrant civil society.

Yet another, related barrier to growth is overregulation of the economy that slows the process of "creative destruction." More than half a century ago, Austrian economist Joseph Schumpeter (1883–1950) introduced this term, which denotes the mechanism that cleanses the economy. The economy lives and grows, Schumpeter showed, through the destruction of old companies, methods, and ideas and the arrival of new companies that are more productive and profitable.

During crises the rate of self-cleansing in an economy significantly increases, causing the losers to increase their resistance as well. Politicians and lobbyists redouble their efforts to save the "dinosaurs" under the banner of helping "the real sector" or saving the symbols of national industry (such as AvtoVAZ in Russia or General Motors in the United States). Sometimes representatives of the old economy win the battle for resources. But their victory is everyone else's loss. Artificial protection of ineffective companies that wield political influence is possible only by using taxpayers' money. Massive inflows of funds to unprofitable firms that should have gone bankrupt or been liquidated slow economic growth for many years.

Putting up barriers to creative destruction is very costly. For example, Philippe Aghion and Peter Howitt (creators of the modern version of Schumpeterian ideas, the economic theory of endogenous growth) show this by contrasting Europe, with its high barriers to entry and strong employment support, and the United States, where barriers are lower.[26] About 50 percent of new US pharmaceutical products are developed by companies that are less than 10 years old; in Europe it is only 10 percent. Twelve percent of the largest companies in the United States were created in the last 20 years; in Europe only 4 percent. In a recent review of empirical research on the effects of forces of creative destruction, macroeconomist Ricardo Caballero concludes that in the long run the Schumpeterian mechanism is

25. *Business Environment and Enterprise Performance Survey*, World Bank and EBRD, www.ebrd.com.

26. Philippe Aghion and Peter Howitt, "Appropriate Growth Policy: A Unifying Framework," *Journal of the European Economic Association* 4 (April–May 2006): 269–314.

responsible for about 50 percent of productivity growth.[27] He also studied how productivity grew in 60 countries and how such growth is affected by social protection mechanisms (for example, by a complicated procedure for firing workers). The conclusion of this research is that excessive job protection leads to 0.9 to 1.2 percentage points slower productivity growth compared with countries in which social protection is lower.

Importantly, after a crisis such overregulated countries grow about 30 percent slower. Another essential element of self-cleansing of the economy is free international trade with low trade barriers and tariffs. For example, in sectors that were significantly affected by lower customs tariffs after signing of the free trade agreement between Canada and the United States productivity growth increased by 15 percent in part because of the 12 percent reduction in inefficient jobs.

Schumpeter's theory offers an important lesson for Russia. During Soviet times the mechanisms of competition and creative destruction were essentially turned off. But these mechanisms are responsible for about half of the long-term growth in advanced economies. The main element of technological progress, entrepreneurship, was punished by imprisonment. We all know the result of the Soviet economic policy—inefficiency of industry and agriculture and underdevelopment of the services sector—which eventually bankrupted the Soviet Union itself. The problem of limited creative destruction is exacerbated in Russia by deficiencies in the corporate bankruptcy code, which limits self-cleansing mechanisms of the economy.

The crisis of 1998 showed that without significant government policy intervention, the Russian economy can speedily return to the trajectory of growth. Now the Russian state has significantly more financial resources than 10 years ago, which not only presents additional opportunities but also leads to temptations to engage in protectionist and interventionist economic policies—give money to large and influential companies, help Russian industry by increasing customs tariffs, or force companies to support excessively high employment. Politicians have to remember that the key to fast recovery from the crisis and the foundation for long-term growth is creative destruction, which has to be supported rather than restrained.

Strategic Priorities for Russia

Fast economic growth in postcrisis Russia will be very difficult, both because the external environment is unlikely to be as benign as it was during Putin's years and because there will be no incentives to undertake reforms. Nonetheless, we deem it necessary to spell out a reform agenda

---

27. Ricardo J. Caballero, "Creative Destruction," in *New Palgrave Dictionary of Economics*, 2d ed., ed. Steven N. Durlauf and Lawrence E. Blume (Palgrave MacMillan, 2008).

in the unlikely scenario that a reform coalition emerges. Our list of reforms does *not* include political decentralization and political liberalization but is likely to result in such social changes. There is no silver bullet for reform and there are no magic recipes for modernization. Most of what we describe is basic economics, which if implemented will result in significantly higher growth rates in Russia. We should emphasize that the list is not about "inventing a bicycle"—most of these reforms were already in Putin's own economic agenda in 2000. This reform plan (the so-called Gref Program, named after its main author, former Minister of Economy Herman Gref) was adopted by the Russian government at the beginning of Putin's first presidential term as the government's official strategy for 2000–10, but most of it was never implemented.

Reforms face general problems in a country suffering from a resource curse. The first is limited capacity of reformers: Reformers in government are scarce and rent seekers abundant. The second problem is limited commitment to reform. Even if reformers have a chance to implement a specific reform package, the resource-curse logic implies such a window of opportunity may not last long. This is why one should start with a short list of reforms to create commitment for further reforms.

There are two devices to create commitment to reforms: a critical mass of stakeholders and outside anchors. A critical mass of stakeholders, namely private owners, who will support reforms can be generated in two major ways. The first is privatization of large companies. The new owners of privatized firms will know that their success is contingent upon building market institutions. Unlike in the 1990s, privatization can now be done in an effective way and will also generate fiscal revenues. Several competitive and open privatization tenders and IPOs have been produced in recent years (including large privatizations of generation capacity during the electricity-sector reform). The capital market is now much more efficient. Corporate accounts are now certainly more informative than in the early 1990s. Unemployment—the nemesis of all privatization supporters—is not going to be a very important issue for Russia postcrisis. Indeed, before the crisis, the *shortage* of workers became a major constraint on economic growth.

Second, further (and drastic) deregulation of small businesses will unlock the entry and growth of such businesses, owners of which are the most faithful proponents of competition, property rights, and contract enforcement. Once a critical mass of small business owners emerges, it will become a powerful lobby against predatory regulation and corruption.

Both these measures will create a (upper) middle class as stakeholders for further reform. It is important to complement these measures with the flat income tax and regressive social tax. Given the persistent attitude toward entrepreneurship as being a "criminal" rather than "lawful" activity, the tax system must provide incentives for entrepreneurs to pay rather than evade taxes.

The next key step is to identify an outside anchor for reforms. Having EU accession as an overarching goal helped Central and Eastern European countries to commit to institutional change. Russia does not have a strong anchor like EU accession. But even weaker anchors like World Trade Organization (WTO) and OECD accessions are helpful. As both can help promote rule of law for both domestic and foreign investors, these goals should be announced and pursued.

Two other major "self-proclaimed" outside anchors are: (1) raise the ruble to the status of an international reserve currency and (2) build an internationally competitive financial sector in Moscow. Both ideas may seem unrealistic at the moment but if pursued with persistence over a long period of time may be successful. As a reserve currency, the ruble may well be in demand as it represents a good hedge against rising oil prices. As long as ruble inflation is low, and the ruble exchange rate is flexible and free of political risks, many oil-importing countries will want to hold rubles or ruble bonds. Russia is a natural economic capital of the postcommunist world and can succeed as an international financial center—provided financial regulation and infrastructure are improved. In both cases, reforms required are exactly those Russia would need to implement anyway. The external anchor helps provide an independent assessment of the reforms' success.

Given outside anchors, macroeconomic policy becomes rather straightforward. Russia should move to inflation targeting (with slowly decreasing inflation targets) and a floating exchange rate. There is, however, an important challenge. Inflation targeting requires a functioning ruble yield curve. This in turn implies that Russia should borrow domestically, which may crowd out private borrowers and result in positive real interest rates. To what extent is it a serious problem? Russia has not experienced real positive interest rates recently. Yet one can argue that with lower inflation and positive real interest rate, household savings will increase and financial markets will become more stable and efficient, resulting in lower cost of long-term capital for business. Inflation targeting is also connected to a political issue. It is difficult to implement as long as the central bank is not independent. Even though independence of the monetary authority is difficult, it is not impossible. Appointing independent members on the yet-to-be-created Monetary Policy Committee is not more difficult than nominating independent directors to 100 percent state-owned companies, which the Russian government successfully did in 2008 and 2009. Eventually, better monetary policy will promote financial development (due to lower inflation and better regulation) and benefit nonresource sectors.

A key issue is the reform of state-owned companies and their eventual privatization. The Russian government consolidated ownership and created large state-owned corporations, which often dominate their respective industries. The overwhelming economic literature argues that state-owned companies are less efficient than the privately owned. Moreover, the inefficiency of state-owned companies is a substantial tax on every other company, drawing necessary financial and labor resources (see chapter 7, which puts forward a reform plan for Gazprom, and Friebel et al.'s paper, which suggests a reform plan for the Russian railroads along the lines of the Latin American railroad reform).[28] On top of restructuring energy and transportation monopolies, Russia should encourage foreign direct investment and raise regulated tariffs to increase energy efficiency.

Several other reforms are necessary but financially costly. The first is army reform (see chapter 8). One may think that this issue has little to do with economics. This is not the case. The current situation in which a large portion of the military is manned by the draft is an important determinant of stratification in society, which fosters and sustains already high inequality in income and opportunity. Michael Lokshin and Ruslan Yemtsov show that the burden of the draft falls disproportionately on poor and less-educated Russians and imposes an additional large implicit tax on their income.[29] The probability of being drafted decreases significantly in cities with more than 100,000 inhabitants. A young male from Moscow or St. Petersburg is six times less likely to be drafted than his counterpart from a rural area. The probability of being drafted in a family from the richest part of society is only 3 percent while in the poorest it is 20 percent. Apart from military service itself, the draft significantly affects the income of families with sons enlisted in the armed forces. Lokshin and Yemtsov show that the draft decreases the income of their families by about 15 percent. This number likely underestimates the economic losses as it does not take into account that a returning draftee has to start his career with less work experience, which in turn affects his salary. And it does not count the fact that the probability of getting injured or dying is significantly higher in the military. That is why the draft acts as an additional tax on the poorest parts of society and reinforces inequality in Russian society.

Many proponents of the status quo argue that the current Russian military is in reality made of volunteers—those who do not want to serve could pay a bribe to avoid service. This logic is fallacious. First, the status quo punishes those who respect the law. Second, the bribes paid by the service dodgers are not collected by the state and do not fund the military. Third, in the military, a "free" draftee is valued at an implicit "price" of zero, which is significantly less than the draftee's value for society or the economy. The solution is evident: A fully volunteer military, in which servicemen and women are paid "market" wages, will clearly improve the efficiency of the military and allocation of resources in society.

---

28. Guido Friebel, Sergei Guriev, Russell Pittman, Elizaveta Shevyakhova, and Anna Tomova, "Railroad Restructuring in Russia and Central and Eastern Europe: One Solution for All Problems?" *Transport Reviews* 27, no. 3 (2007): 251–71.

29. Michael Lokshin and Ruslan Yemtsov, "Who Bears the Cost of Russia's Military Draft?" *Economics of Transition* 16, no. 3 (2008): 359–87.

Another significant problem is the pension system. The Russian population is aging and shrinking, leading to a decrease in the number of working-age people and contributions. In a no-reform scenario, the replacement rate of the public system is projected to decline to about 17 percent in 2030, far below the current level of about 26 percent, which is already widely perceived as inadequate and implies that many state pensions will be below the subsistence level.[30] The pension reform that started in 2001 is not adequate to address these challenges. The current retirement age is too low, and there are multiple incentives for early retirement. A politically costly yet necessary move toward a fully funded system can be achieved only through raising the retirement age and decreasing incentives to retire early. Economic research gives clear prescriptions for how to provide such incentives, for example, by increasing the income replacement rate with the length of employment history.

The question is how to fund these reforms (and others such as education and health-care reform). If done in conjunction with other reforms, part of the costs can be financed with the increased foreign direct investment in Russia (if the other reforms improve business climate and control corruption) and with increased household savings (if the other reforms build a better-functioning financial market and conservative monetary and fiscal policy is sustained). Another option is to borrow abroad, which is a viable route as Russia has virtually no foreign public debt.

The reforms just mentioned are painful, risky, and not exciting. Is there an alternative plan to modernize and diversify? Is it possible to at least lessen the income gap with the rich countries within 10 to 15 years?

Everybody is looking for a silver bullet. There are many such plans— vertical industrial policy, horizontal industrial policy, development institutions, to name a few—but all have been tried in the last 10 years. The level of corruption has remained the same (if not become worse), and the economy has still not diversified. The only difference from 1998 is that Russia is now a much richer country. The low hanging fruit of "catch-up" growth has been picked. So it is time again to listen to "boring accountants" and undertake the boring "not-inventing-the-bicycle" economic reforms. Interestingly, many of these reforms are already outlined in the government's own Long-Term Development Strategy (also known as the 2020 Concept Paper). The problem is that—as with the Gref Program in 2000—the 2020 strategy may not be implemented. This would be equivalent to the "inertia scenario" outlined in the 2020 strategy. Such an outcome is not impossible; it seems to be most likely—given the "resource curse" and lack of incentives to reform.

---

30. David Hauner, "Macroeconomic Effects of Pension Reform in Russia," IMF Working Paper WP/08/201 (Washington: International Monetary Fund, 2008).

What Next?

To sum up, Russia may follow either of two scenarios: (1) difficult economic reforms that will build the foundation for faster economic growth or (2) Brezhnev era–like "70-80" stagnation (and eventual bankruptcy).

If economic reforms are not implemented, Russia is likely to enter a new decade of Brezhnev-style stagnation. A parallel that we already discussed is the "lost decade" of the 1990s in Japan, when the acute phase of the crisis was mostly over but the economy grew very slowly for more than 10 years. During the fat years of high oil prices in Russia, there was some hope that at least a part of the largesse would be spent on infrastructure or education, which would have contributed to long-term economic growth. During the near collapse of the economy in the fall of 2008, we thought that finally the government would realize the need for pushing ahead with radical economic reforms, eventually leading to a modern and fast-growing economy. But while the government's policies were effective in dealing with the immediate crisis, they did not address long-term growth slowdown. Russia still has an ossified, corrupt, and inefficient economy built during the fat years of the oil boom.

The "70-80" plan will conserve the status quo, but the rigid system will not be able to withstand another economic crisis. Russia will not have the benefits of uninterrupted, fast growth, which had allowed it to partially close the gap with OECD economies and to build large reserves that saved the economy in this crisis. The only alternative that we see is economic reforms.

2

Russian Politics in a Time of Economic Turmoil

DANIEL TREISMAN

To explain Russia's politics in the last two decades, most scholars focus on the aims of the country's leaders and the formal institutions they created. I argue here that such accounts miss the central element in Russia's postcommunist political economy. Although the designs of those in the Kremlin obviously made a difference, what mattered more were economic forces that were largely beyond their control. Economic conditions shaped public opinion, which, in turn, determined how the formal institutions worked and whether the leaders would get a chance to implement their ideas. Checks—if not balances—arose spontaneously to constrain presidents who had become unpopular and then melted away when the public recovered confidence in the state's chief executive.[1]

In advancing this argument, I make five claims and offer brief evidence for them. First, Russia's dramatic economic contraction after 1990 and its vigorous recovery after 1998 were caused by factors over which the presidents in power at the time had little control. Boris Yeltsin inherited an economy that was imploding; his successor, Vladimir Putin, took over one that was poised to recover. Second, the economy's fall and rise reshaped public opinion, first destroying Yeltsin's popularity and then helping sus-

Daniel Treisman is professor of political science at the University of California, Los Angeles. He thanks Anders Åslund, Keith Crane, Thomas Graham, Andrew Healey, Andrei Illarionov, Andrew Kuchins, Ed Verona, and other participants in seminars at the Center for Strategic and International Studies and Loyola Marymount University for helpful comments.

1. This chapter draws throughout on my earlier paper "Presidential Popularity in a Young Democracy: Russia under Yeltsin and Putin" (manuscript, University of California, Los Angeles, November 2009) and on my forthcoming book *The Return: Russia's Journey from Gorbachev to Medvedev* (New York: Free Press, 2010).

tain the persistently high ratings of his successor. Third, the incumbent president's ability to enact and implement policies increased and decreased in line with—and, to a considerable extent, because of—changes in that president's popularity. Yeltsin's plummeting ratings emboldened his opponents in the parliament, in regional governments, and elsewhere to block his initiatives and undermine his authority. Conversely, as Putin's popularity soared, such opposition evaporated. Fourth, changes in Russia's formal political institutions during this period explain little about the varying ability of presidents to set an agenda and push it forward. Fifth, the different ideas and aims of Mikhail Gorbachev, Boris Yeltsin, and Vladimir Putin did help to determine Russia's path—but primarily at moments when the incumbent leader was popular. The ideas of unpopular leaders were mostly ignored.

This view of Russian politics differs from conventional accounts in several ways. Both scholars and journalists usually portray ordinary Russian citizens as innocent bystanders in—or victims of—Kremlin politics. I suggest that leaders were actually sensitive to and often constrained by public opinion. Although the public could be fickle, its views were often influential. While missing the importance of public opinion, observers have overemphasized formal institutions. Great significance has been attributed to the extensive formal powers of the Russian presidency since 1993. I argue that these powers meant little when the president was unpopular and were not necessary when his ratings were high. A preoccupation with formal institutions led democracy advocates to condemn details of Russia's political institutions—use of proportional representation in Duma elections, central appointment of regional executives, and a six-year presidential term—that in fact do not distinguish Russia much from many long-established and effective European democracies. The problem was not undemocratic institutions so much as undemocratic *practices*, by which incumbents, shielded by broad and genuine public support, subverted the letter or spirit of relatively democratic laws.[2]

If the character and outcomes of Russian politics depend on public opinion, itself driven largely by economic conditions, the global financial

---

2. See Treisman, *The Return*, chapter 10. Many of the world's democracies—including Austria, Denmark, Spain, and Switzerland—elect their parliaments using the same party-list proportional representation system that Russia introduced for the 2007 election. (Previously, the Duma was elected half on party lists, half in single member constituencies.) Russia's six-year presidential term is on the long side for European democracies, yet until 2002 France's president served for seven years. Putin was widely censured for abolishing elections for regional governors. But among European Union members, a number—including Portugal, Bulgaria, Estonia, and Lithuania—have regional executives that are centrally appointed. None of these countries are widely criticized for this. The greatest problems for democracy in Russia—considerable falsification of election results, administrative and economic pressures on the media, and biased rulings of courts and electoral commissions—were all informal or illegal practices.

crisis of 2008–10 could bring political change. I briefly explore how the early months of the crisis played out and outline three scenarios for what might lie ahead.

Economic Crisis and Recovery

Opinions differ about the quality of Russia's economic management in the 1990s and the wisdom of the reform strategy chosen. Whatever one thinks about this, two points are hard to deny. As Yeltsin took possession of Gorbachev's Kremlin office in 1991, the country was already in a grave economic crisis. And as his successor, Vladimir Putin, took over in 2000, Russia had already begun a vigorous recovery.

Yeltsin's policies in the 1990s may have affected the depth and duration of the economic downturn. But by the time he reached the Kremlin, a severe contraction was unavoidable. This is evident from the fact that output in all the countries of Eastern Europe and the former Soviet Union fell significantly after communism fell. The drop in officially reported GDP per capita in the 15 former Soviet republics ranged from 68 percent (in Tajikistan) to 22 percent (in Estonia).[3] Russia's decline, at 39 percent, was the tenth largest. The Eastern European countries, some of which had started their transitional recessions earlier, also suffered major contractions.

A number of causes contributed to this downturn: chronic inefficiency of Soviet-style planning, worn-out and obsolete capital stock, disruption of production chains, shock of transition to world prices for trade, macroeconomic imbalances created by some of the last communist governments, and—for those like Russia that were major commodity exporters—the fall in world commodity prices.[4] Official statistics greatly exaggerate the decrease in the value of what was produced. Under communism, much of the output counted in the GDP figures was overvalued, consisting of goods of appalling quality that no one would buy freely or state orders for which there was no real demand. Afterwards, much output was produced underground and therefore not recorded in official statistics.[5] But even

---

3. Figures for the fall in real GDP per capita (in constant local currency units) between 1991 and the year in which GDP per capita was lowest, calculated from World Bank, *World Development Indicators*.

4. See, for example, Nauro F. Campos and Fabrizio Coricelli, "Growth in Transition: What We Know, What We Don't, and What We Should," *Journal of Economic Literature* (September 2002), 793–836, and Oleh Havrylyshyn, "Recovery and Growth in Transition: A Decade of Evidence," *IMF Staff Papers* 48 (2001), 53–87.

5. Anders Åslund, "How Small Is Soviet National Income?" in *The Impoverished Superpower: Perestroika and the Soviet Military Burden*, ed. Henry S. Rowen and Charles Wolf, Jr. (San Francisco: ICS Press, 1994), 13–62; Evgeny Gavrilenkov and Vincent Koen, "How Large Was the Output Collapse in Russia: Alternative Measures and Welfare Implications," IMF Working Paper 94/154 (Washington: International Monetary Fund, 1994).

taking such mismeasurement into account, there was almost certainly a significant fall in output. No country found a way to avoid it.

If the crash was universal, so was the recovery. From the late 1990s, rapid growth resumed in all postcommunist countries. The rise in GDP per capita in 1998–2008 among the former Soviet republics ranged from 44 percent (in Kyrgyzstan) to 282 percent (in Azerbaijan). Russia had the eighth strongest rebound. In Eastern Europe as well, the 2000s saw high growth. The recovery was caused in part by the effects of the reforms of the early 1990s, and, in Russia's case, by the resurgence of commodity prices. Again, the fact that recovery came everywhere makes it hard to credit it principally to Putin's economic management.

In short, although the policy choices of postcommunist leaders probably influenced the severity and length of their countries' economic contractions and the speed and vigor of their subsequent recoveries, the experience of contraction in the early 1990s and recovery in the 2000s was common and apparently inescapable. In Russia, Yeltsin inherited an economic catastrophe from his predecessor; Putin received an economy that was ready to rebound.

Consequences of Economics for Politics

The gyrations in Russia's economy had profound effects on public opinion. Evidence suggests they were a major influence on the popularity of the country's successive presidents.

In 1988, several of Russia's most-respected, semi-dissident sociologists founded the polling organization VCIOM in Moscow. It quickly acquired a reputation for professionalism and independence. This was widely thought to be the real reason why in 2003 the Putin administration repossessed the organization, forcing out its director, Yury Levada. Most of Levada's colleagues left to form the Levada Center, which continued the group's polls. From 1989, VCIOM began asking its representative sample of voting-age Russians—at first occasionally, from late 1996 more regularly—whether they approved or disapproved of the country's political leaders. Figure 2.1 shows the percent approving of the country's first four presidents (including Gorbachev, the one and only Soviet president). We see, first, the collapse in Gorbachev's support in 1989–91 and the parallel rise in Yeltsin's, which peaked in December 1990 at almost 90 percent. Then came Yeltsin's long slide to a rating of just 6 percent in late 1999. Approval of Vladimir Putin, appointed prime minister in August 1999, rocketed to 84 percent in mid-January 2000 as he took over as acting president and then remained between 61 and 87 percent during the next eight years. In 2008, his replacement, Dmitri Medvedev, started out a little below Putin's final level.

The patterns of presidential approval shown in figure 2.1 turn out to

Figure 2.1   Approval ratings of Soviet and Russian leaders, 1989–2009

percent approving of the leader

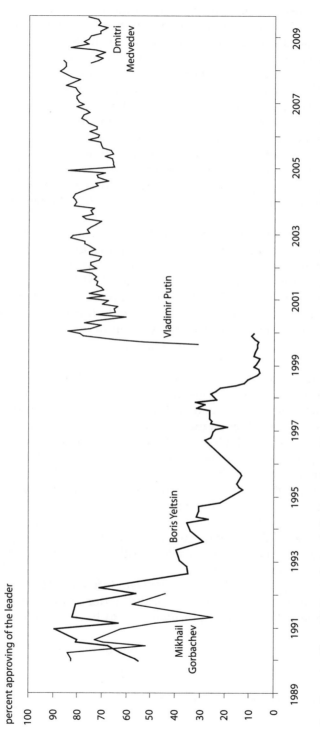

Note: The questions vary slightly in the 1990s, but all ask whether or to what extent the respondent "approves" of the president's performance, actions, or handling of his responsibilities. Putin's approval includes his period as prime minister. Missing values interpolated.

Sources: VCIOM and Levada Center polls, available at http://sofist.socpol.ru and www.russiavotes.org.

be closely related to public perceptions of the state of the Russian economy.[6] From 1993—and then more regularly from mid-1994—the pollsters
of VCIOM asked Russians how they would evaluate the economic situation in Russia and the state of their family's finances, as well as what they
thought awaited Russia's economy in coming months. The relationship
between economic perceptions and presidential approval can be seen in
figure 2.2. The dashed line plots an index of positive economic sentiment
constructed by adding the percentage of respondents that thought Russia's economic situation was "very good," "good," or "intermediate" to
the percentage that said they expected a "significant improvement" or
"some improvement" in coming months. Superimposed on it is a line
measuring the average rating given by respondents to the incumbent
president when asked to rate him on a scale from 1, the worst, to 10, the
best.

It is hard, looking at figure 2.2, not to see a connection between economic sentiment and the public's rating of its president. I confirm the link
between economic perceptions and presidential approval with more elab-
orate statistical tests in a more technical paper.[7] Although it is difficult to
be certain which of the different elements of economic sentiment—evaluations of national economic conditions, family finances, or expectations
about future economic performance—were most important since they are
highly correlated, measures of economic perceptions do a good job of accounting for the trends in the ratings.

Of course, economic factors do not explain all the variation. Other
factors also mattered at various times. Episodes of boorish behavior on
Yeltsin's part cost him popularity. When in Berlin in August 1994 after
too many glasses of champagne he grabbed the baton and energetically
conducted a police band while television cameras rolled, his rating fell by
about one quarter point on the 10-point scale. Putin's resolute response to
the invasion of Dagestan by Chechen guerrillas and the terrorist bomb-
ings of four apartment buildings in late 1999 may have helped propel
his rating upwards, although the economic resurgence would likely have
achieved the same result a few months later. On the other hand, both
the first and second Chechen wars appear to have mostly depressed the
popularity of the incumbent president. Although these and other political factors help to explain some of the peaks and valleys in the rating,
economic perceptions had a more consistent influence. Had the economy
under Yeltsin performed as well as it did under Putin, statistical simulations suggest Russia's first president would have left office extremely
popular.

It could be that the public's perceptions of the economy were them-

6. Treisman, "Presidential Popularity in a Young Democracy."

7. Ibid.

Figure 2.2 Economic sentiment and presidential approval in Russia, 1993–2008

economic sentiment (percent)   presidential approval (10-point scale)

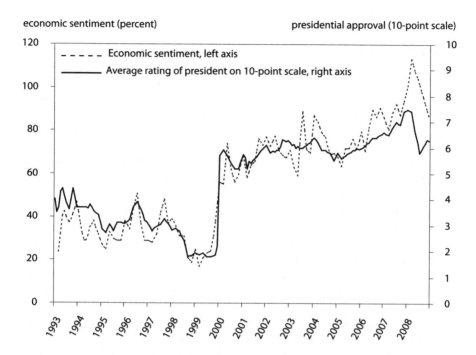

Note: Economic sentiment is percent saying "very good," "good," or "intermediate," when asked "How would you evaluate Russia's economic situation?" plus percent saying "a significant improvement" or "some improvement" when asked "What awaits Russia in coming months in the economy?" Missing values interpolated.

Sources: VCIOM; Levada Center; author's calculations.

selves manipulated by the regime, which under Putin was exerting increasing influence over the mass media. In this case, economics would not be driving politics; politics would be shaping economic perceptions. Analyzing the determinants of economic perceptions, I found that media effects could explain some of the change over time in Russians' views of the economy—in particular, assessments improved more than was warranted during the 1996 and 2004 presidential election campaigns, only to sink afterwards.

Evaluations of the economy were also slightly rosier when Russians had greater confidence in their president. However, on the whole, Russians' assessments of economic conditions tracked objective economic indicators—average real wage, average pension, real wage arrears, unemployment, and job openings. By and large, Russians were not tricked into approving of their president by deceptive media reports about economic performance. Rather, they accurately perceived the contraction of the early and mid-1990s and the rapid recovery after 1998. As the economy deteriorated, their disapproval of Yeltsin intensified; as it recovered, support for Putin reached unprecedented heights.

Presidential Popularity and Political Constraints

As the president's popularity waxed and waned, so did his ability to get things done. Yeltsin's slide in the ratings encouraged ambitious rivals to block his attempts to enact and implement policies, generating deadlock and a widespread sense of impunity. As Putin's popularity soared, most of the obstacles his predecessor had faced evaporated. After his first few months in office, Yeltsin had to fight with skill and stamina for every minor reform. By contrast, Putin enjoyed enviable freedom of action to push his agenda to fruition.

A first potential barrier for the executive was, of course, the parliament. At no point did Yeltsin enjoy a solid base of support in the legislature. But as his popularity dwindled, it grew harder to get loyalists elected or even to hold on to them between elections. In late 1990, pro-government parties held about 24 percent of the seats in the RSFSR Supreme Soviet.[8] Three years later, in the election of December 1993 pro-government parties won 19 percent of seats in the new Duma. In December 1995, they won only about 14 percent. By 1999, however, the tide was turning. That December, on the back of Putin's sprint upwards in the ratings, the pro-government Unity bloc along with the loyalist Our Home Is Russia won 18 percent of seats.[9] By the election of 2003, progovernment parties were winning 58 percent of seats, and in December 2007 they won 78 percent of seats (see figure 2.3).

---

8. I classify pro-government parties as follows. In the RSFSR Supreme Soviet (1990–93): the "Coalition for Reform" bloc, including Democratic Russia, Radical Democrats, Left of Center, Non-Party Faction, and Free Russia (for discussion of this classification, see Josephine T. Andrews, *When Majorities Fail: The Russian Parliament, 1990-1993* (New York: Cambridge University Press, 2002), 128; Richard Sakwa, *Russian Politics and Society* (New York: Routledge, 1993), 67; and Thomas Remington, *Politics in Russia*, 3d ed. (New York: Pearson, 2004), 175). In the Duma, 1994–95: Russia's Choice, Party of Russian Unity and Accord; 1995–99: Our Home Is Russia, Russia's Democratic Choice, Party of Russian Unity and Accord; 1999–2003: Unity, Our Home Is Russia, United Russia; 2003–present: United Russia, Fair Russia. Other sources on the balance of parliamentary factions include Anders Åslund, *How Russia Became a Market Economy* (Washington: Brookings Institution, 1995), 201; Thomas F. Remington, *The Russian Parliament: Institutional Evolution in a Transitional Regime, 1989–1999* (New Haven: Yale University Press, 2001), 178–79, 195; and the website www.russiavotes.org.

9. If one classified the Union of Right Forces (URF), the successor to Russia's Choice, as a pro-government party, the pro-government bloc would swell to about 24 percent. The URF won 6.4 percent of the seats in 1999. However, it was not a reliable partner of the government by this point.

Figure 2.3   Presidential popularity and government support in parliament, 1991–2008

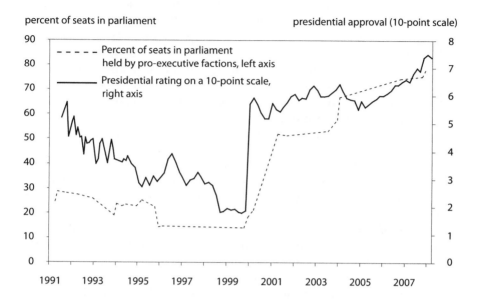

percent of seats in parliament

presidential approval (10-point scale)

Note: Fair Russia, formed in October 2006, is treated as a pro-government party.

Sources: Levada Center, www.russiavotes.org; Thomas Remington, *The Russian Parliament: Institutional Evolution in a Transitional Regime, 1989–1999* (New Haven: Yale University Press), 178–79, 195; Anders Åslund, *How Russia Became a Market Economy,* 201; Josephine T. Andrews, *When Majorities Fail: The Russian Parliament, 1990–1993* (New York: Cambridge University Press, 2002), 128.

The Kremlin's changing ability to win friends in parliament was felt not just at election time. During most legislative terms, factions shrank or swelled as deputies defected from one to another and "independents" joined factions in the hope of getting a committee assignment. The Kremlin forces usually managed to coopt a few additional independents in the first month or two of a session with promises of patronage. But after that, when the president's popularity was falling, the pro-government bloc tended to hemorrhage deputies. Its total fell from 23.6 percent of seats in January 1994 to 22.5 percent in October 1995, and from 14.7 percent in February 1996 to 13.9 percent in October 1999.

The opposite occurred after 1999 as deputies raced to join the faction of the suddenly immensely popular Putin. Between December 1999 and March 2000, Unity swelled from 18.4 to 21.1 percent of the seats. By July 2003, it had persuaded three other factions—Fatherland-All Russia, Russian Regions, and People's Deputy—to join it in a stable coalition comprising 53 percent of the seats. (Fatherland-All Russia merged with United Russia in 2001.) Between December 2003 and October 2007—without any new parliamentary election—the rush to jump on Putin's coattails increased the pro-executive factions from 58 to 75 percent of seats.

The nominal size of factions was not everything. Even though his allies held only about one-quarter of the seats in 1991, at moments when his popularity was soaring Yeltsin could leverage this into large majorities. Bathed in the glow of his victory against the August coup plotters, his rating near an all-time high, Yeltsin managed to convince almost the entire Supreme Soviet to endorse his plans for radical economic reform and to vote him the power to rule by decree and appoint regional governors. But later, as his popularity plunged, he had to fight for each scrap of legislation. Every year, passing the budget required creative deal-making and tactical finesse.

Even when the government got its way, it took longer to push bills through the legislature. The time taken to pass important, nonbudgetary bills increased from fewer than six months in 1994 to almost two years in 1999. It fell rapidly in 2000 with Putin's election and soaring popularity and stayed relatively low throughout his presidency, averaging about six months.[10] The president signed the momentous bill introducing a flat-rate income tax just 65 days after it was introduced in the Duma.[11] The Federation Council proved readier to veto bills introduced by the executive branch under Yeltsin than under Putin. During 1994–99, the Federation Council vetoed 12 percent of such bills, while during 2000–04, it vetoed only 6 percent of such bills.[12] And as Yeltsin's rating fell, he had to fight off repeated attempts to impeach him. The deputies tried in December 1992, March 1993, September 1993, July 1995, and June 1998-April 1999. All attempts failed to receive the required number of votes, although the 1999 effort came quite close. No attempt was made to impeach the more popular Putin.

A second set of obstacles lay in the regional capitals. Yeltsin's plunging rating emboldened the governors to take control of their budgets, assert rights over federal property, even to coopt locally based federal bureaucrats. They ignored government instructions and remitted less tax revenue to the center. Some even supported the Communist extreme opposition. In deciding how far to go in resisting Moscow, evidence suggests the governors took local public opinion into account. In regions where support for

---

10. See Paul Chaisty, "The Legislative Effects of Presidential Partisan Powers in Post-Communist Russia," *Government and Opposition* 43, no. 3 (2008), 424–53, at 448–49.

11. Yegor Gaidar, Current Russian Politics (speech, University of California, Los Angeles, June 14, 2002).

12. Calculated using dataset on Russian bills from 1994 to 2004, collected by Moshe Haspel and Thomas F. Remington. I am grateful to Tom Remington for sharing this. Since the executive is unlikely to introduce bills it expects the Federation Council to veto, it is not surprising that the absolute number of vetoes is relatively low. The contrast, however, suggests that the Putin administration was less frequently subjected to unpleasant surprises.

Yeltsin had been falling relatively faster, the governors were more likely to oppose Yeltsin at critical moments.

One such moment came in September 1993, when Yeltsin declared a state of emergency and ordered the Supreme Soviet to dissolve. A group of deputies refused to leave the building, prompting a constitutional standoff. At this point, 15 of the country's governors spoke out against Yeltsin's action, rallying behind the parliament. Which governors did so was related to local trends in the president's popularity. In regions where support for Yeltsin had fallen in the previous two years, 30 percent of the leaders publicly opposed him; where support for Yeltsin had risen, only 11 percent did. A similar calculus appears to have influenced how regional delegations to the national parliament voted. Deputies from regions where support for Yeltsin had fallen in 1991–93 were more likely to vote against the government's proposals at the March 1993 Congress of People's Deputies session.[13]

By contrast, after Putin's approval rating rose above 80 percent and he won the election in the first round in 2000, opposition from the previously obstreperous governors disappeared. They stood by docilely as he took away their seats in the parliament's upper house, which had conferred legal immunity, imposed a structure of presidential prefects to watch over them, reduced their share of government revenues from 54 percent in 1999 to 35 percent in 2005, and abolished popular elections for their positions.[14] Despite these adverse changes, no governors were overtly fighting the Kremlin, and some seemed positively enthusiastic.

I do not mean to suggest that it was presidential popularity by itself that reshaped the political arena so dramatically. The surge in presidential popularity under Putin was part of a syndrome of positive developments that also included higher tax revenues, expanded government spending (in absolute terms), and revived public optimism, all of which were stimulated by the economic recovery and, in turn, helped underwrite the image of an active, effective president. Yet the president's rating was not just a concomitant of presidential power—it was a signal to potential opponents not to stick their necks out. High approval enabled the president to intimidate, coopt, and coordinate other political actors.

In characterizing political systems, it is customary to focus on the institutions. Yet in Russia in the 1990s and 2000s, such an approach can lead one astray. In fact, the system operated very differently at different times, even without any significant change in the rules and structures of government. Conversely, institutions changed in major ways without much affecting the way the system worked.

---

13. Daniel Treisman, *After the Deluge: Regional Crises and Political Consolidation in Russia* (Ann Arbor: University of Michigan Press, 1999), 122–31, 234.

14. Goskomstat Rossii, *Finansy Rossii* [*Russia's Finances*] (2000, 2008).

The greatest institutional reform in the postcommunist period was the adoption of the new constitution in December 1993. Some viewed this constitution as virtually—or actually—authoritarian in the powers it gave to the president.[15] The previous constitution had assigned sovereign—indeed, dictatorial—authority to the Supreme Soviet. Did this mean that after December 1993 Yeltsin could enact and implement the reforms he favored? Not at all. He remained blocked at every step by the opposition majority in the new Duma, by the defiant ranks of the governors, and by the evasive measures and lobbying of the country's major business interests. There was no noticeable increase in the effectiveness of the executive. Yeltsin struggled for years to institute the free sale of land and a liberal new tax code; he never succeeded.

Another much-discussed institutional change concerned the selection of regional governors. In late 1991, Yeltsin won the right to appoint the governors; then during the mid-1990s, he gradually allowed the regions to elect their leaders; finally in 2004 Putin returned the system to one of presidential nomination. Did the strength of the center vis-à-vis the regional executives increase and decrease in line with these institutional changes? Elected governors were sometimes harder to manage than their appointed counterparts. But this was a relatively small effect. Context was far more important. The greatest regional defiance of central authority came in 1992–93, precisely the period in which almost all the governors were presidential appointees. Putin's success in curbing the governors came not after he reintroduced presidential nomination, but in 2000–02, while they were still popularly elected.

Indeed, the major recentralization of authority and reassertion of presidential power occurred between 1998 and 2002 with almost no significant simultaneous change in political institutions. During his entire eight years in the Kremlin, Putin did not amend the constitution once, although he could have done so quite easily. The changes he did make to the formal government system were relatively minor. And yet his ability to get his way was incomparably greater than Yeltsin's, and the pattern of political outcomes was completely different.

A second common misapprehension is the belief that in Russian politics the opinions of ordinary citizens have been largely irrelevant.[16] In fact, as I have argued, public opinion plays a central role, helping to define the president's freedom of maneuver. A popular president can accomplish far more than an unpopular one. In this, Russia is like many other countries,

---

15. See, for instance, Pavel Felgenhauer, "Yeltsin—The Man who Created Contemporary Russia," *Eurasia Daily Monitor* (Jamestown Foundation, April 24, 2007), www.jamestown.org (accessed on December 10, 2009).

16. For instance, Stephen Holmes, "Simulations of Power in Putin's Russia," in *Russia After the Fall*, ed. Andrew Kuchins (Washington: Carnegie Endowment for International Peace, 2002).

including the United States, where the effectiveness of presidents also depends upon their approval ratings. But the logic in Russia is even starker.

In practice, both Yeltsin and Putin were often solicitous of public opinion, and both adapted their policies in response to it. Even before his first competitive election in March 1989, Yeltsin confessed that he was attentively following "all the official and unofficial public opinion polls (including those of the Americans)."[17] Putin's Kremlin remained an avid consumer of such data, served up for it in recent years by the sociologists of Aleksandr Oslon's Fond Obshchestvennogo Mneniya. Yeltsin's decisions both to pursue radical economic reform in late 1991 and to moderate its pace from late 1992 were in line with public opinion at the time.[18] Putin's emphasis on restoring order, attacking the oligarchs, and increasing the state's role in the economy were all extremely popular.[19] His nods to nostalgia such as the reinstatement of Soviet era music to the national anthem also aimed to buy him popularity—and succeeded.[20] Both his cooperation with the United States after 9/11 and his gradual slide into resentful ambivalence also mirrored the evolution of Russian public opinion. In October 2001, 61 percent of Russians felt "very good" or "mostly good" about the United States, and 62 percent expressed willingness to give blood to help the American victims of the 9/11 terrorist attack. By January 2009, after the Iraq war, US recognition of Kosovo, and Washington's support for Georgia in the 2008 war with Russia, the percentage feeling good about the United States had fallen to 38 percent, and 49 percent "felt bad" about the American superpower.[21]

---

17. Boris Yeltsin, *Ispoved na zadannuyu temu* [*Confession on a Given Topic*] (Moscow: Ogonyok, 1990), 1.

18. The creation of a market economy was favored by 74 percent of Russians, according to one poll in late 1991, although slightly more favored a "gradual" than a "rapid" transition (VCIOM, Omnibus 1991-15, December 1991–January 1992, 3,453 respondents, see http://sofist.socpol.ru.). Sixty-one percent endorsed the privatization of large enterprises; only 13 percent thought that private enterprises were not necessary at all (VCIOM, Fakt 1991-11, November 1991, 1,960 respondents, http://sofist.socpol.ru). Between December 1991 and December 1992, the percentage of respondents favoring a transition to the market "as fast as possible" fell from 33 to 19 percent, and the percentage favoring a gradual transition increased from 41 to 51 percent (VCIOM, Omnibus 1991-15, December 1991–January 1992, and 1992-15, December 1992–January 1993, http://sofist.socpol.ru.)

19. In August 2001, 62 percent of Russians thought the state had "too little" a role in the economy, compared with 3 percent that said it had "too much." In July 2003, 37 percent thought all privatized property should be returned to the state and another 31 percent thought this should be done in cases in which illegality in the privatization process was proven. See www.russiavotes.org.

20. Treisman, "Presidential Popularity in a Young Democracy."

21. Levada Center polls, available at www.russiavotes.org (accessed on November 15, 2009).

Politics in the Financial Crisis

Despite the hopes of some Russian leaders that their country could remain an "island of stability" in the international financial crisis of 2008–10, it too succumbed to the effects of the global meltdown.[22] Industrial production fell by almost 3 percent in the last quarter of 2008 and by 15 percent in the first quarter of 2009, before stabilizing. Compared with a year earlier, real disposable incomes were 6 percent lower in the last quarter of 2008, roughly flat in the first and second quarters of 2009, and lower again in the third quarter.[23] In line with the deterioration, Russians' perceptions of the economy also darkened. The percentage characterizing the state of the Russian economy as "very good," "good," or "intermediate" fell from 64 percent in June 2008 to 50 percent in March 2009. The share expecting some economic improvement in coming months fell from 40 percent in June 2008 to 26 percent that December.

Based on past experience, one might expect the crisis to pull down the ratings of Putin and Medvedev, perhaps even jeopardizing the successful model of governance of the previous eight years. Since Medvedev's inauguration, the ratings of the two leaders have been extremely highly correlated ($r = .88$ in levels and $r = .92$ in first differences). Medvedev's approval tracks Putin's almost exactly, and the gap between them narrowed from about 10 points early in Medvedev's term to about six points in late 2009. As economic sentiment deteriorated, their ratings slipped a little in parallel. The popularity of both surged—Medvedev's jumped 10 points and Putin's 5 points—as Russians rallied behind the Kremlin after the August 2008 war with Georgia. Despite this, between June 2008 and April 2009, Medvedev's rating fell from 73 to 68 percent and Putin's from 83 to 76 percent. However, the economy began to stabilize in the spring of 2009, and economic perceptions improved again. By October 2009, approval had risen to 72 percent for Medvedev and 78 percent for Putin.

If the stabilization of mid-2009 proves temporary and the economy enters a period of sustained, severe decline, one might expect the slide in the leaders' popularity to resume. Of course, they start from an unusually high level, so it could take some time for even a major deterioration to pull the leaders' ratings into dangerous territory. On the other hand, in a grave crisis Russians' sensitivity to economic conditions might increase. During the economic turmoil under Yeltsin, perceptions of the economy had a stronger impact on presidential popularity than in the period of steady in-

---

22. The quote is from Finance Minister Aleksei Kudrin's speech to the Davos Economic Summit in January 2008 (see *Russia Today*, "Russia Is an 'Island of Stability': Finance Minister," January 24, 2008, www.russiatoday.ru).

23. Data downloaded from Roskomstat RF, www.gks.ru (accessed on December 10, 2009).

come growth under Putin, during which Russians apparently acclimated to the new, more positive environment.[24]

Were the ratings of the ruling "tandem" to plunge, history suggests opposition would spontaneously emerge, timidly at first but then more assertively. Most likely, it would come from familiar quarters. Regional governors and legislatures might dare to resist unpopular central projects. Dissent might sound from within the parliament, where factional divisions might appear within United Russia. One might see more public protests, the breaking of previous taboos in the media, more legal challenges against officials, perhaps even some overt disagreements among cabinet members. Of course, history never repeats itself exactly and resistance could also come from new directions. Some unusually independent judge might risk ruling against the Kremlin on some important issue. Institutions created to coopt the elite such as the Public Chamber might start to play a more independent role. Whatever its source, the viability of any resistance would depend on the continued worsening of economic conditions driving down the incumbents' ratings. Other events—military hostilities, terrorist attacks—could intervene.

How the two leaders would react is impossible to predict. A crisis of confidence in their leadership might prompt either a loosening or a tightening of administrative controls and could either reinforce or weaken the bond between them.[25] While nothing is impossible, the chances of genuine conflict between the two appear slim given how closely their political interests are aligned. The almost identical paths of Medvedev's and Putin's ratings show that, nearly two years after the turnover, Russians still see the two as virtually joined at the hip and assign shared responsibility to them for both economic performance and the prosecution of the Georgian war.

Already in early 2009, some rumblings could be heard from the more outspoken governors. Mintimer Shaimiev (of Tatarstan) and Yuri Luzhkov (of Moscow) had already raised the idea of reintroducing gubernatorial elections, earning a quick rebuke from Medvedev.[26] Then in June 2009, Murtaza Rakhimov, the long-serving president of Bashkortostan, lashed out in an interview at the incompetence of the United Russia leadership, saying the party was being run by people who had "never commanded so much as three chickens." He called the rubber stamp politics of the Duma "embarrassing to watch" and warned that "the population is laughing!"[27] This was just before the recovery kicked in; he may have regretted his

24. Treisman, "Presidential Popularity in a Young Democracy."

25. Treisman, *The Return*.

26. Mikhail Vinogradov, "Will There Be a 'Medvedev Thaw'?" *Pro et Contra*, nos. 5-6 (2008).

27. Dmitri Bulin, "Torzhestvo plyuralizma" ["The Triumph of Pluralism"], *Politichesky klass*, May 21–June 6, 2009.

candor as the tandem's ratings revived. But it gave a hint of what might be expected were the economic slide to restart.

The administration in 2009 appeared intensely focused on the possibility of protest. Riot police were flown from Moscow to Vladivostok in December 2008 to arrest dozens of demonstrators incensed by Putin's increase in tariffs on imported automobiles, which had decimated the trade in used Japanese cars.[28] By spring 2009, a program had been installed on the computers of Medvedev and two of his top aides, Sergei Naryshkin and Vladislav Surkov, showing a map of the country highlighting regions in crisis—as classified on the basis of 60 indicators that included Putin's local rating.[29] Then, when unpaid workers in the "one-industry town" of Pikalevo blocked the highway and occupied the local government building, Moscow tried a new tactic—a televised, and completely staged, dressing-down of a Kremlin-friendly oligarch, who was in fact given additional financial aid to quiet the local workers.[30] The spectacle was supposed to encourage other businessmen to dip into their wallets to appease local pockets of protest.

Conclusion

The way in which economic conditions shape Russian public opinion, which, in turn, determines the effectiveness of the government, is hardly unique. Indeed, the striking thing is how closely the logic described here resembles political processes in other electoral democracies, both liberal and illiberal. Russia, often portrayed as unique and mysterious, is in this respect both familiar and intelligible. In the United States, research has traced links from better economic performance to higher presidential ratings, and from presidential popularity to more effective promotion of the president's legislative agenda, at least on salient issues on which the public does not have entrenched views.[31] Similar phenomena have been noted in Latin American states such as Argentina, Brazil, and Uruguay.[32]

---

28. *The Times,* "Moscow Riot Police Flown in to Smash Protests against Car Tariffs in Vladivostok," December 22, 2008.

29. Konstantin Gaaze and Darya Guseva, "Lezte s mest" ["Stand Up"], *Russky Newsweek,* March 16, 2009.

30. Darya Guseva, Artem Vernidub, and Nadezhda Ivanitskaya, "Na Deripasovskoy khoroshaya pogoda" ["The Weather Is Good on Deripasovskaya Street"], *Russky Newsweek,* June 8, 2009; *Moscow News,* "Putin Has Pikalevo Jumping, Money Flying," June 5, 2009.

31. On economics and presidential approval, see, for instance, Robert S. Erikson, Michael B. MacKuen, James A. Stimson, "Bankers or Peasants Revisited: Economic Expectations and Presidential Approval," *Electoral Studies* 19, no. 2 (2000): 295–312. On presidential approval and policy effectiveness, see Brandice Canes-Wrone and Scott de Marchi, "Presidential Approval and Legislative Success," *Journal of Politics* 64, no. 2 (2002): 491–509.

32. Michael S. Lewis-Beck and Mary Stegmaier, "The Economic Vote in Transitional Democ-

On the one hand, this pattern suggests greater accountability than is implied by characterizations of Kremlin politics as the domain of an insulated elite. The public turns out to have an important role in politics. On the other hand, the mode of accountability is somewhat perverse. First, in Russia, where economic conditions depend strongly on international factors like the price of oil, economic performance is a very noisy signal of the incumbent's competence. Presidents end up revered or scorned largely on the basis of fortuitous factors. This is not necessarily irrational—given the ignorance of the public about what drives Russia's economy, it may make sense to simply hold the incumbent responsible. Still, it leads to some major errors. Second, the long lags between policies and their results have meant that Russia's leaders, when they were not being rated based on international conditions, were repeatedly rewarded or penalized for the actions of their predecessors. Gorbachev was a bit of an exception. His own mismanagement arguably played as big a role in the economic disaster on his watch as the problems he inherited. But history played tricks on his two successors. Yeltsin was punished for the catastrophe bequeathed to him by Gorbachev, while Putin was rewarded for a boom caused in part by the market reforms Yeltsin had introduced.

One way to read the message of this chapter would be to conclude that everything in Russian politics is just a function of the price of oil. That would be too reductionist. Of course, oil price changes have been a major determinant of Russia's economic history from the 1980s to the present.[33] But their importance has varied over time, and other factors mattered as well. In the 1980s, the sharp drop in oil prices did not make the collapse of the Soviet economy inevitable. Rather, it prompted Gorbachev to borrow like crazy, triple the money supply, and initiate reforms that were disastrously misconceived.[34] At this point, a different economic strategy might have had quite different results. During the recovery phase, the link between oil prices and growth was far clearer in 2005–09 than in 1999–2001 (when growth owed more to the devaluation) and 2001–04 (when higher output of oil and minerals mattered at least as much as prices). Economists estimate that higher oil prices can explain between one-third and one-half

racies," *Journal of Elections, Public Opinion & Parties* 18, no. 3 (2003), 303–23; Scott Mainwaring, "Multipartism, Robust Federalism, and Presidentialism in Brazil," in *Presidentialism and Democracy in Latin America*, ed. S. Mainwaring and M. Shugart (New York: Cambridge University Press, 1997); David Altman, "The Politics of Coalition Formation and Survival in Multiparty Presidential Democracies: The Case of Uruguay (1989–1999)," *Party Politics* 6, no. 3 (2000): 259–83; Eduardo Alemán and Ernesto Calvo, "Unified Government, Bill Approval, and the Legislative Weight of the President," *Comparative Political Studies* (forthcoming).

33. Yegor Gaidar, *Collapse of an Empire: Lessons for Modern Russia* (Washington: Brookings Institution Press, 2007).

34. Treisman, *The Return*, chapter 1.

of the total growth since 1999.[35] I find clear statistical relationships running from real wages, pensions, and unemployment to economic perceptions, and from these to presidential approval. But I find only weaker relationships between changes in the oil price and economic perceptions.

Even though the oil price is not everything, it has become increasingly important in recent years. With most operational fields approaching exhaustion, increasing output will require major investments to develop new fields—investments that have been discouraged by high taxation of oil profits and insecure property rights. Within the Kremlin as well as outside, a belief has been spreading that the reasons for rapid growth in 1999–2007 no longer apply. The response has been to talk feverishly about innovation policy, diversification strategies, nanotechnology, and so on. Yet, so far, Medvedev's focus on modernization has been undercut by continued evidence of judicial corruption, abusive corporate raiding by state insiders, and security service intimidation at the margins of academia. It is also unclear what niche in the world economy is free for Russia to fill if it diversifies away from minerals, in which it has an obvious comparative advantage.

Of course, economic performance and public opinion are not the only elements in Russia's political economy. I do not mean to suggest that economic fluctuations can explain every uptick and slide in the president's rating or every success and failure in enacting policy. I show elsewhere that the wars in Chechnya also mattered for presidential approval, as did various other temporary factors. Despite Yeltsin's low popularity and formidable constraints, his ministers did manage to push through important reforms in the 1990s, using strategies that coopted some opponents while marginalizing others.[36] The Putin administration, despite more auspicious conditions, did not achieve all of its goals.

In the next few years, Russia seems likely to develop according to one of three scenarios. If oil and gas prices surge again and remain very high, the sense of urgency about reforms will dissipate. "So long as oil prices were growing, many, almost all of us, to be honest, fell for the illusion

---

35. Paavo Suni, "Oil Prices and the Russian Economy: Some Simulation Studies with NiGEM," Discussion Paper 1088 (Helsinki: Research Institute of the Finnish Economy, 2007) estimates that higher oil prices explain about 2.5 points (38 percent) of the 6.5 percent average growth rate in 2001–06. Roland Beck, Annette Kamps, and Elitza Mileva, "Long-Term Growth Prospects for the Russian Economy" (Frankfurt: European Central Bank, 2007), reviewing previous studies, note estimated long-run elasticities of GDP to permanent increases in the oil price of 0.15 to 0.20. Using the monthly prices of European Brent oil, these elasticities imply that the change in oil prices in 1999–2007 can explain 25 to 33 points of the 72 percent increase in GDP (measured in constant rubles) between those years—or, in other words, 35 to 46 percent of the total growth.

36. Andrei Shleifer and Daniel Treisman, *Without a Map: Political Tactics and Economic Reform in Russia* (Cambridge, MA: MIT Press, 2000).

that structural reforms could wait," Medvedev confessed in November 2009.[37] Complacence could return. A resumption of boom times would keep the Kremlin incumbents popular and opposition to their rule muted. If oil prices remain around their current level of $70 to $80 a barrel, the Kremlin's most likely strategy is one of muddling through. This would probably result in somewhat slower growth, with gradually increasing public discontent and louder grumbling among the elite. But, barring some unexpected trauma, a gradual slide would probably not be enough to prompt a major departure from the established model.

If, however, oil and gas prices plunge and stay low long enough to push the economy into deep recession, driving up unemployment and exhausting the government's fiscal resources, more serious opposition could emerge, leading ultimately to challenges to the regime. How the men on the tandem would react is unpredictable. A joint approach seems far more likely than genuine conflict between the two, although for public relations purposes Medvedev might be cast as the advocate of a softer hand. Regimes that have been in power for a long time tend to make mistakes at critical moments, and the current leadership has no experience of governing in bad times. If economic turmoil returns, the centralized structures of the Putin era—the "super-presidency," the "vertical of power" between Moscow and the governors, and the hierarchical United Russia party—may turn out to be less effective at enforcing the leaders' will than in the past. Once again, the context is likely to prove more important than the institutions.

---

37. Medvedev's annual address to the Federal Assembly, November 12, 2009, http://eng. kremlin.ru (accessed on December 11, 2009).

3

Federalism in Russia

EKATERINA ZHURAVSKAYA

Reforms during the 1990s in Russia entailed not only economic liberalization and democratization but also transition from a highly centralized unitary state to a highly decentralized federal state. Since the advent of Vladimir Putin's presidency, former president Boris Yeltsin's experiments with decentralization have been recognized as unsuccessful and as leading to the very collapse of Russia. A consensus has emerged—among scholars, politicians, and the society at large—that the attempt to build a successful federal system in the 1990s badly failed. The new Russian leadership has been consistently taking measures since 2000 to recentralize both public finance and politics. This chapter addresses the following questions: Why did Yeltsin's decentralization fail? What mistakes (if any) were made in the 1990s? How effective is Putin's reversal of Yeltsin's decentralization? Where is the notorious "vertical of power" taking Russia?

These questions have no easy answers, but the experience of other federal states and an examination of Russia's own political economy of intergovernmental relations suggest that the approach being implemented now is no less dangerous than the spontaneous decentralization of the 1990s. Indeed, because of the size of the country and the heterogeneity of its regions, federalism in Russia is inevitable. For the effective functioning of the principles of federalism, Russia needs the "vertical of power," which political economists refer to as political centralization. The "verticals," however, can be different. Other countries' experience with federalism, particularly Mexico and China, shows that the measures that Putin and company are undertaking are unlikely to succeed.

Ekaterina Zhuravskaya is the Hans Rausing Professor of Economics at the New Economic School in Moscow and academic director of the Center for Economic and Financial Research.

Three main lessons emerge from my analysis in this chapter. First, without a strong, functioning, and real opposition and free media, the federal center will not be able to pursue efficient policies, unless one hopes for a miracle. The fact that such a miracle is happening in China is not a guarantee that it can happen on Russian soil. The transition of the last 20 years has clearly demonstrated that transplants do not take root without special conditions, and Russia has clearly violated these conditions.

Second, federalism combined with the absence of elections at the local level can potentially work only when the policy is designed solely to deliver economic growth and is not aimed at providing public goods, such as quality education, health care, and social protection. Such a one-sided goal is politically feasible only in poor countries, but Russia is in the higher middle-income group.

Third, an alternative to Putin's centralization exists, but it entails a complete change of the political system. Obviously it is not easy to implement and obviously the current leadership does not have an interest in trying to do so, but if implemented, it can achieve the balance between political centralization and local accountability necessary for effective federalism. This alternative scenario is in building strong national political parties, together with maintaining political competition by preserving political opposition and free media, as well as holding open and free elections at all levels.

Principles of Federalism

To develop successfully a country needs a system of providing incentives to public officials. Incentives are needed to ensure that bureaucrats and politicians work for the benefit of the people instead of doing nothing or using public office for private gain. The task of creating such a system of incentives for countries with vast territory and diverse population is much more complicated than for small and homogeneous states. First, in these countries, it is much more difficult, compared with small states, to define what is "good for the people." For example, in large and heterogeneous countries, such as Russia, central authorities have much less information about the preferences of people in different parts of the country. And often, the available information is not enough for central provision of public goods to be effective. Second, central management of a large country involves a large state apparatus. Effective control of a large bureaucracy is very complicated, expensive, and not always feasible. For these reasons, authority over public goods provision should be delegated to lower-level governments, in the hope that they will serve the interests of the local population. Because of its vast size and economic and ethnic diversity, Russia cannot be managed efficiently from the center as a corporation in contrast to, for example, Belarus, Mongolia, or Lithuania. Therefore, the answer to the question about whether to delegate authority to the local level is obvious. Instead, the question should be: How should decentralization of authority be designed for federalism to work in Russia?

Based on the experience of developed, wealthy federations, such as the United States and Switzerland, many scholars, including such pillars of economic thought as Friedrich von Hayek and Charles Mills Tiebout, independently came to the conclusion that the delegation of authority to local governments works just fine if three "simple" conditions are met. Two of these conditions are necessary to create political incentives and one to create economic incentives for local authorities. The conditions to create political incentives are: (1) mobility, allowing people to "vote with their feet," and (2) development of democracy, allowing people to "vote with their heart." Poorly performing local politicians lose constituent populations or at least votes in elections. The third condition is necessary to create economic incentives, also known as fiscal incentives. In addition to delegating responsibility to provide public goods, a functioning federalist system must also delegate the authority to every level of government to collect taxes to cover the costs of providing public goods at that level. This way local authorities have incentives to provide these public goods efficiently, i.e., at the lowest cost.

Do these conditions apply to Russian federalism? Are these conditions necessary and/or sufficient for Russia? To understand answers to these questions, it is important to understand the history of Russia's federalism, which I describe briefly in the next section. The history consists of two distinct periods with opposite trends: first, Yeltsin's decentralization of 1991–99; and second, Putin's centralization from 2000 onward. Figures 3.1 and 3.2 portray the dynamics of subnational expenditure and revenue shares, vividly demonstrating the differences between the two periods. Under Yeltsin's rule, regional shares of revenue and expenditure were growing, but when Putin assumed power, regional revenue shares started declining, while shares of expenditure remained approximately constant.

Yeltsin's Decentralization in the 1990s

Russia of the early 1990s inherited a highly centralized Soviet system of intergovernmental fiscal relations, in which the center used financial transfers to the regions as a means to maintain the integrity of the empire. These transfers were purely politically motivated and did not take into account economic considerations.

Fiscal and political decentralization was also driven solely by political motivations. To conduct reforms, President Yeltsin needed the support of regional leaders.[1] The delegation of substantial financial and political autonomy to the regions (in Yeltsin's own words "as much as regions can assume") in exchange for their loyalty was a forced political compromise that allowed liberalization and privatization. Without decentralization,

---

1. As wonderfully described by Andrei Shleifer and Daniel Treisman, *Without a Map: Political Tactics and Economic Reform in Russia* (Cambridge, MA: MIT Press, 2000).

**Figure 3.1   Share of subnational expenditures in total outlays of
national and subnational governments without
extrabudgetary funds, 1992–2006**

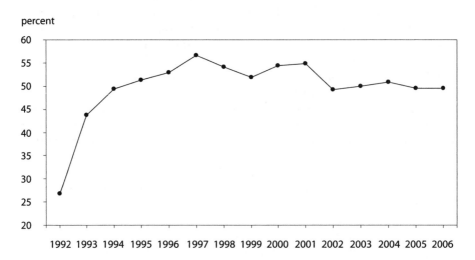

Source: Migara O. De Silva, Galina Kurlyandskaya, Elena Andreeva, and Natalia Golovanova, *Intergovernmental Reforms in the Russian Federation: One Step Forward, Two Steps Back?* (Washington: World Bank, 2009) based on Russian Ministry of Finance data (excluding extrabudgetary funds).

through which the center bought temporary support of governors, basic liberalization reforms would have been politically infeasible.

The transfer of fiscal authority from the center to the regions took the form of chaotic informal bargaining, and cash transfers became a tool in the political game. At different points in time, they were allocated to loyal regions as a reward or to opposition regions as a bribe.[2]

The sequencing of power transfers to the regions was disorderly but far from random. Yeltsin gave political autonomy first to the most politically powerful regions: two metropolitan areas (St. Petersburg and Moscow) and six republics (not counting Chechnya),[3] where elections were held in 1991. In addition, Yeltsin allowed elections first in the poorest regions with the worst fiscal results. At the end of 1991, a five-year moratorium on elections for regional leaders appointed by Yeltsin was proclaimed, but during this period 31 regional elections in the most

---

2. For empirical evidence, see Daniel Treisman, "The Politics of Intergovernmental Transfers in Post-Soviet Russia," *British Journal of Political Science* 26 (1996): 299–335; Vladimir Popov, "Fiscal Federalism in Russia: Rules versus Electoral Politics," *Comparative Economic Studies* 44, no. 4 (2004): 515–41; and Elena Jarocinska, "Are Intergovernmental Grants Tactical? Evidence from Russia," *Economics of Transition* (forthcoming 2010).

3. Elections in Chechnya were considered illegitimate.

Figure 3.2   Share of subnational revenues in total revenues of national and subnational governments without extrabudgetary funds, 1992–2006

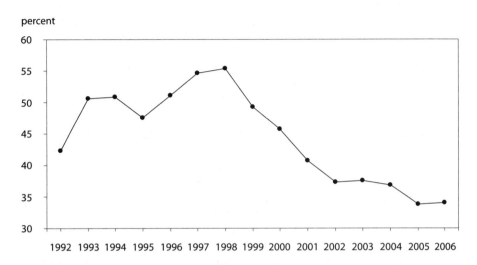

Source: Migara O. De Silva, Galina Kurlyandskaya, Elena Andreeva, and Natalia Golovanova, *Intergovernmental Reforms in the Russian Federation: One Step Forward, Two Steps Back?* (Washington: World Bank, 2009) based on Russian Ministry of Finance data (excluding extrabudgetary funds).

economically troublesome regions took place with his consent (and two without). This evidence illustrates another important political rationale for decentralization: When the economy is not doing well, central authorities are interested in political decentralization to push responsibility for poor performance of the economy onto subnational governments.

Thus, decentralization was conducted purely for political reasons: first, to provide support for liberal reforms at the center, which—as everybody expected at first—were supposed to produce rapid growth, and subsequently, to push responsibility for the failure to deliver the expected economic growth onto the regional governments. Because decentralization at the time was politically motivated, its economic effects were never considered. Historical and economic analyses of the outcome of Yeltsin's chaotic decentralization of the early 1990s suggest it certainly contributed to the reasons why the expected growth did not come about for a long time after transition had started.

Principles of Federalism Violated

Russia of the 1990s provides an important lesson about what happens when delegation of power to local authorities takes place in an environment that is not ideal, i.e., without the benchmark principles of federalism from Western democracies mentioned earlier. Indeed, Russia violated all three principles. Decentralization was characterized by poor local accountability and nontransparent division of expenditure responsibilities and revenue assignments. No one but regional business elites constrained the power of regional governors. Local elections rarely worked as a disciplining device, as the election's outcome depended on the notorious "administrative resource" rather than the performance of the governors. Legislative and judicial powers as well as the local press often were under the direct control of the governors and did not provide checks and balances. In addition, low mobility of the population due to prohibitively high economic costs of migration in most regions made it impossible for people to "vote with their feet," i.e., to escape from the provincial regions to Moscow.[4]

Fragile democratic institutions at the local level made regional governments in Russia easily susceptible to "capture" by new wealth. Politically powerful firms influenced the rules of the game in the economy: They prevented competition by hindering development of businesses and changed the direction and speed of economic reforms.[5] The 1999 Business Environment and Enterprise Performance Survey[6] confirmed that state capture was deeply rooted in economic and political processes of the country: In the composite index of state capture among 20 transition countries, Russia ranked fourth.[7]

Irina Slinko, Evgeny Yakovlev, and I created a measure of state capture in the Russian regions based on Russian legislation in 1992–2000 and evaluated the effects of capture by politically influential firms.[8] Although the study found no robust evidence that capture had a significant impact on aggregate economic growth, it showed that the economy was suffering from state capture by powerful elites. Firms without political influence stagnated; their productivity, sales, and investments declined with an increase in state capture of the regions. Growth of regional small businesses was also hampered; their share of employment and retail turnover went

---

4. Yuri Andrienko and Sergei Guriev, "Determinants of Interregional Mobility in Russia," *Economics of Transition* 12, no. 1 (2004): 1–27.

5. For a theoretical model of state capture with an application to Russia's context, see Konstantin Sonin, "Why the Rich May Favor Poor Protection of Property Rights," *Journal of Comparative Economics* 31, no. 4 (2003): 715–31.

6. European Bank for Reconstruction and Development (EBRD) and World Bank, Business Environment and Enterprise Performance Survey (BEEPS), www.worldbank.org.

7. Joel S. Hellman and Mark Schankerman, "Intervention, Corruption and Capture," *Economics of Transition* 8, no. 3 (2000): 545–76; Joel S. Hellman, Geraint Jones, Daniel Kaufmann, and Mark Schankerman, "Measuring Governance, Corruption, and State Capture: How Firms and Bureaucrats Shape the Business Environment in Transition Economies," World Bank Policy Research Working Paper no. 2312 (Washington: World Bank, 2000).

8. Irina Slinko, Evgeny Yakovlev, and Ekaterina Zhuravskaya, "Laws for Sale: Evidence from Russia," *American Law and Economics Review* 7, no. 1 (2005): 284–318.

down with the growth in regional capture. Regional budgets were also negatively affected: Tax collection decreased and arrears to budgets increased, leading to a deterioration in regional public goods provision.

A survey of mayors of large Russian cities in 1996 showed that in the first half of the 1990s fiscal incentives in the major cities were very weak.[9] Revenue sharing between regional and local governments game no incentive to local governments to increase the tax base or provide public goods. Both the positive and negative changes in large cities' revenue were almost entirely compensated for by changes in shared revenue (through adjustments in tax-sharing rates and size of regional transfers). Alexey Makrushin, Slinko, and I conducted a more general study using the same methodology and data for more than a thousand municipal budgets for the second half of the 1990s.[10] Our results confirmed that the additional revenues of municipalities were expropriated by regional authorities through changes in the percentage of deductions from regulatory taxes and size of the transfer and that this was particularly severe for big urban municipalities. Furthermore, weak fiscal incentives led to local governments' overregulation of private businesses and deterioration in the level and efficiency of public goods provision.[11]

The gross mismatch of expenditure responsibilities and taxing authority at all levels as well as unclear division of authority/responsibility undermined fiscal incentives further. Daniel Berkowitz and Wei Li studied the consequences of overlapping tax bases of different levels of government in Russia in the 1990s.[12] They showed that when governments at different levels simultaneously tax the same base, the tax base becomes a common property resource, which leads to overtaxation. Such poor division of taxing authority in Russia prompted gross tax evasion, discouraged investment, and reduced aggregate tax collections. Berkowitz and Li argued that federal and local tax collections declined steadily in the 1990s, forcing governments at various levels to slash expenditures on public goods such as education, police protection, public health, transport infrastructure, and law enforcement.

Several indepth investigations of intergovernmental relations in Russia of the 1990s showed that corruption, state capture, and subversion of

---

9. See Ekaterina Zhuravskaya, "Incentives to Provide Local Public Goods: Fiscal Federalism—Russian Style," *Journal of Public Economics* 76, no. 3 (2000): 337–68.

10. Alexey Makrushin, Irina Slinko, and Ekaterina Zhuravskaya, "The Reasons for Bad Fiscal Incentives in Russia" (policy paper, Center for Economic and Financial Research at the New Economic School, Moscow, 2002).

11. Zhuravskaya, "Incentives to Provide Local Public Goods: Fiscal Federalism—Russian Style."

12. Daniel Berkowitz and Wei Li, "Tax Rights in Transition Economies: A Tragedy of the Commons?" *Journal of Public Economics* 76, no. 3 (June 2000): 369–97.

budget funds arose from direct violation of the three principles for the establishment of political and economic incentives. These principles are embedded in the constitutions of an overwhelming majority of developed federations, such as the United States and Switzerland, but developing federations routinely violate these principles, and Russia of the 1990s is only one example. However, this is not the only bad news for developing federations.

State-Corroding Federalism

Policies that benefit population in one region may directly harm populations of neighboring regions and, as a result, hurt the country as a whole. Even if such policies do not violate the principles of accountability of local authorities or of correspondence of revenues and expenditures and fully reflect the needs of the local people, delegation of authority to the local level could lead to truly disastrous outcomes for the country as a whole. Thus, additional conditions need to be formulated to avoid disruptive regionalist policies as an outcome of federalism. I return to this issue later as it is highly relevant to the development of Russia's federalism.

Indeed, Russia in the 1990s provides a vivid example of one of the most important costs of federalism in developing federations, namely, severe interregional externalities, which Hongbin Cai and Daniel Treisman called "state-corroding federalism."[13]

In the 1990s, regional authorities helped enterprises in their territories avoid paying federal taxes. This weakened the fiscal capacity of the federal center and undermined the provision of federal public goods. Federal tax collection efforts were impaired because the agents who carried out tax collection and enforcement in the regions—formally federal employees—as well as the regional judiciary—formally independent—were often under the control of regional governments. Aleksei Lavrov, John Litwack, and Douglas Sutherland wrote: "Federal organs operating in the regions typically have close relations with the regional administration, depending on the latter for a number of reasons, sometimes even for the provision of office space."[14] Ariane Lambert-Mogiliansky, Konstantin Sonin, and I documented that regional governments used the regional judiciary to redistribute tax revenue from the federal center to the regions via bankruptcy proceedings.[15] Marina Ponomareva and I showed that politically strong

---

13. Hongbin Cai and Daniel Treisman, "State-Corroding Federalism," *Journal of Public Economics* 88 (2004): 819–43.

14. Aleksei Lavrov, John M. Litwack, and Douglas Sutherland, *Fiscal Federalist Relations in Russia: A Case for Subnational Autonomy* (Paris: OECD Center for Cooperation with Non-Members, 2001).

15. Ariane Lambert-Mogiliansky, Konstantin Sonin, and Ekaterina Zhuravskaya, "Are

governors successfully resisted federal tax collection in their regions.[16] Federal arrears were higher and accumulated faster in regions that were in a better bargaining position than the center or where governors had a larger popular base or were in open political opposition to the center.[17] Moreover, these regions not only managed to disrupt the federal government's tax collection efforts but also were successful in bargaining with the center for official tax deferrals on behalf of regional companies.

Interregional trade barriers were also a pervasive phenomenon in Russia in the 1990s. Berkowitz and David DeJong demonstrated this using evidence on large price dispersions across regions.[18] Yakovlev summarized numerous examples of regional legislation that set tariff and nontariff barriers to trade in Russia's regional alcohol markets;[19] while Sergei Guriev, Yakovlev, and I presented two case studies from beer and copper extraction industries to illustrate that interregional trade barriers were particularly strong in regions where politically powerful regional lobbyists concentrated their business interests.[20] Overall, interregional protectionism created local monopolies and destroyed the single economic space within a country.

Uncontrolled access to credit by regional authorities under the security of the federal budget and production of money surrogates, such as regional "veksels," were very common in the first half of 1990s and led to disastrous macroeconomic consequences.[21]

Overall, the outcome of Yeltsin's decentralization in the 1990s was severe: deterioration of public goods in general and at the local level in particular; increased corruption; high level of state capture at the local

---

Russian Commercial Courts Biased? Evidence from a Bankruptcy Law Transplant," *Journal of Comparative Economics* 35, no. 2 (2007): 254–77.

16. Marina Ponomareva and Ekaterina Zhuravskaya, "Federal Tax Arrears in Russia: Liquidity Problems, Federal Subsidies, or Regional Protection," *Economics of Transition* 12, no. 3 (2004): 373–98.

17. See also Konstantin Sonin, "Provincial Protectionism," *Journal of Comparative Economics* (forthcoming 2010).

18. Daniel Berkowitz and David N. DeJong, "Russia's Internal Border," *Regional Science and Urban Economics* 29, no. 5 (September 1999): 633–49.

19. Evgeny Yakovlev, "Political Economy of Regulation: Case Study of Russian Regional Alcohol Markets," EERC Working Paper (Economics Education and Research Consortium, 2005).

20. Sergei Guriev, Evgeny Yakovlev, and Ekaterina Zhuravskaya, "Interest Group Politics in a Federation," Discussion Paper no. 6671 (Washington: Center for Economic Policy and Research, 2009).

21. See, for example, Ruben Enikolopov, Alexey Makrushin, and Ekaterina Zhuravskaya, "Fiscal Federalism in Russia: Problems and Perspectives" (policy paper, Center for Economic and Financial Research at the New Economic School, Moscow, 2003).

level by local elites; fragmentation of the country's economic (market) space into separate autarchic subnational units; macroeconomic instability caused by the center's loss of monopoly power on issuing money; and corrosion of the central state due to the loss of instruments for efficient collection of federal taxes. By the end of the 1990s, it became apparent that Russia needed a reform of federalism.

Reforming State-Corroding Federalism: Lessons from Other Developing Countries

How can a state-corroding federalist system be reformed? This question was on the agenda when Putin assumed power and is certainly still relevant to Russia's present and future. Since the problems of Russia's federalism are far from unique—Mexico faced similar challenges in the 1920s and 1930s and Argentina and Brazil have been facing them since the second half of the last century—the experiences of developing federations, including more successful ones such as China, are useful in finding an answer to this question.

The solution to the problem of interjurisdictional externalities is in properly designed political incentives for local officials. How can one ensure that local officials carrying out a regional policy take into account the interests of the population of other jurisdictions of the country, while not forgetting about the population of their own jurisdiction? There are two ways to achieve this. William Riker offered one practical way.[22] He argued that the essential condition for the existence of an effective federation—in addition to the three conditions described earlier—is the existence of strong national political parties that create political incentives for local politicians to internalize externalities on neighbors and the center from the regional policy. Strong national parties create political incentives for local politicians by providing prospects for promotion within the party hierarchy based on their actions and by supporting them in local elections (when local policies are benign). Strong national political parties have enabled the most successful developed federations, such as the United States, Australia, and Switzerland, to avoid "too regionalist" policies in their states or cantons. Riker argued that having strong national parties are an additional (fourth) necessary condition for the success of federalism.

Another possible way to prevent regional leaders from pursuing policies that are harmful to the country as a whole is for the center to appoint them. If regional leaders are appointed and not elected, the center can create career concerns for them by basing promotions and demotions on their actions.

---

22. William Riker, *Federalism: Origins, Operation, Significance* (Boston: Little, Brown, and Co., 1964).

Ruben Enikolopov and I used panel data on 75 developing and transition countries over the past 25 years and showed that the presence of strong national political parties indeed has a positive effect on fiscal decentralization (confirming Riker's idea), whereas administrative appointments of local authorities by the center (instead of local elections), on average, do not improve public goods or the quality of governance in developing federations.[23] Interestingly, abolition of local elections, on average, does not necessarily improve federalism even in very young democracies, where, apparently, elections on the ground do not work at all as an institution of accountability. The important reason for this lies in the incentives for rent seeking in the center.

Federalism in China and Mexico

Olivier Blanchard and Andrei Shleifer compared Russia's and China's fiscal decentralizations and argued that China provides a good example of how the center should create conditions under which regional governments have no incentives to pursue policies with negative externalities using such "administrative federalism."[24] It is important to note that even though China is a highly politically centralized unitary state, from an economic standpoint it is a federation; provincial leaders have substantial and exclusive authority over many aspects of regional fiscal and regulatory policy. In particular, provincial leaders in China, i.e., provincial party secretaries and governors, have sufficient discretion over policy that they can substantially affect economic growth in their territory, but there is plenty of evidence that their policies are less "regionalist" than those of many other developing federations (including Russia). Blanchard and Shleifer argued that the provincial leaders' need to please the center for reappointment explains their less regionalist actions. Thus, the Chinese Communist Party is a watchdog ensuring that provincial leaders act in the national interest. Many scholars agree that the unprecedented high economic growth in China over the past 30 years is indeed linked to Chinese federalism, i.e., the synthesis of substantial fiscal autonomy of provinces and strict administrative subordination of provincial governments to the center.

However, Chinese-style federalism has its problems. First, the administrative power of the center leads to a situation where local authorities are not accountable to their population and, therefore, lose interest in the needs of local people and act solely in the interests of the central govern-

23. Ruben Enikolopov and Ekaterina Zhuravskaya, "Decentralization and Political Institutions," *Journal of Public Economics* 91, no. 11-12 (2007): 2261–90.

24. Olivier Blanchard and Andrei Shleifer, "Federalism With and Without Political Centralization: China versus Russia," in *Transition Economies: How Much Progress?* IMF Staff Paper (Washington: International Monetary Fund, 2001).

ment. This, in theory, should undermine one of the main advantages of federalism (why a country would want to decentralize in the first place), namely, the closeness of local governments to the local population, which creates important informational advantages over the central government.[25] Chinese federalism was a result of fast economic growth, which in turn was a consequence of local public policies supporting businesses and market infrastructure. However, little progress is observed in public goods provision to the population, such as education, health care, and social protection, which is still rudimentary.

Why do observers who admire Chinese federalism largely ignore this issue? A country has different priorities at different stages of development. China is a rapidly growing but poor country. At this stage, the central government can afford not to make public goods provision a priority over growth. However, as China develops, priorities will change, and this change will seriously challenge the Chinese system of federalism. The reason is a standard moral hazard problem with multitasking: Multiple goals undermine the power of the incentive scheme created by administrative federalism. As Russia is a lot richer than China, it may not be politically feasible for Russia's central government to deem public goods provision a less important objective and ignore it.

The second fundamental problem with the Chinese system of federalism, and perhaps the most important for Russia, is that this system, as any miracle, cannot be replicated. It is a miracle that in China the central government, whose power is in no way limited due to the autocratic nature of the Communist Party, acts in the interests of national economic growth and not in its own interests of rent seeking.

Analysis of the Chinese experience and that of other countries suggests that a prerequisite for well-functioning administrative federalism is benevolence of the representatives of central authority, i.e., despite the many opportunities for rent seeking, they think and act to accelerate economic growth and improve public welfare. Unfortunately, this condition is grossly violated in most countries, whether young or mature democracies or dictatorships. The fewer the constraints on executives, the more likely the rent seeking at the central level. Thus, for Russia, administrative federalism is a dead end. At present, Chinese federalism, without a doubt, is one of the most interesting and important puzzles for economics and political and other social sciences. No more or less convincing explanation exists yet for why politicians and bureaucrats in Beijing are doing everything they can to support economic growth. And since there is no such explanation, there is no reason to see the Chinese experience as a guide to action but as just a miracle.

Another important example for Russia is the case of Mexico in the

---

25. Friedrich A. Hayek, *Individualism and Economic Order* (Chicago: University of Chicago Press, 1948).

1920s and 1930s, which was developing much like Russia in the 1990s. In the 1950s, the ruling Institutional Revolutionary Party (PRI) gave leaders of Mexican states attractive career prospects in the federal government. The strengthening of the party's political influence in the states streamlined the tax system and substantially restrained the states' protectionist policies. This resulted in significant economic growth coupled with low inflation in the 1950s and 1970s, often referred to as the "Mexican miracle."

Political centralization did not, however, stop at this first stage, which greatly benefited economic growth. Economic and fiscal centralization followed. By the 1980s, the PRI faced no political opposition, and, because of lack of accountability at the center, party elites mainly focused on extraction of rents and strengthening their own power, rather than on effective federalist policies. The central government became interested in gaining control over fiscal resources. Under a one-party system (PRI), there were no commitment devices to stop recentralization. As a result, local authorities lost fiscal autonomy, which significantly reduced their incentives to pursue growth-promoting policies. In the end, in the late 1990s, massive centralization led to a series of crises, and the PRI lost power.

Mexico in the 1980s is a clear example of how the lack of political opposition poses a major systemic threat to administrative federalism: Federal officials who have a great deal of political power cannot commit to refraining from stripping fiscal autonomy of the regions, which in turn undermines the basic idea of federalism. In other words, in the absence of political opposition and political competition, federalism may not be sustainable as the center would want to recentralize all powers, including fiscal powers.

Putin's Centralization: Follow Mexico or China?

To address the severe problems brought about by Yeltsin's federalism, President Putin started reforming the state apparatus soon after assuming power. This reform largely seemed to follow Blanchard and Shleifer's advice. Though never officially declared, Putin took the Chinese example as a model for reform of Russia's federalism. From 2000 to 2004, he undertook a number of important steps to increase the political influence of the central government and reduce that of regions on policy design and its implementation at all levels.

Changes in the formation of the upper house of Russia's parliament (the Federation Council) and the establishment of federal districts and presidential envoys to these districts marked the beginning of this process. Both of these measures took place in 2000. The first significantly reduced the influence of governors on the federal legislation. Governors and the heads of regional legislatures—formerly *ex officio* members of the Federation Council—were replaced by designated professional representatives. The second measure was intended to increase federal control over the implementation of federal legislation on the ground; previously, such control was almost completely absent. Soon after presidential envoys were introduced, it became clear that they were significantly less legitimate and less politically powerful compared with elected governors.

The next reform step was declared on September 13, 2004, when Putin announced significant changes in the formation of the state apparatus. Elections of regional governors were cancelled starting in January 2005 and from then on the president personally appointed governors. Direct majoritarian elections in single-member districts, which previously existed for one-half of the seats in the lower house of Russia's parliament, the Duma, were replaced with proportional representation from party lists with a simultaneous increase in the threshold required for parties to qualify for election. The administration's explanations for these drastic measures came later and were in line with the Chinese model and very much in the spirit of Blanchard and Shleifer: Putin called these reforms "the logical development of Russia's federalism." The need to restore the "vertical of power" was why regional elections were abolished. The need to strengthen the party system was why parliamentary elections were reformed. The latter corresponds quite well with Riker's idea.

Important reforms of intergovernmental fiscal relations also took place starting in 1999. These reforms aimed at and largely achieved streamlining of intergovernmental transfers with the help of a transparent grant-allocation formula and eliminated federal expenditure mandates to regions that were not financed with appropriate federal transfers. These certainly were important changes for the better.[26]

Enough time has passed since these changes were implemented to observe the outcomes of Putin's centralization. In particular, enough data are available to judge whether the reform had the desired effects on the extent of state capture at the regional level and on career concerns for regional leaders.

Yakovlev and I showed that despite political centralization there have been no significant changes in the overall level of state capture at the regional level in Russia between Yeltsin's era and Putin's first term in power.[27] Figure 3.3 portrays the dynamics of two measures of regional capture: the number and concentration of preferential treatment of particular large regional firms by regional governments. The right axis (number of preferential treatments) is the actual average number of firms that received preferential treatment from the regional authorities in each

---

26. I focus on the political side of Putin's reform in this chapter; for a detailed account of the fiscal side, see Migara O. De Silva, Galina Kurlyandskaya, Elena Andreeva, and Natalia Golovanova, *Intergovernmental Reforms in the Russian Federation: One Step Forward, Two Steps Back?* (Washington: World Bank, 2009).

27. Evgeny Yakovlev and Ekaterina Zhuravskaya, "State Capture: From Yeltsin to Putin," in *Corruption, Development and Institutional Design*, ed. János Kornai, L. László Mátyás, and Gérard Roland (New York: Palgrave Macmillian, 2009).

**Figure 3.3   Extent of state capture measured by the number and
concentration of preferential treatments, 1992–2003**

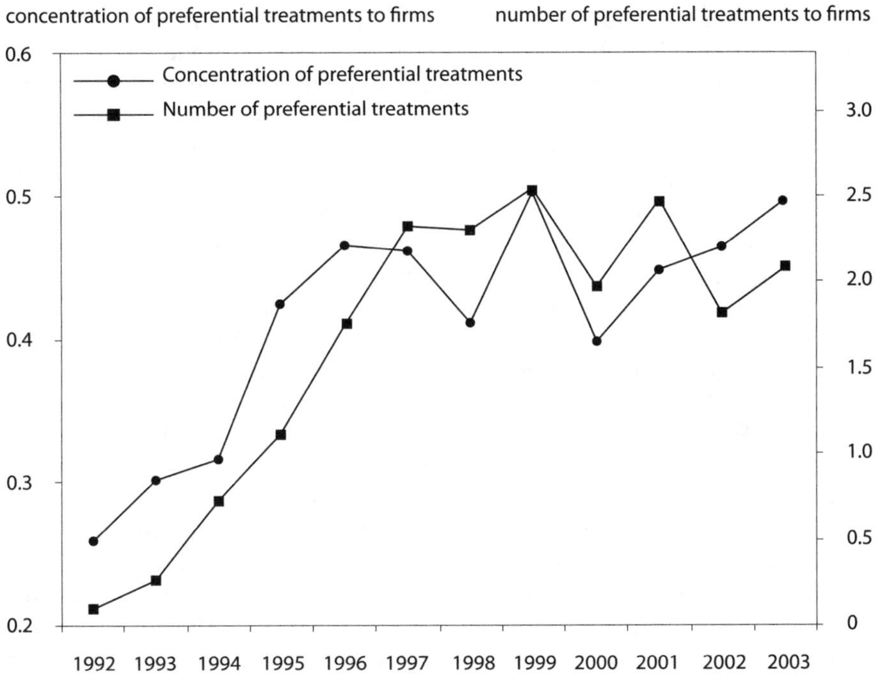

concentration of preferential treatments to firms   number of preferential treatments to firms

Source: Evgeny Yakovlev and Ekaterina Zhuravskaya, "State Capture: From Yeltsin to Putin," in *Corruption, Development and Institutional Design*, ed. János Kornai, L. László Mátyás, and Gérard Roland (New York: Palgrave Macmillan, 2009).

of the years shown. For example, in 1993, one firm in four regions got preferential treatment; in contrast, in 2003, two firms on average in each region got preferential treatment. The left axis (concentration of preferential treatments) is the Herfindahl-Hirschman index of concentration. It shows the probability that the same firm in a region got two randomly drawn preferential treatments in each year. For example, concentration was very low in 1992: If and when several preferential treatments were given, they most certainly went to different rather than the same firms.

Though there were no significant changes in overall level of state capture, there has been an important change in the nature of the most influential groups between Yeltsin's era and Putin's first term in power: Bargaining power within regions has shifted from private firms, particularly those belonging to the largest industrial groups, as well as from firms owned by regional governments to firms owned by the federal government. The latter have become the most politically powerful lobbyists at the regional level. Thus, instead of limiting the extent of state capture, Putin's reform so far has only changed the identity of the captors. This, however, may have actually restrained some of the negative externalities of regionalist policies as firms in federal ownership probably internalize some of these external effects (as Guriev, Yakovlev, and I showed using trade barriers as an example[28]). Yet, the "vertical of power" should have led to a decline in the overall level of capture as the central government was supposed to reinstate equal treatment of firms by regional law and government regulations. Putin's centralization clearly failed to meet this objective.

Over the course of 2005–07, Putin made 74 decisions about appointments of regional leaders. In 2005, 33 governors were reappointed and 9 were dismissed. In 2006, 5 were reappointed and 3 were dismissed. In 2007, 12 governors were reappointed and 12 were dismissed. It is interesting to see whether the decision to reappoint a particular governor depends on the economic performance of the region.[29] A simple calculation of the average annual real growth rate in the regions in 2004–05 and the probability of reappointments of governors by the president based on the growth rate (shown by the solid line in figure 3.4) indicates that, if anything, the correlation between reappointment and economic performance of the region is negative (see figure 3.4). 2004–05 was a period of fast growth—average growth was about 9 percent per annum, i.e., 0.09 on the horizontal axis of figure 3.4. The circles in the figure are the actual dismissals and reappointments in the regions after the 2005 federalism reform, where 1 is reappointment and 0 is dismissal. The figure clearly shows that the relationship between growth rate and reappointments is negative, if anything, which gives no incentives for governors to improve economic performance in their regions.

The pair-wise correlation is statistically insignificant and becomes significant once we control for the 2002 level of per capita gross regional product. It is clear from the figure (and is confirmed by regression analysis) that the statistical significance of the negative correlation depends on a few outliers: replacement of Alu Alhanov by young Ramzan Kadyrov in March 2007 in Chechnya and of Ivan Malahov by Alexander Horoshavin in Sakhalin oblast after the Nevelsk earthquake and reappointment of Roman Abramovitch in Chukotka in November 2005 and of Kirsan Ilyumzhinov in Kalmykia also in November 2005. In any case, there is clearly no evidence of a positive relationship between economic performance and regional reappointments.

---

28. Ibid.

29. Many studies have shown that provincial economic growth is the main determinant of promotions and demotions of Chinese provincial leaders. See, for instance, Hongbin Li and Li-An Zhou, "Political Turnover and Economic Performance: The Incentive Role of Personnel Control in China," *Journal of Public Economics* 89, no. 9-10 (2005): 1743–62; Ye Chen, Hongbin Li, and Li-An Zhou, "Relative Performance Evaluation and the Turnover of Provincial Leaders in China," *Economics Letters* 88, no. 3 (2005): 421–25.

Figure 3.4   Annual average growth rate in the regions and reappointment of governors: Nonparametric average regression (Lowess smoother)

probability of reappointment (line); reappointment or dismissal (circle)

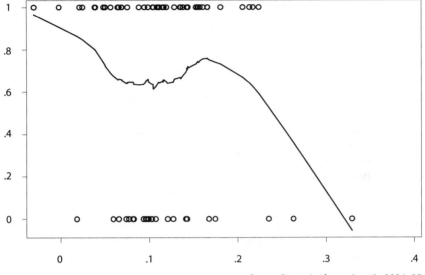

average annual growth rate in the regions in 2004–05

bandwidth = .8

Note: On vertical axis, 1 = reappointment, 0 = dismissal.

Source: Author's calculations.

The most striking example is the reappointment of the governor of the Republic of Kalmykia, Kirsan Ilyumzhinov. For 12 years under the leadership of Ilyumzhinov (before his reappointment by Putin), Kalmykia was one of the least developed and poorest regions. During this time, Kalmykia was the only region in Russia's history to declare bankruptcy as outstanding debts of the republic exceeded its annual budget. Federal investigations suggested that federal transfers systematically disappeared without a trace from Kalmykia's budget. According to Rosstat, in 1993, when Ilyumzhinov was first elected head of the republic, in terms of per capita income of the population, it was the seventh poorest region of all Russian regions (excluding autonomous Okrugs), and after ten years of Ilyumzhinov's governance, Kalmykia dropped to third place. Unemployment in the republic also has grown significantly, and by the time of Ilyumzhinov's reappointment, unemployment was lower than that in only a few regions in the Caucasus. There is little doubt that Ilyumzhinov is grossly unpopular in the republic.[30] Yet, Ilyumzhinov gained the trust of President Putin to lead the region again in 2005.

An important question is why a strong central leader would want to reappoint badly performing governors? One reason is political motivation. Inefficient governors are unpopular and, therefore, cannot become independent political figures and cannot (even potentially) lead the opposition to the ruling central government. Second, and perhaps the easiest explanation, is rent seeking. The central government can use the threat of dismissal to persuade local authorities to give greater part of their rents to federal officials. It is obvious that rent-seeking regional governors can offer a larger sum for their reappointment. Moreover, incumbents have more information and rents and collect them better than outsiders; thus, they can pay more for their jobs.

Of course, it is theoretically possible that changing the system of appointment will radically change the behavior of governors, because their incentive structure would change, which means that it is irrelevant how they behaved before the reform. However, governors who have engaged in rent-seeking behavior for years must have accumulated implicit obligations to special interest groups in their regions, and the interests of these groups do not always coincide with those of the public at large. To break such ties between local governors and local elites, the central reformer interested in streamlining a state-corroding federalist system needs to bring in new people. Thus, even in a case where federal officials have absolute integrity (which I mentioned earlier in the context of transplanting Chinese federalism to Russia), it would make sense to fire most governors who held office under the old system. Yet, as of November 2009, 24 governors in office have been ruling their regions for more than 10 years.

Conclusion

Russia has much to learn from other developing federations. First, for successful development, it needs a federal structure of government, as the country is too large and too diverse to be a unitary state. Second, effective operation of Russia's federalism is possible only if there is a strong political "vertical," which would limit inefficient regionalist policies of individual subjects. However, creation of the administrative vertical by abolishing regional elections, as Putin did, has created two major problems for Russia: (1) inadequate provision of public goods in the absence of accountability of local governments to the local population, and (2) complete depen-

---

30. Tom Parfitt, "King of Kalmykia," *Guardian*, September 21, 2006, www.guardian.co.uk (accessed on April 28, 2010); Regnum News Agency, "Residents of Kalmykia ask EU countries, USA and Canada for political asylum," November 2, 2005, www.regnum.ru/english (accessed on April 28, 2010); and Pravda, "Leader of Kalmyk republic blackmails the Kremlin," November 6, 2004, http://english.pravda.ru (accessed on April 28, 2010).

dence on the utopian assumption of honesty and self-limitation of federal authorities, without which administrative federalism is unsustainable.

The alternative to administrative federalism is creation of a political vertical through strong national political parties. Strong national parties, while preserving local elections, maintain the balance of political incentives for local authorities between the interests of regional and national populations. However, successful operation and sustainability of this approach requires institutional constraints on the central organs of the ruling party as insurance against use of the vertical for personal gain by senior party and government officials. The only effective way to create such a system of checks and balances of federal officials and party bosses is the development of democracy, i.e., strong national opposition parties and independent media, both at national and subnational levels. Unfortunately, it is pretty clear that the Russian leadership interprets the concept of a strong political party system not as having strong opposition but as Mexico's PRI system in the late 1980s.

Even in the zero-probability event that a "Russian miracle" occurs in the absence of political competition, as in China, there will always be a great danger that officials focused on the welfare of the population will be replaced at some point by those focusing mainly on their own well-being. Therefore, long-term success of federalism in Russia depends hugely on promoting democracy at all levels. Russia has a long way to go in establishing democratic institutions (and so far the trend has been in the opposite direction), but it is the only way for Russia's federalism to work.

4

Corruption and Rule of Law

TIMOTHY FRYE

Of all the modernization challenges facing Russia, perhaps none is more complex than reducing corruption and strengthening the rule of law. From human rights to corporate governance to criminal law, Russia's agenda to promote greater legality is daunting. President Dmitri Medvedev may have exaggerated in noting that "no European country can boast of such universal disregard for the law" as can Russia, but he was not far from the mark.

Reducing corruption and promoting the rule of law is both a technical and political problem. The technical challenges include creating proper incentives for bureaucrats and legal officials to serve public rather than private interests. The standard tools of legal reform include improving judicial training, increasing funding for judges and bailiffs, and computerizing case loads to improve efficiency. On this dimension, Russia has not done badly in recent years.[1]

Yet bolstering the rule of law also involves strengthening supporting institutions, such as promoting a free press, empowering autonomous social organizations, and encouraging the spread of nongovernmental organizations to monitor violations of human rights, bureaucratic misconduct,

Timothy Frye is Marshall D. Shulman Professor of Post-Soviet Foreign Policy at Columbia University and director of the Harriman Institute. He thanks the editors and Harley Balzer for comments and the National Council on Eurasian and East European Research, the Center for International Business and Economic Research, and the Institute for Social and Economic Research and Policy at Columbia University for generous funding.

1. Peter Solomon, "Putin's Judicial Reform: Making Judges Accountable as well as Independent," *East European Constitutional Review* 11, no. 1/2 (Winter/Spring 2002): 117–24; Peter Solomon, "Assessing the Courts in Russia: Parameters of Progress Under Putin," *Demokratizatsiya* 16, no. 1 (Winter 2008): 63–73.

and consumer fraud. Here, Russia has fared badly, in large part because these aspects of the rule of law cut to the core of politics.

At the fundamental level, the challenge of modernizing legal institutions in Russia is inherently political because while corruption and weak rule of law impose tremendous costs on society at large, they also produce concentrated benefits for powerful constituencies within the state and society. Rather than viewing corruption and weak rule of law as driven by technical problems, moral failings of state officials, or the Soviet legacy, it is far more productive to recognize the underlying political nature of the problem. Each sweetheart tax deal to companies owned by relatives of powerful state officials, each government contract directed to United Russia supporters rather than to the best qualified firm, and each call from a governor to a judge to decide a case in a supporter's favor is political capital that incumbents are loath to abandon. While Russia has made progress in rationalizing its legal institutions in the last 20 years, political obstacles to improving the rule of law remain the greatest barrier to modernization.

In this chapter, I address the following questions: How has the quality of governance in Russia evolved in the last decade? Have the centralization of power in the Kremlin, increased spending on the judiciary, and high growth rates brought a degree of order to the daily transactions of businesspeople? Or has the weakening of checks on central state power heightened perceptions of corruption and undermined the security of property rights? Original data from two large surveys of Russian businesses in 2000 and 2008 reveal that businesspeople perceive that corruption has increased since 2000 (discussed in detail further into the chapter). This perception is especially surprising because many firms that existed in 2000 were likely driven out of business due to corruption, which means that only those firms for whom corruption is less of a problem have survived and were surveyed in 2008. Such a "survivor" bias in the surveys should have led to lower estimates of corruption; however, businesspeople report higher rates of corruption in 2008 than in 2000.

In addition, businesspeople report that in recent years the security of property rights has become more contingent on political connections. Investment decisions greatly depend on whether businesspeople believe that they can take the state to court. Moreover, political connections in legal disputes remain a powerful asset. Controlling for all other factors a small firm can increase its perceived chances of winning a property dispute with another small firm by 9 percentage points if it has good relations with the regional government. Taken together, these results indicate that the playing field for businesses in Russia has become increasingly uneven in the last decade.

Table 4.1 Corruption and business climate in Russia compared with selected developing and transition countries

Country	Corruption Perceptions Index ranking	Ease of Doing Business ranking
Poland	49	72
Brazil	75	129
China	79	89
India	84	133
Russia	146	120
Ukraine	146	142
Venezuela	162	177
Uzbekistan	174	150

Sources: Corruption Perceptions Index, Transparency International, 2009; World Bank, *Doing Business 2010*, www.doingbusiness.org.

Context

Russia is far from the only low- to middle-income country struggling under the weight of weak rule of law and extensive corruption (table 4.1). A quick glance at two common measures helps put Russia's problems in perspective. Transparency International's Corruption Perceptions Index relies on up to 13 surveys to rank countries, and the World Bank's Doing Business ranking uses formal, legal indicators, such as the number of procedures required to start a firm, to rank countries according to their business climate. Compared with a small group of other developing and transition countries, Russia fares better on some measures and worse on others.

Corruption is perceived to be considerably greater in Russia than in Poland, Brazil, India, and China, on par with Ukraine, but less than in Venezuela or Uzbekistan. Given Russia's highly educated populace and relative wealth, its level of corruption is surprising. However, in light of its dependence on natural resources for state revenue and the institutional legacy of Soviet rule, its vast corruption is less noteworthy. Russia ranks somewhat better in the Doing Business ranking, which uses de jure rather than de facto assessments of the ease of doing business in a country. In evaluating corruption and the rule of law in Russia, it is important to bear the broader comparative perspective in mind.

These problems are hardly new to Russia. Under tsarist rule close ties between state officials and firms limited judicial discretion, and even after the legal reforms of 1864, state officials spent much of the following decades undermining this legislation.[2] In the Soviet period, law was reduced still further to an instrument of state power. Nikita Khrushchev captured the sentiment of the Communist Party elites toward the rule of law: "Who is the master, the Party or the law? We are masters over the law, not the law over us."[3] In the 1990s President Boris Yeltsin introduced sweeping rule of law reforms, including life tenure for judges, and expanded court authority over commercial, constitutional, and administrative disputes. The Yeltsin administration also created justices of the peace, which eventually led to significant declines in caseloads of overworked judges in the courts of general jurisdiction and courts of arbitration.[4] In addition, the Yeltsin administration transferred the administration of courts from the executive branch to a judicial body under the authority of the Supreme Court.[5]

The impact of these reforms, however, was limited by severe shortages of federal funds. Court facilities were crumbling, pay for judicial officials declined significantly in real terms, and bailiffs often lacked the resources to enforce decisions against state and private parties. With federal support declining, regional officials often helped fill the shortfall but typically in exchange for favorable treatment. Reliance on local officials for unofficial financial support, housing, and logistics drastically limited the reach of central organs of power in Russia's regions in the 1990s.[6]

President Vladimir Putin came to power vowing to establish "a dictatorship of the rule of law," and thanks to the ruble devaluation of 1998 and the boom in oil prices, the Russian state no longer lacked the resources to support judicial reform. The Putin administration pushed through new criminal codes (2002) and civil codes (2003). While far from ideal, these new procedural codes helped to establish formal, legal rules of the game. Courts were pushed to create websites to post their decisions and improve physical infrastructure such as their buildings. In addition, on President Putin's watch, jury trials expanded to all regions in Russia (except Chechnya) despite opposition from the prosecutor's office and many judges. Perhaps most importantly, the Putin administration dramatically increased funding for the courts. The Plan for the Improvement of the Courts for 2002–06 called for 44 billion rubles in new spending, and ad-

---

2. Thomas Owen, "Autocracy and the Rule of Law in Russian Economic History," in *The Rule of Law and Economic Reform in Russia*, eds. Katharina Pistor and Jeffrey Sachs (Boulder, CO: Westview Press, 1997), 23–39.

3. Konstantin Simis, *USSR: Secrets of a Corrupt Society* (New York: Simon and Schuster, 1982), 30.

4. Peter Solomon, "The New Justices of the Peace in the Russian Federation: A Cornerstone of Judicial Reform," *Demokratizatsiya* 11, no. 3 (Summer 2003): 363–80.

5. Solomon, "Assessing the Courts in Russia: Parameters of Progress Under Putin," 66.

6. Kathryn Stoner-Weiss, *Resisting the State: Reform and Retrenchment in Post-Soviet Russia* (New York: Cambridge University Press, 2006).

ditional monies were made available in the Plan for 2007–11. Judges' base salaries are now on the order of $1,000 per month, which is fairly high for many Russian cities.[7] Even an otherwise highly critical Council of Europe report from 2009 on judicial institutions in Russia noted that the "strong improvement in the social status of judges and prosecutors in recent years has all but eliminated their dependence on executive bodies for housing and other basic needs."[8] Thus, there are reasons to expect improved performance of judicial institutions in Russia under Putin.

Yet, great damage has also been done to the supporting institutions that are essential to the rule of law. Media freedom has declined sharply. Freedom House ratings of media freedom fell from 4.75 in 2000, which was better than the average non-Baltic country of the former Soviet Union (5.25), to 6.25 in 2008, worse than the average of the same group (5.92). More generally, the raucous and open, if hardly unbiased, media of the Yeltsin era has been replaced by a staid, nontransparent, and even more biased media in the Putin years.

The Putin administration has made considerable efforts to keep in line business organizations that have been instrumental in defending members against predatory officials.[9] Nongovernmental organizations that monitor corruption, human rights abuses, and protect consumer rights have also been squeezed, particularly those relying on foreign sources of funding.

Perhaps as important, spectacular violations of property rights in high-profile cases have done tremendous damage to Russia's reputation for recognizing basic legal norms. A few of many examples suffice: The bankruptcy and subsequent resale of oil giant Yukos in 2003, the forced sale of foreign-owned shares to Gazprom in the Sakhalin II project in 2006, and the expropriation of three subsidiaries of the international investment fund Hermitage Capital in 2008 have further cemented Russia's reputation for weak property rights. In addition, the failure to resolve high-profile murders of lawyers, journalists, and human rights activists on Putin's watch has brought a cloud of suspicion over the government's willingness to instill the basic legal norms of its European neighbors.

The Putin Report Card: Corruption

To explore changes in the legal environment under President Putin with greater precision, I commissioned the Levada Center to conduct two surveys of 500 businesspeople in eight regions in 2000 and 2008. These eight

---

7. Solomon, "Assessing the Courts in Russia: Parameters of Progress Under Putin," 68.

8. Pamela Jordan, "Strong-Arm Rule or Rule of Law? Prospects for Legal Reform in Russia," *Jurist* (2009), available at http://jurist.law.pitt.edu (accessed on December 28, 2009).

9. Dinissa Duvanova, "Bureaucratic Corruption and Collective Action: Business Associations in Eastern Europe and Eurasia," *Comparative Politics* 39, no. 4 (July 2007): 441–63.

Table 4.2   Characteristics and distribution of firms and respondents in 2000 and 2008 surveys

Characteristic	2000 survey	2008 survey
Average age of respondent (years)	46	47
Percent of male respondents	74	70
Average firm size (number of employees)	840	436
Adjusted average firm size[a] (number of employees)	488	436
Modal firm size (number of employees)	150	130
Business organization members (percent)	31	32

a. Adjusted by dropping the ten largest firms in 2000.

Table 4.3   Obstacles to doing business in Russia, 2000 and 2008

Obstacle	2000	2008
Finding qualified labor	2.60	3.16
Competition	2.89	3.22
Taxes	4.29	3.49
Finding credit	2.75	2.65
Stability of laws	3.46	3.15
Regulations	1.98	3.15
Corruption	2.43	2.74

Note: Responses rated on a scale of 1 to 5, where 1 equals not at all an obstacle and 5 equals a very serious obstacle.

regions are Voronezh, Nizhnii Novgorod, Ekaterinburg, Moscow city, Smolensk, Bashkortostan, Tula, and Novgorod. We surveyed firms from 23 sectors of the economy, including heavy and light industry, finance, trade and construction, but did not include agricultural firms. Interviews were conducted face to face in the respondent's place of work, and 20 percent of firms were called after the survey to check the veracity of responses. The questionnaires went through extensive pilot testing and did not require disclosure of sensitive financial information. The distribution of firms in both surveys was roughly similar as indicated in table 4.2. We asked respondents to rate several obstacles to doing business on a scale of 1 to 5, results of which are reported in table 4.3.

The responses indicate some improvements in the business environment during Putin's presidency, as firms reported that labor shortages and competition were more important obstacles and that taxes and stability of laws were less significant problems in 2008 than in 2000. Most surprising is that these positive changes were also accompanied by sharp increases

Table 4.4 Extent of bribery in government, 2000 and 2008

Level of government	2000	2008
Federal	1.83	2.61
Regional	1.92	2.74
Municipal	2.09	2.81
Inspectors	2.35	3.14

Note: Responses rated on a scale of 1 to 5, where 1 equals not at all a problem and 5 equals a very serious problem.

in complaints about corruption and its close relative, burdensome regulation. On a scale of 1 to 5, businesspeople in 2000 rated corruption as 2.43, but this rating increased to 2.75 in 2008. In addition, regulations as a problem for firms were rated as only 1.98 in 2000 but soared to 3.15 in 2008.

To probe perceptions of corruption in somewhat more detail, we asked respondents to rate on a scale of 1 to 5 the extent to which bribery was a problem at the federal, regional, and municipal levels of government. We also asked respondents to rate bribery among inspectors (table 4.4).

At each level of government businesspeople perceived stark increases in levels of bribery during the years of the Putin presidency. Bribery was most severe at lower levels of government, including the municipal government and inspectors (ratings of 2.81 and 3.14, respectively).[10] Even in the wake of an unprecedented economic boom, businesspeople perceived corruption to be a more significant problem in 2008 than in 2000. Russia is not growing out of its corruption problem.

These results are surprising in light of three common biases, which may have led businesspeople to give somewhat more positive responses in 2008 than in 2000. First, responses may suffer from a "halo effect," i.e., respondents give higher scores for institutional performance during good economic times than during economic downturns, even if institutional performance is largely unchanged. Second, respondents may have been less likely to criticize the government given the more autocratic nature of state power in 2008. Finally, weak rule of law and high levels of corruption may have driven firms that could not survive the harsh environment out of business and thus from the sample, thereby biasing the sample in favor of firms for which corruption and burdensome regulations are not especially severe problems. This form of "survivor bias" is likely to be more pronounced among small firms that typically experience the greatest costs of corruption. Each of these effects should have deflated perceptions of the severity of corruption and regulation in 2008 relative to 2000, but we find

10. Tula and Novgorod had relatively low ratings on bribery in both 2000 and 2008, while Moscow had bribery ratings far higher than average in both surveys. Other regions experienced substantial increases between 2000 and 2008.

Table 4.5   Perceptions of performance of state courts of arbitration, 2000 and 2008 (percent saying "yes" or "more or less yes")

Courts can...	2000	2008
...defend interests against another firm	76	89
...defend interests against regional government	39	59

significant increases in both. Respondents might also have inflated evaluations of improvements in the business environment.

Legal Institutions

To examine changes in perceptions of the performance of judicial institutions, we asked respondents to evaluate the courts' capacity to protect their legal interests in disputes with different parties. Here the focus is on Russia's state courts of arbitration, which are the main public fora for resolving disputes between firms and between firms and the state, rather than on courts of general jurisdiction, which hear most criminal cases. Almost every region has an arbitration court. These courts have been a focus for reform over the last 20 years.[11]

To explore how managers perceive the performance of state courts of arbitration, we asked:

> In the case of an economic dispute with a *business partner* do you believe that the state arbitration courts could protect your legal interests?
>
> (1) yes (2) more or less yes (3) more or less no (4) no

> In the case of an economic dispute with the *local or regional government* do you believe that the state arbitration courts could protect your legal interests?
>
> (1) yes (2) more or less yes (3) more or less no (4) no

The question establishes a fairly low bar for confidence in the courts. It does not ask the managers whether courts will always defend their rights. It only asks whether the managers expect that the courts can do so. In 2000, 76 percent of managers believed that the courts could protect their legal interests in a dispute with another firm, while 89 percent believed so in 2008 (table 4.5).

Managers were significantly less confident in their ability to use courts against the regional government in both surveys. In 2000, 39 percent of managers expressed confidence that the courts could protect their rights in a dispute with the regional government. In 2008, this figure increased to 59 percent of respondents (table 4.5). The 2008 figure seems high but may

---

11. Solomon, "Putin's Judicial Reform: Making Judges Accountable as well as Independent."

reflect several different factors.[12] First, as noted earlier, the halo effect may be at work as the first survey was conducted in the wake of the financial crisis of 1998 and the second at the peak of an unprecedented eight-year economic boom in Russia. Second, as the Putin administration weakened governors' power between 2000 and 2008, business managers may have expected to have greater leverage over governors in legal disputes in 2008 compared with 2000. Third, increased funding for the judiciary and the legal reform passed in 2000 may have improved the performance of the courts. Fourth, between 2000 and 2008, firms that could not use courts against the regional government were more likely to have gone out of business. If so, then on average, more firms that remained in business (and hence in the sample) would expect that they can use courts against the state.[13] Note also that the question does not ask how respondents can use the courts to protect their rights. Some respondents may believe that they can bribe judges to win their case.

It is difficult, however, to make simple comparisons between the two surveys. While these data suggest that firms in 2008 had confidence in the ability of courts to protect their property rights in disputes with private firms and state agencies, as already noted, it may be due to the halo effect, survivor bias, or changes in respondents' willingness to criticize the government. We are on firmer ground when making comparisons between firms within a single survey.

Moreover, while it is important to understand firms' evaluations of the performance of courts, what we would really like to know is how perceptions of the performance of the courts influence economic behavior. For example, do firms that have confidence in the courts to protect their rights in disputes against the state invest at higher rates than those that do not? If so, this would be evidence of an uneven playing field for firms.

To get at this issue, we asked a series of questions about the security of property rights. More specifically, we asked managers whether they planned to make a major new investment in the coming 12 months, whether they had bought new capital equipment, whether they had conducted a major renovation of their building or constructed a new building. Undertaking each of these activities indicates that the respondent has some

---

12. I also conducted this survey in 2005 and 2007 and found that roughly 54 and 46 percent of firms, respectively, believed that the courts could protect their rights against the regional government. Small differences in the question's wording may also have affected the results. The latter survey was financed by the Higher School of Economics and conducted in concert with Andrei Yakovlev and Yevgeny Yasin.

13. There is some evidence for this view. For example, in 2000 and 2008 we asked managers to rate the performance of the governor in their region on a scale of 1 to 5. In 2000, managers who could and could not take the regional government to court rated the governor as 2.64 and 2.85 (t = 2.4), respectively. In 2008, these figures increased to 3.15 and 3.67 (t = 5.1), respectively. This form of survivor bias would likely inflate the number of firms that believe they can use courts against the regional government.

confidence in the rule of law and enforcement of property rights because they require significant upfront costs with only the promise of future gain. If managers expect that their property rights will be violated and that the legal system will do little to protect them, then they are unlikely to take these risky steps.

Forty-nine percent of managers in 2008 were planning to make a new investment in the coming year, while 85 percent claimed to have bought new capital equipment in the last two years. Three-quarters of respondents had conducted a major renovation of their place of business in the last two years and just under one-quarter (24 percent) had built a new building within the last two years. These raw figures are not especially revealing about the quality of the legal environment as investment could be driven by many factors, including the economic boom or the significant expansion of credit during Putin's presidency. The biases mentioned earlier should be less important in exploring differences in responses within a single survey because the halo effect is likely to equally influence firms that believe they can take the state to court and those that do not.

Managers who expected to be able to use the courts against the regional government were much more likely to take actions that indicate some confidence in the rule of law and security of property rights than those who did not (table 4.6). They were significantly more likely to be planning a new investment in the coming year (54 percent versus 40 percent), to have bought new capital equipment in the last year (89 percent versus 79 percent), and to have conducted a major renovation of their place of business (77 percent versus 70 percent). They were also more likely to have built a new building in the last 12 months, although this difference falls just short of statistical significance (26 percent versus 21 percent, p = .14). These results indicate the importance of placing legal constraints on the regional government in order to foster investment.[14] Managers who viewed themselves as unable to use courts against the regional government were much less likely to invest than their competitors who expected that they could use courts to protect themselves. Thus, the playing field in 2008 is decidedly tilted in favor of more legally powerful firms relative to less legally powerful firms.[15]

These differences are even more pronounced if one examines perceptions of the ability of firms to use courts to protect their rights against

---

14. These relationships hold in more demanding analyses as well. For example, controlling for region, sector, and the age of the manager, respondents who believe that they can use the courts against the regional government were significantly more likely to have built new buildings and be planning to make an investment in the coming year.

15. This relationship was also present in 2000, although the magnitude of the effect of being able to use courts against the regional government appears to have been smaller than in 2008.

Table 4.6 **Investment decisions based on firms' perceived ability to use courts to protect their property rights against regional and federal governments, 2008** (percent saying "yes" or "more or less yes")

Investment decision	Firms that cannot use courts against the regional government	Firms that can use courts against the regional government	Firms that cannot use courts against the federal government	Firms that can use courts against the federal government
Plan new investment in coming year	40	54***	35	58***
Bought new equipment in last two years	79	89***	78	88***
Conducted major renovation in last two years	70	77*	69	76
Built new building in last two years	21	26	18	27**

Note: *, **, *** indicate significant differences at the .10, .05, and .01 levels, respectively.

the federal government, as depicted in the last two columns of table 4.6. In three of the four cases, differences in responses between groups that believe they can and cannot use courts in dispute with the federal government are statistically significant. In the fourth, the difference between groups lies just beyond standard levels of significance (p = .12).

The differences in the responses between these two groups illuminate a central reality for firms in Russia: Property rights remain quite contingent on a firm's ability to protect itself against predation by the state. Ideally one would like to make investment decisions primarily on economic grounds in an environment in which legal power matters less than economic efficiency, but this is far from the case in Russia.

It is interesting to note that there is no relationship between levels of investment and managers' perceptions of the capacity of courts to protect their rights in disputes with other private firms: Both firms that did and did not have confidence in the courts to protect their rights in disputes with private firms invested at roughly equal rates. Thus, the problem of strengthening property rights in Russia has less to do with the capacity of the state to make and enforce decisions in disputes between private firms and more to do with increasing legal constraints on the power of state officials.[16]

---

16. The evaluations of the ability of the courts to protect property rights against the regional government and against private firms did not vary between those that had and had not actually used courts to resolve a dispute in the last two years. Thus, the experience of actually

The Power of Friends in High Places

To explore the value of having close relations with the regional government, we tried a slightly different strategy in the 2008 survey. Rather than asking the same question of all respondents and reporting the average response, I created four slightly different hypothetical disputes (with firms of different sizes and having different relations with the regional government) and randomly assigned one to each questionnaire. I asked whether respondents expected that the courts would protect their rights in the hypothetical dispute assigned to them. Because the versions of the question were randomly assigned, the differences in responses can be attributed only to the small differences in the question. In other words, the results here are quite powerful because the design of the question implicitly controls for all factors that may be affecting responses, such as the size, location, and sector of the firm in the hypothetical dispute as well the individual characteristics of respondents.

To be specific, we asked:

> Let's say that your firm fulfilled a large order worth about 10 percent of your annual revenue for a [small company with about 100 employees/a large company with about 3,000 employees]. The buyer paid 50 percent in advance but is now refusing to pay the rest of the bill because it claims that the product is defective. You are sure that the product is in good working order. What do you think, can your firm defend its legal interests by turning to the state courts of arbitration?
>
> (1) yes (2) more or less yes (3) more or less no (4) no
>
> Half of the respondents were also told that "the buyer firm has close relations with the regional government."[17]

It is not surprising that firms on good terms with the regional government were thought to receive better treatment from state courts of arbitration. The size of the benefits of political connections is more interesting. When respondents were told that the disputant had only 100 employees, 79 percent said that the courts could protect their rights (table 4.7). How-

---

using the courts did not seem to have a significant impact on perceptions of the performance of state courts of arbitration.

17. The four versions were:
   (1) Let's say that your firm fulfilled a large order worth about 10 percent of your annual revenue for a small company with about 100 employees.
   (2) Let's say that your firm fulfilled a large order worth about 10 percent of your annual revenue for a large company with about 3,000 employees.
   (3) Let's say that your firm fulfilled a large order worth about 10 percent of your annual revenue for a small company with about 100 employees. In addition, the buyer firm has close relations with the regional government.
   (4) Let's say that your firm fulfilled a large order worth about 10 percent of your annual revenue for a large company with about 3,000 employees. In addition, the buyer firm has close relations with the regional government.

Table 4.7 **Percent of respondents who expected the courts would protect their firm's rights in a hypothetical dispute** (percent saying "yes" or "more or less yes")

If the disputant was a...	No information on disputant's relations with the regional government	Disputant had good relations with the regional government
Small firm (100 employees)	79	70
Large firm (3,000 employees)	70	64

ever, when told that the disputant also had good relations with the regional government, this figure declined by 9 percentage points, to 70 percent. When told that the disputant was a large firm with 3,000 employees, 70 percent expected that the courts could protect their rights, but the number declined to 64 percent when the large disputant also had good relations with the regional government. Because this analysis controls for all other factors that could be helping a firm protect its property rights, the benefits of political connections appear to be substantial.

Caveats and Observations

Some caveats are in order. This analysis focuses almost exclusively on nonstrategic firms, and the results should not be generalized to the large politically important firms in the natural resources sector of the economy. Nor should they be extended to foreign firms whose relations with the state likely differ from those of run-of-the-mill Russian firms in the surveys. The latter are less likely to grab headlines than are Russia's natural resource giants or high-profile foreign companies but nevertheless merit attention as they employ most Russians, are critical for efforts to diversify the economy away from oil and gas, and are understudied. Moreover, these firms would most benefit from reduction in corruption and improvements in the rule of law.

These results focus only on firms' relations with the state and tell us little about the state of the rule of law and corruption in criminal or human rights cases. There is, however, evidence that the courts of general jurisdiction that handle most criminal cases have historically performed significantly worse than the courts of arbitration under study here.[18] Finally, these results were obtained before the financial crash of the fall of 2008. The

18. Kathryn Hendley, Peter Murrell, and Randi Ryterman, "Law, Relationships, and Private Enforcement: Transactional Strategies of Russian Enterprises," *Europe-Asia Studies* 52, no. 4 (June 2000): 627–56; Kathryn Hendley, Peter Murrell, and Randi Ryterman, "Law Works in Russia: The Role of Law in Inter-Enterprise Transactions," in *Assessing the Value of the Rule of Law in Transition Economies*, ed. Peter Murrell (Ann Arbor: University of Michigan Press, 2002).

increased role of the state in the economy and the heightened dependence of many firms on the state for resources after the crisis do not bode well.

President Medvedev's Turn

President Medvedev has put great rhetorical effort into promoting rule of law reform. He has decried Russia's "legal nihilism" and its "eternal corruption which has debilitated Russia as long as one can remember."[19] As a lawyer without experience in the security services, his criticisms have evoked optimism in some quarters about Russia's commitment to enforcing rule of law.

His record to date on legal reform has, however, been modest and at times contradictory despite his rhetoric. In the summer of 2008, he signed amendments to the law on nongovernmental organizations, which eased rules for registration but did little to ease other regulatory burdens on these organizations. He has highlighted the importance of judicial independence but also backed a proposal to change the rules for selecting the chair of the Russian Constitutional Court, which would allow him, rather than other justices, to elect the chair. In addition, during his tenure the state brought another criminal case against Yukos' Mikhail Khodorkovsky and ended jury trials in cases involving treason and other politically sensitive topics.

Medvedev has been maddeningly vague on the details of his proposed policies and taken few steps to put his ideas into action. His recent decision to downsize the police by 20,000 and to raise the salary of those remaining on the forces captures the duality of his approach. On one hand, the decision to reduce the police force raises the possibility that the government can weed out "bad apples" and reward those who follow the law. On the other hand, the move gives the Interior Ministry a year to implement the policy, allows it to count positions that have gone unfilled toward the 20,000 figure, and relies on the Interior Ministry itself to implement the reform. Moreover, Medvedev assured that no senior Interior Ministry officials would be dismissed and put the incumbent head of the Interior Ministry in charge of anticorruption efforts, a move that hardly inspires confidence. Given the numerous recent scandals involving the militia, including a murderous rampage by a Moscow police officer in a grocery store in April 2009 and a video appeal by a policeman from Novorossiisk decrying corruption among his peers, these steps hardly echo the radical rhetorical flourishes of Medvedev's speeches on the need to reduce corruption and strengthen the rule of law. For his efforts, Alexei Dymovsky, the whistle-blowing policeman who appeared in a YouTube video publicizing corruption

---

19. Dmitri Medvedev, "Krasnoyarsk speech," February 15, 2008, www.medvedev2008.ru; "Go Russia!" [in Russian], *Gazeta.ru*, September 10, 2009, www.gazeta.ru.

among his peers, was recently charged with "fraud committed by a person using his official position" by the prosecutor general.

On a potentially more hopeful but tragic note, President Medvedev dismissed 20 employees of the Federal Penitentiary Service, the head of Moscow's prisons, and the head of the tax crimes department of the Moscow branch of the Interior Ministry, Anatoli Mikhalkin, in the wake of the death while in detention of Sergei Magnitsky, a lawyer for Hermitage Capital.[20] Magnitsky had made detailed charges of state property theft by subordinates of Mikhalkin in the Interior Ministry.

One may attribute President Medvedev's lack of concrete measures to his cautious nature or weak position relative to his mentor, Prime Minister Putin, who has much better relations with the security services. Yet, President Medvedev has been in office for almost two years, and each month that passes without concrete actions to improve the legal environment, optimism about his intentions and capacity to make real changes in Russia dims.

To be sure, President Medvedev's task has been complicated by the global economic crisis, which has hit Russia especially hard. The expansion of state ownership in high-profile firms and increased role of state banks may have made macroeconomic sense, but in Russia these steps are also likely to have the side effect of increasing opportunities for corruption and abuse of state power. As many firms have become more dependent on state banks and state ownership, their vulnerability to abusive state officials has increased. This suggests that corruption and political connections will continue to define the business environment at least in the short run.[21]

Implications

Given Russia's long history of failed reforms, autocratic government, and heavy reliance on natural resources, is it reasonable to expect significant improvements in the rule of law? Certainly, these factors are not encouraging, but it is also the case that Russia's corruption ratings are worse than expected given its level of education and wealth. Nonetheless, while there is still much work to be done, Russia has made considerable progress in modernizing the technical aspects of its legal institutions over the last 20 years.

---

20. Nataliya Vasilyeva, "Russia's Medvedev Fires 20 Prison Officials after Death of Jailed Lawyer," *Washington Post*, December 12, 2009, www.washingtonpost.com (accessed on April 28, 2010); Charles Clover, "Medvedev Fires Head of Moscow Tax Crime Unit," *Financial Times*, December 16, 2009, www.ft.com (accessed on April 28, 2010); and Gregory L. White, "U.S. Investor's Lawyer Dies in Moscow Jail," *Wall Street Journal*, November 18, 2009, http://online.wsj.com (accessed on April 28, 2010).

21. One issue worth watching is how quickly and transparently Russia privatizes assets in which the state has taken positions during the crisis.

However, strengthening the rule of law requires changes in political relations that level the playing field between the powerful and the powerless, and on this front Russia has made far less progress. Indeed, some argue that Russia has moved from state capture by private business to capture of private business by the state.[22] Barring significant political liberalization that increases the power of the voter to constrain state officials, Russia will continue to face daunting problems with legality. Some modest proposals to improve the quality of the rule of law in Russia include finding ways to check state power short of political liberalization. As noted earlier, Russian courts do not work badly in run-of-the-mill disputes between private firms but are much less effective in politically sensitive or high-profile cases involving large stakes.

One suggestion to curtail state power is to empower autonomous business organizations that can protect the interests of their members. As Dinissa Duvanova[23] shows, firms in Russia often join business associations to defend themselves against petty corruption. Similarly, William Pyle[24] finds that members of business organizations in Russia are more willing to contest government predation, to lobby for institutional reform, and to invest in physical capital.

Russia would also benefit by redrawing its legal districts. As it stands, Russia's legal jurisdictions coincide with its political jurisdictions—that is, almost every region has one arbitration court and therefore is vulnerable to pressure from a single governor. Redrawing the jurisdictions so that each arbitration court includes several regions might increase the independence of arbitration court judges by reducing their dependence on any single governor. Similarly, it would be helpful to rotate judges among several regions to make it harder for them to form close relations with governors. Surely, governors (and many judges) would oppose this move, but the benefits to society as a whole could be significant.

---

22. Andrei Yakovlev, "The Evolution of Business-State Interaction in Russia: From State Capture to Business Capture," *Europe-Asia Studies* 58, no. 7 (November 2006): 1033–56.

23. Duvanova, "Bureaucratic Corruption and Collective Action: Business Associations in Eastern Europe and Eurasia."

24. William Pyle, "Organized Business, Political Competition and Property Rights: Evidence from the Russian Federation," *Journal of Law, Economics and Organization* (forthcoming).

5

Role of High-Technology Industries

KEITH CRANE AND ARTUR USANOV

Politicians worldwide are fond of supporting high-technology industries—that is, industries that develop and deploy new technologies to create products or services not previously available. These industries, where expenditures on research and development (R&D) as a share of total sales are much higher than average,[1] are considered especially attractive because demand for their products often grows rapidly. These industries also tend to pay wages substantially higher than average. Production processes often have less impact on the environment than some traditional industries. In some instances, R&D undertaken by high-technology industries has spillover effects that benefit other sectors in the economy.

Russia is no different. Both President Dmitri Medvedev and Prime Minister Vladimir Putin envision increased output from high-technology industries as driving Russia's economic growth.[2]

This chapter assesses whether these hopes are likely to be fulfilled. We first assess Russia's heritage in high-technology industries, then evaluate five high-technology industries with significant sales in Russia and abroad: software, nanotechnology, nuclear, aerospace, and armaments. We look at

Keith Crane is director of the RAND Corporation's Environment, Energy, and Economic Development Program. Artur Usanov is completing his doctoral studies in policy analysis at the Pardee RAND Graduate School.

1. T. Hatzichronoglou, "Revision of the High-Technology Sector and Product Classification," OECD Science, Technology and Industry Working Paper (Paris: Organization for Economic Cooperation and Development, 1997), http://puck.sourceoecd.org.

2. Russian Federal Government, *Concept of Long-Term Social and Economic Development of the Russian Federation Until 2020* (November 2008); Dmitri Medvedev's article, "Go Russia!" September 10, 2009, http://eng.kremlin.ru/speeches (accessed on November 3, 2009).

each sector's organization, sales, strengths, weaknesses, and impediments to growth and how policies pursued by the Russian government would affect that sector. We conclude with an assessment of likely prospects for growth for each sector and the likely future role of high-technology industries in the Russian economy.

Russia's Heritage in High-Technology Industries

One of the legacies that Russia inherited from the former Soviet Union was a large cadre of well-trained scientists and engineers, a system of national laboratories and research institutes, and design bureaus and enterprises that had succeeded in building some highly sophisticated machinery and equipment. With these resources, the Soviet Union managed to achieve notable technological feats, including launching the first satellite, Sputnik 1, into space; putting the first human into space; manufacturing the world's first supersonic transport aircraft; and building the world's first nuclear power plant to generate electricity for a power grid. The Soviet Union also produced a number of sophisticated weapons systems, including advanced fighter aircraft, intercontinental ballistic missiles, and nuclear weapons. In fact, most of the Soviet Union's major achievements in civilian technologies were tied to its military program.

After the collapse of the Soviet Union, high technology was no longer the key focus of Russian policymakers. With the exception of software, output from high-technology industries fell sharply (along with output from most other industries). Aerospace and armaments were hit especially hard, as domestic procurement fell by 80 percent in the 1990s.[3]

High-technology industries played a small role in driving the increases in Russian GDP between 1998 and 2008, when growth in GDP averaged 6.8 percent per year. However, growth in output of machinery and equipment—the sector where most high technologies are lodged—has been rapid since 1998, eclipsing the overall rate of growth in GDP.

Russia's recovery was primarily driven by the same factors driving growth in other transition economies: market disciplines and shift from state to private ownership. These changes massively improved the efficiency with which capital and other resources were used. During this period, labor productivity in manufacturing rose at double-digit rates. Sectors of the economy that had been relatively neglected during the Soviet era or suffered the most severe declines in output during the first decade of the transition led the recovery: retail and wholesale trade, construction, transportation, and telecommunications (figure 5.1). Despite the importance of oil, refined oil products, and natural gas in Russian exports and tax revenues, changes in output of oil and natural gas did not directly drive growth

---

3. Institute for International Strategic Studies, *Military Balance* (London, various years).

Figure 5.1   Sectoral contributions to Russia's growth in GDP between 1998 and 2008

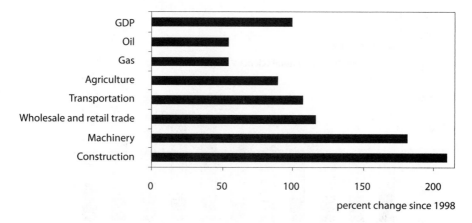

Note: For machinery production, data on "machine building and metal processing" are used for 1999 and 2000 and "production of machinery and equipment" for 2001 to 2008.

Source: Rosstat, *Annual Statistical Yearbook*, various years.

in output, although revenues from these exports played an important role in attracting the financial flows that boosted construction and retail trade.

The Soviet industrial base still forms the core of Russia's high-technology industries: advanced materials, nuclear power, aerospace, and other sectors of the defense industry. Software is the only substantial high-technology sector to have emerged since the collapse of the Soviet Union.

The Soviet education and research establishment remains the source of human capital for Russia's high-technology sectors. Russia inherited the Soviet Union's extensive system of science and technology education. Although the educational system has changed, Russia still scores well in various international comparisons of high school and college students' knowledge of science, mathematics, and engineering—the educational basis of high-technology industries. Moreover, the number of students graduating with university degrees has risen sharply since Soviet times (figure 5.2). Although the number of graduates with degrees in mathematics and natural sciences has stagnated, those with engineering degrees has increased in recent years, from 146,000 in 1990 to 207,000 in 2007.

The Soviet Union's massive system of research laboratories and development institutes shrank following the country's collapse. Of the countries that emerged from the Soviet Union, Russia has done the best job of maintaining at least some of these laboratories, but employment and the number of active laboratories have fallen sharply. The number of R&D personnel in Russia shrank from 1.94 million in 1990 to 793,000 in 2008.[4]

4. Ministry of Education and Science of the Russian Federation, *National Innovation System*

Figure 5.2   Graduates from Russian private and public universities, 1990, 1998–2007

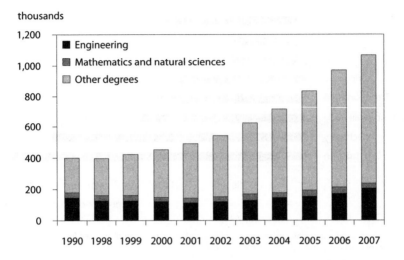

thousands

Source: Authors' calculation based on data from the Russian Education Statistics website, http://stat.edu.ru.

For example, the total number of individuals employed in the Soviet nuclear industry (weapons and civilian uses) was estimated at 200,000 to 222,000 in 1991. Research is now confined to a few core laboratories.

R&D expenditures also shrank. In 2008 they amounted to 1.14 percent of GDP, well below the average OECD level but above that of most countries with a similar level of per capita GDP. The Russian Federal Space Agency (Roscosmos) has been the main recipient of public funds for nondefense R&D, followed by the Russian Academy of Sciences, the Federal Agency for Science and Innovation, and the Russian Academy of Medical Sciences.[5] The share of universities in R&D funding remains small. Unlike in most OECD countries, the public sector finances most Russian R&D—61 percent—while the business sector accounts for 29 percent and foreign sources, 9 percent.[6]

The Russian Academy of Sciences inherited most of the All-Union facilities for basic science research after the collapse of the Soviet Union. However, it too has shrunk over the past two decades. Laboratories not associated with the academy have experienced even sharper reductions.

While traditional sources of support for high-technology industries

---

and State Innovation Policy of the Russian Federation (background report to the OECD Country Review of the Russian Innovation Policy, Moscow, 2009), chart 5.6, http://mon.gov.ru (accessed on January 14, 2010).

5. Ibid, chapter 5.

6. Ibid., chart 5.5, data for 2006, but the composition has not changed significantly since then.

have faltered in Russia, a number of new sources have sprung up over the course of the transition. Foreign companies have spurred growth in Russia's high-technology industries through subcontracting, joint ventures, wholly owned research laboratories, or funding research by independent laboratories or academic institutions. Russian scientists are also frequently engaged as consultants. These new activities have markedly changed R&D in Russia and the nature of Russian high-technology industries.

Current Role of High-Technology Industries

According to the Organization for Economic Cooperation and Development (OECD), nine main product groups (based on the Standard International Trade Classification [SITC] codes) encompass products produced by high-technology industries: (1) aerospace, (2) computers and office machines, (3) electronics and telecommunications, (4) pharmaceuticals, (5) scientific instruments, (6) electrical machinery, (7) chemicals, (8) non-electrical machinery, and (9) armaments.[7] Of these, Russia has internationally competitive products in

1. software in the computer and office machines industry;
2. specialty materials, including nanotechnologies;
3. nuclear technologies in the nonelectrical machinery sector;
4. aerospace; and
5. armaments.

We investigate each of these five industries in this section. The Concept for Long-Term Social and Economic Development of the Russian Federation until 2020 adopted by the Russian government in November 2008 adds shipbuilding and radioelectronics to these sectors. However, outside some specialized applications in defense, these two sectors are well behind their international competitors. Moreover, shipbuilding is not usually considered a high-technology industry. President Medvedev has also mentioned pharmaceuticals, an industry in which Russia has not registered substantial exports or shown much innovation.

Software and Information Technology (IT) Services

The Russian software industry has been a success story. From a humble beginning in the early 1990s, the industry's dollar revenues have grown at double-digit rates. In 2008, gross revenues ran about $5.5 billion, almost half of those from exports.[8] The total Russian market, as shown in

---

7. Hatzichronoglou, "Revision of the High-Technology Sector and Product Classification."

8. Russian Software Developers Association (Russoft), *6th Annual Survey of the Russian*

Figure 5.3   Russian market for software and information technology services, 2005–09e

billions of US dollars

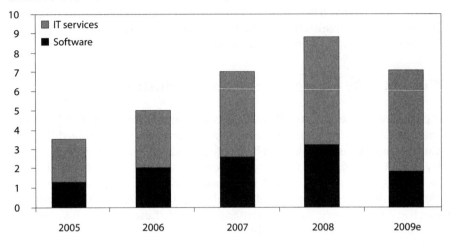

e = estimate

Source: CNews Analytics, 2009, www.cnews.ru.

figure 5.3, is substantially larger because of sales by foreign firms like Oracle and Microsoft in Russia. However, the Russian industry is smaller than India's; the Indian software and IT services industry had revenues of $60 billion in 2008.[9]

The Russian software and IT services industry is young. Almost all existing IT companies are startups by Russian entrepreneurs. Initially, most of these entrepreneurs had worked in government-owned IT centers, research institutions, or defense companies. The industry benefited from its young age, absence of legacy assets, and small size—the government did not bother to regulate it, which would likely have hindered its growth. The low capital intensity of the industry kept barriers to entry and exit low.[10] As a consequence, the IT sector has always been one of the most open industries in Russia.

Software Export Industry (St. Petersburg, 2009), 20, www.russoft.org (accessed on January 14, 2010). This number includes sales by Russian companies only, which might be tricky to define in offshore software development. Normally these are companies that have either headquarters or most of their developers located in Russia.

9. Data from NASSCOM, the trade body of India's IT industry, www.nasscom.org (accessed on January 14, 2010).

10. McKinsey Global Institute, *Unlocking Economic Growth in Russia* (Moscow, 1999), www.mckinsey.com (accessed on January 14, 2010).

In 1999, McKinsey Global Institute found the software sector had the highest labor productivity in the Russian economy, at 38 percent of the US level, double the average of the ten sectors studied.[11]

Russia's rapid growth between 1999 and 2008 substantially increased demand for the industry's products and services from business, government, and consumers. Another factor driving growth in the software industry was more robust enforcement of intellectual property rights and antipiracy measures: Software piracy declined from 87 percent in 2004 to 68 percent in 2008.[12] As a result, from 2005 to 2008, sales of software and IT services in the Russian market more than doubled, although the economic crisis in 2009 resulted in a large drop in IT spending (figure 5.3).

Probably the best indicator of the Russian software industry's competitiveness and strength is its rapidly growing exports (figure 5.4). Offshore programming in Russia began to gain momentum after the dot-com bubble burst in 2000–01 when US and European companies aggressively sought ways to cut costs.[13]

While lower labor costs were the main initial driver of offshore programming, IDC, a global research firm that focuses on the information and communications technology (ICT) sector, finds "strong technical skills, sound methodologies, and high education levels, which allow delivery of high-end, technically complex projects, as key strengths of the Russian software and services industry."[14] Russia has higher wages in the IT sector than India or China and so is unlikely to challenge India's leadership in the offshore information technology–business process outsourcing (IT-BPO) market. However, it is likely to continue to increase its presence in the high-end segment of the offshore development market and in packaged software.

The Russian Software Developers Association (Russoft) divides software exports from Russia into three groups:

1. *Packaged software.* This consists of commercially available programs for sale or lease. The largest Russian packaged software company is

---

11. The McKinsey Global Institute found that in project services (consulting, implementation, including offshore programming, and training in IT) labor productivity was 72 percent of the US level while it was only 13 percent in packaged software due to the small scale of operations, piracy, and low value added; see McKinsey Global Institute, *Unlocking Economic Growth in Russia.*

12. Data are from BSA and IDC, quoted in Russoft, *6th Annual Survey of the Russian Software Export Industry,* 16.

13. D. J. Petersen, *Russia and the Information Revolution* (Santa Monica, CA: RAND, 2005), www.rand.org.

14. Marianne Kolding and Vladimir Kroa, *Russia as Offshore Software Development Location: Should You Consider This Your Next Move?* (White Paper sponsored by Russoft, March 2007), www.russoft.org. This white paper was based on in-depth, executive-level interviews with 20 Western European and US-based companies that have used Russian software and services companies for offshore development projects.

Figure 5.4   Exports of Russian software, 2002–09f

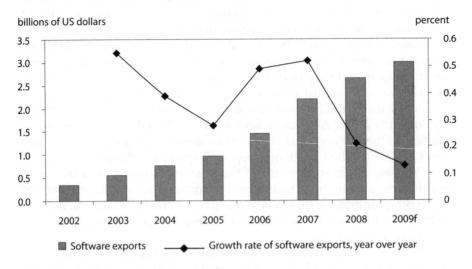

f = forecast

Source: Survey of software companies by Russoft, 2009.

Kaspersky Lab, which develops antivirus software and had revenues of $360 million in 2008, of which $260 million were from exports.[15] Its products regularly receive high ratings from major software publications. Agnitum and Doctor Web are two smaller Russian antivirus software developers. Other Russian software companies with significant sales in international markets are Transas (navigational systems, training simulators, and fleet management systems), ABBYY (provider of document conversion, data capture, and linguistic software), PROMT (automated translation systems), and Parallels (virtualization and automation software).

2. *Offshore programming (software development services).* In this case, a foreign company contracts with Russians for software development or IT services for its clients. The foreign company keeps the resulting intellectual property. This is the largest source of Russian software exports (figure 5.5). Companies engaged in subcontracting are less well known, but some, such as EPAM Systems, Exigen Services, and Luxoft, work with thousands of programmers and development centers across the world. They are truly global companies. There are also hundreds of Russian companies with fewer than 100 employees. Russoft estimates total employment in this sector at about 50,000 in 2008.

3. *Captive software development centers.* Attracted by Russia's research expertise in some areas and its large pool of highly skilled professionals

---

15. Russoft, *6th Annual Survey of the Russian Software Export Industry*, 20.

Figure 5.5   Composition of Russian software exports, 2008

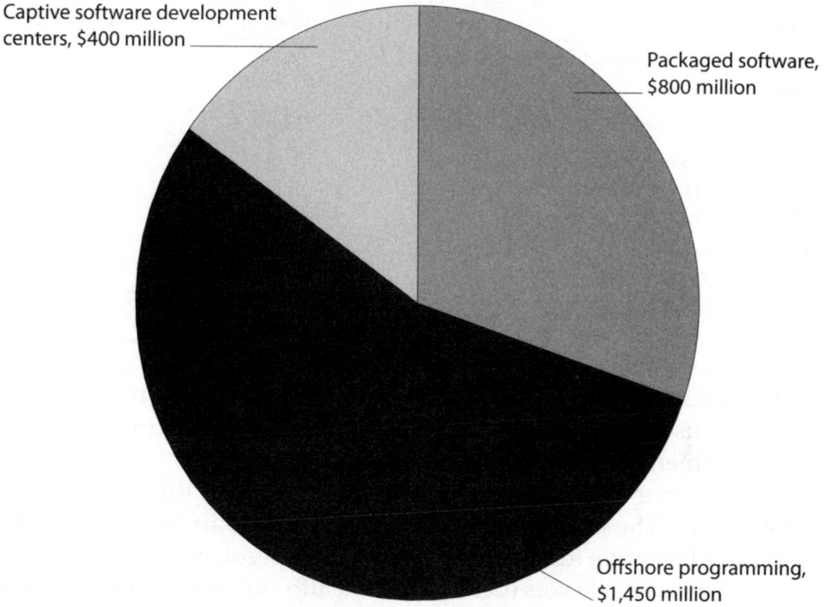

Captive software development centers, $400 million

Packaged software, $800 million

Offshore programming, $1,450 million

Source: Survey of software companies by Russoft, 2009.

with scientific backgrounds, a number of major international firms have established dedicated offshore programming and R&D centers in Russia. These companies include Alcatel, Ericsson, Google, Intel, Motorola, Samsung, and Sun Microsystems, among others.

The development of Russia's IT sector will depend on making the country's business environment friendlier, especially for offshore software companies, which have to compete in the global market. A common theme across most indices measuring Russia's performance is that Russia scores well on its highly educated population. As noted earlier, Russian education in science and mathematics remains strong as demonstrated by the performance of Russian students in international contests. However, some software companies complain that university curricula do not reflect the requirements of today's marketplace. On the other hand, as the CEO of a large Russian software company observed in an interview with one of us, in general the industry is very pleased with the quality of recent Russian graduates. He saw no decline in the competitiveness of Russian students. Rather, students had an increased appreciation for and knowledge of the software industry.

Russia's overall rating, however, is dragged down by unfriendly business regulations and corruption (table 5.1). For example, Russia does rela-

Table 5.1   Russia's ranking in selected information and communication technology surveys

Survey	Rank	Percentile
IT Industry Competitiveness Index (Economist Intelligence Unit, 2009)	38/66	42
A.T. Kearney Global Services Location Index, 2009	33/50	34
International Telecommunications Union, Information and Communication Technology Development Index, 2009	50/154	68
World Economic Forum, Networked Readiness Index, 2008–2009 rankings	74/134	46

tively well on the International Telecommunications Union's Information and Communication Technology Development Index, which measures ICT access, use, and skills, but on ratings that take into account regulation and government policies it scores much more poorly.[16]

A key barrier to the development of the industry is Russia's lax tax administration.[17] The tax authorities do not closely audit companies, which is sufficient incentive for companies to use independent contractors—who avoid paying payroll taxes (pension and health care taxes) or value-added tax (VAT)—as opposed to hiring full-time employees, which is more expensive. In this business environment, traditional incentives like promotions, stock options, or other means of inducing loyalty and commitment are much less effective. This proclivity to use independent contractors rather than full-time employees makes it difficult for companies to build project management skills, as companies lack the staff and loyalty needed to run large projects.

However, the greatest barrier to the development of the industry is thuggery and corruption that Russian entrepreneurs face from the police and other government officials.[18] Bribing inspectors, tax collection agents, and the police places a substantial burden on companies. The police penalize companies by demanding years of records on flimsy grounds. If no irregularities are found, the police have been known to manufacture irregularities and threaten company managers with imprisonment unless they are bribed. Some police officers have threatened to kidnap or beat up family members if they are not bribed. This climate of intimidation and fear discourages entrepreneurs from expanding their businesses and puts a premium on moving assets outside of Russia.

---

16. Ibid.

17. Keith Crane's interview with CEO of a Russian software company, November 16, 2009.

18. Ibid.

Table 5.2   Public and private spending on nanotechnology, 2008–15
(billions of rubles)

Category	2008	2009	2010	2011	2012–15
R&D	8.2	9.8	11.2	13.1	25.7
Infrastructure	10.9	9.1	9	2	0
Rusnano spending	20.3	21	22.8	19.5	80.5
Private investment in Rusnano projects	n.a.	n.a.	6.5	7	40
Other	0.1	0.3	0.4	0.6	0
Total	39.5	40.2	49.8	42.2	146.2
In billions of US dollars (30 rubles = $1)	1.3	1.3	1.7	1.4	4.9

n.a. = not available

Source: Ministry of Education and Science of the Russian Federation, Federal Target Program for Development of Nanoindustry until 2015, 2008, http://mon.gov.ru.

Nanotechnology

The Russian government has made development of nanotechnology a state priority. Nanotechnology has received more attention than almost any other technological sector in post-Soviet Russia. The push to make Russia a technological leader in this field comes from the very top.

The government has set up several programs to support and direct the development of nanotechnology, providing substantial sums of money for research and related infrastructure (table 5.2). In 2007, it created a state-owned corporation, Rusnano, with chartered capital of 130 billion rubles ($5 billion) to support commercial initiatives in this area. By the end of 2009, Rusnano had approved investments of 91 billion rubles in 61 projects (including in other investment funds)[19] and become the largest investor in high-technology industries in Russia. However, the 2007–09 crisis has set back the company's and the Russian government's plans for nanotechnology. In 2009, at the request of the Russian government, Rusnano transferred approximately half of its funds back to the federal budget to help cover other government expenditures.[20]

The current state of nanotechnology in Russia reflects both the strengths and weaknesses of Russia's research and innovation system. Russian scientists have been relatively productive in theoretical research on nanotechnology. Russia ranked sixth in the number of nanotechnology publications in

19. "Rusnano Recaps 2009," press release, December 23, 2009, www.rusnano.com.

20. "Rusnano transferred 66.4 billion rubles to the state budget," press release, December 17, 2009, www.rusnano.com. The government plans to return these funds to Rusnano in 2010–12.

1995–2007, behind the United States, China, Japan, Germany, and France.[21] The Russian Academy of Sciences began publishing its *Journal of Nano and Microsystem Techniques* in 1999. Russian public spending on nanotechnology projects and initiatives in 2008 exceeded $1 billion, behind only the United States and Japan.[22]

Russia's performance has not been as strong in the commercialization stage of the innovation process: It ranks 16th in the number of patents related to nanotechnology, 0.2 percent of the global total.[23] Innovation activity in nanotechnology by Russian firms has been modest. President Medvedev lamented the lack of interest of Russian businesses in nanotechnology at a forum organized by Rusnano in October 2009.

In addition to Rusnano, Russia is home to some private companies engaged in nanotechnology. NT-MDT (www.ntmdt.com) was set up in 1989 by Viktor Bykov, head of a research laboratory at the Physical Problems Research Institute. NT-MDT specializes in designing and manufacturing scanning probe microscopes and other equipment for nanotechnology research. The firm has about 10 percent of the world market for these microscopes and 90 percent of the market in Russia and countries in the Commonwealth of Independent States (CIS). In 2007, it had revenues of about $65 million. The *National Report on Innovations* in 2008 singled out this firm as possibly the best commercial success of Russia in the nanotechnology market. NT-MDT has a large network of international suppliers and two branches abroad, one in the Netherlands and the other in Ireland. The firm invests 15 to 20 percent of revenues in R&D and actively collaborates with outside research laboratories or organizations.[24]

Optogan (www.optogan.com) was founded in Finland in 2004 by a team of Russian scientists from the Ioffe Institute in St. Petersburg. Optogan develops and produces high-brightness light-emitting diodes (LEDs). Its proprietary technology and product designs have enabled tangible improvements in performance and reductions in the cost of LED lighting. Optogan has R&D facilities in Finland and a pilot manufacturing line in Germany. Rusnano together with the private investment fund Onexim Group, owned by billionaire Mikhail Prokhorov, and another Russian company bought Optogan in December 2008. Optogan is currently ramping up volume manufacturing in St. Petersburg. Total investment in the project is 3.4 billion rubles. The investors hope that the company's revenue will reach 6 billion rubles in 2013.

---

21. Lux Research as quoted in *Innovatsionnoe razvitie—osnova modernizatsii ekonomiki Rossii* [*Innovation Development—Foundation for Russia's Economy Modernization*] National Report, State University—Higher School of Economics, 2008), 127, available at www.hse.ru.

22. Ibid., 120.

23. Ibid., 127.

24. Ibid., 151–55.

Nuclear Industry

Russia's civilian nuclear industry is broad-based, encompassing nuclear power plant design and construction, power-sector equipment, and the entire nuclear fuel cycle. It is the direct outgrowth of the Soviet nuclear weapons program. In 2007, both the civilian and military sides of the industry were integrated under the State Atomic Energy Corporation, Rosatom. One of the goals set by the federal government for the corporation was to strengthen the country's position on the global market for nuclear technology. Most of the civilian assets in the nuclear sector have been transferred to a joint-stock company, Atomenergoprom, which is a subsidiary of Rosatom.

Atomenergoprom is a vertically integrated holding company. It owns companies at all stages of the value chain in the nuclear power sector, from uranium mining and fuel fabrication, nuclear reactor design and manufacture to design and construction of nuclear power plants. Total sales were 290 billion rubles ($11.7 billion) in 2008.

Atomenergoprom is one of the world's largest nuclear companies. It is the largest in the world in terms of exports of nuclear power plants. It is currently constructing five reactors outside Russia. It owns and operates ten power plants with a total capacity of over 23 GW, making it the second largest company in the world in terms of electricity generated by nuclear power plants. It is also the second largest company in the world in terms of uranium reserves, including joint ventures abroad, and the fourth in terms of production of uranium ore.[25]

Russia has a strong competitive position in the nuclear fuel cycle, especially in uranium conversion and enrichment. It has the world's largest uranium enrichment capacity (40 percent of the global total).[26] It owns 100 percent of the shares of Russia's four enrichment plants: Angarsk Electrolysis Chemical Complex (Angarsk, Irkutsk region), Electrochemical Plant (Zheleznogorsk, Krasnoyarsk region), Urals Electrochemical Combine (Novouralsk, Sverdlovsk region), and Siberian Chemical Combine (Seversk, Tomsk region). The companies have a total capacity of 26 million kilograms separative work units (SWU).

Uranium enrichment adds the largest value to uranium in its transformation into nuclear fuel, accounting for 30 to 50 percent of the final reactor fuel price.[27] Russia has the lowest costs of enrichment in the world, making it one of the most competitive Russian industries on the world

---

25. Atomenergoprom company profile, www.atomenergoprom.ru/en.

26. Rosatom, Uranium Enrichment Division, www.rosatom.ru/en.

27. Commonwealth of Australia, *Uranium Mining, Processing and Nuclear Energy—Opportunities for Australia?* (report to the Prime Minister by the Uranium Mining, Processing and Nuclear Energy Review Taskforce, December 2006), 35–37.

market.[28] Russia's competitive advantage in this sector is based on its efficient gas centrifuge technology and large scale of facilities and is due in part to decisions made on R&D and investment in the 1990s. Russia invested in the development and deployment of a new generation of gas centrifuges in the 1990s; other industrial sectors did not enjoy this support.[29] In addition, uranium enrichment is a capital-intensive business, and the large scale of production facilities in Russia helps to reduce average costs.[30]

Price is the main factor in determining competitiveness in uranium enrichment. Two of Russia's major competitors—USEC in the United States and the European consortium controlled by Areva—use a different technology, gas diffusion, which requires much more electricity and therefore is costlier.

Because it is the lowest-cost producer, Russia has enjoyed growing exports of uranium enrichment services and radioisotopes to all major markets (figure 5.6). These exports are carried out through another Atomenergoprom subsidiary, Tenex, which supplies nearly one-third of Europe's nuclear reactor fuel needs. It also takes highly enriched uranium extracted from nuclear warheads and mixes it with less enriched uranium to create fuel for civilian use in the United States. These sales are made through the Megatons to Megawatts contract also known as the HEU-LEU agreement. However, Tenex's further expansion on the European and American markets is limited by quotas and other trade barriers protecting domestic enrichment companies.

Russia has proposed an International Uranium Enrichment Center at the existing enrichment plant in Angarsk. This center would provide assured nuclear fuel cycle services to states on a nondiscriminatory basis. Russia has proposed to enrich uranium for Iran in such a facility in exchange for Iran ending its nuclear enrichment activities. The center would be jointly owned by Russia and other states. It would help to increase demand for Russia's uranium enrichment services.

Russia exported its enrichment technology to China in the 1990s. It built centrifuge enrichment plants in Shaan-xi and Lanzhou.[31] However, these plants used an older generation of centrifuges. Russia built these plants with an understanding that they would serve only China's domestic customers.

---

28. G. Rothwell, "Market Power in Uranium Enrichment," SIEPR Discussion Paper no. 08-32 (Stanford Institute for Economic Policy Research, March 2009), http://siepr.stanford.edu.

29. O. Bukharin, "Understanding Russia's Uranium Enrichment Complex," *Science and Global Security* 12 (2004): 193–218.

30. Urals Electrochemical Combine is the largest enrichment plant in the world with a capacity of 12.5 million kilograms SWU (Rothwell, "Market Power in Uranium Enrichment").

31. Bukharin, "Understanding Russia's Uranium Enrichment Complex."

Figure 5.6   Exports of enriched uranium and enrichment services by Tenex, 2006–08

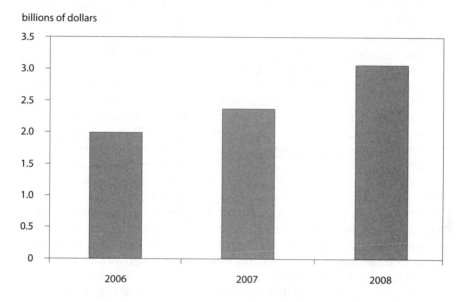

billions of dollars

Source: Tenex, 2008 Annual Report, 61, www.tenex.ru (accessed on January 14, 2010).

Retirement of less efficient gas diffusion plants by Areva and USEC is likely to increase competitive pressure in the industry but in the medium term is unlikely to undermine Russia's cost advantage. Emerging new technologies, such as laser isotope separation, may present a bigger threat in the long term.

Russia is also a major producer of nuclear fuel assemblies for nuclear power stations. It has 17 percent of the global nuclear fuel market, supplying every sixth reactor in the world with assemblies. However, in this sector its supplies are limited mainly to Soviet- or Russian-built reactors.

Russia also has considerable experience in nuclear reactor design and construction. Concerned about scarcity and sustainability of uranium supplies, it has been interested in fast neutron reactors. These reactors would allow the world to extend existing uranium resources by up to a factor of 60 and potentially to use thorium, which is much more abundant in nature than uranium, as nuclear fuel.[32] Russia's BN-600 (560 MWe) reactor in Beloyarsk is the largest fast neutron reactor in the world and has supplied electricity to the grid since 1980. Russia is building an even larger reactor, BN-800, which is scheduled to start commercial operation in 2012. In October 2009 Russia announced it would design and build two similar reac-

---

32. World Nuclear Association, "Fast Neutron Reactors," www.world-nuclear.org.

tors in China, which would be the first time commercial-scale fast neutron reactors have been exported.[33]

Another sign that Russian nuclear reactor technology has some advantages is the decision by German engineering giant Siemens to leave its nuclear reactor joint venture with Areva and form one with Rosatom. This venture will develop a new-generation nuclear reactor that will compete with Areva's Evolutionary Power Reactor.[34]

The United States and Russia have cooperated on a gas turbine-modular helium reactor.[35] However, this and other possible cooperation projects between Russia and the United States in the nuclear sector are hindered by the fact the US Congress has not yet ratified the US-Russia Agreement for Peaceful Nuclear Cooperation (123 Agreement) signed on May 6, 2008.[36]

Until recently, the depressed state of the world market for new nuclear power plants limited Russia's exports of nuclear reactor technology. The Chernobyl catastrophe seriously damaged market confidence in Russian-designed reactors. Nevertheless, Rosatom's operator for constructing Russian-design nuclear power plants in other countries, Atomstroyexport (ASE), has won several recent tenders. Its main successes had been in countries where competition was limited and where the host government lent support to Russian nuclear plants, such as Iran, China, and India. However, in recent years, a number of other countries have expressed interest in nuclear power, which has increased Russian exports (figure 5.7). In October 2006 ASE was chosen over a Skoda-led consortium to build a plant in Bulgaria consisting of 1060-MWe AES-92 VVER units with third-generation reactors, making it the first Russian nuclear power project in the European Union.

Russia's political leadership has made a strong commitment to nuclear power. On the one hand, it sees nuclear power as a way to free more natural gas for export by replacing gas-fired electricity generation with nuclear power plants. On the other hand, nuclear power and related industries are one of just a few high-technology sectors in which Russia has a serious R&D development base and can compete with more developed countries on the world market. The state has invested substantial sums in R&D, funded construction of new nuclear plants in Russia, and provided strong political support for Russian nuclear power projects abroad. Recent consolidation of all nuclear assets under Rosatom is aimed at strengthening the international position of Russia's nuclear sector.

---

33. "China Signs Up Russian Fast Reactors," *World Nuclear News*, October 15, 2009, www.world-nuclear-news.org.

34. "Siemens, Rosatom may sign JV deal in 2009," Reuters, October 1, 2009, www.reuters.com.

35. General Atomics Energy Group, "GT-MHR: Inherently Safe Nuclear Power for the 21st Century," http://gt-mhr.ga.com.

36. Anton Khlopkov, "U.S.-Russian Nuclear Energy Cooperation: A Missed Opportunity," *Bulletin of the Atomic Scientists*, August 31, 2009, www.thebulletin.org.

Figure 5.7   Russian exports of nuclear fuel and nuclear power plants, 1996–2008

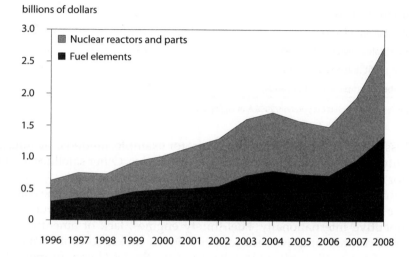

billions of dollars

Source: UN Comtrade Database.

Aerospace

Russia's aerospace industry consists of rockets, satellites, and civilian aircraft. Of these, Russia's rocket industry is the strongest. Russia remains a leader in launchers; once the US space shuttle is retired in the next decade, Russia's Proton rocket will remain the only well-tested rocket capable of ferrying people and heavy payloads into space. It has the best record among major launchers.

Since the 1990s, the Russian space program has depended upon commercial launch contracts and collaborative activities with other countries and foreign companies for survival. For example, Pratt and Whitney markets Russia's RD-120 rocket engine in the United States. Although the Russian government funded the program in the 1990s, budgets were small. In recent years, revenues have recovered as the Russian federal government budget has grown. Even in the crisis year of 2009, the budget for space programs ran 82 billion rubles, roughly $2.5 billion.

The space industry remains primarily under government control. The Russian Federal Space Agency (RKA) is in charge of all civilian space operations. NPO Energia, a company in which private shareholders have a controlling stake, and two state-owned companies, Khrunichev and TsSKB-Progress, manufacture Russia's rockets.

In addition to rockets, Russia has produced communications, geopositioning, and other satellites. In contrast to launchers, communications satellites have not been competitive internationally. Wider use of GLONASS,

Table 5.3   Russian aircraft industry, military and civilian, 2008

	Aircraft industry	United Aircraft Corporation
Number of companies	106	18
Sales (billions of rubles)	226.6	105.3
Export sales (billions of rubles)	65.7	44.7
Gross profit (billions of rubles)	7.1	0.9
Number of employees (thousands)	355.3	92.1

Source: United Aircraft Corporation, 2008 Annual Report.

a Russian satellite navigation system, is, for example, hindered by inferior quality and the higher cost of GLONASS receivers. Other satellites tend to be for military use only.

Russia's civilian aircraft industry has not fared well since the collapse of the Soviet Union. Under central planning Soviet aircraft were never competitive internationally. Fuel-thirsty engines, lack of amenities, and inferior controls and avionics confined Soviet makes to captive markets among Soviet allies. After the collapse of the Soviet Union, former allies stopped purchasing these models. Even Russian airlines preferred Western makes. Consequently, Russia has succeeded in exporting just a few Soviet-era planes since the collapse of the Soviet Union, even though the industry has experimented with putting Western engines on its airframes. Civilian transport aircraft manufacturers have survived through sales of military transport aircraft, tankers, and other military aircraft.

The Russian government has attempted to consolidate the aircraft industry by creating a holding company, United Aircraft Corporation (UAC). The major Russian transport aircraft design bureaus (Sukhoi, Tupolev, Ilyushin, and Yakovlev) and production facilities have been merged into this company. Table 5.3 shows the composition of the entire industry, military as well as civilian, and the role that UAC plays in the industry.

In UAC, as in the other new agglomerates that the Russian government has fashioned out of the disparate companies that emerged from the former Soviet military complex, the new chief executive officers have had a hard time establishing control. The managers of the individual plants still wield a substantial amount of power.[37]

Russia has attempted to reenter the commercial aviation market. Sukhoi has embarked on a commercial airline venture, entitled Sukhoi Superjet, a modern regional jet seating 75 to 95 people. Characteristic of most commercial civilian aircraft activities in Russia, the venture involves a Western partner, Finmeccanica, an Italian aerospace and mechanical engineering firm. Design and manufacturing of the aircraft are led by Sukhoi

---

37. Conversation with an aircraft manufacturing executive in Moscow, October 2006.

Civil Aircraft, in which Alenia Aeronautica, a subsidiary of Finmeccanica, owns 25 percent plus one share.[38] In addition, Finmeccanica owns 51 percent in SuperJet International, which is responsible for marketing, sales, and aircraft delivery for the Sukhoi Superjet in Europe, North and South America, Africa, Japan, and Oceania as well as for worldwide logistics support. The engine for the aircraft was developed by PowerJet, a 50-50 joint venture between France's SNECMA and Russia's NPO Saturn. The consortium has received a number of orders for the plane, for example, from Aeroflot as well as several airlines outside Russia, including Hungary's Malev, Armenia's Armavia, and Indonesia's Kartika Airlines. The first deliveries will reportedly be made in 2010.

Russia has had more success in providing design services and components to the civilian aerospace industry. United Technologies' Pratt and Whitney division has invested in Russian aircraft engine turbine manufacturers. Boeing has a large design bureau in Moscow. EADS also subcontracts design and other activities to Russian companies.

Armaments

Russia's defense industry is emerging from a rough period. After the collapse of the Soviet Union, the industry experienced an initial fall in domestic funding for procurement of at least 80 percent compared with Soviet times.[39] Domestic procurement funding fell sharply again after the 1998 financial crash; it recovered to 1997 levels only in 2007. The part of the former Soviet industry located outside of Russia suffered even deeper declines.

The Russian defense industry survived by cutting salaries, often by not paying wages, and reducing production. Employment fell as workers left for jobs with a higher or steadier paycheck and because the cash-strapped defense industry hired few new workers. Closing plants and consolidating enterprises proceeded much more slowly. Outright layoffs, however, were rare. The industry stayed alive only due to exports.

Today the industry is composed of fewer than 1,500 enterprises, consisting of research institutes, design bureaus, and production facilities, a heritage of Russia's Soviet past.[40] The sector has been partially privatized, primarily through insider privatizations that took place in the 1990s. Roughly two-fifths of the enterprises are mainly private (the state has less than a 25 percent stake) and two-fifths are 100 percent state-owned. The state maintains sizable shares in the rest. These enterprises are often

---

38. Sukhoi Company, "Sukhoi Superjet 100," www.sukhoi.org.

39. Institute of International Strategic Studies, "Russian Military-Industrial Overview," *Military Balance* (London, various years).

40. Global Security, "Military Industry Overview," www.globalsecurity.org (accessed on January 14, 2010).

only partially independent; most are affiliated with large consortia like the Sukhoi group. Because these enterprises sell almost all their output to these consortia, revenue figures for Russia's largest defense firms provide a lower bound for the final output of Russia's defense industry.

Russia's defense companies are relatively small. The largest, Almaz-Antei Air Defense Concern, had military sales of $4.3 billion in 2008, placing it 16th on a list of the world's largest defense firms. Sukhoi, the next largest company, had revenues less than half those of Almaz-Antei (table 5.4).

The Putin administration made a concerted effort to consolidate the industry by creating large holding companies. The Russian government has continued these efforts under Medvedev. Initially, the government used Russia's state-controlled arms export company, Rosoboroneksport, as the vehicle to consolidate the industry, especially in aerospace. The government also created the United Shipbuilding Corporation by merging a large number of naval shipbuilding companies. OPK Oboronprom, partially owned by Rosoboroneksport, took stakes in a number of helicopter manufacturers to consolidate that industry. At the end of 2007, the government created Russian Technologies and transferred its stakes in 439 firms to this company, including Rosoboroneksport and Oboronprom, almost all of which are in the defense sector. Russian Technologies now accounts for 23 percent of all sales in the defense sector.[41]

Although the industry was overdue for rationalization and has done a poor job of consolidating on its own, this new policy has already had some negative consequences. Russian military analysts complain about large price increases for weapons now that procurement budgets are rising again.[42] A single seller makes it more difficult for the Russian government to negotiate lower prices.

In the immediate aftermath of the collapse of the Soviet Union, Russian arms manufacturers saw exports fall along with domestic procurement. Eastern European clients disappeared along with the Warsaw Pact; Iraq ceased to be a customer because of the embargo; and the superiority of US weaponry to Soviet models during the first Gulf War turned former Soviet customers to arms from other countries. In 1991, exports reportedly fell to $6.6 billion compared with $19.8 billion in 1989. Russian exports continued to fall for most of the 1990s.

During the 2000s, exports have provided a lifeline to Russia's defense industry. Russian arms exports have exceeded procurement expenditures in every single year since 1998 (figure 5.8). In some years, arms exports were more than double domestic spending on procurement.

---

41. Russian Technologies, www.rostechnologii.ru/company.

42. Viktor Baranets, "Will Russia Buy American Tanks?" *Komsomolskaya Pravda*, April 25, 2007, 7.

Table 5.4   Russian armaments industry, 2008 (millions of US dollars)

Company	Rank	2008 defense revenue	2008 total revenue	Percent of revenue from defense
Almaz-Antei	16	4,335.20	4,616.80	93.9
Aviation Holding Company Sukhoi[a]	40	2,039.20	2,169.40	94.0
Severnaya Verf	n.a.	n.a.	1,895.30	n.a.
Tactical Missiles	55	1,152.60	1,213.30	95.0
Irkut[a]	56	1,149.80	1,255.20	91.6
Russian Helicopters	64	845.10	1,657.10	51.0
Uralvagonzavod	80	646.80	1,848.10	35.0
KB Priborostroyeniya	84	607.00	610.00	99.5
Ufa Engine Building	89	541.00	601.00	90.0
Sevmash	n.a.	n.a.	539.50	n.a.
RTI Systems Concern	99	396.10	471.50	84.0

n.a. = not available

a. Sukhoi and Irkut are subsidiaries of the United Aircraft Corporation (UAC). However, they still report their results independently while UAC has not published its consolidated reports for the last two years.

Sources: Defense News, Top 100 for 2008, 2009, www.defensenews.com (accessed on January 14, 2010); for Severnaya Verf and Sevmash, Expert-400 Ranking of the Largest Russian Companies, available at http://raexpert.org (accessed on January 14, 2010).

Exports have grown rapidly in large part because of India and China. These two countries are Russia's two most important clients, accounting for as much as 70 percent of total sales in recent years. Rapid economic growth in both countries has permitted large increases in defense spending, especially on procurement. Moreover, both countries face difficulties in obtaining modern weapons from other sources: The European Union and the United States have embargoed arms exports to China; India's nuclear program has hindered its ability to import from the United States. In both countries, Russia has been seen as a less politically motivated arms supplier.

India has been a major customer of the Soviet and later Russian defense industry since 1959. In 1993, a new Treaty of Friendship and Cooperation was signed between the two countries, putting their relationship on firmer ground in the post-Soviet era. Part of this agreement was a defense cooperation accord aimed at ensuring continued supply of Russian arms and spare parts for India's military and the promotion of joint production of defense equipment. Since this agreement was signed, Russia has sold a vast array of high-quality military equipment to India. Among the Russian equipment purchased by India are land assault hardware such as T-90 tanks, the Smerch multiple-launch rocket systems (MLRS), long-range howitzers, and infantry vehicles. India has also worked with Russia

Figure 5.8   Russian procurement and exports of weapons, 2001–08

billions of US dollars

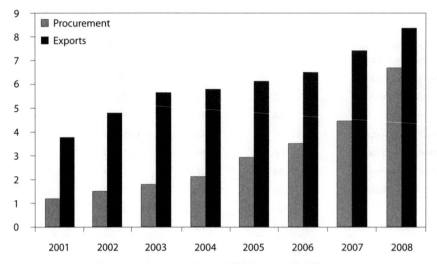

Sources: Procurement: International Institute for Strategic Studies, *The Military Balance*, various years; Exports: Federal Agency for Military-Technical Cooperation, www.fsvts.gov.ru.

on overhauling its diesel submarine fleet and has acquired the BrahMos antiship missile. India has also been a major buyer and joint producer of Russian aviation equipment. Of particular note, the Su-30MKI was specifically designed for India. In 2000 Hindustan Aeronautics Limited (HAL) signed an agreement with Rosoboroneksport for license manufacture of 140 Su-30s. This is in addition to the delivery of 50 of these aircraft purchased directly by Russia.

For its part, China has procured over $15 billion of Russian equipment since 1999, averaging at least $1 billion a year since 1992.[43] Among the systems China has obtained are Su-27 and Su-30 multirole fighters and Il-76 military transport planes. The Chinese navy has acquired Sovremenny class destroyers with Sunburn antiship missiles and Kilo class diesel submarines. The one weapon category Russia has been reluctant to sell to China is land assault hardware. Unlike India, Russia has not sold China tanks or MLRS.

Some attribute part of the rapid development of China's defense industrial base in recent years to its purchases from Russia, which have at times (though not always) come with access to the underlying military technology. Tai Ming Cheung's comprehensive study of the transforma-

---

43. Vladimir Paramonov and Aleksey Strokov, "Russian-Chinese Relations: Past, Present, and Future" (Defense Academy of the United Kingdom, September 2006).

tion of China's defense technology industrial base (DTIB) concludes that the ability of the DTIB "to learn and absorb already existing technologies and techniques has been significantly enhanced by the acquisition of civilian and foreign, especially Russian, defense technology and industrial hardware and knowledge."[44]

The preponderance of exports in sales of Russian arms manufacturers has begun to shift. On the one hand, rapid growth in defense budgets in Russia is pushing up domestic procurement spending. On the other, growth in arms exports to China and India may be leveling off as those two countries are attempting to replace imports from Russia with domestic production. In 2005 China decided not to import additional Su-30s and also stopped production under license of the Su-27, preferring to manufacture its own model.[45] In India, the Su-30 is being assembled under license, not imported directly from Russia. Russian officials have expressed some concern that Indian and Chinese demand for defense equipment will decline in the next five to ten years. The Chinese government is more interested in developing indigenous defense capabilities, rather than buying foreign equipment. Future purchases may be limited to imported components such as jet engines that will be used in Chinese aircraft.

Russian exports to India are under pressure for different reasons. Russian officials are concerned that India's improving relationship with the United States will lead to a shift in arms purchases from Russia to Western suppliers. The Russian press gave wide coverage to a comment by Nicholas Burns, former US undersecretary of state for political affairs, when he predicted that 2008 would represent a breakthrough for US-India relations, with "US firms well positioned" to compete in the Indian market.[46] The potential for future US-India arms deals is closely tied to the two nations' nuclear cooperation agreement, which will allow India access to US nuclear fuel and reactors.

With Russia's arms exports to China and India unlikely to grow, Russian firms have sought to expand their sales to other markets. In 2006 Russia exported arms or military services to 61 countries, including Venezuela, which signed a series of agreements with Russia for 24 Su-30 fighters, 53 military helicopters, and 100,000 Kalashnikov assault rifles for a total of over $3 billion. Russia and Venezuela have also been exchanging military personnel, such as pilots and technicians, with Russian instructors providing assistance to Venezuelan pilots. Russian defense officials have agreed

44. Tai Ming Cheung, "Leaping Tiger, Hybrid Dragon: The Search for Technological Innovation and Civil-Military Integration in the Chinese Defense Economy" (PhD thesis, Department of War Studies, Kings College, University of London, September 29, 2006).

45. Piotr Butowski, "Drop in Russian Aircraft Sales to Hit Industry Hard," *Jane's Defence Weekly*, July 13, 2005.

46. "Russian weapon makers switch sales tactics with China as Beijing slows arms shopping spree," *International Herald Tribune*, November 28, 2006.

to allow Venezuela to set up a factory capable of producing 50,000 Russian assault rifles annually.

Another region where Russia continues to sell arms is the Middle East. In 2000 President Putin cancelled an agreement with the United States to restrict Russia's arms and nuclear sales to Iran. Since then, Russia has been a major arms supplier to the Iranian military. In 2005 Russia agreed to sell Iran 29 Tor-M1 (SA-15 Gauntlet) surface-to-air defense systems and to upgrade Iran's Su-24 and MiG-29 aircraft. Russia has also had success in exporting arms to Algeria, Syria, the United Arab Emirates, Indonesia, and Yemen.

Future Role of High-Technology Industries

As Russia emerges from recession in 2010 or 2011, drivers of growth are likely to shift. On the one hand, red-hot growth in construction and whole-sale and retail trade came to an abrupt end in 2009; output of oil and natu-ral gas has fallen and shows little sign of rapid expansion. World oil prices are also down from their highs of 2008. On the other, the fall in the real effective exchange rate of the ruble has improved the competitive posi-tion of manufacturing, including high-technology industries. In addition, continued, if halting, integration of the Russian economy into the global economy has opened up new markets for these and other industries.

The perceptions and aspirations of Russia's current leaders are to a large extent based on previous Soviet technological achievements. Rus-sian leaders worry that the concentration of Russia's exports in energy and raw materials might make it a "raw material appendage" not just to Europe but also to China. They perceive growth in high-technology indus-tries as key to defining Russia's future place in the world economy, with implications for economic growth and national security.

In our view, Russian policy to encourage growth in high-technol-ogy industries has not been very effective. Russian policymakers have attempted to foster high-technology industries by consolidating existing manufacturers into large state-controlled agglomerates—"national cham-pions." The creation of these "strategic" enterprises has been most pro-nounced in armaments, the nuclear industry, and aerospace. The major rationale for consolidation has been to achieve a larger scale (as many of these industries are capital-intensive) so these companies are better placed to invest in developing new products and to compete internationally. The government's desire to avoid competition among domestic high-technol-ogy companies has been palpable. Russian policymakers perceive such competition as wasteful as opposed to a force for innovation as it is in the United States. Russian policymakers have also pushed for greater coop-eration between state-owned strategic companies and international com-panies. The Sukhoi Superjet project is an example of such cooperation.

The Russian government has greatly increased budgetary expenditures on high-technology sectors. In addition to larger budgets for aerospace and substantially larger procurement budgets for defense, it has made substantial investments in nanotechnology through Rusnano. It has also created an investment fund for ICT companies and the Russian Venture Company to encourage private investments in high-technology firms. The software industry, which until recently was below the radar of Russian policymakers, finally attracted government support at the end of 2009 in the form of reduced payroll taxes.

Despite the attention these industries have attracted, hopes that high-technology industries will be the main driver of Russian growth seem misplaced. Russia's Ministry of Education and Science report estimates that high-technology industries accounted for 9.8 percent of industrial output in 2008;[47] industry contributed 30.6 percent to Russia's GDP in 2008, suggesting that the share of high-technology industries in Russia's GDP may have run 3 percent of GDP. Software and telecommunications, which are not included in industrial output, would add to this total. Although not negligible, these industries are not of a size to drive aggregate economic growth. What then is the likely contribution of these industries to Russian economic growth in the coming years?

Software and Information Technology Services

The software and IT industry provides a number of lessons for other Russian industries on how to succeed in the global marketplace. The industry

- is closely integrated into the world economy;
- is characterized by substantial inward and outward foreign investment;
- competes with global players without government protection; and
- operates without excessive government regulation or involvement.

The software and IT industry is the healthiest of the five industries assessed in this chapter; it has registered the fastest growth. In contrast to the nuclear, aerospace, and armaments industries, this industry consists entirely of new startups, albeit many of these entrepreneurs were trained and worked in Soviet-era defense laboratories or enterprises. The industry depends heavily on foreign sales, especially to developed-country markets. Not surprisingly, sales dropped in 2009 because of the global downturn. However, the industry is poised to resume growth as the global economy recovers. The large number of companies, the high quality of

---

47. Ministry of Education and Science of the Russian Federation, *National Innovation System and State Innovation Policy of the Russian Federation,* table 1.5.

the workforce, and a good reputation for innovation and quality make this a vibrant sector that should do well in the coming years. Because of high salaries, it continues to attract and retain a highly trained, ambitious workforce.

As mentioned earlier, the key challenge to continued growth in Russia's software industry is corruption, especially within the Russian police.[48] Threats to corporate officers, including family members, to extract bribes create a precarious working environment. Other problems endemic to Russia are less threatening. Corporate raiders, who use illegal means to take control of Russian companies, have difficulty acquiring software companies because it is tough to seize intangible, as opposed to tangible, assets. Intellectual property rights are not a major impediment to growth.[49] Software companies farm out coding of software to freelancers, who do not have access to the entire product. Companies have been able to prevent product theft successfully.

Nanotechnology

Nanotechnology is difficult to define as an industry. Successful companies in Russia, like NT-MDT, are really manufacturers of scientific equipment. These market niches can be highly profitable. Market leaders need to invest heavily in R&D to maintain their positions. However, demand for scientific apparatus tends to be limited, so although profitable, companies in these industries often do not experience rapid growth in sales.

The amorphous nature of nanotechnology makes it difficult to predict future sales or even the development of the industry. However, Russian manufacturers of specialty materials and scientific equipment will continue to play a role in the global industry. This said, we are skeptical that nanotechnology sales will be so large or will grow so rapidly in the years ahead that they will provide a major boost to Russian growth.

Nuclear Industry

Russia's nuclear industry is well poised to continue to take market share in uranium enrichment. With its superior centrifuge technology and low electric power costs, Russia should do well in this segment of the industry, especially as countries become increasingly concerned about climate change and greenhouse gas emissions and opt for nuclear power. The Russian-US HEU-LEU agreement has helped create a market for Russian fuel. Once ratified by the US Congress, the US-Russia civilian nuclear power agreement, the 123 Agreement, should also be helpful.

48. Keith Crane's interview with CEO of a Russian software company, November 16, 2009.

49. Ibid.

Russia's nuclear industry faces greater challenges in selling new nuclear power plants. Even though it is constructing five plants in other countries, the Chernobyl disaster, competition from Western, Japanese, and Korean manufacturers, and concerns about dependability and safety are likely to hinder its ability to win substantial shares of the global market, especially in developed countries. Developing-country markets, the major area of growth, are likely to be easier, especially if the Russian industry collaborates with Western manufacturers, as it has in Bulgaria.

Aerospace

Space is not a dynamic industry in the global economy. Commercial satellite launches have been fewer than expected as fiber optic cables have satisfied most of the increased demand for communications capacity despite the extraordinary growth of the internet. Most launches are still purchased by governments. The space program in the United States appears to be in a period of retrenchment, and in Europe it also faces budgetary pressures. Although China and India have expanding programs, they tend to favor their own manufacturers. Russia's good track record and budgetary pressures in the United States provide room for continued sales of launches and rockets as demand for observation satellites remains, but the industry does not show signs of dynamic growth. New rocket designs appear to be keeping Russia competitive.

Civilian aviation presents a different story. Within Russia, there is a debate about whether the Russian industry will be able to maintain stand-alone capacity to assemble civilian aircraft or would be better off collaborating with Western manufacturers. Western companies have complimented Russian capabilities in design, precision engineering, especially turbine blades, and sophisticated materials but have difficulty in acquisitions or greenfield investments, in part because of security concerns and high levels of corruption. In our view, despite the concerns of Russia's military establishment, the answer is clear: Russian companies have done well collaborating with the international industry but have failed when they have attempted to go it alone. Russia's successes with joint ventures and the failure of former Soviet products on international markets show the future of the industry.

Armaments

As of 2008, Russia's defense industry was enjoying its best years since Soviet times. Export orders were up. The Russian government had promised to spend 5 trillion rubles ($190 billion) on procurement between 2007 and 2015. Industry sales ran close to $10 billion a year.

Although order books are full, the outlook is less rosy. The industry faces a number of challenges. The most important problems are technological, financial, and management-related. As noted earlier, Russia's defense companies are relatively small. European manufacturers like BAE Systems, Finmeccanica, EADS, and Thales had sales more than twice those of Russia's largest defense contractor, Almaz-Antei. US companies are even larger. These Western companies have the wherewithal and the client base to invest heavily in new technologies. They purchase components and designs from each other, stimulating technological change. They have experience in large projects involving integration of systems. They also face pressures from shareholders to increase profits by reducing costs and expanding sales.

Russian defense enterprises face competitive pressures to sell more and cut costs but lack the funding to keep pace with R&D in Western Europe and the United States. They have relied on existing technologies for most of their production for close to 20 years. R&D had been a small fraction of Soviet efforts. Russian companies are also financially weak: About a third are at risk of bankruptcy. Because of the lack of resources for the past two decades, the capital stock and workforce of the defense industry are aged: Seventy percent of its production assets are fully depreciated, and the average age of the workforce is over 55 in a country where male life expectancy hovers around 60 years. The three-quarters state-owned, one-quarter private ownership structure for the new defense holding companies does not promise improvements in efficiency. Whereas Russia's private companies have performed well even compared with established multinationals, its state-controlled companies have not. Companies like Gazprom are overstaffed, sluggish, and inefficient.

Russia's defense industry will increasingly suffer from the virtual hiatus in the development of new weapons systems during the 1990s. It will also suffer from the heavy hand of the state in enterprise management and reduced domestic competition. More importantly, unless Russia's defense industry interacts more closely with European and US manufacturers, the gap between most Russian technologies and those being developed by Western manufacturers will continue to widen. The efficiencies and technological benefits that Western companies enjoy from trade and exchanges of technologies, even in the face of export controls and other limitations, will give Western manufacturers a continued technological edge over their Russian competitors.

Conclusion

High-technology sectors of the Russian economy contributed roughly 3 percent to Russia's GDP in 2008 and, broadly defined, accounted for roughly 10 percent of industrial output. Growth in these sectors would provide tangible benefits to Russia, leading to increased high-wage employment and nonenergy exports and development of supplier industries.

This said, growth in high-technology sectors will not drive growth in aggregate output. The economic drivers of the past decade will remain the more important drivers of growth: rising productivity across all sectors; growth in services, especially financial and business services; retail and wholesale trade; telecommunications; and government expenditures financed by taxes on exported energy.

We find that those companies or sectors that are most integrated with and most open to the global economy have the most favorable outlooks. Russia has shown it has a comparative advantage in software, especially programming of more complex software. It has an established set of home-grown software companies, which are closely integrated into the global industry. In addition, Russia has dominant firms in markets for scanning probe microscopes (nanotechnology) and uranium enrichment, where Russian technology is at the forefront.

The record of the past two decades indicates that future success in these sectors will depend on increased integration into the global, especially European, economy. In aerospace, sales of rockets, aircraft components, aircraft design services, and the new Sukhoi Superjet have depended on collaborating with foreign manufacturers. Prospects for Russia's armaments companies are dimmer because they remain much more insular than firms in other sectors.

Despite concerns voiced by many Russians about the quality of the Russian education system, more people are graduating with university degrees than in the past, many with degrees in engineering and the sciences. Our interlocutors from Russian and foreign high-technology companies active in Russia praised the quality of new and existing Russian staff engaged in R&D. Russia's human capital is improving.

The Russian government's policy of consolidating enterprises into state champions does not appear to have been successful. In the case of the defense industry, where it has been pursued most aggressively, consolidation appears to have chiefly resulted in higher prices of weapons for the Ministry of Defense. These agglomerates do not appear to have aggressively rationalized their holdings. In some instances, the mergers may have provided a lifeline to failing plants, covering their losses with profits from more efficient factories.

The biggest impediment to growth of Russia's high-technology sectors is the pervasive corruption in tax collection and law enforcement. Threats of physical violence and incarceration by the Russian police discourage investment and provide compelling reasons for Russian entrepreneurs to invest abroad. Cleaning up the tax administration and police force by holding senior officials accountable and firing corrupt staff is the single most important near-term policy measure that the Russian government should undertake to foster this sector. In the long term, successful prosecution and incarceration of corrupt security services officials would significantly benefit this and other private-sector industries in Russia.

6

Climate Change and Role of Energy Efficiency

SAMUEL CHARAP AND GEORGI V. SAFONOV

In prepared remarks before a meeting with several ministers and senior aides on February 18, 2010, President Dmitri Medvedev delivered a highly unusual speech on climate change for a senior Russian official.[1] Just two months earlier, the Copenhagen climate talks had produced a document far less ambitious than had been hoped, and many observers had consigned the subject of climate change to the back-burner of international politics. It seemed Russia would have done the same, since its leadership's attitude toward global warming had ranged from denying its existence to seeing it purely as a means of augmenting Russia's role in international affairs.

Yet Medvedev, in contrast to both his previous statements on the topic and those of his predecessor and the current prime minister, Vladimir Putin, outlined an approach to Russian climate change policy that sounded strikingly similar to those of Western European countries:

> [The disappointing outcome at Copenhagen] is not a reason to sit back now and do nothing, because we are responsible for the state of our planet.... We need to decide today how to make the most effective use of what has been achieved... and outline the best ways for aiding less developed countries to fight climate threats. The new climate agreement represents a real chance for mass introduction [of] energy-efficient and low-emission technology.... We are going to improve our energy efficiency and reduce our emissions regardless of whether or not there is an international agreement. This is in our own interest from both an economic and environmental point of view.

Samuel Charap is a fellow in the National Security and International Policy Program at the Center for American Progress. Georgi V. Safonov is the director of the Center for Environmental and Natural Resource Economics at the State University–Higher School of Economics.

1. Opening remarks at Meeting on Climate Change, February 18, 2010, http://eng.kremlin.ru (accessed on February 20, 2010).

Medvedev went on to urge the assembled officials to create incentives for the private sector to play a role in addressing climate change and called for adapting the government's climate doctrine, a framework for policy that he signed in late 2009, to current developments, making it a "living document" and not a "sacred cow." A month later, he repeated these ideas in a speech to the Security Council, a body consisting of Russia's most influential decision makers.[2]

In short, Medvedev asserted that climate change is real, that global warming threatens Russia's future, that Russia has a responsibility to address it both domestically and in international forums, that doing so can be economically beneficial, and that old policymaking patterns—a regulation-first approach to the economy and paper-tiger framework documents that become irrelevant soon after they are released—need to change if any progress is to be made. The speech is striking both because it is essentially the first time a Russian leader has made this argument coherently and because it is totally divorced from the reality of Russia's current approach to climate change, which can be charitably characterized as lackluster. Indeed, Medvedev has become known for making grand, forward-looking speeches, most of which seem fanciful and generally produce little substantive change.

This chapter demonstrates that scientific and economic data in fact support Medvedev's assertions. However, it also shows that Russia has either failed to live up to his stated goals or only begun the process of realizing them. Despite Medvedev's call to action, Russia has not been a leader on climate issues; in fact, it has either taken a passive stance or used the issue as leverage on other questions in global talks and failed to implement a serious domestic mitigation or adaptation program. The second half of the chapter focuses on energy efficiency. It demonstrates that the Russian government stands to reap huge benefits from increasing the efficiency of its economy and that this step in itself will lead to significant reductions in greenhouse gas emissions. Under Medvedev's leadership, some steps have been taken in this direction, but much remains to be done. Greater efficiency will not realize the full potential of emissions reduction in Russia, but it represents a crucial element in achieving this goal. The chapter concludes with proposals for the United States to engage Russia on energy efficiency. Such engagement would benefit both sides and would help add substance to the bilateral relationship on economic issues. But for international cooperation on these issues to gain traction, Russia needs to take a proactive stance on addressing climate change, a stance that is clearly economically beneficial given the emissions reductions that can be achieved by increasing efficiency. Medvedev's lofty words must be matched by concrete changes in policy.

---

2. Opening remarks at Security Council Meeting on Climate Change, March 17, 2010, http://eng.kremlin.ru.

Russia and Climate Change

Russia has been and continues to be responsible for a large share of cumulative anthropogenic carbon emissions into the atmosphere. Today, Russia is the third largest emitter of carbon dioxide (CO_2), behind only the United States and China (figure 6.1). Perhaps more importantly, before the economic crisis hit, Russia's per capita emissions were growing and were projected to approach the US level by 2030. Russia's third rank is all the more striking given that its emissions dropped by 40 percent in 1990–98 following the dramatic decline in energy consumption and industrial production precipitated by the economic contraction of the early post-Soviet period. As late as 2007, emissions have remained at only 66 percent of 1990 levels (figure 6.2).[3]

Russia is not only a major contributor to global warming; it is also especially vulnerable to its effects. Temperatures in Russia are rising faster than the world average. In 2008 the Russian Federal Service for Hydrometeorology and Environmental Monitoring (Rosgidromet) issued an extensive report that demonstrated that winter temperatures increased by 2 to 3 degrees Celsius in Siberia over the past 120 to 150 years, while the average global temperature rose in that period by only 0.7 degrees.[4] Rosgidromet's calculations demonstrate that Russia will experience global warming to a significantly greater extent than most other countries.

Despite the belief, widely held across its society, that, given its cold temperatures, Russia could benefit from global warming, climate change is, according to the World Bank, a "major threat to Russia" and will have significant negative effects—economic and social—there, not to mention the potentially devastating impacts on its ecosystem.[5] Already Russia is experiencing more floods, windstorms, heat waves, forest fires, and melting of permafrost. In Yakutsk, collapsing ground caused by permafrost melt has damaged the structural integrity of several large apartment buildings, a power station, and a runway at the local airport. The total number of structures damaged as a result of uneven foundation subsidence increased by 61 percent there in the 1990s compared with the previ-

---

3. According to recent estimates, the global economic crisis led to a 7 to 8 percent decline in Russia's emissions, so in 2009 CO_2 levels could be the lowest in two decades.

4. For the English language summary of the report, see Federal Service for Hydrometeorology and Environmental Monitoring, *Assessment Report on Climate Change and Its Consequences in the Russian Federation: General Summary*, 2008, http://climate2008.igce.ru (accessed on January 31, 2010). The full version in Russian is also available at the same website.

5. See World Bank, *Adapting to Climate Change in Europe and Central Asia* (Washington, June 2009), www.worldbank.org (accessed on January 31, 2010) and "Russia Needs to Act Swiftly to Reduce Vulnerability to Its Changing Climate," in *Russian Economic Report* 19 (Washington: World Bank, June 2009), www.worldbank.org (accessed on January 31, 2010), 22–28.

Figure 6.1 Energy-related carbon dioxide (CO$_2$) emissions by selected countries and regions, 2007

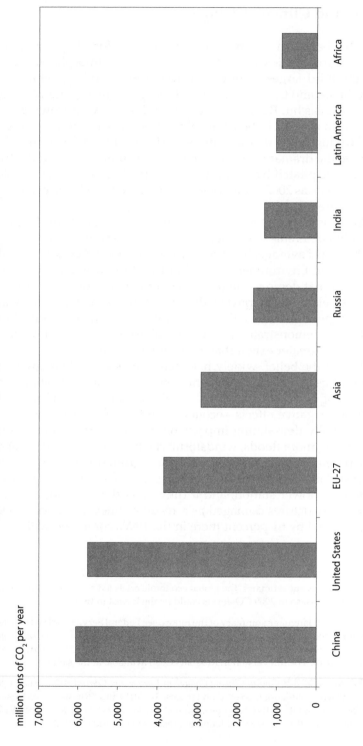

million tons of CO$_2$ per year

Source: United Nations Framework Convention on Climate Change (UNFCCC), National Greenhouse Gas Inventory Data for the Period 1990–2007, October 21, 2009, http://unfccc.int.

Figure 6.2   Russia's greenhouse gas emissions, 1990–2007

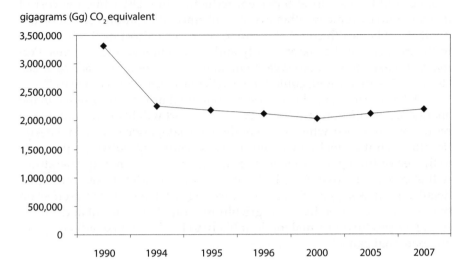

gigagrams (Gg) CO_2 equivalent

Source: Generated from the UNFCCC Data Interface, http://unfccc.int, December 2009.

ous decade.[6] Extreme events, snowmelt, and warmer temperatures have precipitated significant tree loss and degradation. And such phenomena are only going to become more common with rising temperatures. Areas of discontinuous permafrost (which covers over 60 percent of Russia's territory) are particularly at risk; melting will have social[7] and economic effects because of the large amount of oil and gas infrastructure in these areas—93 percent of natural gas and 75 percent of oil production occurs in permafrost zones. Indeed, climate change poses a direct threat to the energy sector, which plays a crucial role in the economy. Most of the extraction and other structures were built on pile foundations using permafrost soils as a base, and therefore their stability is dependent on that permafrost not melting. Already over 7,400 accidents related to melting of permafrost and soil degradation in West Siberia were reported in 2007, while up to $1.8 billion is spent annually on accidents and upkeep of pipelines.[8]

6. World Wildlife Foundation Russia, *Climate Change Impacts in the Russian Arctic: Searching for Ways for Adaptation*, 2009, www.wwf.ru (accessed on March 3, 2010).

7. Communities will have to be resettled since up to a quarter of housing stock in the far north will be destroyed by 2030. This figure was cited by First Deputy Minister of Emergency Situations Ruslan Tsalikov. See "Global'noe poteplenie unichtozhit Sever Rossii" ["Global Warming Will Destroy Russia's North"], February 11, 2009, www.indigenousportal.com/Climate-Change (accessed on March 2, 2010).

8. Oleg Anisimov, ed., *Osnovnye prirodnye i sotsial'no-ekonomicheskie posledstviia izmeneniia klimata v raionakh rasprostraneniia mnogoletnemerzlykh porod: prognoz na osnove sinteza nabliudenii*

Overall, according to Minister of Natural Resources Yuri Trutnev, climate change could cause up to 5 percent reduction in GDP, while the cost of dealing with extreme weather events will amount to around $2 billion annually.[9] Public health could also suffer, since permafrost melt poses a risk to the integrity of the water supply and sewer engineering systems. Permafrost weakening on Novaya Zemlya, where several radioactive waste storage sites are located, could have particularly dire consequences.[10]

Global warming could entail some potential upsides for Russia. In the energy sector, offshore production and transport will likely benefit due to reductions in sea ice, which will lengthen the navigation season in the Arctic, although it is unclear whether these benefits will outweigh the costs to the sector from permafrost melt. Some claim that warmer temperatures will also benefit Russian agriculture. However, studies based on highly detailed models suggest that global warming will have a net zero effect on the sector.[11] Moreover, Russian agriculture is highly inefficient and suffers from low productivity, making it unlikely to be able to take advantage of any potential gains.[12]

Russia's Role in International Climate Policy

Despite both Russia's central role in causing, and thus potentially abating, global warming and its vulnerability to rising temperatures, Moscow has often assumed a passive role in the construction of the international climate regime and scrupulously avoided commitments that would force it to take steps to reduce emissions. Its major contribution—ratification of the Kyoto Protocol when its signature was needed for the treaty to take effect—was driven largely by political factors and has required no meaningful changes in its policies.

Russia has also "contributed" to international efforts to control emissions through the wrenching economic contraction, and resulting drop in emissions, it experienced in the 1990s. For example, were it not for Russia's drop in emissions in that period, the quantitative target of reducing

i modelirovaniia [*The Main Environmental and Socio-Economic Consequences of Climate Change in Regions with Widespread Permafrost: A Prognosis Based on a Synthesis of Observation and Modeling*] (evaluation report, Greenpeace Russia, November 2009), www.greenpeace.org (accessed on March 3, 2010).

9. Yuri Trutnev, presentation at a Meeting of the Presidium of the Government, April 24, 2009, www.priroda.ru (accessed on January 31, 2010).

10. World Wildlife Foundation Russia, *Climate Change Impacts in the Russian Arctic*, 47, 51.

11. William R. Cline, *Global Warming and Agriculture: Impact Estimates by Country* (Washington: Petersen Institute for International Economics, 2007), 59.

12. World Bank, *Russian Economic Report* 19, 26.

the emissions of Annex I Parties[13] to the UN Framework Convention on Climate Change (UNFCCC), which Russia ratified in 1995, to 1990 levels by 2000 would have been impossible.

The Kyoto Protocol to the UNFCCC, which was initially adopted in December 1997 but entered into force only in February 2005 after Moscow ratified it, provides legally binding commitments for developed countries and some transition economies, including Russia, to modulate emissions to an agreed-upon level by 2012 relative to the baseline of their 1990 emissions. Russia only agreed not to exceed 1990 levels, rather than reducing its emissions below that baseline. As a result of the post-Soviet emissions drop, without any additional efforts Russian emissions will not return to 1990 levels before at least 2020. In December 2009, Russia was 40 percent below the baseline.

Therefore, Moscow's participation in Kyoto required it to make no additional efforts to meet its obligations. Further, Russia stood to gain billions of dollars through the various flexibility mechanisms, such as trading of carbon credits, outlined in the Protocol. Nonetheless, Russia withheld its approval for seven years.

The Protocol could not have come into force unless at least 55 countries representing at least 55 percent of global carbon emissions ratified it. When the first round of commitments was announced, enough countries were willing to ratify the treaty but their emissions did not add up to the share of global carbon output required for enactment. Once the United States declared that it would not join, Russia's participation was necessary to meet that goal. In other words, because of its contribution to global warming as the third largest emitter, Russia's eventual decision to participate in Kyoto proved crucial in bringing the treaty into force.

While Russia's decision to ratify the Protocol is often cited as a demonstration of its productive role in contributing to international efforts to control global warming, Moscow's motives were far less altruistic. Indeed, it is widely believed that then president Putin agreed to sign the Kyoto Protocol in return for the European Union's granting of certain concessions in its negotiations with Russia on its bilateral World Trade Organization (WTO) accession protocol—in effect giving its blessing to Russia's membership.

Since 2008 the international community has been negotiating a follow-on agreement to the Kyoto Protocol that should provide a longer-term framework for international efforts to combat climate change. Russia's behavior in this period made it clear that its participation in Kyoto had not transformed it into a leader in the international effort to address climate change. In its submission to the UNFCCC prior to the Poznan Conference

---

13. Annex I countries include developed economies and some emerging economies such as Russia, Ukraine, and Belarus. These countries have special obligations under the convention.

of Parties (COP) in December 2008, Russia declared the goal of a 25 to 40 percent reduction from 1990 levels by 2020 "unreasonable" and asserted that legally binding commitments must be interpreted as "non-enforceable, non-punitive as well as flexible."

In June 2009, President Medvedev announced Russia's post-Kyoto proposed target as 10 to 15 percent below the 1990 baseline. It would be a stretch to call this ambitious: It translates to an effective 30 to 35 percent emissions *increase* from the 2007 level and implies an *acceleration* in annual emissions growth. Although Medvedev upped his pledge in December 2009 to a 20 to 25 percent drop, this still is not as ambitious as it could be; independent studies have shown that at least a 30 percent reduction is possible.[14] His own goal of a 40 percent decline in energy intensity (energy expended per unit of GDP) by 2020 would necessitate a greater decrease in emissions below the 1990 baseline than he seems willing to commit to in the context of the climate talks.[15]

Its track record at recent multilateral meetings demonstrates that Russia has largely been a passive player in international climate policy. At meetings of the parties to the UNFCCC and other climate-related gatherings such as the Major Economies Forum (MEF), Russia is notable for its silence; its negotiators are not active participants, let alone leaders, in the talks and take little initiative. Its attitude was neatly summed up by one of the government's lead climate experts: "The solution to climate change negotiations lies between the US and China."[16] In other words, Russia is content to sit on the sidelines until the other players come to an agreement and then decide whether to participate.

On the one hand, this may be a deliberate strategy: While the other major emitters debate and look for compromise, Russia has complete freedom of maneuver. It can agree on a strict emissions reduction target or disagree with it; agree on financing adaptation needs of least developed countries or object to it; or accept flexibility mechanisms or continue avoiding their use. On the other hand, pure bureaucratic and political factors might be at play: Without a strong signal from the political leadership that an ambitious treaty is a priority, working-level officials will be highly unlikely to take the initiative on their own. As the Russian saying goes, initiative is punishable.

Russia's behavior at the 15th COP, or COP-15, which was held in December 2009 in Copenhagen, represented a slight, but nonetheless important, departure from this trend. The goal of the Copenhagen meeting was to reach a legally binding agreement on further greenhouse gas emissions

---

14. Oldag Caspar, "Russia in the UN Climate Talks" (unpublished manuscript, Helsinki: Finnish Institute of International Affairs, June 2009).

15. Georgi Safonov's calculations.

16. Samuel Charap and Georgi Safonov's interview with Sergei Tulinov, advisor to the director of Rosgidromet, October 2009.

cuts, create an arrangement to finance adaptation and mitigation in developing countries, and delineate mechanisms for international cooperation in emissions reductions, among other issues. Given its contribution to global warming and status as a Kyoto signatory, Russia's position at the COP-15 was important. Further, if it were to have demanded to be compensated for the massive amount of carbon credits it had accumulated under Kyoto, Moscow could have torpedoed an agreement or at least made a functioning carbon market impossible.[17]

What changed at Copenhagen was the Russian leadership's engagement with the issue. Medvedev not only attended but also created an entry in his video blog on the subject[18] and made a major speech at the conference. In his address, he said that "Russia is ready to play the most active part in all of this processes [sic]. We recognize our share of the responsibility and this is the guideline in our efforts."[19] Such rhetoric represents a departure from his predecessor; indeed, it is hard to imagine the current prime minister giving such a speech.

Russia did end up signing the so-called Copenhagen Accord at the COP-15, but, as per the pattern described earlier, it played no significant role in formulating it. There was one breakthrough at Copenhagen: Russia agreed to provide funding for the Copenhagen Green Climate Fund, which will finance adaptation and mitigation activities in least developed countries. Russia had previously refused to participate in any such assistance projects.

On February 1, 2010, Russia submitted its plans for reducing greenhouse gas emissions as the Copenhagen Accord requires.[20] Strangely, its submission appears to have been a step backward: Russia committed to a 15 to 25 percent reduction from the 1990 baseline, as opposed to the 20 to 25 percent that Medvedev had proclaimed less than two months earlier. The commitment was conditioned on the participation of all major emitters in a legally binding agreement and on Russia's forest sinks being taken into account in calculations of its overall emissions. This latter demand has become a top priority for Russian international climate policy. On average, Russian forests absorb about 300 million tons of CO_2 per annum. However, Russia supports allowing countries not to account for emissions from

17. See Anna Korppoo and Thomas Spencer, "The Dead Souls: How to Deal with the Russian Surplus?" Briefing Paper 39 (Helsinki: Finnish Institute of International Affairs, September 4, 2009).

18. See recording on Dmitri Medvedev's blog: World's Major Greenhouse Gas Emitters Must Simultaneously Make the Necessary Commitments, December 14, 2009, http://eng.kremlin.ru (accessed on January 31, 2010).

19. Speech at Climate Change Conference Plenary Session in Copenhagen, December 18, 2009, http://eng.kremlin.ru (accessed on January 31, 2010).

20. See UNFCCC, Quantified Economy-Wide Emissions Targets for 2020 for Annex I Parties, http://unfccc.int (accessed on February 1, 2010).

forest management until this sector becomes a net source of emissions and favors accounting approaches that would allow for "hiding" of expected increased emissions from growth in the forestry sector.[21] In other words, commercial motives seem to be at work in addition to other factors.

Despite the increased engagement in Copenhagen, Russia's relatively unambitious submission shows that it largely remains a passive actor on climate issues. Further, it underscores that Russia's climate policy continues to be based on the view that the drop in emissions that resulted from the post-Soviet economic contraction represents a "contribution" to global efforts to control climate change. The wrenching social impact of economic contraction, and thus the "contribution," is considered a "sacrifice" made by the Russian people in the fight against global warming.[22] As a result, Russian policymakers consider that their country is entitled to avoid an affirmative stance on emissions reductions, which they consider a threat to economic growth.

Climate Policy at Home

Russia does not have a discrete climate change policy, but instead the government considers policies and measures in the energy sector, industry, municipal heat supply, forestry, and other areas as having side benefits in terms of greenhouse gas emission reduction or sinks. The secondary impacts of other policies and measures are as close as Russia gets to a "climate policy."

That said, on the eve of his departure for Copenhagen in December 2009, President Medvedev took a major step forward in climate policy and signed the Russian climate doctrine[23] (box 6.1). The doctrine marks the first attempt at institutionalizing climate change policy. Among other steps, it acknowledges the harmful effects of climate change, states the need to take into account climate-related consequences in economic, social and other policies, and outlines measures for adaptation—which could address the potential damage from permafrost melting, infrastructure collapse, South-to-North spread of infectious diseases—and mitigation.

However, the doctrine is an inadequate framework for policymaking. It does not establish concrete goals for mitigation and adaptation, mechanisms for such activities, or a framework for international cooperation.

---

21. See Anna Korppoo and Thomas Spencer, "The Layers of the Doll: Exploring the Russian Position for Copenhagen," Briefing Paper 46 (Helsinki: Finnish Institute of International Affairs, November 5, 2009), 6–7.

22. Samuel Charap's interview with Arkady Dvorkovich, economic advisor to the president of Russia, October 2009.

23. Climate Doctrine of the Russian Federation, http://eng.kremlin.ru (accessed on January 31, 2010).

Box 6.1   Russia's climate doctrine

The climate doctrine offers goals, principles, and means to unify government policy on climate change. According to the doctrine, "the strategic goal of climate policy is to achieve secure and sustainable development of the Russian Federation, including institutional, economic, environmental, and social as well as demographic aspects of development in the context of changing climate and emerging challenges...."

The main tasks of climate policy are formulated in the doctrine as follows:

- establishment of legal and regulatory frameworks and government regulations in the area of climate change;

- development of economic mechanisms related to the implementation of measures aimed to adapt to and mitigate human impact on climate;

- scientific, information, and personnel support for the development and implementation of measures aimed at adapting to and mitigating human impact on climate; and

- international cooperation in the development and implementation of measures aimed at adapting to and mitigating human impact on climate.

Further, the document places much more emphasis on adaptation than mitigation. One observer called the doctrine a "call to take cover."[24] The doctrine is to a significant degree window dressing, creating the appearance that the Russian government really cares about climate change while not outlining a program that would amount to a serious attempt to address it. That said, at the meeting of the Security Council in March 2010 mentioned earlier, Medvedev issued a presidential instruction to the government to "approve a package of measures for implementing" the doctrine by October 1, 2010, including "drafting the necessary laws and regulations."[25] Time will tell whether Putin's government takes his request seriously.

Politics of Climate Change Policy

As this review demonstrates, climate policy has not been a major priority for the Russian government. Russia has shown no inclination to lead in international climate talks nor has it taken major steps in the domestic context to mitigate climate change or address its impact. This stance could

---

24. Kristin Jørgensen of the Bellona Foundation in the *Moscow Times*, May 14, 2009.

25. Opening Remarks at Security Council Meeting on Climate Change, March 17, 2010, eng. kremlin.ru.

be the result of the elite's continuing skepticism about the anthropogenic nature of climate change and the negative impact global warming will have on Russia. In 2003, then president Putin famously quipped, "For a northern country like Russia, it won't be that bad if it gets two or three degrees warmer," since "we would spend less on fur coats" and "our grain production would increase."[26] More recent statements, such as Federation Council Speaker Sergei Mironov's comment that the "impact of greenhouse-gas emissions on the climate has not been studied sufficiently," and therefore the Kyoto Protocol has little meaning, indicate that similar views persist, even if the top leadership has changed its tune. (Mironov also claimed that a process of global cooling was taking place, and cited the paintings of the Dutch Masters, which featured bright landscapes, as evidence.)[27]

Climate skepticism is in fact rife throughout Russian society, even in certain quarters of the scientific community. Indeed, in the weeks leading up to the COP-15, and while it was taking place, these skeptics were particularly vocal. In early November 2009, Russia's state-owned Channel 1 aired a documentary called "The History of Deception: Global Warming," which purported to demonstrate that the link between human activity and climate change was fabricated by a media conspiracy. The bulk of the mid-December issue of the respected *Kommersant-Vlast'* political magazine was devoted to climate skepticism, with one article alleging that efforts to address climate change are in fact a cover for funneling money to a cottage industry of scientists, green-tech firms, and corrupt developing countries. The week before the COP-15, the Russian Academy of Sciences Institute of Oceanography issued a report claiming that human activity is not a major factor in climate change, while the director of the research institute of the Ministry of Energy attributed global warming to the slowing of the Earth's rotation.

Perhaps as a result of this drumbeat of pseudoscience, only 40 percent of Russians consider climate change a serious issue, as opposed to 70 percent of Turks.[28] There is also a chronic ignorance of environmental problems in the country. The lack of public pressure and the dominance of climate change skepticism have attached no political costs to keeping climate change a low priority issue for the Kremlin.

---

26. Quoted in Maria Antonova, "World Bank Warns on Climate Change," *Moscow Times*, October 29, 2009.

27. Simon Shuster, "Mironov Tells Kyoto Experts the World Is Getting Cooler," *Moscow Times*, May 28, 2007; Simon Shuster, "Russia Still Dragging Its Feet on Climate Change," November 4, 2009, TIME Special on COP-15: Climate-Change Conference, www.time.com/time/specials (accessed on April 16, 2010).

28. World Bank, *Russian Economic Report* 19, 23.

Energy Efficiency and the Economic Benefits of an Affirmative Climate Policy

As the previous section demonstrates, Russia has not adopted the affirmative approach to climate policy that Medvedev advocated in his February and March 2010 speeches. The unambitious approach to emissions reductions appears to be a function of the perception that taking action will limit Russia's potential to develop its economy. This line of thinking fails to appreciate the role energy efficiency can play in this equation and the positive economics of increased efficiency in the Russian case.

If Russia were to adopt a comprehensive energy efficiency program, it could reduce its CO_2 emissions by 793 million tons per annum, which represents around half of its total emissions in 2005. Put another way, Russia could reduce greenhouse gas emissions by 20 percent compared with 1990 levels through energy efficiency measures alone. Although energy efficiency has become a priority for Russia in recent years, policies are changing very slowly and, until Medvedev's recent speeches, policymakers have yet to link efficiency policy with measures to address climate change. In the Russian case, gains from efficiency make addressing global warming a potential driver of economic growth, modernization, and innovation. Russia has incentive to pursue these gains in any case; the argument here is that climate policy should be explicitly linked to the drive to increase efficiency.

Russia's energy efficiency deficit is striking. It is the world's eighth largest economy but the third largest consumer of energy. Of the world's top ten economies, none consumes more energy per unit of GDP than Russia. In fact, Russia's energy intensity is two to three times higher than in any industrial country (figure 6.3), higher than any of the other BRICs (Brazil, India, and China), and over two times higher than the world average. Even Canada, which has similar climatic conditions, consumes around three times less energy per unit of GDP. The energy intensity of the economy is a fundamental challenge to Russia's future development.

Russia's energy intensity is a function of inefficiencies at all levels, from the end users to the producers of energy (figure 6.4). Households cannot adjust the temperature of their radiators and often do not even have the option of switching them off. As a result, many regulate heat by opening windows, which accounts for a loss of energy comparable to the entire volume of energy produced by Russia's nuclear power plants.[29] In total, Russia loses over 60 percent of heat due to outdated municipal heating networks. An enormous amount of power is also wasted by end users who have no incentive to conserve due to the artificially low price of electricity.

---

29. Vyacheslav Kulagin, "Energy Efficiency and Development of Renewables: Russia's Approach," *Russian Analytical Digest* 46 (September 25, 2008), 4.

Figure 6.3   Energy intensity of selected countries, 2007

ton of coal equivalent per $2,000 of GDP measured in purchasing power parity

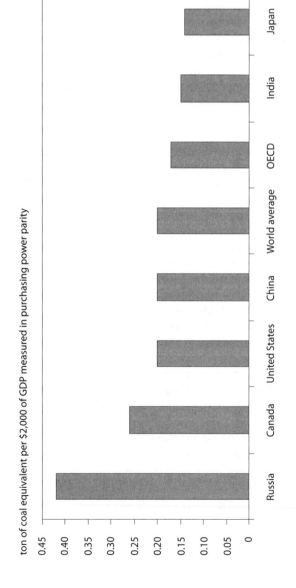

OECD = member states of the Organization for Economic Cooperation and Development

Source: International Energy Agency, *Key World Energy Statistics,* 2009.

Figure 6.4   Energy-saving potential in Russia, by sector

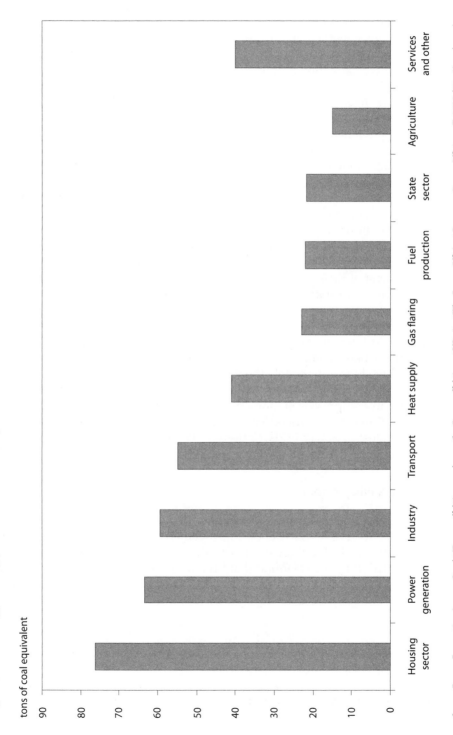

Source: Energy Forecasting Agency, Proekt "Energoeffektivnaya ekonomika: Energoeffektivnost" [Project "The Energy Efficient Economy: Energy Efficiency"], 2008, http://e-apbe.ru (accessed on January 15, 2010).

Modernization-driven energy efficiency is rare in Russian industry. Most of the existing industrial capacity was installed several decades ago and is highly inefficient. Further, few attempts have been made to rectify this situation: Depreciation of capital stock is over 46 percent in the natural resource extraction sector, 53 percent in transport, 54 percent in communications, 70 percent in the thermal power sector, and about 80 percent in hydropower.[30] Not only is industry dated, but it also suffers from the Soviet legacy: Before 1991, targets were set to *increase* the power consumption to personnel ratio (*energovooruzhennost'*), which was considered a sign of the country's industrial progress. This misguided Soviet policy was a roadblock to increasing efficiency in the Russian metallurgy, oil and gas, and chemical sectors.

One of the main concerns about effectiveness of energy-saving policy is the role of monopolies in Russian economy. Energy suppliers are often interested in higher demand for energy, not improvement of energy efficiency, energy saving, or introduction of alternative energy sources. Large oil and gas companies as well as electricity suppliers are natural monopolies in most of Russia's regions, and they will likely limit the effectiveness of policies and programs planned by the government.

Energy producers waste staggering amounts of energy resources. The efficiency of power plants, especially coal-fired ones, 40 percent of which were built over 40 years ago, is far below the world average. Russian oil producers flare as much as 38 billion cubic meters of associated gas annually, which is approximately the volume of gas Russia sold to Germany, its largest customer, in 2006. In that same year 39 billion cubic meters were burned in compressor stations or leaked.[31] The electricity grid and heat distribution network are no less wasteful: The energy consumed by power stations, lost in power grids, or used in the heat network is approximately equivalent to Poland's annual power consumption.

Energy-Saving Potential

Various domestic and international organizations have estimated Russia's potential for energy efficiency improvement. In the most authoritative study, the World Bank together with the Russian Center for Energy Efficiency (CENEF) in 2008 found that Russia could save 45 percent of its total primary energy consumption if it were to implement a comprehensive

---

30. Rosstat data for 2009 and Audit Chamber report on RAO UES investment program, 2006, www.ach.gov.ru (accessed on January 31, 2010).

31. PFC Energy, *Using Russia's Associated Gas* (report prepared for the Global Gas Flaring Reduction Partnership and the World Bank, December 10, 2007), www.worldbank.org (accessed on January 18, 2010.

reform program.[32] According to their calculations, with the right policy measures Russia could save:

- 240 billion cubic meters of natural gas,
- 340 billion kilowatt hours of electricity,
- 89 million tons of coal, and
- 43 million tons of crude oil and petroleum products (measured in crude oil equivalents).

In total, Russia could achieve savings equivalent to all energy produced and imported (net of exports) by France or the United Kingdom. And the Russian economy could benefit from $120 billion to $150 billion in energy cost savings and increased gas exports *annually*.[33] It is important to note that the World Bank/CENEF study assumes implementation of a reform program that would cost the economy $320 billion (although its authors claim that this amount would be paid back in four years).

Another study, by McKinsey & Company, outlined 60 measures aimed at increasing energy efficiency over two decades. The program would keep Russia's energy consumption at today's levels while its economy doubles in size, cutting energy intensity by a total of 64 percent compared with 2007 (figure 6.5).[34] These measures would cost €150 billion over the 20-year period, but the report contends that Russia could see savings of over twice that amount in the same period. This amounts to an average rate of return above 30 percent.[35] Other studies assume less ambitious plans but nonetheless demonstrate the astronomical potential for savings.[36]

Impact of the Economic Crisis

As has been the case in practically every aspect of Russian policy, the global economic crisis has had a major impact on energy efficiency plans and programs. On the one hand, the crisis affected the government's approach to energy efficiency reform. Unlike the business-as-usual approach seen in previous years, more aggressive policy measures were adopted.

---

32. World Bank, *Energy Efficiency in Russia: Untapped Reserves* (Washington, 2008).

33. Ibid, 5–6.

34. This number assumes a natural improvement of 40 percent in energy efficiency by 2030; it adds around 24 percent to that—more than the total annual consumption of Canada today.

35. McKinsey & Company, *Pathways to an Energy and Carbon Efficient Russia* (Moscow, 2009), www.mckinsey.com (accessed on January 31, 2010).

36. See, for example, Energy Forecasting Agency, *Proekt "Energoeffektivnaya ekonomika: Energoeffektivnost"* [*Project "The Energy Efficient Economy: Energy Efficiency"*], 2008, http://e-apbe.ru (accessed on January 15, 2010).

Figure 6.5   Reduction in energy intensity assuming implementation of McKinsey program

tons of coal equivalent per €1,000 of GDP

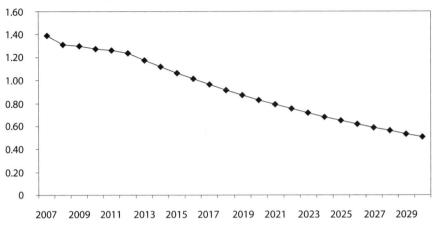

Source: McKinsey & Company, *Pathways to an Energy and Carbon Efficient Russia* (Moscow, 2009), www.mckinsey. com (accessed on January 31, 2010).

For example, the government's anticrisis program included requirements for recipients of funds from the stimulus package to have an energy efficiency plan. On the other hand, the crisis forced substantial reductions in corporate investment programs, including modernization of energy infrastructure and energy transportation networks. This is particularly true of the electricity sector, which saw a 4.5 percent drop in demand in 2009, as well as the other sectors affected by the global decline in demand, such as metallurgy and chemicals.

What's at Stake for Russia?

In addition to the benefits for emissions reductions, reducing Russia's energy intensity is a critical component of its future development, for several reasons.[37]

- *Ensuring energy security.* Energy generation capacity limits and increasing demand by domestic industries mean that improvement in energy efficiency is a key component—and perhaps the only possible component that can be realized in the near future—for ensuring adequate energy supply.
- *Maintaining competitiveness.* Greater energy efficiency would allow companies to remain competitive by cutting overall production costs.

---

37. All statistics are from World Bank, *Energy Efficiency in Russia*, except where noted.

■ *Increasing oil and gas exports.* Russia's high energy intensity costs the government about $100 billion per year in forgone export revenues, or about 35 percent of the 2008 federal budget.

■ *Economizing budgetary outlays.* Over $3 billion can be saved annually from federal and local budgets by reducing inefficient use of energy.

■ *Benefiting the nation's health.* Energy saving would reduce air pollution, in particular by cutting nitrogen oxide, sulfur oxide, particulates, and other harmful substances in the atmosphere. According to recent estimates, air pollution causes over 88,000 premature deaths in Russia, and total damage from related illnesses and mortalities is about $14 billion per year.[38]

■ *Diversifying the economy.* Greater energy efficiency would free up capital for investment in other sectors and help diversify the economy.

Energy Efficiency Policy

In Russia policymaking on energy efficiency is nominally based on several framework documents. For example, the Energy Strategy to 2030 provides the long-term (20-year) vision for the development of the energy sector and outlines policies and measures required to reach priority targets. In contrast, federal programs cover medium-term and interim targets. While various normative acts on energy efficiency have been passed over the course of the post-Soviet period, only in the past two years has the government moved decisively to address the issue. Russia's current priorities in energy efficiency policy are determined by the following legal acts:

■ In June 2008, President Medvedev signed a decree calling for an overall reduction of energy intensity by no less than 40 percent by 2020 vis-à-vis 2007 levels. The decree also included provisions on rational and environmentally sound use of energy and budgetary support for renewable energy projects.

■ In November 2009, the government approved the Energy Strategy to 2030,[39] which is part of a $2 trillion–plus three-stage plan to develop the energy sector in the country by 2030. The main goal of the first stage is to minimize the impact of the ongoing economic crisis on the energy sector and pave the way for postcrisis development. The second stage would focus on improving energy efficiency. By the end of the third stage, Russia is expected to have switched to highly efficient

---

38. Laura A. Henry and Vladimir Douhovnikoff, "Environmental Issues in Russia," *Annual Review of Environment and Resources* 33 (2008): 437–60.

39. See Energeticheskaya strategiya Rossii na period do 2030 goda [Energy Strategy of Russia for the Period up to 2030], available at www.minenergo.gov.ru, for the original text (accessed on January 31, 2010).

use of traditional energy and to have greatly increased the role of alternative energy.

- Later in that same month, President Medvedev signed the Law on Energy Saving and Improvement of Energy Efficiency (hereafter, the Law on Energy Efficiency). This is the primary normative document setting out the Russian government's policy in this sphere. It sets both the general framework for federal policy aimed at substantial improvement of energy efficiency and specific priority targets and mechanisms to achieve them. The range of these targets is fairly wide, from consumer products and construction requirements to creation of markets for energy-efficient technologies (box 6.2).

- The planned State Program on Energy Saving and Energy Efficiency Improvement to 2020 will determine federal policy and measures to reduce energy intensity by 2020.

Politics of Energy Efficiency

As the previous section shows, there has been significant legislative activity, most importantly the presidential decree and the Law on Energy Efficiency, in the energy efficiency sphere since mid-2008. To a significant degree, credit for this shift is due to President Medvedev, who has made energy efficiency a primary component of his modernization agenda, which is the centerpiece of his presidency. At a meeting of the State Council in July 2009, he said: "Energy efficiency needs to serve as a foundation, with other development priorities based on it. To put it differently, energy efficiency must support all the other priorities for technological modernization.... We seem to be falling behind in every respect...not only because of the difficulties we faced in the 1990s and even earlier, but also because of our mindset, because we have never tried to save energy.... It is true that we are the world's leading nation in terms of energy resources. This does not mean, however, that we should consume these resources irresponsibly."[40] While the distance between words and deeds is a long one in the Russian context, it is nonetheless important that the president has made efficiency a top priority.

In fact, in addition to the presidential decree and the Law on Energy Efficiency, some other concrete steps have also been taken. For example, energy efficiency is the first of five priorities for the newly created Commission on Modernization and Technological Development of the Economy. Medvedev appears to be using the commission as a platform for establishing himself as an independent political actor. Its meetings receive

---

40. Opening remarks at Expanded State Council Presidium Meeting on Improving Energy Efficiency of the Russian Economy, July 2, 2009, http://eng.kremlin.ru (accessed on January 31, 2010).

Box 6.2   The Law on Energy Efficiency

The Law on Energy Efficiency was adopted on November 23, 2009. Some of the primary envisioned actions include incremental regulation of incandescent lamp use, culminating in an outright ban in 2014; installation of metering equipment for water, power, and heat use in the residential sector by 2011; and energy labeling of household appliances by 2011.

The law requires regular obligatory energy audits (at least once in five years) for all state-owned and state-regulated enterprises, as well as the top energy-producing and energy-consuming companies. The first energy audit is due by the end of 2012, which will provide unprecedented nationwide data on energy inventory. Another new approach is the creation of long-term energy-servicing contracts, rather than annual ones, which undermined incentives for energy saving in municipal heating and water treatment facilities.

The law requires organizations accepting financial support from the state to produce energy-saving and energy-efficiency plans and creates provisions for the monitoring and enforcement of this requirement.

It also provides for financial support for energy-efficiency and energy-saving programs in education; public awareness campaigns; regional and municipal programs; and subsidization of energy-efficient technologies.

---

heavy media coverage, and it has been allocated 10 billion rubles in the 2010 budget.[41]

At its first meeting devoted to energy efficiency, the commission approved six projects: installing devices to meter and regulate energy consumption; replacing existing lighting systems with more efficient technologies; initiating pilot projects to modernize certain city districts and towns; increasing the efficiency of government services such as health care and schools; replacing the technology of heat supply; and creating projects in alternative and renewable energy.

Yet, despite the new legislative initiatives and the president's focus on the issue, the politics of energy efficiency are for the most part not conducive to addressing the problem. On the societal level, awareness of the importance of saving energy and knowledge of the means of doing so are extremely low. Information on the efficiency of consumer goods is scarce, and Soviet-era attitudes toward energy usage (i.e., taking cheap energy as a given and treating utility services as public goods) persist. Industry managers also have yet to adopt a productive approach to the issue.

---

41. See Natalia Kostenko, "Podpitka innovatsii" [Nourishing Innovation], *Vedomosti*, October 28, 2009, www.vedomosti.ru (accessed on November 1, 2009).

On the conceptual level, the proliferation of strategies and other conceptual documents undermines goal-oriented behavior and long-term planning. The Law on Energy Efficiency, the Energy Strategy to 2030, the State Program on Energy Saving and Increasing Energy Efficiency to 2020, the Long-Term Concept of Socio-Economic Development to 2020, and the General Scheme of Location of Objects of Energy Consumption are among the multitude of documents that touch on energy efficiency. Many of these documents contradict one another. Russia has had strategy documents for energy efficiency for over 15 years, but they have had little impact.

On the bureaucratic level, Medvedev faces several hurdles to realizing his goals. First, his programs tend to focus on ends and ignore the means of achieving them, thus leaving implementation to the bureaucracy, which is notorious for its low implementation capacity and weak institutions. This is particularly true in the energy efficiency sphere, where the lead agency, the Ministry of Energy, largely remains a "line ministry"—i.e., it sees its essential function as lobbying the interests of the industry. The Ministry of Economic Development appears to be the most proactive government entity on these issues, but it lacks the institutional clout and legal authority to take the lead.[42] The situation is further complicated by the existence of a plethora of deputy prime ministers, at least three of whom have jurisdiction over efficiency-related issues.

Medvedev's program also reflects a nonmarket approach to encouraging the private sector to adopt energy-saving measures. Instead of creating incentives for businesses to adopt energy-saving technologies, the Russian government's initiatives reflect its proclivity for heavy-handed interference in the economy. In contrast to his February 2010 speech, Medvedev himself suggested that law enforcement agencies should be responsible for monitoring adoption of energy-saving technologies: "Let the FSB [Federal Security Service] and the militia report on this—that's an excellent source of information."[43] Such an approach is unlikely to yield sustainable results.

That said, the government's unwillingness to turn to incentives as opposed to rigid enforcement might reflect an acknowledgment of the monopolized nature of the Russian economy, and particularly the energy sector. The monopolies or oligopolies that exist in oil, gas, and electricity not only are inherently resistant to greater efficiency but also often render moot the economic incentives created by regulations.

Finally, social, economic, and political costs are associated with increasing energy efficiency. In no area is this more true than residential gas prices. Although the Russian government is widely considered immune

---

42. Samuel Charap and Georgi Sofonov's interview with Oleg Pluzhnikov, department director, Ministry of Economic Development, October 2009.

43. "Rossiiskii put' k energoeffektivnosti" ["Russia's Path to Energy Efficiency"], *Nezavisimaya Gazeta*, October 2, 2009, www.ng.ru (accessed on November 1, 2009).

to public opinion, decision makers do appear to take social consequences into consideration when contemplating increasing gas prices. This phenomenon can be seen in both the government's reluctance to raise prices significantly before the 2007–08 electoral cycle and its reduction in planned price increases during the economic crisis.

Efficiency Is Only Part of the Puzzle of Addressing Climate Change

The difficult politics of increased efficiency notwithstanding, it is clear that Russia stands to make major economic gains from an ambitious efficiency program. And, as noted earlier, Russia can go a long way toward reducing its emissions through such a program. However, as Medvedev himself noted in the February 2010 speech, structural changes in Russia's economy can be a significant piece of the puzzle of reducing its emissions. Indeed, the increased share of the services sector in the economy and the decline of some Soviet-era heavy industry since the late 1990s have been important factors in reducing Russia's emissions. If Medvedev's modernization agenda is realized, these trends will continue.

The Russian government could also adopt a more aggressive program of climate change mitigation. The McKinsey study concluded that Russia's total emissions reduction potential is approximately 45 percent of the 1990 baseline by 2030 (figure 6.6). The economically beneficial efficiency measures in the study would account for almost a third of this potential. The rest could be achieved through an aggressive investment program of €410 billion over 20 years, which would result in €90 billion in savings. Specific measures would include carbon capture and storage; fuel mix changes in the power and heat sector; and agriculture and forestry sector investments. Although some of these measures do not provide a direct economic benefit, they do entail potentially significant indirect benefits, including the "green jobs" and development of new technologies that Medvedev referenced in his February 2010 speech, through the stimulus spending required to implement them. Indeed, multiple new studies suggest that these benefits outweigh the costs in other country settings.[44] For example, one study of this dynamic in the United States demonstrated that investing $150 billion in clean energy would create an estimated 1.7 million new jobs.[45]

---

44. For a partial list, see Center for American Progress, The Hub: Resources for a Clean-Energy Economy, www.americanprogress.org/projects/energy_hub. This perspective is of course not shared by all economists who have looked at the issue.

45. Robert Pollin, James Heintz, and Heidi Garrett-Peltier, *The Economic Benefits of Investing in Clean Energy* (Amherst and Washington: Political Economy Research Institute at the University of Massachusetts and Center for American Progress, June 2009), www.americanprogress.org (accessed on January 13, 2010).

148

Figure 6.6   Greenhouse gas emissions abatement potential in 2030

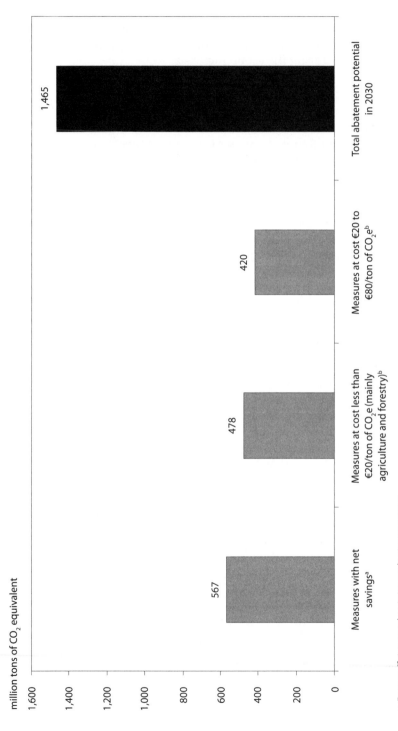

million tons of CO_2 equivalent

a. Energy efficiency and emissions reductions measures.
b. Emissions reductions measures.

Note: In 2007 Russia emitted approximately 2,200 million tons of coal equivalent compared with 3,300 million tons of coal equivalent in 1990.

Source: McKinsey & Company, *Pathways to an Energy and Carbon Efficient Russia* (Moscow, 2009), www.mckinsey.com (accessed on January 31, 2010).

An Opportunity for US-Russia Engagement

Moscow's newfound interest in energy efficiency and its role in the international climate regime open new avenues for US-Russia bilateral engagement. This is particularly true in the energy efficiency sphere, for several reasons. First, it is a domestic policy priority of both President Medvedev and US President Barack Obama. It is unusual to have convergence between domestic political priorities and potential avenues of bilateral cooperation in the US-Russia relationship. This factor not only creates avenues for such synergies but also makes it more likely that the presidents will exercise political will to push policies through the bureaucracy, where great ideas are often undermined or delayed in both countries. Second, it is a win-win issue—both countries stand to gain from such cooperation. This contrasts with other issues on the bilateral agenda, such as Iran, which entail one side asking the other to act on one of its policy priorities. Finally, it presents the possibility of involving the private sector and creating joint public-private partnerships, which would provide economic benefits for both sides and help cement the foundation of the relationship. Without strong business links between the two countries, the bilateral relationship will lack an anchor that could mitigate the impact of disputes on the political level.

Several European countries have developed significant ties with Russia on energy efficiency issues. Germany, for example, has established a joint energy efficiency center with Russia. The United States, however, lags far behind its European allies. The US Secretary of Energy and the Russian Minister of Energy signed a memorandum of understanding on energy efficiency cooperation, but the document envisions standard interactions between the respective bureaucracies; it is far from ambitious. A group in the Bilateral Presidential Commission deals with energy efficiency, but little concrete progress has been made thus far.

More imaginative approaches are needed to make energy efficiency a central issue in the US-Russia relationship. The United States can use its experience in working with China on industrial energy efficiency as a model. For example, the Lawrence Berkeley National Laboratory collaborates with Chinese scientists and the Chinese government on an industrial energy efficiency program to benchmark China's top 1,000 energy-consuming enterprises based on international standards. The United States and Russia can take advantage of public-private partnerships, sharing any new energy-saving technologies that emerge from this collaboration.[46]

Addressing climate change directly also presents opportunities for bilateral cooperation. Currently, Russia is not linked to any emissions

---

46. See Andrew Light, Julian Wong, and Samuel Charap, "U.S.-Russia Climate and Energy Efficiency Cooperation: A Neglected Challenge" (Washington: Center for American Progress, June 30, 2009), www.americanprogress.org (accessed on January 31, 2010).

trading system and lacks the institutional capacity to do so. Although the United States does not have a national cap and trade system, it does have a number of highly successful markets such as the 1990s sulfur dioxide trading scheme and regional (Western Climate Initiative, Regional Greenhouse Gas Initiative, and Midwestern Initiative) and voluntary (Chicago Climate Exchange) carbon emissions trading initiatives. The United States can create incentives for these trading centers to collaborate with Russian partners to launch pilot emissions trading schemes there. Developing Russia's capacity in emissions trading will help place it in a better position to join a multinational trading scheme as a full participant if and when it agrees to begin stemming its current emissions.[47]

---

47. Ibid.

7

Gazprom: Challenged Giant in Need of Reform

ANDERS ÅSLUND

The 2008–10 global financial crisis has shaken all, not least Russian perceptions of last decade's energy boom. Gazprom, Russia's natural gas monopoly, just over 50 percent of which belongs to the Russian state, is a national champion with enormous resources. But its business strategy faces serious challenges. Because of its size and importance for the Russian economy, much of Russia's future depends on how the government handles Gazprom's current dilemma.

Gazprom's traditional business model is inadequate. The company has piped gas from its giant fields in West Siberia to a steadily growing European market, and when necessary it has cheaply bought additional gas from Central Asia. Now, everything has changed. Gas prices have tumbled and decoupled from oil prices, as liquefied natural gas (LNG) and shale gas are competing with piped natural gas. Increasingly, spot markets are offering an alternative to long-term contracts. Much of the European demand for Russian gas is gone and not likely to come back any time soon, but Gazprom has minimal physical possibility to export anywhere but Europe in the foreseeable future. With its West Siberian gas fields past their peak, Gazprom's supply is in decline. Rather than selling their gas cheaply to Russia, the Central Asians are exporting to China through new pipelines. Gazprom is losing out in supplies, sales, and profits but insists on building new pipelines to Europe.

Anders Åslund is a senior fellow at the Peterson Institute for International Economics. He has greatly benefited from comments from Sergei Guriev, Ed Chow, Andrew Kuchins, Pavel Baev, Harry Griffith, and participants in a seminar at the Center for Strategic and International Studies (CSIS) on February 18, 2010. Anna Borshchevskaya provided excellent research assistance. Any mistakes that remain are his own.

In this chapter I first summarize Gazprom's traditional strategy, then record how the financial crisis has challenged Gazprom, report and assess the Gazprom management's response, and finally outline an alternative Russian gas policy.

Gazprom's Traditional Strategy

Gazprom draws on two traditions. One is that of Soviet ministries. In parallel with a few other Russian industries, notably railways and atomic energy, Gazprom was formed out of a Soviet ministry—the Ministry of Gas Industry. In contrast, most other Soviet industrial ministries, such as oil, coal, and electricity, were broken up into individual enterprises, which were largely privatized and encouraged to compete on domestic and foreign markets. But Gazprom and Rosatom (Russia's State Atomic Energy Corporation) stayed consolidated monopolies. Like the Soviet railways, they have retained many features of Soviet ministries.

The other Gazprom tradition, the state-owned national oil and gas company, is characteristic of most member countries of the Organization of Petroleum Exporting Countries (OPEC). These companies are forming a state within the state, dominating their respective countries both economically and politically. Gazprom has a few peculiarities in comparison with such national champions. Although it has acquired substantial oil production and power assets, it remains predominantly a gas company. Unlike most national champions in OPEC countries, Gazprom has substantial and widespread private ownership. Both these traditions involve extensive state monopolies.

Gazprom was formed by Viktor Chernomyrdin, the young, impressive professional who was appointed the last Soviet minister of gas industry in 1985. It was transformed into an enterprise association before the collapse of the Soviet Union. Chernomyrdin, who was Russia's prime minister from December 1992 until March 1998, granted Gazprom special privileges. In late 1993 it was awarded multiple monopolies and tax privileges, and in 1994 a large-scale insider privatization was launched. Gazprom's dominant features were huge resource endowment, extreme monopoly, favorable taxation, and insider privatization.[1] It also has many specific features.

First, Gazprom is big. It accounts for about 8 percent of Russia's GDP, one-fifth of its exports, and one-fifth of its market capitalization. In these three dimensions as well as tax payments, Gazprom is Russia's largest

---

1. Jonathan P. Stern, *The Future of Russian Gas and Gazprom* (Oxford: Oxford University Press, 2005) offers an upbeat view of Gazprom, while Clifford G. Gaddy and Barry W. Ickes, *Russia's Virtual Economy* (Washington: Brookings Institution) show the complexity of Gazprom's barter deals and cross-subsidization.

corporation, though its staff of some 330,000 is far smaller than that of the Russian Railways.

Second, Gazprom maintains monopolies over exports, trunk-line transportation, and development of new major fields. Russia has the world's largest gas reserves, and Gazprom's great advantage is its control of one-quarter of the world's gas reserves, through licenses granted by the government. Government protection is its greatest strength.

Third, gas prices are controlled far below the market level, and Gazprom rations its supplies. For the last several years, domestic prices have been gradually raised and are supposed to reach the market level in 2011, but the discrepancy between domestic and world prices varies with the vagaries of the international market. At times, domestic prices have been as low as one-fifth of world prices.

Fourth, Gazprom has far lower tax rates than the oil industry. In 2007 Gazprom paid $7.3 in taxes per barrel of oil equivalent produced, while private companies paid $31 to $34 or nearly five times more.[2] The low taxes are justified with low regulated gas prices, but as a consequence Gazprom openly negotiates with the state on its taxes. Gazprom hardly makes any profits on its domestic sales, unlike independent producers, notably Novatek, which are making huge profits on such sales because of their greater efficiency.[3]

The Soviet gas industry expanded greatly in the 1970s and 1980s, when the large West Siberian gas fields were developed. The gas fields were developed later than the oil fields, and in the 1990s the gas industry managed to maintain nearly stable production, while Russian oil output plummeted by half. From 1999 to 2004, however, Russian oil production rose sharply, while gas output remained stagnant. From 2003 to 2008 Gazprom's production was almost perfectly flat at 550 billion cubic meters, accounting for almost 85 percent of Russia's gas output (figure 7.1).

Russia's gas production rose slightly because of independent producers. In reality, Gazprom's own production has long been in decline, but it keeps its production constant by taking over the assets of independent producers. Some 40 billion cubic meters of associated gas is flared in Russia each year since Gazprom does not allow the producers in question access to its pipeline system.[4]

When its gas output expanded in the 1970s and 1980s, the Soviet Union initially satisfied its own gas needs, then those of its Eastern European satellites. In the early 1980s, the Soviet Union built politically controversial long pipelines to Western Europe, selling large volumes to primarily

2. Vladimir Milov, *Russia and the West: The Energy Factor* (Institut français des relations internationales and Center for Strategic and International Studies, July 2008), 3.

3. A large minority share of Novatek is now owned by Gazprom, so it is a related company.

4. Nadia Popova, "Bill Gives Priority to Gas Power," *Moscow Times*, August 13, 2009.

Figure 7.1   Gas production, Russia and Gazprom, 2000-09

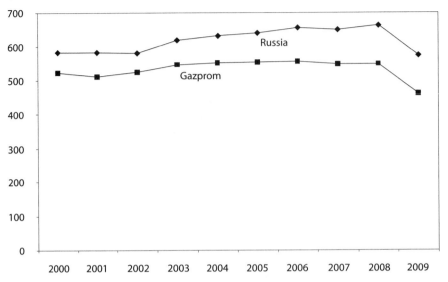

billions of cubic meters

Sources: Gazprom Databook, 2007 and June 2009, www.gazprom.com; Russian Federal Statistical Service; Kremlin.ru; and International Energy Agency.

Germany and Italy. These sales were based on long-term contracts, with prices changing quarterly related to various oil prices with a delay of half a year.

As the outer Soviet empire and the Soviet Union itself collapsed, Russia's gas sales changed geographic orientation. All the postcommunist countries reduced overall production and energy intensity, allowing Gazprom to redirect its sales from the Commonwealth of Independent States (CIS) and Eastern Europe to Western Europe. During the long economic boom starting in 2000, Gazprom thrived on steadily increasing gas demand from Western Europe, as the European Union's own gas production dwindled; gas was a favored source of energy, generating less carbon dioxide than oil and coal. Russian gas supplies were considered very reliable. Production costs in existing giant gas fields in West Siberia were low, allowing Gazprom to reap huge profits.

Gazprom has enjoyed monopoly over foreign trade in piped gas, though sometimes it allowed related intermediaries to participate in this trade. The value of its exports tripled from 2002 until 2006 because of rising oil and gas prices. Russia's export volume was actually more or less constant around 195 billion cubic meters. Its net export volume, however,

Figure 7.2   Russia's exports and imports of gas, 2000–08

billions of cubic meters

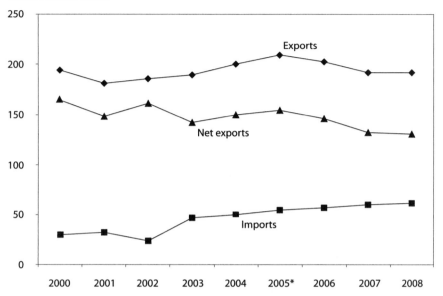

* = includes natural gas, exported from underground gas storage houses in Ukraine.

Sources: Central Bank of Russia, www.cbr.ru; Gazprom Databook, June 2009, www.gazprom.cpm; UN Comtrade Database (accessed on November 28, 2009 and February 16, 2010).

plummeted from 164 billion cubic meters in 2000 to 131 billion cubic meters in 2008, as Russia imported more gas from Central Asia (figure 7.2).[5]

Russia's exports to the CIS declined from 60 billion cubic meters in 2000 to 37 billion cubic meters in 2008, while those to Europe rose steadily from 129 billion cubic meters in 2002 to 184 billion cubic meters in 2008 (figure 7.3). Thus, Russia is now a net importer of gas from the CIS.

Sales seemed to be on autopilot, and the perception was that Russia could double its gas sales to Europe from 2006 to 2015. The big question was where Gazprom would find additional supplies. The long-term solution was perceived to be the development of some of Russia's known giant fields. The main focus was on the Yamal Peninsula in the far north or the offshore Shtokman field in the Barents Sea, but their development would be very expensive. The Gazprom management compared the costs with the low domestic gas prices and repeatedly postponed these two large developments.

---

5. Previously, Turkmenistan exported more of its gas directly to countries such as Ukraine without Gazprom's involvement.

Figure 7.3   Russia's gas exports to CIS and Europe, 2000–09

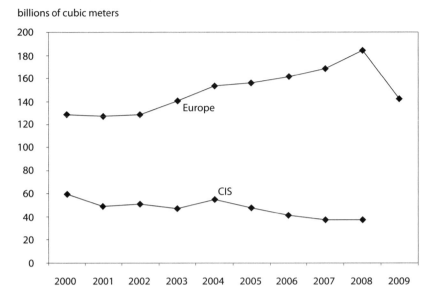

billions of cubic meters

CIS = Commonwealth of Independent States

Note: The year 2005 for CIS includes natural gas, exported from underground gas storage houses in Ukraine.

Sources: Central Bank of Russia, www.cbr.ru (accessed on February 16, 2010); Gazprom, www.gazprom.com (accessed on February 16, 2010).

Instead, Gazprom increased its exports to the European market by increasing its purchases of Central Asian gas, and the Russian state helped Gazprom to control gas supplies from Central Asian countries such as Turkmenistan, Kazakhstan, and Uzbekistan. For years, Gazprom could dictate its export prices at a level far below the European prices plus transportation costs, awarding Gazprom large arbitrage rents.

Around 2005 Gazprom played with alternative themes. A major idea was to diversify its sales to reduce its dependence on the European market by supplying gas to the United States, China, and Japan, mainly through LNG to be produced at the Shtokman field for the United States and on Sakhalin for China and Japan. Another idea was to build new pipelines to Europe, mainly Nord Stream from Russia to Germany through the Baltic Sea and South Stream through the Black Sea over the Balkans to Italy. Pipelines to China were discussed more tentatively. Senior Gazprom officials traveled the world discussing developments in Nigeria and elsewhere, but most of these plans remained tenuous. Only in 2009 did Gazprom open its first LNG plant in Sakhalin Energy, a project initiated by Royal Dutch Shell, but Gazprom had forced the foreign companies involved to sell their majority share to it in 2006.

Gazprom seemed a money machine. In 2006 the Russian government finally liberalized trade in the previously restricted stocks of Gazprom. As a consequence of great foreign demand, Gazprom's market capitalization peaked at $350 billion in May 2008, when it was the third most valuable corporation in the world. In June 2008 Gazprom's CEO Alexei Miller boldly predicted that the oil price would rise to $250 per barrel "in the foreseeable future." The ensuing month, the oil price peaked at $147 per barrel. Investment banks and energy consultants wrote rave reviews about Gazprom's splendid future. Its officials long predicted that their company would soon be worth $1 trillion and become the biggest company in the world. Gazprom did not have a very clear strategy, but it seemed to be able to afford it.

Gazprom's great benefits did not necessarily favor the Russian state or its shareholders, but certainly its management. Its governance has persistently been poor and for a purpose. In their excellent book, *Putin and Gazprom*, Boris Nemtsov and Vladimir Milov argue that Gazprom's real aim is to transfer assets to officials through kickbacks on pipeline construction and equity purchases, illicit transfer of Gazprom shares, and transfer pricing in international sales.[6]

Challenges Hit Gazprom

The global economic crisis hit Gazprom hard. In January 2009 the oil price plummeted to $32.40 per barrel and Gazprom's market capitalization bottomed out at $85 billion. A year later, the oil price recovered to $75 per barrel, and Gazprom's market capitalization stabilized around $140 billion, just 40 percent of its peak value. It remains Russia's largest company in terms of market capitalization, but it has underperformed in comparison with any relevant asset class.

Its net profit, which exceeded $25 billion in 2007 and 2008, is likely to stop at some $19 billion in 2009 (figure 7.4). Meanwhile, Gazprom's overall investment continues to rise and in 2010 is planned at $30 billion, far exceeding net profits.[7] As a consequence, Gazprom has a persistent negative cash flow with a net debt of over $40 billion.

In each recession, some structural weaknesses are revealed, and Gazprom may be experiencing the beginning of a substantial structural crisis. Because of its unique role in Russia's economy and politics, this concerns

---

6. Boris Nemtsov and Vladimir Milov, *Putin and Gazprom* (Moscow, 2009); Global Witness, *It's a Gas—Funny Business in the Turkmen-Ukraine Gas Trade* (report, Washington: Global Witness Publishing, 2006).

7. UBS, "Gazprom Export—Key Takeaways from Conference Call," *Russian Daily News*, April 28, 2009.

Figure 7.4 Gazprom's net profit and capital expenditures, 2004–09e

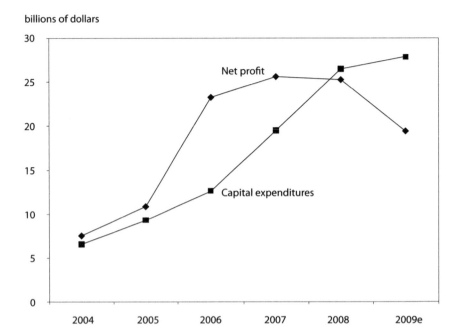

billions of dollars

e = estimate

Source: UBS Investment Research, July 15, 2009.

the country's economic and political model. The current financial crisis should not be seen as the cause but as a catalyst.

In the first quarter of 2009 an external shock hit Gazprom. Russia's gas exports plunged, compelling Gazprom to cut its production. By June it had reduced its production by 36 percent in annualized terms.[8] Exports started recovering in April and production in July, but Russia's export volume for the year contracted by 11 percent, and the lack of demand forced Gazprom to cut its production from 550 billion cubic meters in 2008 to 462 billion cubic meters in 2009 or by 16 percent.[9] Three factors caused this sudden drop: two weeks of supply cut, temporarily high gas prices, and the great recession.

There are at least six reasons to believe that this was not a temporary phenomenon but a new trend: Gazprom's unreliability as a supplier; new competition from LNG and shale gas; changing relative prices; structural

---

8. UBS, "Gas Industry –56.2% y-o-y Reduction in Russian Gas Exports," *Russian Daily News*, December 18, 2009; UBS, "Gazprom Export—Key Takeaways from Conference Call," *Russian Daily News*, December 18, 2009.

9. UBS, "Gazprom: 3Q09 IFRS Results Review," February 2, 2010.

decline in the demand for gas; decreased energy intensity in Russia, Ukraine, and Belarus; and Gazprom's underperformance relative to independent producers.

First, Gazprom has long advertised itself as a "Reliable Gas Supplier to Russian and Foreign Consumers,"[10] but it has established a firm record to the contrary. In January 2006 its cuts of deliveries to Ukraine harmed eight countries, and a few were hurt by cuts to Belarus in 2007. In January 2009 Gazprom eliminated all deliveries for two weeks to 16 European countries because of a dispute with Ukraine. The European customers were neither guilty nor forewarned, and several of them, especially in the Balkans, suffered badly.

Gazprom has used considerable discretion in its deliveries for many years, but until 2006 it made a sharp distinction favoring its European customers, while treating post-Soviet countries badly. A study by the Swedish Defense Research Agency established that Russia used "coercive energy policy," such as supply cuts, coercive price policy, and sabotage 55 times from 1991 until 2006. Of these incidents, the authors reckoned that 36 had political and 48 economic underpinnings, that is, both motives were present. Gazprom was the dominant actor in 16 of these cases, and Itera, an allegedly related gas trading company, accounted for another 9. Thus coercive measures in Russia's gas policy toward post-Soviet countries do appear habitual. The main targets have been Lithuania, Georgia, Belarus, Ukraine, and Moldova.[11]

Gazprom has justified its multiple cuts in supply with payment arrears and resistance to higher prices by post-Soviet countries, but often they have been accompanied by loud public political polemics by Russian officials. For many years, Gazprom offered much lower prices to these nations, which often accumulated large unregulated debts. Gazprom was patient because it tried to exploit these debts for debt-equity swaps attempting to acquire their pipeline systems. However, after Gazprom had succeeded in doing so, for example, in Moldova and Belarus, it continued disrupting supplies so it did not improve energy security. Since 2005, Gazprom has tried to extract the higher European prices from its post-Soviet customers, but it has done so in fits and starts with policies varying by country, making political motives all too evident. Moreover, Gazprom has often insisted on including nontransparent intermediaries, which have benefited from transfer pricing.[12]

---

10. Gazprom Today, www.gazprom.com (accessed on December 23, 2009).

11. Jacob Hedenskog and Robert L. Larsson, *Russian Leverage on the CIS and the Baltic States* (Stockholm: Swedish Defense Research Agency, 2007), 46–57; Robert L. Larsson, *Russia's Energy Policy* (Stockholm: Swedish Defense Research Agency, 2006), 296–97.

12. Simon Pirani, ed., *Russian and CIS Gas Markets and their Impact on Europe* (Oxford: Oxford University Press, 2009); Walerij Paniuszkin and Mikhail Zygar, *Gazprom: Rosyjska broń* [*Gazprom: The Russian Weapon*] (Warsaw: W.A.B., 2008).

Its agreement with Ukraine in January 2009 might set a new trend. Its characteristics, as amended in November, are a long-term agreement, a European gas price formula, reasonable transit tariffs, and no middleman. However, the volume agreed was far too large, and it had to be cut by about half for both 2009 and 2010 as Ukraine approximately halved its gas imports from Russia at the new, higher gas prices.

Naturally, the victims of these vagaries defended themselves. Some of Gazprom's major customers—Ukraine, Germany, Austria, and Hungary—have accumulated gas stocks for three months or more, but such large stocks involve substantial costs, which have to be included in the cost of purchasing gas from Gazprom. All are trying to diversify their energy supplies and diminish their dependence on piped gas. As a consequence, Gazprom's partial downstream monopoly as supplier of gas to much of postcommunist Eastern Europe is gradually being dismantled. Now countries such as Poland and Hungary receive half their gas from other sources. Gazprom delivers 40 percent of the European Union's gas imports and one-quarter of its total supplies.[13]

Gazprom's second problem is that it is encountering new competition from LNG and shale gas. Traditionally, Gazprom delivers gas only to Europe and it does so through pipelines. LNG technology has existed for a long time, but until recently it was too expensive and only now has it taken off. LNG allows gas producers far away, notably Qatar in the Persian Gulf, to freeze their gas in expensive liquefaction plants. The LNG is shipped like oil in supertankers to regasification terminals, from where it is distributed through pipelines. In the last few years, huge investments have been directed to all three stages of LNG, flooding the European gas market with comparatively cheap LNG through multiple new regasification terminals.[14]

At the same time, the United States has started mass producing cheap shale gas, replacing most of the anticipated American demand for LNG, which is now being redirected to the European market. The International Energy Agency predicts that this will remain the case for the next three to five years, and it does not expect European gas demand to return to the level of 2008 until 2012 or 2013.[15] The steadily increasing demand for gas has turned into a medium-term glut.

Third, the gas surplus is changing market conditions and depressing international gas prices. LNG trade is reminiscent of oil trade and is domi-

13. Peter B. Doran, "Collective Energy Security: A Road Map for Europe," Report 24 (Center for European Policy Analysis, 2009), 11.

14. Richard Pomfret, "Energy Security in the EU and Beyond" (paper presented to the CASE Conference "The Return of History," Warsaw, November 20–21, 2009).

15. International Energy Agency, *Natural Gas Market Review* (Paris, 2009); Paul Betts and Andrew Hill, "Gas Glut That Risks Spoiling Russia's Power Games," *Financial Times*, December 16, 2009.

nated by the spot market, whose prices vary greatly, at times half the Russian gas prices in 2009. At present, a new customer has little reason to opt for piped Russian gas when cheaper LNG is available.

Also, Gazprom's contract terms are being challenged. Since it started selling gas to Europe in the early 1980s, Gazprom has insisted on long-term contracts with prices linked to a mixture of oil indices half a year earlier. Such contracts were attractive when oil prices were rising but not when prices fell. In the first half of 2009 Russian gas to Europe was seriously overpriced, which depressed demand. The recovery in the second half of 2009, when Russian gas was much cheaper, was only partial.

The hard question for Gazprom is whether European gas prices have decoupled from the oil price for good, leaving Gazprom's gas overpriced. The Gazprom view is that this is a temporary phenomenon, while independent consultants claim it is a long-term condition.[16] Gazprom insists on its long-term contracts with a clause called "take or pay," forcing its customers to pay even if they do not accept deliveries.

A fourth challenge concerns the demand for gas after the crisis. The customary precrisis idea was that gas was one of the best fuels, emitting far less carbon dioxide than coal or oil, but it is primarily used in three spheres: power generation, heating, and process industry (chemical and metallurgical industry). In power generation, gas competes with coal, and great energy savings can be made through greater energy efficiency in power stations. Much of the heating costs can be saved through better insulation. Chemical and metallurgical industries are probably experiencing a structural downsizing. In a recent study, McKinsey & Company points out that Russia can make its greatest energy savings in these very sectors.[17] Therefore, much of the demand for gas might disappear in the medium term.

Fifth, after high energy prices from 1973 to 1980, the world saw massive and unanticipated energy saving. Similar energy savings are likely this time around. Three countries that can save energy most easily are Russia, Ukraine, and Belarus. Today, Russia consumes twice as much primary energy as China and six times as much as the United States for each $1 of GDP in purchasing power parities.[18] The situation is similar in Ukraine and Belarus, two of Gazprom's largest export markets. As a consequence, gas demand from these three countries is likely to decline.

The decline in demand for gas will be all the greater if the ambitious targets for a reduction of greenhouse emissions by 50 percent by 2050, as were discussed at the Copenhagen climate conference in December 2009, are implemented (see chapter 6). In a paper with long-term scenarios for

---

16. Panel discussion on gas demand at Troika Dialog's Russian Forum 2010, Moscow, February 3-4, 2010.

17. McKinsey & Company, *Pathways to an Energy and Carbon Efficient Russia* (Moscow: McKinsey & Company, Inc., 2009), 4.

18. Ibid.

Russia's energy demand, Sergey Paltsev, John Reilly, and Natalia Tourdyeva find that Russia's gas demand might peak in 2010.[19] The gas glut might be not only medium term but also long term.

A sixth challenge to Gazprom is independent producers in Russia. With its unwieldy bureaucracy, Gazprom can produce only from giant fields, but Russia has plenty of accessible small and medium-sized fields. It does not need to develop inaccessible new giant fields for the foreseeable future if it utilizes medium-sized fields. Agile independent companies are already doing that. Novatek and big private oil companies produce gas far cheaper than Gazprom, and unlike Gazprom they manage to sell increased gas volumes on the domestic market with profit.

Gazprom has repeatedly used its monopoly power and political muscle to purchase independent producers cheaply to recover its share of production. Many Russian and foreign companies have faced such a fate. Eventually, the question must arise why the Russian government allows Gazprom to waste billions of dollars every year.

In sum, Gazprom may have far too much gas in the medium term because of energy savings both at home and abroad, especially in industries using gas. But the prices that Russian gas can fetch abroad are likely to stay low and probably decouple from oil prices. Even if domestic gas prices in Russia rise, Gazprom's finances are likely to be squeezed.

Gazprom's Response to the Crisis

The Gazprom management—that is, the Russian government—does not seem to have understood the severity of these dramatic changes. After a long time in denial, it has reacted in an ad hoc manner. At the time of this writing, Gazprom is gradually molding a new defensive strategy. It is trying to maintain the old demand while letting go of new markets and cutting output.

The crucial issue for Gazprom is European demand, which generates all its profits. Instead of apologizing to its European customers for the supply cut in January 2009, Gazprom has aggressively insisted on its old long-term contracts with its take-or-pay clauses. It is bound to lose customers with this high-risk policy in a buyers' market. In February 2010, Gazprom finally started easing this policy, allowing four major European client companies to buy 10 to 15 percent of their contracted gas at lower spot market prices.[20]

Gazprom has constrained its supplies by reducing its purchases of

---

19. Sergey Paltsev, John Reilly, and Natalia Tourdyeva, "Russia and the World Energy Markets: Long-Term Scenarios" (paper presented at the GTAP 12th Annual Conference on Global Economic Analysis, June 10–12, 2009, Santiago, Chile).

20. "Gazprom Price Change to Last 3 Years," *Moscow Times*, March 1, 2010.

Central Asian gas and by postponing the development of new giant fields. In 2008 Gazprom contracted 70 billion to 80 billion cubic meters a year of Central Asian gas at prices above current market prices. In April 2009 Gazprom suddenly and unilaterally halted the gas flow from Turkmenistan, which caused an explosion in the pipeline on Turkmen territory, blocking further gas sales to Russia. After the Turkmens repaired the pipeline, Gazprom refused to take the agreed volumes at the contracted price, although it had a take-or-pay contract. Turkmenistan had prior bitter experiences from the gas glut of 1997–98, when Russia embargoed all its gas exports for 18 months until it built an alternative pipeline to Iran.[21] In December 2009 Russia and Turkmenistan agreed to reduce Turkmenistan's deliveries to Russia from 50 billion cubic meters in 2009, of which Russia took only 12 billion cubic meters, to up to 30 billion cubic meters in 2010.[22]

Since Gazprom has been forced to reduce its output from existing fields, it has neither need nor financing for the expensive new mastodon fields, Shtokman in the Barents Sea, Yamal in Northern Russia, or Kovykta in East Siberia. Gazprom has acted rationally, quietly, and without drama delaying the development of all these new fields.

One inconsistency remains in Gazprom's new defensive strategy. The company insists on building two new pipelines, Nord Stream through the Baltic Sea to Germany and South Stream through the Black Sea and Balkans to Italy. These two pipelines are intended to circumvent the transit countries Ukraine, Belarus, and Poland, but South Stream would pass through more transit countries. After the many coercive measures by Gazprom against their customers, Gazprom, not any transit country, appears to be the problem, which Gazprom refuses to acknowledge. Nord Stream, with a capacity of 55 billion cubic meters, would cost at least $15 billion and South Stream, with a capacity of 60 billion cubic meters, about $28 billion. By contrast, the March 23, 2009 EU-Ukraine declaration on the gas transit system through Ukraine could solve the problems with Ukrainian gas transit for a paltry investment of $3.5 billion and secure all the necessary capacity.

Gazprom's investment structure is a traditional peculiarity. It has invested more in pipelines than in development and production and large amounts in acquisitions outside the gas sector. In 2005 more than half of its large capital budget went to pipelines and only one-third to production and development. But the Gazprom management has sobered up somewhat. In 2007 and 2008 Gazprom spent 43 percent of its capital investment on production and just over a third on transportation (figure 7.5). Yet, the existing pipeline network is poorly maintained, and these massive invest-

21. Vladimir Soccor, "Strategic Implications of the Central Asia-China Pipeline," *Eurasia Daily Monitor* (Jamestown Foundation, December 18, 2009).

22. Isabel Gorst, "Russia Welcomes End to Turkmen Gas Dispute," *Financial Times*, December 23, 2009.

Figure 7.5   Gazprom's capital expenditures, 2003–08

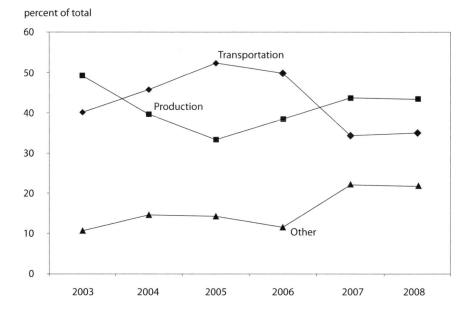

Source: Gazprom Databook, June 2009, www.gazprom.com (accessed November 28, 2009).

ments expanded the total Russian gas network by only 8.6 percent from 2000 to 2008.[23]

Gazprom has no comparative advantage in pipeline construction. Few companies procure at higher prices. Anecdotal evidence suggests that it usually costs Gazprom three times as much to build a pipeline as anybody else. When Gazprom built Blue Stream, Hermitage Capital Management showed that Gazprom's cost per kilometer of pipeline was 119 percent higher than on the Turkish side.[24]

Nor does Gazprom have any apparent comparative advantage in the transportation of gas, being notorious for including shady intermediaries, which later prompt it to shut off its deliveries. In March 2010, Gazprom sensationally announced that it would audit its related export intermediaries, which seemed to be an attack on customary corrupt schemes.[25]

With reduced gas exports to Europe, Russia has no need for additional

23. Goskomstat (Russia's Federal State Statistics Service), Russia in Figures for 2009, 2008, and 2007.

24. Vadim Kleiner, "How Should Gazprom Be Managed in Russia's National Interests and the Interests of Its Shareholders?" (Hermitage Capital Management, June 2005), 40–41.

25. Yelena Mazneva, Inna Reznik, and Maxim Tovkailo, "Gazprom Middlemen Face Audit on Exports," Moscow Times, March 5, 2010.

pipeline capacity. It makes no commercial sense to build either Nord Stream or South Stream. Nor would it make any political sense, as Gazprom regularly causes delivery disruptions.

For all these reasons, demand from Gazprom's final European consumers is likely to stay low for years. Eventually, Gazprom's friendly intermediaries—the big European gas companies—have little choice but to renegotiate their long-term contracts with Gazprom. The post-Soviet countries have already reduced their dependence on Russian gas deliveries for many years, and the two remaining big customers, Ukraine and Belarus, can easily reduce most of their gas consumption. Ukraine, which has even greater energy intensity than Russia, could save all its gas imports from Russia in the medium term by becoming as energy efficient as Poland or Slovakia. Nor are Gazprom's domestic sales of some 270 billion cubic meters safe. If prices double within a few years as is currently planned, Russian gas consumption will plummet, as Russia is ripe for energy savings. If the independent producers are permitted reasonable market conditions, they will beat Gazprom in both production and sales. All this would be good for Russia but not for Gazprom.

The Central Asian gas market is going through a metamorphosis. Most of the Central Asian gas supply is likely to go to China without Russian intermediation. China has already built a gas pipeline to Turkmenistan. By 2013, China is planning to buy 40 billion cubic meters of natural gas from Turkmenistan, while the Russian-sponsored new pipeline project on the eastern shore of the Caspian Sea from Turkmenistan to Russia, which President Putin announced in May 2007, is going nowhere and will most likely never be built.[26]

In 2007 Gazprom forced TNK-BP to abandon the giant gas field Kovykta in East Siberia, from which it could have been profitable to build a pipeline to China. Now Kovykta will remain stranded and barely exploited for years to come. Gazprom is also set to abandon the project to build a pipeline with a capacity of 80 billion cubic meters of gas from West Siberia to China, which President Putin presented with great fanfare in 2006, though it never appeared plausible.[27] The only Russian gas to be sold to China is LNG from Sakhalin Energy. Turkmenistan and Kazakhstan are likely to outcompete Russia on the Chinese gas market.

Without investment in new giant gas fields, notably Yamal, or without allowing independent producers more freedom, Gazprom's output is set to decline steeply beginning in 2011. It may lose as much as one-third of its production capacity in half a decade, as the four giant fields in West Siberia that currently dominate its production have all passed their peak

---

26. Pavel K. Baev, "China Trumps Gazprom," *Moscow Times*, December 17, 2009.

27. Catherine Belton, "Dispute Puts Gazprom China Pipeline on Hold," *Financial Times*, June 18, 2009.

and are in decline. Given that Russian gas demand may fall even further, such a development no longer seems problematic but an appropriate adjustment of supply to contracting demand.

If Gazprom does not change its pipeline construction plans and starts building both Nord Stream and South Stream in 2010, these two pipelines might become two of the most wasteful white elephants ever. Russia will not have gas for them for the foreseeable future, and it is far cheaper to use the existing pipelines through Ukraine. Their construction would not lead to any diversification but further tie Russia to the old pipeline transportation and the stagnant European gas market when it should try to diversify its markets. Nord Stream seems to have advanced too far to be stopped, while the construction of South Stream can still be halted.

As a consequence of less demand, less production, lower prices, and excessive capital investment, Gazprom will be a smaller, less profitable, and less valuable company. Within five years, its supply of gas could decline by 200 billion cubic meters or about one-third, while losing domestic and foreign sales of similar magnitude. Russian society will forgo huge wealth that its gas industry could have generated, but it also means that Gazprom will cease to be a state within the state, and Russia could become a more normal and open society.

An Alternative Russian Gas Policy

The current recession has exposed Gazprom's weaknesses and offers an excellent opportunity for reform as long outlined.[28] The crucial insight is that what is good for Gazprom's management is bad for Russia, because Gazprom is the primary cause of Russia's energy curse. The less energy rents it generates, the lesser the curse will be.[29] The danger is to be content with marginal improvements when truly profound changes are required.

The first step should be to separate Gazprom from the state. Either the president or the prime minister concludes virtually all important international gas deals. Even if the majority of Gazprom remains state-owned, it must gain integrity as an autonomous joint stock company. Therefore, it should be deprived of its regulatory functions, which should be transferred to an independent regulatory agency.

Since the Gazprom management has failed so miserably, a clean sweep of the existing management and installation of a new, competent management from the private sector are desirable. Another immediate decision

28. Rudiger Ahrend and William Tompson, "Russia's Gas Sector: The Endless Wait for Reform?" OECD Economics Department Working Paper 402 (Paris: Organization for Economic Cooperation and Development, September 2004).

29. Yegor T. Gaidar, *The Collapse of the Empire: Lessons for Modern Russia* (Washington: Brookings Institution, 2007).

should be to abandon Nord Stream and South Stream, since neither appears commercially viable.

In a rational market economy, a conglomerate such as Gazprom would not exist. All kinds of noncore assets from farms to television companies should be sold off.[30] Production of gas should be separated from transportation and sales in different companies. At least underperforming production companies should be put up for sale. Since Gazprom lacks the administrative ability to develop small and medium-sized fields, the Ministry of Natural Resources should take back all its neglected or mothballed licenses. Gradually, such licenses should be auctioned off, which would strengthen independent gas producers. No doubt, they would quickly outcompete Gazprom in production in the same way Russia's private oil producers dominate that industry.

The gas pipeline system could stay state-owned but be separated from production and opened up on equal pricing conditions to independent producers. As a consequence, flaring could be sharply reduced and Russia would benefit from a huge, cheap, additional supply of gas, at the same time air pollution would be reduced. This would be a large, swift gain for Russian welfare.

In accordance with long-accepted policy, domestic and CIS prices should be gradually raised to the market level, which would be considerably lower than in Europe because of large transportation costs for gas. For domestic Russian prices, the current target date is 2011. When market prices have been reached and a competitive gas market established, the gas market can be deregulated. Then differential taxation between the oil and gas industry will no longer be justified, and equal taxation should be attempted. That should increase Russia's federal tax revenues.

The combination of reduced flaring, introduction of market prices, and market allocation of gas will lead to greater efficiency, huge savings of energy, and reduction of air pollution, which will benefit the welfare of the Russian people. Presumably, this will lead to a substantial decline in gas consumption in Russia and other post-Soviet countries. If more gas is needed, independent companies can extract it from existing small and medium-sized gas deposits at much lower cost than from the distant giant fields in the far north. Then, Russia could manage without developing Yamal or Shtokman for quite some time. Instead, it could direct financial resources to the maintenance of the existing pipeline system to reduce losses. If independent producers are given more freedom, Russia's many accessible small and medium-sized fields could be developed.

Gazprom must also try to win back the trust of its foreign customers, whom it has abused in the last several years. To begin with, it should apologize for cuts in recent years and offer credible guarantees that it will

---

30. Admittedly, many enterprises have apparently been privatized through asset stripping. See Nemtsov and Milov, *Putin and Gazprom.*

not do so again. It may need to reconsider its centralized sales model. Gazprom should build up storage in its customers' markets to reassure them that sudden delivery cuts will no longer occur, and it can start participating in spot sales. Gazprom should adopt a more flexible, decentralized, and customer-oriented business model,[31] but such a policy requires a different kind of company, which is an additional reason to break up Gazprom.

It will be much easier to render Gazprom transparent and improve its governance on a competitive market. Gazprom will stop being a slush fund for Russian politics. For the European Union, Gazprom's new weakness offers an outstanding opportunity to clean up gas trade with Russia. The European Union and Russia should come together and reform the European and Russian gas sectors, which are both in crisis. The centerpiece of an all-European gas reform should be marketization and the unbundling of transportation and production of gas.

The Europeans could take up Russian President Dmitri Medvedev's recent proposal to draft a new legal framework for energy cooperation meant to replace the Energy Charter of 1994, which almost all other European countries have ratified. Both Russia and Europe need an agreed legal framework for international energy cooperation. If Russia accepts the application of the Energy Charter's transit protocol, it could benefit from export revenues from international usage of its extensive trunk pipeline network.

Gazprom's current crisis offers the best opportunity ever for Russian and European energy reform. The arguments for a profound reform of Russia's gas sector have never been stronger.

---

31. I owe this policy suggestion to Vladimir Milov.

8

Military Reform against Heavy Odds

PAVEL K. BAEV

The Russian military is undergoing a radical and painful reform that will drastically reshape its doctrine, training, technology, materiel, and organization. Observers argue that this is the greatest reform that the Russian military has gone through since the 1860s, when Russia moved to a German-style mass army based on conscription. Today, the Russian military is following the US lead: moving toward small but well-equipped rapid deployment forces, leaving large tank armies in the past. The success of this overhaul, however, is by no means guaranteed.

Russia inherited the bulk of the Soviet military machine, which was far too large for its needs and resources. Nor was it appropriate for its actual challenges, as the disastrous war in Chechnya showed. In the 1990s, the dearth of resources was acute; however, since neither politicians nor the military knew what to do, no significant reform occurred. In the 2000s, thanks to oil-fueled prosperity, the military and military-industrial complex enjoyed massive increases in funding, but inefficiency became a growing concern. The Russian military has maintained its Cold War posture, becoming increasingly top-heavy and rusty. While funding of the military is now more adequate, manning of the forces has become a growing problem. The long overdue military reform is thus necessary.[1]

Pavel K. Baev is a research professor at the International Peace Research Institute, Oslo (PRIO). He is grateful to the Norwegian Defense Ministry for sustained support for his research on the Russian military.

1. There is a body of analysis on the rationale for military reforms; see, for instance, Steven E. Miller, and Dmitri Trenin, eds., *The Russian Military: Power and Policy* (Cambridge, MA, and

The financial crisis took the Russian leadership by surprise, and it coincided with the escalation of the Russian-Georgian conflict into full-blown war for five days in August 2008. Both the financial crisis and the Russian-Georgian war provided crucial impetus to military reform, whose guidelines and timetables were decided in the fall of 2008.

The Russian military consists of three branches—ground forces (Sukhoputnye Voyska, SV), navy (Voyenno-Morskoy Flot, VMF), and air force (Voyenno-Vozdushnye Sily, VVS)—and three independent "combat arms," not subordinate to any of the three branches: airborne troops (Vozdushno-Desantnye Voiska, VDV), strategic rocket forces (Raketnye Voyska Strategicheskogo Naznacheniya, RVSN), and space troops (Kosmicheskiye Voyska, KV).

This chapter evaluates the attempted military transformation and assesses the risks of failure. It first briefly describes the ongoing reforms and then investigates their underlying ideology. It evaluates the leadership of the reforms and examines specific issues in the strategic forces, the army, the navy, and the air force. Finally, it addresses the problem of resource allocation for military modernization.

Origins and Design of the Military Reform

In the 1990s, the transformation of the Russian armed forces was radical in quantitative terms but qualitatively minuscule: The total number of soldiers was reduced by a factor of four to just over one million men in uniform, but the command structure and organization remained intact. Many reform proposals were drafted and some were attempted but abandoned after encountering shortage of funds and resistance from the military. The last time reform was seriously considered was in summer 2003 when the liberal Union of the Rightist Forces (SPS) party proposed to cancel the draft in its election campaign, but it failed to enter the State Duma.[2] Defense Minister Sergei Ivanov reassured the military high command that the period of military reforms was over. However, in his 2004 address to the parliament President Vladimir Putin emphasized that "modernization of the army is a task of national importance."[3]

London: MIT Press, 2004); Aleksei Arbatov, "Russian Military Policy Adrift," Briefing Paper 8, no. 6 (Moscow: Carnegie Center, November 2006); Aleksandr Hramchihin and Igor Plugatarev, "The Agenda for a New Army," *Nezavisimoe Voennoe Obozrenie*, February 8, 2008; Vitaly Shlykov, "Secrets of Serdyukov's Blitzkrieg," *Russia in Global Affairs* (November-December 2008), 8–25. My most recent study is Pavel K. Baev, "Neither Reform nor Modernization: The Russian Armed Forces under and after Putin's Command," in *The Politics of Security in Modern Russia*, ed. Mark Galeotti (London: Ashgate, 2010), 69–88.

2. Dale R. Herspring, "Vladimir Putin and Military Reform in Russia," *European Security* 14, no. 1 (March 2005): 137–55.

3. The minister elaborated his thesis in Sergei Ivanov, "Russia's Geopolitical Priorities and Armed Forces," *Russia in Global Affairs* (January-February 2004): 38–51; Vladimir Putin,

Yet hardly any modernization occurred during Putin's second presidential term. The nominal defense budget increased annually by 20 to 25 percent, but it was roughly in line with the overall growth of state expenditures and amounted to 2.5 to 2.7 percent of GDP. Official information on the structure of defense expenditures is scant, but the prioritization of procurement (which increased by up to 40 percent annually) failed to increase deliveries of key weapons systems to the armed forces.[4] These low returns on loudly trumpeted military investments possibly prompted Putin to replace Ivanov with a more capable executive.

In February 2007, Anatoly Serdyukov was appointed minister of defense. This choice was very surprising, because he had previously led the Federal Tax Service and had devoted most of his career to furniture trade and had no military background. Serdyukov's outsider perspective might have been valuable. The distortions in the Soviet-style military were dangerous because of the combination of rising costs and diminishing capabilities, which rendered the armed forces both ineffective and unsustainable. Serdyukov started his attack on the dilapidated military organization by calling for optimization and enhancement, avoiding the loaded term "reform."

The reorganization of the armed forces, announced without warning in mid-October 2008, included four key elements. The first element is a deep cut in the number of officers from 335,000 to 150,000 by 2012, while the number of junior officers (lieutenants) will grow from 50,000 to 60,000. Such draconian decimation involves early retirement of at least 60,000 mid-career officers.[5] The second element is disbandment of all "reduced strength" units in conventional forces, so that the total number of ground force units will decline from 1,890 to 172, from 340 to 180 in the air force, and from 240 to 123 in the navy. The third element is elimination of regiments and divisions in both the army and the air force, so that the army will change to a two-level battalion-brigade structure and in the air force squadrons will be subordinated to air bases. Finally, the system of military education will be downsized, with many colleges closed and traditional academies relocated from Moscow to new education centers.[6]

Altogether, this reform amounts to a profound change comparable to the military reforms conducted in the 1860s by Dmitri Milyutin after

---

"Address to the Federal Assembly," May 10, 2006, available at www.kremlin.ru/eng.

4. This apparent paradox is examined in Margarete Klein, "Russia's Military Capabilities: 'Great Power' Ambitions and Reality," SWP Research Paper (Berlin: Stiftung Wissenschaft und Politik [German Institute for International and Security Affairs], October 2009).

5. An officer earns pension after 20 years of service; see Vadim Solovyev, "New Decembrists," *Nezavisimaya Gazeta*, November 21, 2008.

6. This part of the reform is not analyzed in detail here, but a serious disruption of the education process (not least due to the retirement of many professors who preferred to stay in Moscow) is evident; see Shlykov, "Secrets of Serdyukov's Blitzkrieg."

Russia's defeat in the Crimean war and in the 1920s by Mikhail Frunze after the end of the Civil War. It is more profound than Nikita Khrushchev's famous "1.2-million cut" in the early 1960s.[7]

Under a previously approved plan, troop numbers were to have declined to 1.1 million personnel by 2011 and to 1 million by 2016. Serdyukov ruled that the size would be trimmed to 1 million personnel by 2013, three years earlier than previously planned. He did not venture into strategic matters but went for the easiest targets. The central point of his plan is, nevertheless, quite ambitious and amounts to the dismantling of extensive infrastructure for mass mobilization for a large-scale conventional war.

Despite all the outcry in, and sabotage from, the overgrown military bureaucracy, execution of the plan was sustained through the first crucial year. By early 2010, the point of no return had been reached in all four directions of reform. The armed forces, however, are far from acquiring a lean new look, particularly since their tasks remain ambivalently defined and combat capabilities cannot be measured against them.

The Thinking behind the Military Reform

Preparatory work for the reform was conducted quietly during the second half of Putin's second presidential term. This rather peaceful period saw a sharp decline in antiterrorist operations and a significant stabilization of the Northern Caucasus. Deployment of Russian troops beyond the national territory reached a new low, with the withdrawal of three Russian bases from Georgia. Yet, tensions with the United States and the North Atlantic Treaty Organization (NATO) were growing, starting with Putin's famous Munich speech in February 2007. Self-assertive rhetoric was backed by increasing demonstrations of Russia's military might, from the resumption of strategic bomber patrol flights over neutral waters off the Arctic, Pacific, and Atlantic Oceans to joint military exercises with China to Northern Fleet cruises to Venezuela, Cuba, and Libya.[8]

These performances were not all that impressive, revealing rather than camouflaging the deficiencies in the Russian military machine, but they generated an impression that Russian power could be projected.[9]

---

7. On the history of reforming the Russian military, see Alexander M. Golts and Tonya L. Putnam, "State Militarism and Its Legacies: Why Military Reform Has Failed in Russia," *International Security* 29, no. 2 (Fall 2004): 121–58.

8. The limitations of this military self-assertion are discussed in Jan Leijonhielm, ed., *Russian Power Structures: Present and Future Roles in Russian Politics* (Stockholm: Swedish Defense Research Agency, December 2007); Pavel K. Baev, "Russia's Security Policy Grows Muscular: Should the West Be Worried? Briefing Paper 15 (Helsinki: Finnish Institute of International Affairs, February 2008).

9. Zoltan Barany, "Resurgent Russia? A Still-Faltering Military," *Policy Review* no. 147 (Febru-

The Russian-Georgian war further exposed shocking gaps in air support and command and control.[10] The militaristic discourse, while gaining popularity, did not make it into key official documents: The Foreign Policy Concept (approved in July 2008) did not mention military instruments, and the National Security Strategy (approved in May 2009) elaborated on nonmilitary security challenges, including health care and culture.[11] Strategic thinking, however, remained in limbo during the initial stage of the reform because adoption of a new military doctrine was postponed. Defense Minister Serdyukov was free to formulate the key guidelines for transforming the military structures as he saw fit, but as a civilian he refrained from painting a big strategic picture, limiting his task to organizational and budget matters.

President Dmitri Medvedev should have performed the key role in defining security interests and the means for their advancement in line with Putin's idea of "an innovative army" spelled out in his farewell address to the State Council in February 2008.[12] Only two sentences in Medvedev's manifesto-article "Go Russia!" addressed military matters: "Of course Russia will be well-armed. Well enough so that it does not occur to anyone to threaten us or our allies." A much sharper point marked a departure from Putin's foreign policy line: "But resentment, arrogance, various complexes, mistrust and especially hostility should be excluded from the relations between Russia and the leading democratic countries."[13] Up to early 2010, Medvedev had preferred to avoid identifying military threats and priorities in modernizing the armed forces; in keeping with this, he chose not to address the annual gathering of the high command in late 2008 and not to hold the ceremonial meeting on February 23, 2009 (Defender of the Fatherland Day), which are his traditional functions as commander in chief.

After much delay, however, the long-awaited military doctrine was finally approved in February 2010. The text of this lengthy document pro-

---

ary-March 2008), available at www.hoover.org (this and all other websites sourced in this chapter were accessed on December 25, 2009).

10. Sober analysis can be found in Aleksandr Tsyganok, "Lessons of the Five-Day War in the Caucasus," *Nezavisimoe Voennoe Obozrenie*, August 29, 2008; and Roger McDermott, "Russia's Conventional Armed Forces and the Georgian War," *Parameters* (Spring 2009): 65–80.

11. The texts of key documents are available at the Security Council of Russia website, Documents Related to Various Aspects of Russia's Security, www.scrf.gov.ru. On the National Security Strategy document, see Fedor Lukyanov, "A Positive but Confusing Strategy," *Moscow Times*, May 20, 2009.

12. Ariel Cohen, "Russia on the March: The Return of the Red Square Parades," Heritage Foundation Web Memo 1805, February 11, 2008, available at www.heritage.org.

13. The extensive debates on this article published in the liberal *Gazeta.ru* hardly touched upon military issues.

vides no explanation for the long delay.[14] The doctrine essentially states that the Russian armed forces should be ready for every type of military conflict—from space wars to peacekeeping operations—and must build corresponding capabilities, for which all necessary resources would be provided. Perhaps the most significant article in the document defines conditions for the use of nuclear weapons. There had been many informed speculations that the document would justify preventive/preemptive strikes, even in local conflicts; in fact, the document confirms only retaliatory strikes: The first use of nuclear weapons is defined as possible only when a conventional aggression threatens "the very existence of the state."[15]

The list of "external military dangers" starts with the alleged "intention" to grant NATO "global functions" and to deploy its military infrastructure close to Russia's borders, including by enlargement. This statement appears unduly confrontational and has invoked criticism from the alliance leadership, but in reality it is a purely political postscript to the sharp argument about NATO enlargement in 2007–08. What the doctrine does not say is that the dismantling of the Soviet mechanism of mass mobilization amounts to scrapping of the model of protracted conventional war, which means that Russia is not even envisaging any confrontation with NATO in the West or with China in the East.[16] The hidden but entirely practical key assumption is that the Russian armed forces are expected to be engaged only in low-intensity operations—from counterterrorism to power projection—in the post-Soviet South.[17]

The doctrine thus has very little if any connection to the ongoing reform, in which elimination of "skeleton" units from the armed forces is presented simply as a way to get rid of useless "empty shells" and cut down the number of officers. The only useful purpose of this document is to shelter the high command from criticism on the lack of strategic vision and to stifle public debates. Having thus covered his lack of leadership, Medvedev duly held the ceremonial meeting on February 23, 2010 and presided over the session of the Defense Ministry Board on March 5, 2010, asserting that the transformation of the military structures proceeds on schedule and is encountering only minor complications.[18]

---

14. The text is available at the Security Council of Russia website, www.scrf.gov.ru, and there is no official English translation. A competent overview was done by Viktor Litovkin, "Doctrine of Striking Back," *Nezavisimoe Voennoe Obozrenie*, February 12, 2010.

15. Nikolai Patrushev, secretary of the Security Council of Russia, was the main source for those speculations; see Vladimir Mamontov, "Russia Is Changing, and Its Military Doctrine Is Changing Also," *Izvestia*, October 14, 2009.

16. Aleksandr Hramchihin, "All in All—85 Permanent Readiness Brigades," *Nezavisimoe Voennoe Obozrenie*, October 16, 2009.

17. Stanislav Kuvaldin, "Army for Modest Power," *Expert*, October 12, 2009.

18. Irina Granik and Ivan Konovalov, "Defense Exists in General," *Kommersant*, March 6, 2010.

The main problem with Medvedev's ideas and Serdyukov's action plan is that the major cuts in the number of officers will lead to a deterioration in combat readiness of the forces as only professional sergeants and soldiers can offer real combat readiness for rapid deployment operations. The high command has been avoiding the crucial issue of draft, expecting that the reduction of the conscription period from 24 months first to 18 months and then to 12 months will reduce social tensions.[19] A temporary drop in draft dodging and the drafting of college graduates have eased immediate manpower shortages, but demographic and health problems in Russia will shrink the conscript pool, rendering unsustainable the plan of taking 600,000 soldiers annually into the armed forces.[20] What is needed is a big cut from the psychologically convincing total strength of 1 million uniformed personnel to a new target figure of 600,000 to 700,000, which is more appropriate for strategy and budget.

A Team of Reluctant and Accidental Reformers

Serdyukov is closely associated with the execution of this revolutionary reform project. His appointment as defense minister in February 2007 broke the pattern of leaving the military to deal with its own problems. The choice of a "nobody" for this high-profile post appeared rather odd and was interpreted as a maneuver either to promote Sergei Ivanov or remove him from the Ministry of Defense in a complicated political scheme surrounding presidential succession in the 2008 elections. Serdyukov did not rush to reorganize the military but started with streamlining the money flows in the notoriously nontransparent defense budget. He quickly discovered the limits of this cost cutting because the problem was galloping monopoly prices of military goods and services. By the end of 2007, the top brass had stopped referring to him as a "furniture trader."[21] He survived the cabinet reshuffling in September 2007 (when his father-in-law, Viktor Zubkov, became prime minister) and was reappointed in May 2008, when Prime Minister Putin formed his cabinet.

This confirmation of authority granted Serdyukov a mandate for resolving the conflict with the top brass triggered by his modest proposal for

---

19. According to Levada Center polls, support for keeping the draft system increased from 32 percent in February 2006 to 41 percent in 2007, 45 percent in 2008, and 47 percent in February 2009, while support for a change in the all-volunteer system declined, respectively, from 62 percent to 54 percent, 48 percent, and 43 percent. See Levada Press Center, "The Attitudes toward Military Reform and Army Draft," Levada Center Polls, March 30, 2009, available at www.levada.ru.

20. Aleksandr Golts, "Reflections of a Seasoned Liberal on the Military Reform Plan," *Ezhednevny Zhurnal*, June 11, 2009, http://ej.ru.

21. For a balanced evaluation, see "The First Truly Civilian Defense Minister," *Nezavisimoe Voennoe Obozrenie*, December 28, 2007.

replacing military officers with civilians in noncombat positions (e.g., in medicine and logistics). Compared with some earlier clashes—particularly between Defense Minister Igor Sergeev and Chief of General Staff Anatoly Kvashnin at the start of Putin's reign—this conflict appeared trivial, but the exercise of political power was swift and brutal. Yuri Baluyevsky, the chief of general staff and a career *genshtabist*, probably expected that hawkish statements about direct threat from US antimissiles planned for deployment in Poland would help him defend his turf. Serdyukov was not impressed and secured Medvedev's consent to fire him in July 2008. Within a month, several of Baluyevsky's deputies and aides resigned.[22]

The purging of the general staff completely disorganized the chain of command during the war with Georgia in early August 2008, particularly since the experienced Aleksei Maslov was replaced as the commander of the ground forces in late July. The whole upper echelon of the high command became dysfunctional, so key decisions in the crucial hours at the start of the war were apparently made at a remarkably low level in the military hierarchy. General Vladimir Shamanov, the chief of the Ministry of Defense Main Directorate for Combat Training, who returned to active service in October 2007, probably played a key role. Colonel General Sergei Makarov, commander of the North Caucasus Military District, and General Anatoly Khrulev, commander of the 58th Army, who both served under Shamanov in the Second Chechen War, also may have issued orders for combat deployment.[23]

Medvedev was shocked by the imperative to take responsibility for a war not of his making, claiming that he "remembers by minute" that "most difficult day" of his life. He became concerned about independent decision making by a gang of "Chechen warriors." Putin, who had taken pains to keep them under control during the Second Chechen War, apparently concluded that only further purges would control the office corps. Already in mid-October 2008, Serdyukov announced a draconian plan for reforming the military structures: He targeted one particular imbalance—high proportion of officers—envisaging the elimination of some 200,000 positions in only two years. This reorganization involves early involuntary retirements of tens of thousands of officers for whom housing had to be provided, and it also aims to cut down the apparatus of the high command by about 60 percent from some 22,000 to 8,500 officers.[24]

22. Vadim Solovyev and Vladimir Ivanov, "Serdyukov Decimates the General Corps," *Nezavisimoe Voennoe Obozrenie*, July 11, 2008.

23. Shamanov organized the "Caucasus-2008" exercises in July (which were not attended by the high command); Khrulev led the troops in the field and went into South Ossetia with the first column that was ambushed outside Tskhinvali. My more detailed analysis of this decision making is in Pavel K. Baev, "Vae Victors: The Russian Army Pays for the Lessons of the Georgian War," *PONARS Eurasia Memo* 46 (Washington: Georgetown University, December 2008).

24. For an initial feasibility assessment, see Vadim Solovyev, "Military Reform of 2009–2012," *Nezavisimoe Voennoe Obozrenie*, December 12, 2008.

Because of the financial crisis, resources available for military reform were reduced. In the first half of 2009, Serdyukov had to make corrections to the downsizing schedule and postpone salary raises as well as expansion of contract service. Meanwhile, Medvedev and Putin turned their attention to social issues in the armed forces and pledged to prioritize rearmament in the postcrisis period, while glossing over the problems with incoherent logic of transformations and declining combat readiness.[25]

Serdyukov's small team in the Defense Ministry was besieged by angry generals. He ordered General Nikolai Makarov, the chief of general staff, known for his loyalty to bosses, to provide justifications for the cuts and reorganizations, but Makarov was heavily criticized for poor performance.[26] Seeking to neutralize discontent among the top brass, Medvedev promoted General Shamanov, an influential advocate of reforms, to commander of the prestigious airborne troops (VDV). Although he confirmed his support for modernization, Shamanov immediately cancelled all cuts as well as the shift to brigades in the VDV, stating that these elite forces would be reinforced.[27] Medvedev's trust in this supposed champion of reforms, who is a decorated veteran of the Chechen war, was further undermined when Shamanov personally dispatched special forces to stop a criminal investigation of an enterprise owned by a relative. Shamanov had to admit to "inappropriate behavior" but was only reprimanded.[28]

Serdyukov steadfastly proceeded with his reforms, rendering them irreversible, but he closely guards all information perhaps due to personal preferences and because military opinions only diminish the efficiency of decision making.[29] Resistance among the top brass against reforms has continued to grow and necessitated further replacements in January 2010, which might have strengthened Makarov's position in the general staff but hardly promoted any reformers.[30] Absence of transparency and information could become a weakness of the reforms as it would lead to poor understanding of the necessary further changes, which the opposition could exploit.

25. Vadim Solovyev and Vladimir Ivanov, "The Reform Has Gone an Unpredictable Way," *Nezavisimoe Voennoe Obozrenie*, May 29, 2009.

26. Konstantin Vershinin, "Military Brain with an Unprofessional Bend," *Nezavisimoe Voennoe Obozrenie*, October 16, 2009.

27. Vadim Solovyev and Vladimir Ivanov, "Generals in Counter-Offensive," *Nezavisimaya Gazeta*, May 29, 2009.

28. The scandal was triggered by reports in Roman Anin, "General and Glyba," *Novaya Gazeta*, September 21, 2009 and Pavel Felgengauer, "18 Brumaire of Vladimir Shamanov," *Novaya Gazeta*, September 28, 2009.

29. Elena Melnichuk and Vasily Toporov, "Unsinkable," *Profil*, October 12, 2009.

30. Viktor Myasnikov, "In the Army: Quiet Rebellion of Generals Is Suppressed," *Nezavisimaya Gazeta*, January 18, 2010.

Reform of the Army Is Radical but not Radical Enough

Ground forces are the main target of Serdyukov's reforms, and so far they have shown little resistance to his radical intentions to decimate their numbers, break their traditional organizational structures, and do away with their philosophy of protracted large-scale tank battles. The numbers given by the high command amount to a truly revolutionary downsizing: The total strength of the army will be halved to 270,000 troops; the overall number of units will plummet from 1,890 to 172; and of the current 22,000 tanks, only 2,000 will remain.[31] It is not clear what tasks this mini-army will be able to perform, but the current bloated army is hardly able to carry out any tasks.

The long-discussed reorganization from the three-level battalion-regiment-division structure to the two-level battalion-brigade structure makes sufficient sense to overcome the objections of traditionalists. Far more significant is the relatively uncontroversial disbandment of hundreds of "skeleton" units, which implies not only the end of the grand Soviet plan for mass mobilization but also a shift from the previous *matryoshka*-doll model, with a small elite army inside a larger low-readiness army. That model was far from efficient, and Alexei Arbatov argued perceptively that the large, socially disaffected army was hardly useful for anything except auxiliary functions, while still demanding a big share of funding, and the elite army was too small and could not shield itself from the rot spreading from the conscript units.[32]

One valuable feature in the abandoned model, however, was that the permanent readiness units were supposed to be fully professional and include only soldiers serving on two- to four-year contracts. This requirement was not consistently implemented but has now been abandoned.[33] Even the elite 76th Airborne Division (which is not split into brigades, thanks to Shamanov's protection)—the pilot unit in the "professionalization" experiment—now needs 1,500 conscripts to fill its ranks.[34] With the draft period cut to 12 months, training of soldiers has been reduced to basic tasks. Corruption, brutal bullying (*dedovshchina*) in the barracks, draft dodging, and the unhealthy lifestyle of Russians will all lead to a drop in real combat worthiness of permanent readiness units.

---

31. Extensive explanation of these reform targets can be found in Nikolai Makarov, "Full Text of Presentation at the Ministry of Defense," *Kommersant-Vlast*, July 13, 2009.

32. Arbatov, "Russian Military Policy Adrift," 7.

33. This issue gained attention when it was revealed that the permanent readiness units deployed in South Ossetia in August 2008 had many conscripts, four of whom were killed in action; see Valery Panfilov, "War with No Contract," *Lenta.ru*, August 20, 2008, http://lenta.ru.

34. Aleksandr Golts, "Reforms Go Full Circle," *Ezhednevny Zhurnal*, August 4, 2009, http://ej.ru.

Even more problematic is the situation with professional noncommissioned officers.[35] Serdyukov's plan is muddled in this regard; he envisions a larger number of lieutenants (which doesn't correspond with lower output from military colleges) but the disbandment of the corps of warrant officers (*praporshchiki*). Some of the latter might be promoted to lieutenants and others might become sergeants. The key issue, however, is the lack of experienced leaders at the level of squad or tank or gun crew, and it is unclear whether the single sergeant school established in December 2009 can cover this need.[36] At the same time, the program for recruiting up to 250,000 soldiers on contract has been slashed to 180,000, which is bound to fall further.[37] As a result, in the next few years, permanent readiness units will consist mostly of poorly trained conscripts, with perhaps five to seven sergeants (serving on two-year contracts) per platoon commanded by a former *praporshchik*.

The only way to check this degradation of combat worthiness is to reexamine the transition to professional soldiers. The cost could be affordable, since the army is no longer competing in a tight labor market and offers a reasonably attractive job package in a depressed economy. But the focus of the current plan is on modernization understood as increased acquisition of more modern weapons systems, mainly armor.[38] The persistence of this tank philosophy is understandable and much of the current armaments are hopelessly obsolete, but the long-promised delivery of the T-95—the new generation main battle tank—will not solve two key shortcomings revealed by the war with Georgia: communication and mobility.[39] Putin held a special meeting in Voronezh on developing a brigade-level computerized command-and-control system, but the current design is estimated to cost close to $250 million per brigade and is based on the problem-ridden GLONASS system.[40]

35. Vitaly Shlykov argued that building a corps of professional sergeants (perhaps in five to seven years) should have been the starting point for reorganizations; see "Current Problems and Logic of the Military Reform," *Nezavisimoe Voennoe Obozrenie*, May 14, 2009.

36. Roger McDermott, "Russian Military Plans New NCO Training Center," *Eurasia Daily Monitor*, September 8, 2009.

37. Vladimir Muhin, "Draft as a Rescue-Wand," *Nezavisimoe Voennoe Obozrenie*, October 9, 2009.

38. Putin visited Uralvagonzavod (the main producer of tanks) in Nizhny Tagil in December 2009 and assured that massive direct support for this enterprise would be followed by a significant increase in orders by the Ministry of Defense; see Yulia Mironova, "Armored Troop Carrier; Vladimir Putin Delivered Money to the Largest Tank Plant," *Vremya Novostei*, December 9, 2009.

39. Aleksandr Golts, "The End of the 'Tank Philosophy'," *Ezhednevny Zhurnal*, July 17, 2009, http://ej.ru; Mikhail Rastopshin, "Tank for the Wars of the Past," *Nezavisimoe Voennoe Obozrenie*, May 15, 2009.

40. Viktor Myasnikov, "Putin Turned the Army toward the Internet," *Nezavisimaya Gazeta*, January 19, 2010.

As far as mobility is concerned, the decision in 2003 to once again subordinate army aviation to the air force (because of heavy losses of helicopters in Chechnya) has turned out to be a mistake that is expensive to reverse. It took about a week to transport several battalions from the Moscow oblast to Belarus by rail for the Zapad-2009 large-scale military exercise, and it would be impossible to deploy a brigade to Central Asia.[41] Only the airborne troops maintain the ability for reasonably rapid deployment, and General Shamanov, who shelters them from reforms, is lobbying to acquire An-124 Ruslan heavy transportation planes for the transport aviation.[42]

Overall, the army needs reforms the most, and while they are focused accordingly, their design flaws could result in extreme deterioration of this central branch of the armed forces.

The Overexploited Navy and the Undertrained Air Force

The navy and the air force are secondary in Serdyukov's reform plan, which does not address their modernization. In 2007–08, they demonstrated the revival of Russia's military might. The navy sailed toward Cuba, Venezuela, and even the pirate coast, while strategic bombers conducted sporadic training flights in the Atlantic and Pacific corridors.[43]

Both the air force and the navy grant top priority to upgrading their strategic elements—the long-range aviation and ballistic missile nuclear submarines (SSBNs). The bulk of resources allocated to the navy are concentrated on the Borey class of fourth-generation nuclear-powered missile submarines, which are intended to replace the aging Delta III and Typhoon class submarines. The Borey class submarine was redesigned to accommodate the new Bulava submarine-launched ballistic missile (SLBM) in place of the abandoned R-39UTTH Bark missile. The first Borey class submarine, Yuri Dolgoruky, has gone through sea trials, but the vessel's commissioning is in jeopardy due to a series of test failures of the Bulava SLBM.[44] Two more Borey class submarines are under construction in Severodvinsk. All five remaining Delta III SSBNs will be retired by 2013,

---

41. Viktor Litovkin, "Blazing Fire and Steel," *Nezavisimaya Gazeta*, October 2, 2009.

42. Vasily Sychev, "The Return of Ruslan," *Lenta.ru*, December 25, 2009, http://lenta.ru.

43. In 2008, the official figure was more than 60 flights with total duration of 660 hours, which means one pair of bombers going over the north Atlantic and another over the north Pacific every month, plus a couple of exercises; see "More Than 60 Bombers Flew Out on Patrol in 2008," *RIA Novosti*, December 23, 2008, www.rian.ru.

44. After the spectacular test failure of Bulava in December 2009, the navy command decided to postpone the construction of the fourth Borey-class submarine; see Albert Dubrovin and Sergei Makeev, "Bulava Might Take Off but It Won't Fly," *Nezavisimoe Voennoe Obozrenie*, December 11, 2009.

and only six Delta IV submarines will remain operational—and hardly stay in service longer than 2020.

Nearly all vintage landing ships and minesweepers have to be retired before 2020. Despite the steady decline in the size of the navy, the admirals keep presenting plans for deploying five to six aircraft carrier groups.[45] The minor naval clash during the Russian-Georgian war has given their plans new impetus, and they are now focused on buying the French helicopter carrier Mistral and then building several ships of this class.[46] The issue of costs is conveniently left out of these debates. Meanwhile, the navy is reducing expenditures on constructing a new base in Novorossiisk, which is supposed to replace the main Russian base of the Black Sea Fleet in Sevastopol by 2017, but if it is not built in time, withdrawal will not be possible.

For the air force, Serdyukov's reforms aimed at replacing all air divisions and regiments with 55 air bases, cutting some 50,000 officers, and the plan is progressing on schedule. Modernization, however, is promised mostly for the medium term. The air force command has subscribed to Putin's proposal of serial production of the Tu-160 strategic bombers, but it took three years for the Kazan plant to assemble the first bomber, which was delivered in April 2008.[47] The promise to develop a new "invisible" strategic bomber by 2015 is not credible, but then at least 25 out of 64 aging Tu-95MS (Bear H) bombers must be retired. Tactical aviation received two new planes in 2008, for the first time in more than 15 years, but the plan to acquire 8 to 10 Su-34 fighter bombers a year has been curtailed. An unexpected gift for the Russian air force in 2009 were 34 MiG-29, which were delivered to the domestic market when Algeria refused to honor the contract for purchasing them and no other foreign buyer was interested.[48]

The main practical problem for the air force, however, has been lack of training. Even with increased funding in the last few years, the average level in full readiness units of tactical aviation has not exceeded 60 to 65 flying hours a year.[49] Due to prolonged poor training, demands to quickly raise the quality of performance have led to many accidents; after a crash of the Su-27 fighter aircraft in January 2009, Russia grounded the

---

45. One competent assessment of the naval posture is Mikhail Barabanov and Mikhail Lukin, "Where the Russian Navy Is Going," *Kommersant-Vlast*, February 25, 2008.

46. Viktor Litovkin, "The Navy Command Is Hunting for Phantoms," *Nezavisimaya Gazeta*, November 2, 2009.

47. Pavel Sergeev, "White Swan," *Lenta.ru*, April 30, 2008, http://lenta.ru.

48. Ivan Konovalov, "Armed Forces Will Rearm," *Kommersant*, March 6, 2009.

49. This figure given by the commander of the air force, General Alexander Zelin, is a big improvement from 20 to 25 hours, which was the norm in the 1990s, but most probably is reached only in several units; his point on the need for a massive increase in funding appears more believable; see Vadim Solovyev, "Worries and Expectations of the Commander of the Air Force," *Nezavisimoe Voennoe Obozrenie*, August 7, 2009.

whole fleet; the same story was repeated in June 2009 after two crashes of the Su-24. The crash of two Su-27 fighter jets from the Vityazi (Russian Knights) pilot group in August 2009 highlighted the problems of maintenance and training.[50] Russia suffered surprisingly heavy losses of aircraft in the war with Georgia, including Su-25 close air support aircraft, Su-24 tactical bombers, and Tu-22M3 long-range bomber. Poor training of pilots and friendly fire were responsible for half the damage.[51]

The success of reforms in the navy and the air force will be determined not by scrapping deteriorated hardware or structural reorganizations but by greater attention to logistics, training, and substantial rearmament. Combat training improved somewhat in the second half of the 2000s, but maintenance remains poor. Rearmament has been promised toward the second half of the 2010s, but the scope of these promises is so high that their credibility is diminishing.

Financial Matters and the Dysfunctional Military-Industrial Complex

With the disintegration of the Soviet military-industrial complex, two major issues in every reform project discussed since the Russian armed forces came into existence in 1992 have been how to finance modernization and reconnect the defense industry with the military.[52] Preparing his plan in the time of plenty, Serdyukov assumed that sufficient funding would be available, while Sergei Ivanov, who was elevated to the post of first deputy prime minister, was supposed to sort out the military industry.

As the financial crisis unfolded, Serdyukov had to assert that his reforms would be accomplished without any increases in the military budget. Given the shortage of funding in the crucial initial phase, that promise has dwindled to a commitment to minimize the sequestration of defense expenditures. The federal budget for 2009 was revised several times, and the allocations to the military (amounting to 12.2 percent of the total) were trimmed from 1.38 trillion rubles to 1.21 trillion rubles, with the share of defense expenditures close to 3 percent of GDP.[53]

The costs of decimating the officer corps have been underestimated.

---

50. Igor Naumov, "Sukhoi Counts Losses," *Nezavisimaya Gazeta*, August 19, 2009.

51. Anton Lavrov, "Russian Air Force Losses in the Five-Day War with Georgia," in *Tanki Avgusta* [*The Tanks of August*], ed. Mikhail Barabanov (Moscow: Center for Analysis of Strategies and Technologies (CAST), 2009), 109–118.

52. Julian Cooper, "Society-Military Relations in Russia: the Economic Dimension," in *Military and Society Post-Soviet Russia*, eds. Stephen L. Webber and Jennifer G. Matters (Manchester: Manchester University Press, 2006), 131–58.

53. Vladimir Muhin, "The Army Has Opened the Emergency Reserve," *Nezavisimaya Gazeta*, October 27, 2009.

The most expensive item is housing, because the state is obligated to pro-vide an apartment for every retiring officer. The Ministry of Defense was able to acquire less than half the apartments it needed in 2009, and it will be unable to provide all the promised apartments in 2010.[54] The expected income from sales of military land and buildings has been much less than expected, while the costs of closing and moving military academies have skyrocketed. The large expenditures on retirement packages have neces-sitated postponement of the promised sharp increases in officer salaries and dented financial incentives for contract soldiers.[55] As a result, instead of cutting out deadwood, the armed forces are losing their most valuable cadres and failing to attract the necessary expertise.

Shortage of funds has also caused delays in technical modernization, but Serdyukov has avoided all conflicts with his predecessor, Ivanov, who now supervises the defense industry. To Putin's satisfaction, Ivanov re-ports steady increases in defense orders, emphasizing that the State Arma-ments Program 2015 is firmly on track. Meanwhile Serdyukov is reporting a very different picture to Medvedev: In October 2009, the commander in chief suddenly criticized the "poor returns" on the massive investments in the defense industry and called for cutting production costs as a matter of "survival."[56]

Even arms characterized as modern are superficially upgraded So-viet-era designs that cannot be produced in significant quantities because crucial components are no longer available.[57]

The situation is particularly acute in the aircraft industry, which keeps speculating about a fifth-generation fighter when in fact it can produce neither reasonably modern electronic equipment nor high-precision muni-tions.[58] Another sad story is the Bulava SLBM, whose last nine test failures were caused by malfunctioning components. Ivanov pointed to dozens of subcontractors affiliated with the Votkinsk plant to explain these setbacks, which shows that quality control has not been enforced.[59]

The easiest way out of this conundrum is to concentrate efforts on a

---

54. Vladimir Ivanov, "Deputy Minister Stumbles Over Housing Issue," *Nezavisimoe Voennoe Obozrenie*, December 4, 2009.

55. Vladimir Muhin, "Military Sales without Significant Profits," *Nezavisimaya Gazeta*, January 14, 2010.

56. English translation of this statement is not available at the presidential website; the Russian transcript is "The Beginning of the Meeting on the Issues of Development of the Military-Industrial Complex," October 26, 2009, available at http://news.kremlin.ru.

57. Aleksandr Golts, "Instructions for Repairing a Broken Washtub," *Ezhednevny Zhurnal*, October 30, 2009, http://ej.ru.

58. Mikhail Rastopshin, "Imitation of the New Weapons Design Process," *Nezavisimaya Gazeta*, October 23, 2009.

59. Viktor Litovkin, "Bulava Is Undeliverable," *Nezavisimaya Gazeta*, October 30, 2009.

few promising directions and import new technologies, abandoning the Soviet model of producing all arms. Some steps in this direction have been taken (described in greater detail in chapter 5); for instance, the contract on importing reconnaissance drones from Israel (following Georgia's example) has been approved despite objections from domestic producers. Advancing a few sensational proposals, like purchasing France's Mistral helicopter carrier, Medvedev is not prepared to contemplate the full scope of a reorientation toward external suppliers that would involve shutting down dozens of domestic plants and research institutes of dubious value. With the average age of employees at the 1,300 defense enterprises hovering around 55 years and the share of worn-out equipment close to 75 percent, the atrophy of the Soviet defense industrial base will soon become irreversible.[60]

The armed forces cannot acquire any meaningful new look without new weapons systems, and after two lost decades of surviving on Soviet stocks the need for rearmament is indeed pressing. The defense industry is lobbying for new contracts but can offer only expensive upgrades of old Soviet models, and the government is promising to address all existing needs but does not have sufficient funds to purchase even limited quantities of these arms.

Conclusion: Profound Change but Limited Success

In the second year of profound reform, the Russian armed forces are in a precarious situation. Further transformation is necessary, but discontent in the ranks and opposition among the top brass are spreading and funding is becoming scarce. The way the reforms were designed risked failure to begin with, and their execution has only aggravated that risk. In hindsight, the narrow focus and great secrecy make sense as the only practical way to launch the reforms, but this selective breakthrough needs to lead to a deepening and widening of reform, maintaining the dynamics of changes while setting new targets. Instead, some backpedaling is taking place, especially in the VDV under Shamanov's command. The original plans are being stubbornly implemented, but little fresh effort is being added. Such slow, fragmented advance is due primarily to postponed problems, which have to be reckoned with along the way.

Information about the progress in building an army with a new look is disconcertingly incomplete, because Serdyukov discourages discussions of the reforms inside the military and refuses to engage in public debate. This self-isolation of a small team of reformers is to a large degree due to their inability to develop a convincing concept of reforms that logi-

---

60. Aleksandr Hramchihin, "OPK Has Rallied Against Common Sense," *Nezavisimaya Gazeta*, August 12, 2009.

cally connects strategic risk assessments with resource allocation and desired military capabilities. The new military doctrine contains no realistic guidelines and has no relevance for the ongoing transformation because the high command is not prepared to abandon the vision of a looming confrontation with NATO or to spell out concerns about the growth of China's military power. The armed forces are required to prepare for every kind of contingency, but the conventional capabilities that could be built by the mid-2010s would be usable only in local conflicts. Building an army that would not be able to counter acute security threats is one kind of risk, but arriving at an unsustainable military force because of demographic/draft problems is an entirely different kind of risk.

The financial crisis has interrupted Russia's economic growth, necessitating sober adjustments in the leadership's behavior and foreign policy—examined in chapter 9—and ambivalent shifts toward greater realism are indeed taking place. The defense policy, however, remains out of touch with reality. Pledges to build up military might were not convincing in the last years of Putin's petro-prosperity, but now promises to deploy every conceivable weapons system—new heavy intercontinental ballistic missiles and "invisible" strategic bombers, several aircraft carrier groups, and 20 giant Ruslan transport planes—look grotesque, particularly in the wake of the Bulava fiasco. This irresponsible attitude of the leaders toward military reform could be detrimental to the already traumatized armed forces and turn them into a maverick political force.

Serdyukov's position as the one in charge of the experimental transformation of the military is no less vulnerable than Yegor Gaidar's was in 1992–93, especially since Medvedev has not taken responsibility for setting the guidelines for reforms but has merely declared—including in his 2009 address to the parliament—his commitment to modernization and social protection of servicemen. Gaidar always had the larger picture in mind, while Serdyukov apparently operates within set boundaries and prefers not to worry about where his endeavor is really heading. It is remarkable that the resistance to painful and poorly explained reforms has not yet taken more open forms, but this opposition—not only among retired generals and expelled officers but also in the ranks—could be mobilized as the recession begins to break political passivity in society. Firing Serdyukov might seem to be an easy way out for Medvedev, but such scapegoating could work only if his own position were more secure than it currently is. Alienating the army might prove to be too dangerous a gamble.

9

Russian Foreign Policy: Modernization or Marginalization?

DMITRI TRENIN

The global economic crisis of 2008–09 has had a profound effect on Russia. The country entered the crisis hoping to remain an "island of stability," immune from financial troubles plaguing the Western world. The skyrocketing price of oil, just before the crisis struck, had strengthened the financial power of the Russian state. As a member of the virtual BRIC group of fast-growing, major non-Western economies,[1] Russia counted on the crisis, if anything, to facilitate its advancement through the ranks of the international economic power hierarchy. The troubles of the US dollar appeared to make a compelling case for the Russian ruble as a regional reserve currency. Not only was a multipolar world, no longer dominated by the United States, a near reality but also, as many Western institutions—in finance, government, and ethics—became discredited, the political systems of China and Russia showed remarkable resilience.

Within a few months, however, many of these hopes were dispelled as illusions, and many high ambitions were set back. Having lost 8 percent of its GDP in 2009, Russia was more severely hit than any Group of Twenty (G-20) country. However, the crisis failed to produce a social backlash that domestic adversaries of the Russian government hoped for. President Dmitri Medvedev praised the continuing social and thus regime stability as the biggest achievement of 2009. Russia did shed about $200 billion currency reserves while trying to salvage the ruble, but with more than

Dmitri Trenin is director of the Carnegie Moscow Center and has been with the center since its inception. This chapter draws on his article "Reimagining Moscow's Foreign Policy," Foreign Affairs 88, no. 6 (November/December 2009).

1. A group named after a 2001 Goldman Sachs report that lumped together the world's four largest emerging markets, Brazil, Russia, India, and China.

$400 billion remaining, it has enough to feel reasonably secure. Observers who had calculated that the mounting economic difficulties would make Moscow's foreign policy more pliable were largely confounded as the oil price rebounded quickly enough in 2009 before their hypothesis could really be tested.

Yet, at the beginning 2010 there was a widespread feeling of malaise within Russia. The "Gilded Age" of the 2000s had suddenly lost much of its luster. It is becoming clear that unless the country modernizes, Russia will further marginalize its position in global affairs. Russia's foreign policy is as much in need of a fundamental overhaul as are its economy and social and political systems.

Still Searching for a Global Role

Twenty years after the Soviet withdrawal from Afghanistan and the fall of the Berlin Wall, and 18 years after the breakup of the Soviet Union, Russia has shed communism and lost its historical empire. But it has not yet found a new role; instead, it sits uncomfortably on the periphery of both Europe and Asia while apprehensively rubbing shoulders with the Muslim world.

Throughout the 1990s, Moscow attempted to integrate into, and then with, the West. These efforts ended in failure, both because the West lacked the will to adopt Russia as one of its own and because Russian elites chose to embrace a corporatist, conservative policy agenda at home and abroad.

As a result, somewhere between 2003 and 2005 Russia abandoned its initial goal of Western integration and returned to its default option of behaving as an independent great power. It redefined its objectives: soft dominance in the immediate post-Soviet neighborhood; independence from, and equality with, the world's principal power centers of China, the European Union, and the United States; and membership in the global multipolar order.

Half a decade later, this policy course has revealed its failures and flaws. Most are rooted in the Russian government's inability and unwillingness to reform the country's oil-dependent economy, the noncompetitive nature of Russian politics, and the trend toward nationalism and isolationism. In terms of foreign policy, Russia's leaders have failed to close the books on the lost Soviet empire. It is as if they exited the 20th century through two doors at the same time—one leading to the globalized market of the 21st century and the other opening into the Great Game of the 19th century.

As the economic crisis has demonstrated, the model Russia's contemporary leaders have chosen—growth without development, capitalism without democracy, and great power policies without international appeal—can run only so far. Russia will not only fail to achieve its principal foreign policy objectives but also fall further behind in a world increasingly defined by instant communication and open borders, endangering not merely its status but also its existence. Russia's foreign policy needs more than a reset: It requires a new strategy and new policy instruments and mechanisms to implement it.

Project CIS on Life Support

When Russia, during Vladimir Putin's second term, abandoned its aspirations to join the West, it set about working on what could be called "project CIS." This effort attempted to turn the Commonwealth of Independent States—a loose association of ex-Soviet republics minus the three Baltic countries—into a Russian power center. Russia did not aim to restore the Soviet Union but to ensure political loyalty of these new states to Moscow, a privileged position for Russian business interests, and the predominant influence of Russian culture. After the 2008 war in Georgia, President Medvedev called the region "a zone of privileged interests" of the Russian Federation.

Russia's victory in that war seemed to strengthen its claim to that role. Moscow defended South Ossetia from the advances of the Georgian military and sent troops to allow the breakaway republic of Abkhazia to evict Georgian forces from the strategic Kodori Gorge. In a departure from its long-standing adherence to post-Soviet borders, Moscow recognized the independence of South Ossetia and Abkhazia, two enclaves that had seceded from Georgia in the early 1990s.

In contrast, the war made the United States appear ineffectual and irrelevant. First, the George W. Bush administration failed to restrain Mikhail Saakashvili from taking reckless action against South Ossetia, provoking Russia's darkest suspicions about Washington's motives. It then failed to come to Tbilisi's rescue once the war began, raising questions among US allies along Russia's borders about its credibility as a guarantor of security. Europe seemed equally disjointed. In a largely symbolic move, the North Atlantic Treaty Organization (NATO) froze relations with Russia because of Moscow's disproportionate use of force, while also putting enlargement plans for Georgia and Ukraine on the back-burner, essentially fulfilling a long-time Russian wish. The media briefly discussed sanctions by Western countries against Russia, although such measures were never under serious consideration.

A year and a half later, the picture looks less rosy for Russia. No other country in the Collective Security Treaty Organization (CSTO)—the mutual security pact of six CIS states—has recognized the independence of Abkhazia and South Ossetia. Russia has tried to cast this in a more positive light: Prime Minister Putin says that such de jure recognition is unnecessary and what really matters is Russia's protection and support for the two provinces; for his part, Medvedev reports that several foreign leaders privately complain that they would recognize Abkhazia and South Ossetia if only they could, citing diverse reasons—from sensitivity to ethnic disputes to outside pressure. Although both Putin and Medvedev may be right, the wider context is clear: Not a single Russian ally wants—or can afford—to be seen as Moscow's satellite.

Other indicators suggest that Russia's plans for a regional political system centered on Moscow are not taking shape. In 2005 there was glee in Moscow when Uzbek President Islam Karimov closed US military bases in his country and rejoined the CSTO and later the Russia-led Eurasian Economic Community (EurAsEc). That same year, Karimov brutally suppressed a revolt in the city of Andijan, making him a pariah in the West and something of a prodigal son in Moscow. The mood has changed since then, however. Uzbekistan is unhappy with the terms of its economic cooperation with Russia, angry about Russia's plan to establish a second military base in neighboring Kyrgyzstan, and warming to the presence of the US military.

Even smaller countries in Central Asia are feeling similarly emboldened to contradict Moscow's preferences. For years Russia had publicly expressed its desire to see a US air base in Kyrgyzstan closed. And in early 2009 Kyrgyzstan obliged: It was seeking a large economic assistance package from Russia and sought to please Moscow by expelling the US military from the facility. But some months later the seemingly disorganized and cash-strapped Kyrgyz government managed a double act: It allowed the United States to stay, raised the rent on the use of the base, and also received the Russian aid package worth around $2 billion. Moscow was left bewildered by Bishkek's volte-face and had to be content with the promise of its own base in Kyrgyzstan.

After the war in Georgia, Russia was very keen to demonstrate that drawing new borders around Abkhazia and South Ossetia was a special case and that it was serious about its responsibility as a peacekeeper and facilitator in the contested enclaves of Nagorno-Karabakh and Transnistria. Medvedev held a series of joint meetings with the presidents of Armenia and Azerbaijan and conferred with the president of Moldova. Yet, there has been no breakthrough in any of these conflicts, and it has become clear that Moscow is unable to single-handedly broker any peace settlement.

Before the global economic crisis struck in fall 2008, the Kremlin was confident that Russia was on the rise as an economic and geopolitical powerhouse. In June 2008 Medvedev hailed the Russian ruble as the region's future reserve currency. Since then, Russian reserves have shrunk, and the ruble has lost much of its value and potential appeal as an international currency. When Moscow offered Minsk $500 million worth of rubles instead of dollars—in a reversal of an earlier agreement—the Belarusians felt short-changed and insulted.

The crisis has hit Russia harder than any other major country. The Russian economy has only grown more dependent on oil and gas since its default in 1998. As global commodity prices dropped, so did Russia's GDP, falling more than 10 percent between mid-2008 and mid-2009. Still, other CIS countries have been affected even more severely: Ukraine's GDP contracted nearly 20 percent. Conscious of this, Moscow is attempting to use the crisis as an opportunity, offering cash to its neighbors in the hope that economic assistance can buy a measure of political influence. Kyrgyzstan, as seen earlier, played this game to its benefit. Ukraine never claimed the $5 billion Russia offered it to help with its energy needs and instead chose to bypass Russia and secure a much smaller sum from the European Union to modernize its gas transportation network. As for Belarus, Minsk collected most of the $2 billion package offered by Moscow but then quickly became embroiled in a dispute with Russia over issues ranging from the two countries' trade in dairy products to conditions for industrial privatization in Belarus.

At the same time, Moscow suspended its 16-year quest for membership in the World Trade Organization (WTO). Instead, it championed the creation of a supranational customs union comprising Belarus, Kazakhstan, and Russia, which has yet to be implemented and may take a long time shaping up. Although Russia was certainly frustrated with protracted negotiations and saw an opening for crisis-related opportunism, Moscow's decision to abandon WTO membership showed its ambition and desire to reorder its foreign policy priorities. The snag—and irony—was that as Moscow took this momentous decision, its spat with Minsk exposed the officially existing (on paper) Russo-Belarusian union state as a sham. The union's 10th anniversary in December 2009 was marked by new bitter rows over Moscow's withdrawal of oil and gas subsidies for Minsk.

Since 2003, when the United States invaded Iraq, Mikhail Khodorkovsky's Yukos company got in trouble, and oil prices started their spectacular five-year-long rise, Moscow had championed its new position as an energy power, comparing its oil and gas resources to the nuclear arsenal that once gave the Soviet Union superpower status during the Cold War. But the use of energy as a weapon proved to be a disaster, as the state oil giant Gazprom's clumsy gas cut-offs to Ukraine in 2006 and 2009 made clear. Over the past several years, Gazprom has been scrambling to buy the gas produced by other CIS countries and to maintain control over its export routes. In 2003 it acquired rights to the entire gas production of Turkmenistan for the next 25 years; and in 2007 Russia agreed with Kazakhstan, Turkmenistan, and Uzbekistan to build a new pipeline from the Caspian Sea.

By 2009, however, much of this unraveled. Gazprom's relations with Turkmenistan have soured: A newly price-conscious Russian government refused to buy any gas from Turkmenistan in the spring of 2009, leading the Turkmen government to look West for new customers. By the end of the year, China completed a gas pipeline that begins in Turkmenistan and heads east—the Caspian region's first pipeline that does not traverse Russian territory. Ironically, it is Beijing, not the West, that has broken Moscow's historical monopoly on gas transit from the region.

Thus, the fear of a Russian "gas caliphate" in Central Asia was revealed as a myth. At the beginning of 2010, there was no gas war between Moscow and Kiev: On the eve of Ukrainian presidential elections, the Russians had resolved to reach an agreement on prices and transit fees without recourse to ultimate measures. In its previous gas crises with Ukraine, Russia did the wrong things (shutting off supplies to Ukraine and thereby to Europe) for the right reasons (claiming a fair price for its product). The result was doubly damaging for Russia: Its reputation as a reliable gas exporter was left in tatters, and Europe finally decided it needed to find alternative energy sources. As a result, the Nabucco pipeline—which Europe imagined as an alternative supply route of natural gas and Russia long derided as infeasible—started to look more realistic. Russia, for its part, has been able to sign a deal with Turkey on Blue Stream II, which could potentially reach Israel. In the end, Europe will continue to depend heavily on Russian gas supplies, but Russia will have to tolerate multiple pipelines from the Caspian going in all directions.

Finally, the demonstration of Russian military power in Georgia has done nothing to forestall a deteriorating security situation in Russia's own North Caucasus region. The republics of Ingushetia and Dagestan are especially dangerous flashpoints, and Chechnya, newly pacified after years of war, is again experiencing a spate of terrorist attacks. Moscow's strategy of buying off corrupt local elites in the region has not purchased stability. Islamist radicals thrive on official corruption, interclan warfare, and the heavy-handedness of the police and security services. As a result, Russia's grip on the North Caucasus is loosening, and the failure to stabilize the situation there could result in terrorists and extremists turning the mountainous region into a base along the lines of Pakistan's northwestern frontier province. Conscious of the seriousness of the situation, Moscow decided in early 2010 to carve out the North Caucasus from the Southern federal district and place it under control of a special viceroy.

South of the mountains, the situation presents different challenges. Abkhazia and South Ossetia may be the only places in the former Soviet space that firmly fall into the Russian sphere of influence. But each poses a problem. In Abkhazia, Putin has said that Russian recognition was enough. But in the long term, Abkhazia wants to become a genuinely independent state and not a protectorate on Russia's Black Sea coast. The Abkhaz presidential election of December 2009 was generally free and fair—ironically, more so than elections in the Russian Federation itself. In South Ossetia, the situation is the reverse: Contrary to Russia's wishes, it probably cannot become a viable state, but its otherwise seemingly natural accession to the neighboring North Ossetia in Russia would be seen by Russia's neighbors as evidence of Moscow reverting to the historical pattern of territorial aggrandizement.

Russia may have many interests and a measure of influence, but it does not have—and is unlikely to have—anything it can call a "zone." Yet, Russia is hampered by its territorial thinking, a view in which the world is set up as a handful of imperial poles battling for influence in smaller countries. Such an understanding ignores the real nature of contemporary global politics and will surely lead to failure.

At the same time Russia aspires to primacy in the former Soviet space; it craves equality with the United States and the European Union in the Euro-Atlantic area. In a 2007 speech at the Munich Security Conference, Putin made clear that Russia no longer accepted the rules of the game set after the collapse of the Soviet Union, when Russia was weak. Putin's declaratory revisionism was backed up by Russia's suspension of its responsibilities under the Conventional Forces in Europe Treaty. Then, as tensions over Georgia rose in 2008, Moscow resumed its air patrols off the coasts of Europe and North America and sent its bombers and navy ships on missions to Venezuela. The message from Moscow was clear: Ignoring Russian security interests could be hazardous.

Although the Kremlin did succeed in proving its strategic independence from the United States, there could be no talk of Russia's overall equality with America and Europe. Moscow's problem with the West is that it would not become a junior partner of the United States/European Union and would not be accepted by them as an equal. Thus, while Medvedev was right to call attention to the issue of Russia's absence from meaningful European security structures, the notion of a treaty that would de facto block further NATO enlargement has been roundly rejected, as has the idea that Europe's security should be jointly managed by a troika of the United States and NATO, the European Union, and Russia and the CSTO. The draft text of such a treaty, made public in November 2009, leaves one with the conclusion that, while the issue of an inclusive security space in the Euro-Atlantic is as relevant as ever, the specific proposal for creating a latter-day League of Nations is definitely flawed.

Similarly, the idea of a grand bargain—Washington's acquiescence to Moscow's dominance in the former Soviet states on Russia's borders in exchange for Russia's support for US and Western policies in the Middle East and elsewhere—is a chimera. Unlike during the Great Game of the 19th century, the political futures of these countries—such as Georgia, Moldova, and Ukraine—will not be decided by strategists in Washington or Moscow but by people on the ground. Thus, the issue of NATO membership in Ukraine has been put on a back-burner not by Moscow's opposition to it, or lack of interest in Washington, but rather by the Ukrainian people themselves, who, in the 2010 presidential election, voted out the one Ukrainian leader for whom joining NATO was an article of faith: Viktor Yushchenko.

In the 21st century, the power of attraction trumps that of coercion, which runs contrary to the view of many in the Russian leadership that the world is composed of sovereign empires competing over zones of influence. Russia, a nuclear superpower, is fighting a losing battle for influence in Ukraine, Moldova (where the post-Soviet generation looks to the European Union), and even Belarus (where younger urbanites consider themselves European). Georgia is overwhelmingly pro-Western, largely because Moscow's policies over the last two decades have made the population vehemently anti-Russian. Azerbaijan, in contrast, has managed to do business with Western oil companies while staying on friendly terms with Moscow and avoiding being dominated by it. Armenia notionally depends on Russian security guarantees but as a result of the continued Russia-Georgia confrontation it is more physically isolated from Russia. Recently, Armenia engaged in a dialogue with Turkey, which ultimately promised to lift a 16-year-old economic blockade imposed by Ankara at the height of the conflict over Karabakh.

This suggests that the vision of a "binary Europe"—made up of the NATO/EU community in the west and the center and a Russian-led bloc in the east—is less likely now than at any moment since the end of the Cold War. Even if bodies such as the CSTO and the customs union become more competent and effective, their effectiveness will be limited by Moscow's desire to turn them into its own policy instruments—a development that clashes with the interests of Russia's closest partners in Belarus and Kazakhstan.

Russia's Great Power Pretensions Need a Reality Check

The Kremlin leadership consciously ignores the relative modesty of Russia's economic potential, its dependency on raw materials, and its technological backwardness. Russia has slightly over 140 million people, produces around 2 percent of global GDP, has a level of economic productivity four times lower than that of the United States, and is dependent on fluctuations in the price of oil. Such a country may wield a measure of power and influence with distant partners and near neighbors but needs a monumental effort to upgrade its economic clout, technological prowess, and societal appeal before it can claim the status of a world-class power center.

In the tsarist and Soviet past, Russia compensated for its weakness and backwardness with superior manpower, political centralism, and militarization of its industry. Today, it is unable to do the same. The country is in the midst of a demographic crisis that threatens to cut its population to 120 million or less by mid-century. Raw military power is also on the decline. Russia's remaining nuclear arsenal aside, its defense industry is no longer capable of producing a full range of weapons systems and it has been forced to buy arms from abroad, such as drones from Israel and ships from France. The continuing test failures of the Bulava ballistic missile suggest that even Russia's superior nuclear weapons sector is plagued with deficiencies.

Three hundred years ago, the newly reformed Russian army defeated Swedish forces at the Battle of Poltava, heralding Russia's emergence as a European power. This long historical era has now come to an end. Russia is the European Union's largest and most important neighbor, but emphasizing power relationships is not to Russia's advantage. The currency of world politics has changed, and Russia will have to work hard to acquire it. Unfortunately, Russia's leadership is looking not so much to build a new power base at home but to find detours to borrow power from others.

In the summer of 2009, Ekaterinburg, the regional capital of the Urals, hosted three international summits at nearly the same time: the CSTO; the Shanghai Cooperation Organization (SCO); and the first meeting of the leaders of the BRIC countries.

Moscow has been keen to promote closer links among the leading non-Western powers in order to expedite the withering of US global hegemony and to establish a multipolar world order in its place. In his 2007 speech in Munich, Putin sounded like not only the leader of Russia but also the spokesman for the non-West. He was the only major world figure willing—and who thought he could afford—to openly challenge US foreign policy.

But the BRIC summit provided little more than a rare photo-op. The effects of the economic crisis made many analysts talk about BIC—rather than BRIC—because Russia's resource-based economy has been much harder hit than China's, India's, or Brazil's. Russia's approach to foreign policy bears little resemblance to that of the other BRIC countries. China, India, and Brazil are all WTO members and have been active in the Doha Round of trade negotiations, whereas Russia has deprioritized its accession process to the WTO. Geopolitically, China is cautious and India is insular, but Russia is assertive and openly revisionist. Russia's plans to use the BRIC to boost itself to a higher international orbit are unlikely to do the trick. The Chinese and the Indians are notorious *Alleingaengers* and now tend to look down on the Russians. Brazil, meanwhile, is just getting on its feet as an emerging world power.

Although Russian-Chinese collaboration is growing—as within the SCO—China is emerging as the state driving the bilateral agenda. For the first time in three hundred years, China is more powerful and dynamic than Russia—and it can back up its economic and security interests with hefty infusions of cash. In recent months, Beijing has offered $10 billion to countries in Central Asia; provided a currency swap to Belarus, which was haggling with Russia over the terms of the dollar credit; and found a billion dollars of aid for faraway Moldova, double Moscow's promised sum. It is worth remembering that China refused to recognize the independence of Abkhazia and South Ossetia in August 2008, setting an example for the SCO's Central Asian members, who followed Beijing's lead.

The conclusion is not that Russia has no useful role to play in its own neighborhood, in the Euro-Atlantic area, or on the global stage. Russia's foreign policy priorities and objectives must change. Seeking political status and economic rents will end in failure and, in the process, waste precious resources and only breed more disappointment and resentment among Russia's elites and public. Russia needs a new foreign policy commensurate with its needs, size, and capacity—one that is shaped by the realities of the 21st century's globalized environment. In short, Russia needs to focus on overcoming its economic, social, and political backwardness, with foreign policy as a resource toward meeting this supreme national interest.

Sketching Russia's Way Forward

Moscow's first priority should be Russia and its people, geared toward strengthening the country's own economic, intellectual, and social potential. Attempts to restore a "soft" equivalent of an empire would not add to Russia but only take away from it. This does not mean that Russia should ignore its close neighbors (which would be impossible) or shy away from close cooperation with them (which would be foolish). Instead, Russia's looming demographic crisis requires it to learn to win over people rather than "collect" lands and integrate many of them as full citizens.

Soft power should be central to Russia's foreign policy. Across the post-Soviet world, Russia possesses precious and virtually unused elements of this kind of power: Its language is widely used from Riga to Almaty, and Russian culture, from Pushkin to pop, is still in big demand. If Russia rebuilds its infrastructure, opportunities for higher education—especially in science—and research and development could become exceedingly attractive for its neighbors. And if Russia manages to fundamentally change how its political system and economy are run, the benefits become even more dramatic: Russian business interests would no longer be perceived as agents of the Kremlin and could become more welcome abroad; a Russian language television channel could become a Russophone version of Al Jazeera, and the Russian Orthodox Church could gain authority outside Russia if it were seen as a transnational institution and not an extension of the state. But such a vision would require transcending the model of a Russia defined by its leader—whether Yeltsin, Putin, or Medvedev—and instead envisage a Russia of multiple actors where the nation, and not the authorities, is sovereign.

Under such a strategy, policy toward Ukraine could become a touchstone. Rather than pressuring its neighbor not to defect to the West, Russia must reach out to the Ukrainian people directly, to attract new business opportunities, new workers, and new students. The Caucasus is another test: Solving the conundrum of Russia's relationship with Georgia and the final status of Abkhazia and South Ossetia are a sine qua non of Russia assuming the role of a benevolent regional leader. Meanwhile, settling the conflicts in Nagorno-Karabakh and Transnistria will require Russia to work alongside the European Union, the United States, Turkey, Ukraine, and the parties to the conflicts themselves.

Russia needs hard power, too, but the kind that addresses the challenges of the present, not the past. It needs a well-trained and well-equipped mobile army to deal with crises along its vast border, as well as a modern air force and navy. In many cases, Russia will not be acting alone. It will need to master the mechanisms of military and security cooperation in Eurasia with its allies in the CSTO, its Euro-Atlantic partners in NATO, and its Asian neighbors such as China, India, and Japan.

Rather than focusing on status and the international pecking order, Russia now must overcome its "institutional deficit" in relations with the West. Accordingly, it needs to identify modernization—not only technological or economic but sociopolitical as well—as its top priority. Consistent with this view, the principal task of Russian foreign policy—alongside protecting national security—must be to tap external resources for domestic transformation.

Such a vision prioritizes relations with developed countries that can provide technology, expertise, and investment. Luckily, the European Union, Japan, and the United States are Russia's direct neighbors, a fact that Russia can use to further regional development in areas near these shared borders, from the Kola Peninsula to Kamchatka and the Kurile Islands. Due to its geographical proximity and Russia's European roots, the European Union is Russia's most important partner for modernization. A 2005 EU-Russian agreement defined four areas for cooperation—economy, justice and internal security, culture and human contacts, and external relations—which are precisely the areas in which closer ties with the European Union would contribute to Russia's own transformation.

Russia's goal should not be to join the European Union but to create a common European economic space with it. When Russia finally joins the WTO, a free trade area between the European Union and Russia—with Belarus, Kazakhstan, Ukraine, and others joining in—will become possible. Energy could likely form the underlying basis for this common space, but to do so EU-Russian energy trade must be transformed from an area of contention into a tool of integration. Visa-free travel would also be a central human element of this new arrangement. As a guiding principle, former EU Commission president Romano Prodi's formulation—the European Union and Russia "sharing everything but the institutions"—remains sound and valid.

As Europe's own experience shows, such a common economic space can exist only in an atmosphere of trust and confidence. Therefore, Russia must seek to create a Euro-Atlantic security order that would finally demilitarize relations from Vancouver to Vladivostok, as was once said at the end of the Cold War. To this end, Russia must be convinced to give up its lingering suspicion of US power and intentions, and countries in Central and Eastern Europe must similarly be induced to let go of their fear of Russia. On the US side, this means moving away from the institutionalized hostility enshrined in mutually assured destruction, by pursuing a policy centered on collaboration on strategic defenses rather than on regulating strategic arsenals. Russia, meanwhile, should end its obsession with NATO and instead use joint projects with the alliance and its member states for its own defense modernization (but not seek NATO membership—to both keep its strategic independence and maintain relations with China on an even keel). Also, Russia's reconciliation with its Central and Eastern European neighbors is indispensable: For Moscow, Europe no longer starts on the Elbe but on the Narova and the Niemen. In Europe, multilateralism has taken over from multipolarity, and it is time for Moscow to pay attention.

China is one of Russia's leading trade partners and a fast-growing market that could also become a major source of capital investment. In addition, Beijing is an indispensable partner in assuring security and stability in Russia's near abroad, from Central and Northeast Asia to the greater Middle East. As such, there is no alternative to friendly and cooperative relations with Beijing. A key challenge for Russia's foreign policy will be to learn to live alongside a China that is strong, dynamic, assertive, and increasingly more advanced. This will require keen knowledge and deep understanding of Russia's great neighbor.

Russia's territory extends all the way to the Pacific, making it more of a Euro-Pacific power than a Euro-Asian one. The United States is its neighbor to the east, right across the Bering Strait. In fact, there are far fewer points of contention between Washington and Moscow in the Pacific than there are in the Atlantic or the Caspian. Russia's 21st century frontier lies to the east, where it has both a need and a chance to catch up with its immediate neighbors: China, Japan, and Korea. The global power shift toward the Pacific necessitates a new focus in Russia's foreign policy.

A new emphasis on the Pacific Rim would develop not only the Russian Far East but also the many time zones that lie between Vladivostok and St. Petersburg. Such a focus would turn Siberia—Russia's long-time periphery—into a genuinely central region. It would also push Russia to pursue economic opportunities in the Arctic Ocean, which is emerging as a potentially rich and productive area. The Arctic, which brings together Europe, North America, and Russia, is an area whose very harshness prizes cooperation.

Russia would better serve its interests by strengthening ties to the world's most relevant and influential actors, rather than focusing on power balances and exclusive zones. And instead of favoring the United Nations merely for the privilege of a veto right in the Security Council, Russia needs to engage in producing global public goods. Thus, closer to home it should focus on conflict resolution, as in the Caucasus and Moldova; in Asia and the Middle East, on reducing religious extremism and building political stability. With an indigenous Muslim population that has grown by 40 percent since 1989, Russia has a role to play in the Christian-Muslim dialogue. Finally, Russia could select functional areas where it could make a difference—whether energy security, climate change, clean water, or international law. Devising, together with the European Union, a new international energy charter; reducing its own vastly inefficient use of energy; protecting clean water and forest resources of Siberia; and helping find political and legal formulas to resolve conflicts in the neighborhood could become Russia's significant contributions to international well-being.

Acquiring a new role after 500 years as an empire, 70 years as an ideological warrior, and 40 years as a military superpower will be difficult. Russia's post-Soviet comeback proved those anticipating Russia's descent into irrelevance wrong. It will certainly survive the present economic crisis. But Russia has a long way to go before it becomes a modern state capable of pursuing a foreign policy in line with its needs and not its nostalgias. It will not formally join the West as its former satellites have done and as its erstwhile borderlands may do. But as Russia becomes more modern as a result of domestic transformation—and adapts its foreign policy accordingly—it can emerge as a serious, desirable, and indispensable partner, as well as a significant global actor.

Over the long term, the present global economic crisis can be a major driver of change. It is widely recognized that Russia cannot return to the model of growth without development, which characterized the precrisis "fat years" of high and rising energy prices. Russians also note that the world around them is surging ahead, drawing lessons from the crisis. Russian leaders, of course, are extremely jealous of the power they wield domestically, but they are also jealous of the place their country occupies in the international system. Paradoxically, great power mentality, which used to be an obstacle to modernization, may push it in the future, but only if great powerdom is redefined in terms of technological advances, economic competitiveness, social attractiveness, and a capacity to produce global public goods. This will require a broad and comprehensive, rather than limited and "conservative," vision of modernization.

Putting too much faith in a handful of leaders is certainly a risky proposition. Other potential drivers of change may be a financial crunch that would require a fiscal reform abolishing a low flat income tax. The Russian budget is feeling the pain of deficit, and the country is about to resume borrowing abroad for the first time since the 1998 default. For a decade, Russians have enjoyed a regime that, in fact, did not require the growing middle class to pay much in terms of taxes. Seen from the other end, the federal budget has not depended much on citizens' contributions. In a way, the state and the people have lived in different financial worlds. When and if this changes, the issue of government accountability may arise for the first time in post-Soviet Russia.

Finally, an hour of truth is nearing on a number of fronts. Russia's conventional forces, even when they are eventually reformed—which will take more than a decade—will have only a limited capacity to act beyond the country's borders. More important, the Russian defense-industrial base will have to be fundamentally restructured to support even that capacity. The Russian civilian aircraft industry will have to decide whether it partners with Airbus or Boeing, or both. The Russian car industry has already essentially turned itself into an assembly line for European, American, and Japanese manufacturers. Russia's integration with the global economy will continue, making it harder to indulge in nostalgias of the imperial, and isolationist, past.

For Russia, the age of empire is definitely over, but postimperial adjustment continues. Russia's task is harder than that of Europe's former great powers, who were helped into their postimperial phases by security integration with the Atlantic alliance and economic and eventually political integration with what is now the European Union. Those countries, however, have lost both their imperial possessions *and* great power status: There are no great powers in today's Europe.

Russia's ambition is precisely to remain a great power, i.e., an independent strategic player on the global level and a center of attraction in Eurasia. This is difficult, especially given Russia's relative backwardness and declining population, but not absolutely impossible. Realizing this ambition will require the Russian people as a whole, including the country's elite, to go through a seminal transformation, economic, social, political, and cultural. This transformation will obviously take many years, even decades, but the next ten years are crucial. They will provide the answer to whether Russia is headed north or south.

10

Foreign Economic Policy at a Crossroads

DAVID G. TARR AND NATALYA VOLCHKOVA

Russia is the largest economy outside the World Trade Organization (WTO) and—along with Azerbaijan, Belarus, Kazakhstan, Tajikistan, and Uzbekistan of the Commonwealth of Independent States (CIS)—is among the 29 countries that were attempting to accede to the WTO in April 2010.[1] The Working Party on the accession of the Russian Federation to the WTO, established in June 16, 1993, comprises about 60 countries and is the largest such Working Party in the history of the WTO. By the spring of 2007, Russia had successfully concluded bilateral agreements with all the Working Party members who sought such an agreement except Georgia.[2] The focus now is on the multilateral phase of the negotiations, where considerable progress has been made so that by mid-2008 only three issues remained to be resolved: (1) level of permitted trade-distorting subsidies in agriculture, (2) export taxes on Russian timber, and (3) rules on state trading enterprises. These issues, however, remain on the table.

During the years of the Vladimir Putin presidency, Russia actively sought membership in the WTO, which was seen as part of an open economy model of economic development. However, in recent years, in its efforts to diversify its economy away from energy and raw material dependence, Russia has employed several industrial policy and import-

David G. Tarr is a consultant and former lead economist with the World Bank and adjunct professor of international economics at the New Economic School, Moscow. Natalya Volchkova has been assistant professor of economics at the New Economic School since 2007.

1. As of June 2009, 153 countries were WTO members. Trade among them represented 97 percent of the world's trade turnover, including over 94 percent of foodstuffs.

2. Georgia had agreed to a bilateral agreement on Russian WTO accession but has withdrawn from that agreement.

substitution industrialization measures. We discuss why we believe that Russia's trade and foreign direct investment (FDI) policies for the future are at a critical crossroads. We begin by summarizing the estimates of what Russia will gain from WTO accession and why. Estimates place these gains at about $53 billion per year in the medium term and $177 billion per year in the long term, due largely to Russia's own commitments to reform in the business services sectors. In the next sections, we summarize the principal Russian reform commitments in the WTO and compare them with those of other acceding countries. We find that the demands on Russia are comparable to those on other transition countries. We then discuss prospects for the Russia-Belarus-Kazakhstan customs union and related WTO accession issues. In a separate section we explain why Russian WTO accession will result in the elimination of the Jackson-Vanik Amendment against Russia. In the last sections we discuss Russian policies to attract FDI and argue that uniform tariffs would yield substantial benefits for Russia, but preshipment inspection would yield marginal benefits at best. We conclude that Russian WTO accession is crucial for Russia. Due to pressure from the international community, WTO accession represents a unique historical opportunity for Russia to overcome the usual domestic political economy forces that have led to excessive protection. On the other hand, the economic gains to the international community from Russia's accession will likely be small. For Russia to successfully diversify its economy, it will have to reform its institutions to improve the business climate, especially for small and medium enterprises.

Gains from WTO Accession to Russia

The WTO accession process is an important tool that countries can use for economic development. WTO accession affects a wide range of policies and institutions, including tariff policy, customs administration, standards, rights of foreign investors (especially in services), agricultural policy, intellectual property, and possibly government procurement. It therefore represents a time for evaluating a country's regulations and an opportunity to implement important trade, FDI, and institutional changes. In many cases, Russia implemented changes prior to accession to adapt to post-WTO requirements; in other cases, commitments may be implemented only several years after accession due to a negotiated adjustment period. These cumulative changes will move the economy toward an open trade and investment model of economic development and away from an import-substitution industrialization economic model.

The World Bank has commissioned several studies on the consequences of WTO accession for the Russian Ministry of Economic Development and Trade. Jesper Jensen, Thomas Rutherford, and David Tarr estimated that in the medium term, Russia should annually gain about 3.3 percent of

Russian GDP (or about $53 billion per year based on 2008 GDP at market exchange rates).[3] In the long term, when the positive impact on the invest- ment climate is incorporated, the gains should increase to about 11 percent of the value of Russian GDP per year (or about $177 billion per year at market exchange rates).[4]

Rutherford and Tarr examined household and poverty impacts and found that virtually all households should gain from WTO accession.[5] They found that skilled labor and urban households gain relatively more than average due to the increase in FDI in the skill-intensive business ser- vices sectors. Rich households gain less than the average household, since increased competition from foreign investment results in capital gaining less than labor. The poorest households are estimated to gain at about the level of the average household.

Given the vast geographic diversity of Russia, Rutherford and Tarr employed a ten-region model of Russia to estimate how impacts would vary across regions.[6] They estimated that all regions should gain substan- tially, but those most successful at attracting FDI and creating a good in- vestment climate would gain the most.[7]

In a study for the Russian Ministry of Communications, Jensen, Ruther- ford, and Tarr examined the impacts on Russia's telecommunications sector and found that skilled workers in the sector would gain substantially from FDI.[8] Russian firms that become part of joint ventures with foreign inves- tors would likely preserve or increase the value of their investments; but

---

3. Jesper Jensen, Thomas Rutherford, and David Tarr, "The Impact of Liberalizing Barriers to Foreign Direct Investment in Services: The Case of Russian Accession to the World Trade Organization," *Review of Development Economics* 11, no. 3 (August 2007): 482–506.

4. Russia's GDP at market exchange rates is estimated at $1.61 trillion by the World Bank, $1.68 trillion by the IMF, and $1.76 trillion by the CIA, making it either the eighth or ninth largest economy in the world. Based on purchasing power parity (PPP) exchange rates, Russia's GDP was $2.3 trillion in 2008, making it the sixth largest economy in the world— larger than the United Kingdom or France. At PPP exchange rates, the estimated gains per year for WTO accession would rise to about $76 billion per year in the medium term and $253 billion per year in the long term.

5. Thomas Rutherford and David Tarr, "Poverty Effects of Russia's WTO Accession: Modeling Real Households and Endogenous Productivity Effects," *Journal of International Economics* 75, no. 1 (2008): 131–50.

6. Thomas Rutherford and David Tarr, "Regional Impacts of Russia's Accession to the WTO," *Review of International Economics* 18, no. 1 (2010): 30–46.

7. They estimate that as a percent of consumption in the medium term the three regions in their model that will gain the most are the Northwest (11.2 percent), St. Petersburg (10.6 percent), and the Far East (9.7 percent) while the Urals (6.2 percent) gains the least.

8. Jesper Jensen, Thomas Rutherford, and David Tarr, "Telecommunications Reform within Russia's Accession to the WTO," *Eastern European Economics* 44, no. 1 (January-February 2006): 25–58.

Russian capital owners in the telecom sector who remain wholly independent of multinational firms would likely see the value of their investments decline. Households dependent on capital income from such independent firms would likely lose from WTO accession. Rutherford and Tarr estimated a similar distribution of gains in other business services sectors.[9]

In summary, these studies indicate that Russia will reap substantial gains from WTO accession: The benefits are widespread and would reduce poverty, regions with a better investment climate would reap greater gains, and, crucially, most of the gains would be due to Russia's commitments to implement its own reforms. Reforms in the services sectors are the most important of Russia's own reforms that produce the gains.

However, these studies did not find that WTO accession would contribute positively to the diversification objective of the Russian government. The sectors they estimated would expand the most are nonferrous metals, ferrous metals, and chemicals, while light industry, food processing, and construction materials are likely to contract. These estimates suggest that less than 10 percent of the gains come from improved market access for Russian exporters. Russia has already negotiated most favored nation (MFN) status or better with all its significant trading partners. While Russian exporters will be accorded additional legal benefits in antidumping cases once Russia is a WTO member—and this is the source of the gains estimated in these studies—many economists are skeptical of the fairness of antidumping proceedings. This suggests that significant differences in determinations against Russian exporters in antidumping cases should not be expected, and improved market access therefore cannot be the source of substantial gains to Russia from WTO accession.[10]

Given that the benefits to Russia of WTO accession come from its own internal reforms, and since Russia could unilaterally implement these reforms, some infer that Russia will gain little from WTO accession. We take the opposite view, since the process of WTO accession is a unique historical opportunity to achieve reform.

The key reason that WTO accession is important is the political economy dimension. Since the benefits to industries that achieve protection are concentrated, industry groups typically lobby for protection. On the other

9. Rutherford and Tarr, "Poverty Effects of Russia's WTO Accession."

10. In addition, members of the WTO obtain rights in international trade. Members are granted permanent most favored nation status to the markets of other member states. So Russia will not have to be concerned about annual renewals of MFN status. Members can also use the WTO's dispute settlement procedures to protect their trade interests, such as in antidumping cases. Trade disputes among WTO members are resolved based on WTO legal agreements under which smaller countries have the potential to win disputes against large countries. All WTO agreements require unanimous consent of all the members, which helps provide a voice for the smaller member countries. On the other hand, nonmembers are affected by the new rules of this dominant organization in international trade with no voice in their formation.

hand, since the benefits to consumers are diverse and less concentrated, they typically do not lobby against protection but hope others with similar interests will lobby on their behalf. This "free rider problem" in political decision making results in an absence of representation of the views of the consumer and broader economic interests from political discussions of tariffs. Lobbying and political economy considerations often allow special interests to strongly influence policy so that reforms are slow. WTO accession, however, requires across-the-board reform in many sectors, and the pressure of a WTO negotiation engages policymakers at the highest levels of government. Experience has shown that high-level policymakers, who have the economywide interest in mind, often intervene to impose reform on slow-moving ministries. In the case of Russia, the process began to move when Putin made WTO accession a priority in his first term.

It is difficult to argue that Russia would have made reforms as widespread and as deep as it has without the external pressure of WTO accession. Reforms that are accomplished in the context of WTO accession would not normally be achieved so quickly. That is, WTO bindings and external pressure make it easier for a government to adopt a trade policy designed to promote growth and reduce poverty. Moreover, unlike unilateral reforms, once a country commits to a reform at the WTO, it is bound by an international commitment that is difficult to reverse in the future by a less reform-minded government. The process of negotiating bilateral market access with the countries in its WTO Working Party on accession has dramatically increased reform of Russia's trade and foreign investment regimes, thereby helping the country move toward an open economy model of economic development.[11]

Russia's Commitments to Foreign Exporters and Investors

Nonagricultural Market Access

Russia agreed to reduce its bound MFN tariffs to about 8 percent on average. Shepotylo and Tarr show that for 2005, Russia's MFN tariffs were about 12.1 percent on a simple average basis or 14 percent on a trade-weighted basis, taking into account the ad valorem equivalents of Russia's specific tariffs.[12] Thus, a cut of average Russian tariffs to 8 percent implies a decline of about 50 percent on average.

---

11. For details, see US Trade Representative, Fact Sheets on the Russia-United States Bilateral Agreement on Russian WTO Accession, November 2006, www.ustr.gov.

12. Oleksandr Shepotylo and David Tarr, "Specific Tariffs, Tariff Simplification, and the Structure of Import Tariffs in Russia: 2001–2005," *Eastern European Economics* 46, no. 5 (September–October 2008), 49–58.

Services

The business services sector has been the subject of some of the most intense negotiations associated with Russian accession. Russia has made numerous commitments in this area. It has agreed to increase the maximum share that foreign banks and insurance companies can attain from 15 to 50 percent and will phase out the prohibition of foreign participation in mandatory insurance lines. Russia reportedly agreed to terminate the Rostelecom monopoly on long-distance fixed-line telephone services as part of the Russia-EU bilateral agreement. (Multinational operators are already operating in the Russian mobile telephone market.) Russia will ensure national treatment and market access for a wide variety of professions, including lawyers, accountants, architects, engineers, marketing specialists, and health care professionals. Foreign-owned companies will be permitted to engage in wholesale and retail trade, franchising, and express courier services.[13] The European Union has negotiated intensely for the rights of companies other than Gazprom to construct a gas pipeline, but no success in this area has been reported.

In the banking sector, Russia was willing to allow subsidiaries of international banks. Subsidiaries must be registered as Russian entities, and the capital requirements would be based on capital in the Russian entity. But opposition galvanized around branch banking. Branches do not have a separate legal status or capital apart from their foreign parent bank. In general, entry into a country's banking sector is easier when branches are permitted, and the US Treasury has been attempting to ensure branch banking is permitted in all countries admitted to the WTO. The Russian central bank maintained that it could not regulate or supervise branches adequately and that depositors would therefore be at risk.

Banking interests in Russia succeeded in getting Putin himself to say that branch banking was a deal breaker for Russian WTO accession. Based on its bilateral agreement with the United States, Russia succeeded in avoiding a commitment on branch banking, becoming the only acceding country that is not a least developed country to avoid such a commitment.[14] Like many items in accession negotiations, succeeding in avoiding a commitment is a pyrrhic victory as Russia will lose the benefits from greater FDI. Nonetheless, multinational banks operating as subsidiaries have greater market access and national treatment rights under the bilateral US-Russia agreement and Russia should benefit from their greater involvement over time.

---

13. For details, see David G. Tarr, "Russian Accession to the WTO: An Assessment," *Eurasian Geography and Economics* 48, no. 3 (May–June 2007), 306–19.

14. Russia will have to reopen discussions on this issue upon consideration of membership in the OECD.

Agriculture

Agricultural issues have been among the most contentious in Russia's WTO accession negotiations. The key unresolved issue is agricultural subsidies. Russia, however, has made considerable commitments in market access as well as sanitary and phytosanitary negotiations. Disputes with the United States on beef, pork, and poultry exports were among the most significant. Under its bilateral market access agreement with the United States, Russia has made substantial concessions.

For poultry and pork products, instead of joint inspection of facilities, Russia agrees to allow the US Department of Agriculture Food Safety and Inspection Service to inspect and certify new facilities or facilities that need to remedy a deficiency. For beef, Russia and the United States agree to timely joint inspections of all facilities that will export to Russia. Once a joint inspection has been completed, the inspection process for poultry and pork exporters will apply. Russia made significant additional commitments to the United States to limit risks of trichinae in pork and of modern biotechnology products.

Are WTO Accession Demands on Russia Excessive?

Many observers have frequently alleged and come to believe that demands on Russia are either political or excessive by the standards of other countries that have acceded to the WTO. We believe, however, that the evidence contradicts this allegation. Aside from a couple of well-publicized cases where unusual demands were placed on Russia,[15] the demands are typical of the WTO accession process in the past 12 years. The process of acceding to the WTO since 1998 is a difficult one in which all acceding countries have been asked to take on very significant commitments to foreign exporters and investors. Compared with the commitments of these countries, the commitments required of Russia do not appear excessive.

Goods

Russia has agreed to bind its tariffs on goods at an average level of 8 percent, after an adjustment period.[16] This is slightly higher than that of most

---

15. One such example was the pressure on Russia to unify its domestic and export prices of natural gas. This demand, which occupied negotiators for considerable time and was eventually dropped by the European Union, would have imposed a very high cost on Russia. David Tarr and Peter Thomson, "The Merits of Dual Pricing of Russian Natural Gas," *World Economy* 27, no. 8 (August 2004): 1173–94.

16. US Trade Representative, Fact Sheets on the Russia-United States Bilateral Agreement on Russian WTO Accession.

countries that have acceded to the WTO since 1998.[17] The average tariffs for other acceding countries are: Saudi Arabia, 10.5 percent; Former Yugoslav Republic of Macedonia, 6.2 percent; Armenia, 7.5 percent; Chinese Taipei, 4.8 percent; China, 9.1 percent; Moldova, 6.0 percent; Croatia, 5.5 percent; Oman, 11.6 percent; Albania, 6.6 percent; Georgia, 6.5 percent; Jordan, 15.2 percent; Estonia, 7.3 percent; Latvia, 9.4 percent; and the Kyrgyz Republic, 6.7 percent.[18] Thus, by the standards of countries that have acceded to the WTO in the last eight years that are not least developed countries, Russia appears to have concluded market access negotiations with bound tariffs slightly higher than average, especially in comparison to the other transition countries, i.e., the Working Party has no excessive demands here.

Services

In the area of services, no simple measure like an average tariff is available. But an examination of commitments of the countries that have acceded to the WTO since 1998 shows that all of them have assumed a rather high and comprehensive level of commitments in terms of sectors included.[19] More detailed qualitative analysis of banking and insurance[20] does not suggest an above average level of commitments in these important sectors. On the contrary, as mentioned earlier, Russia has been able to avoid committing to branches of banks, unlike almost all of the other acceding countries.

Agriculture

The level of agricultural support permitted has become a major point of controversy for Russia, which is attempting to negotiate a high permitted Aggregate Measure of Support (AMS). However, despite the increase in Russian agricultural subsidies in recent years, the de minimis level of subsidies under WTO rules should allow Russia to subsidize at its present levels or higher.

17. World Trade Organization, "Technical Note on the Accession Process," Note by the Secretariat, WT/ACC/10/Rev.3 (November 28, 2005), www.wto.org.

18. Two least developed nations acceded with relatively high bound tariffs: Cambodia, 17.7 percent; and Nepal, 23.7 percent. But the WTO accords preferential status to developing countries.

19. World Trade Organization, "Technical Note on the Accession Process," table 5.

20. Tarr, "Russian Accession to the WTO: An Assessment."

Green Box Subsidies—Unconstrained

The WTO allows without constraint an extensive list of subsidies in agriculture that are not considered trade distorting—the so-called Green Box subsidies.[21] The worldwide trend is to move agricultural support away from trade-distorting subsidies toward Green Box measures. It is generally recognized that trade-distorting subsidies are a highly inefficient way of helping agricultural producers compared with Green Box measures. These measures, which focus on research and development and agricultural services to improve productivity, are more effective at creating a competitive agricultural sector in the long run.

Amber Box Subsidies: De Minimis Level

Trade-distorting subsidies to production—the so-called Amber Box subsidies—are constrained, but the de minimis levels of support allow developing countries to provide state support to agriculture of up to 20 percent of the value of aggregate agricultural output. Amber Box subsidies are either product-specific or non-product-specific. For developing countries, if product-specific Amber Box subsidies are below 10 percent of the gross value of agricultural production in the specific sector, the level of support is considered de minimis. In addition, a developing country may provide further Amber Box support on a non-product-specific basis and have it be defined as de minimis provided it is not above 10 percent of the gross value of agricultural production. Countries can self-classify their support between product- and non-product-specific support, subject only to dispute settlement, which is rarely used in this area.[22]

As part of their accession commitments, however, the countries of the former Soviet Union that have acceded to the WTO have had to accept developed-country de minimis limits (sometimes with an adjustment period). That is, Estonia, Latvia, Lithuania, Georgia, Armenia, Moldova, and the Kyrgyz Republic have all accepted 5 percent limits on product-specific agricultural subsidies and 5 percent limits on non-product-specific support. It is likely that Russia is being pressured to accept the same smaller developed-country de minimis limits on Amber Box subsidies. Regardless

---

21. Green Box subsidies include a wide range of publicly funded measures including research and development, pest control, general and specialist training, extension and advisory services, inspection services for health and sanitary reasons, marketing and promotion services, infrastructure services, including electricity, roads, and environmental expenditures, targeted support to low-income population through food stamps or subsidized prices, direct payments to producers to support income provided it has minimal trade-distorting features, crop insurance subsidies for natural disasters, adjustment assistance through producer retirement programs, and indirect income support not related to prices.

22. The de minimis levels of support for developed countries are one-half the allowed levels for developing countries. Post-accession, countries self-declare whether they are developed or developing.

of whether Russia declares itself a developed or developing country post-accession, if it agrees to the smaller level, its de minimis level of agricultural subsidies would be that for developed countries.

Aggregate Measure of Support (AMS) and the Russian Support Level

Incumbent members of the WTO, like the European Union, Canada, the United States, and Norway, have a base period for trade-distorting agricultural subsidies during which more substantial trade-distorting subsidies than the de minimis levels are permitted. The precedent among acceding countries, however, is that the three-year period prior to accession forms the base period for permitted trade-distorting subsidies, which are negotiated down from that base. Russia failed in the bilateral discussions to achieve its objective of defining 1992–94 as the base period for trade-distorting agricultural subsidies. It now hopes to be able to negotiate about $9 billion in subsidies.

The total value of state support to Russian agriculture in 2008 was about 163 billion rubles (or about $6.5 billion).[23] The Ministry of Finance data include all support to agriculture, including many items that would be considered Green Box (i.e., unconstrained) support. The total value of Russian agricultural output (including hunting and fishing) in 2008 was 1,776 billion rubles.[24] Subsidies of 163 billion rubles are about 9 percent of the value of agricultural output. The $9 billion in Amber Box subsidies sought by Russia is about 12 to 13 percent of the aggregate value of Russian agricultural output.

If Russia were constrained by developed-country de minimis levels post accession, it would still be permitted the $9 billion in agricultural support, provided about $2 billion of that support is through Green Box subsidies. According to press reports, at least $2 billion of existing support is likely to be classified as Green Box support.

In summary, the de minimis levels of agricultural support in Russia appear to allow Russia to subsidize agriculture at its present level of support or considerably more to the extent it uses Green Box subsidies (which are more effective at helping farmers). Thus, unless Russia seeks to use Amber Box subsidies to a significantly larger extent than at present, we do not understand why this is a crucial issue for Russia.

---

23. Ministry of Finance of the Russian Federation, *Budget for the Years 2008–2010*, www1.minfin.ru.

24. See Federal State Statistical Service of Russia, *Nominal Value of GDP Produced*, www.gks.ru.

Remaining Issues in WTO Accession

Often the most difficult issues remain at the end of accession negotiations. Although Russia has resolved some of the most contentious ones (such as gas pricing and branch banking, where Russia achieved its objectives in the negotiations), several thorny issues remain.

Conflict with Georgia

The conflict between Russia and Georgia regarding Abkhazia and South Ossetia has spilled over to the WTO negotiations. Georgia signed its bilateral agreement on Russian WTO accession in 2004, then withdrew its support. Moreover, Georgia has objected to the agenda of the multilateral meetings and blocked any formal meetings of the Working Party on Russia's WTO accession. The Working Party has therefore been meeting on an "informal basis." Agreement on Russia's intellectual property regime was accomplished in this manner.

Article XII of the WTO Articles on Accession states that "Decisions on accession shall be taken by the Ministerial Conference. The Ministerial Conference shall approve the agreement on the terms of accession by a two-thirds majority of the Members of the WTO." Russia has apparently investigated whether it can bypass Georgia based on this two-thirds majority rule. As a practical matter, this rule is an illusion and all accession decisions are taken by unanimous consensus as are all other decisions of the WTO (except dispute settlement). The Working Party would have to write a final report on Russia's WTO accession, without which the matter will never come to a vote before the WTO ministerial meeting. Just as Georgia has been able to block the Working Party from meeting, it will be able to block the report from going to the ministerial. So again, consensus is required and Georgia has a blocking vote. Thus for Russia to accede to the WTO, Georgia will have to agree.

Agriculture

As discussed earlier, Russia is having difficulty achieving its objective of about $9 billion in permitted trade-distorting subsidies. Other countries like Kazakhstan and Azerbaijan would like similar departures from the WTO precedent. If the Working Party allows Russia a larger trade-distorting subsidy than suggested by precedent, it will find it more difficult to negotiate previous limits with subsequent applicants for WTO membership. Australia and New Zealand are likely to resist a change in precedent that would allow an increase in trade-distorting subsidies.

Export Taxes on Timber—Dispute with the European Union

In early 2007, the Russian government announced an increase in the export tax on timber, to be phased in over 18 months. Export taxes on softwood or poplar timber, which in early 2007 were the greater of either 6.5 percent or 4 euros per cubic meter, were progressively raised, reaching the maximum of 25 percent or 15 euros per cubic meter as of April 1, 2008. The plan was to increase the export taxes further in January 2009 to the maximum of 80 percent or 50 euros per cubic meter.[25] To date, however, the Russian government has postponed implementation of the 80 percent export tax. The increase in the export tax is part of the government's effort to diversify its industry and is intended to dramatically reduce log exports, provide cheaper inputs to wood processors, and attract FDI to its wood-processing sector. Finland, which is the most heavily affected by the export tax measure, has strenuously opposed it; so has Sweden. As bilateral talks with Russia failed, these two countries succeeded in getting the European Union to negotiate the matter as part of Russia's WTO accession negotiations, but the issue remains unresolved.[26]

Regarding Russia's national interest in the matter, increasing value added is not a goal to be pursued at any cost. If value added were the only criterion, bananas could be grown at exorbitant cost in greenhouse conditions in northern Siberia. Rather, production according to comparative advantage is the appropriate criterion. But Finland's strong concerns suggest that Russia has some monopoly power in its trade with Finland, and given the competitive nature of the logging industry, an export tax would be needed to exploit it.

By extending the model of Tarr and Thomson,[27] Khramov, Korableva, and Kovaleva[28] show that Russia does have an optimal export tax to exploit its monopoly power on timber exports. However, they estimate that the export tax is about 11.5 percent. Thus, the actual export tax applied since April 2008 is more than twice the optimum level and dramatically less than the approximately 80 percent proposed for the future. When the costs to the logging industry are taken into account, the timber export tax imposes a lot more costs on the Russian economy (and the logging sector in particular) than benefits.

---

25. In 2005, Russia introduced a 6.5 percent export tax on logs. As of July 1, 2007, export taxes were raised to the maximum of 20 percent or 10 euros per cubic meter.

26. International Centre for Trade and Sustainable Development, "Russia and Finland at Loggerheads Over Timber Taxation" (Geneva), http://ictsd.net.

27. Tarr and Thomson, "The Merits of Dual Pricing of Russian Natural Gas."

28. Vadim Khramov, Larisa Korableva, and Anna Kovaleva, "Export Taxes on Russian Timber Case of Finland and Sweden" (photocopy, New Economic School, May 2008).

Rules on State Trading Enterprises

Russia is willing to accept the usual restraints on state trading enterprises for WTO members. It objects, however, to US demands for more stringent restraints on such enterprises.

Acceding as a Customs Union: What Does It Mean for Russia's Trade Policy?

Customs Union and WTO Accession

In June 2009, Prime Minister Putin announced that Russia would abandon its effort to join the WTO as a single country and seek membership as part of a three-country customs union with Kazakhstan and Belarus. However, President Dmitri Medvedev and some officials from his office promptly indicated that single country accession was still preferred.[29] Considerable confusion prevailed in the Russian government until October 15, 2009, when Maxim Medvedkov, the lead Russian negotiator on WTO accession, announced that the three countries would seek to accede to the WTO as single countries rather than as a customs union.

Although Russia, Belarus, and Kazakhstan have returned to independent accession negotiations, Medvedkov announced that they hoped to accede to the WTO on the basis of a common external tariff that was implemented on January 1, 2010.[30] The return to the negotiating table as independent countries apparently reflects the enormous complexity that negotiating as a common customs entity entails. If the three countries were to jointly apply to the WTO for accession as a customs union, a new WTO working party on the accession of the customs union would have to be formed. This new working party would have to be convinced that the conditions of agreement would be applied throughout the three countries. These commitments include but are not limited to commitments on bound tariffs; rights of foreign investors in services (a rather complicated area of negotiation); Technical Barriers to Trade (TBTs); Sanitary and Phyto-Sanitary Measures (SPS); Trade Related Investment Measures (TRIMs); agricultural trade-distorting subsidies; and intellectual property commitments. All this is sufficiently difficult as no customs union has acceded to the WTO, only individual countries.

The biggest problem with the October 2009 announcement is the

---

29. "Russian President: WTO Membership via Customs Union with Kazakhstan, Belarus, 'Problematic,'" Breaking News 24/7, July 10, 2009, http://blog.taragana.com.

30. Frances Williams, "Russia Scraps WTO Customs Union Bid," *Financial Times*, October 15, 2009, www.ft.com.

statement, repeated by Belarusian representatives,[31] that the three countries would accede to the WTO simultaneously. Since Belarus is far behind Russia in its WTO accession negotiations, simultaneous accession would mean that Russia would have to wait, potentially many years, until Belarus is ready to join the WTO.

Medvedkov announced that the common external tariff would not violate any bound tariff agreement at the WTO. However, the chief negotiator for Kazakhstan, Zhanar Aitzhonova, implicitly acknowledged that the customs union tariff will violate commitments Kazakhstan has made in its bilateral market access agreements on its WTO accession.

Prospects for the Customs Union

As with earlier agreements on the Eurasian Economic Community (EurAsEc), questions remain whether the common external tariff will be implemented outside Russia. As Michalopoulos and Tarr explain in detail, EurAsEc adopted the Russian tariff, which protected Russian industry and made the other countries pay higher prices for Russian goods compared with cheaper third-country imports.[32] Thus, the common external tariff was reportedly implemented on only 50 to 60 percent of the tariff lines outside Russia. In the current three-country customs union, a formal supranational tariff-setting authority should begin operating in January 2010, but the common external tariff has already been established. As in EurAsEc, the tariff structure is likely heavily biased in favor of protecting Russian producers. Thus, there is reason to believe that over time, Russia's trade partners will avoid implementing the common external tariff.

While negotiation of a common external tariff is notoriously difficult in a customs union, members of the customs union could potentially provide substantial trade benefits to each other in other areas. Two such areas include improving trade facilitation and reducing nontariff barriers.

The Jackson-Vanik Amendment

The Jackson-Vanik Amendment of the United States requires an annual review of emigration policies in countries such as Russia and other former

---

31. See "Response by Press Secretary Andrei Popov to a media question over a situation in the accession of Belarus to the WTO," NewsBY.org, October 19, 2009, www.newsby.org.

32. Constantine Michalopoulos and David Tarr, "The Economics of Customs Unions in the Commonwealth of Independent States," *Post-Soviet Geography and Economics* 38, no. 3 (1997): 125–43; and "The Economics of Customs Unions in the Commonwealth of Independent States," World Bank Policy Research Working Paper no. 1786 (Washington: World Bank, 1997), http://econ.worldbank.org.

communist countries in order for the United States to grant them MFN status. This is a significant irritant to Russia, but the United States is currently under no commercial pressure to remove it. Once Russia becomes a WTO member, however, there will be commercial pressure on the United States from its own exporters and investors, at which point the United States will almost certainly terminate the amendment's application to Russia.

The WTO requires that permanent MFN status be granted unconditionally to all members, but the provisions of Jackson-Vanik are inconsistent with this requirement. Once Russia becomes a WTO member, the United States has two options: (1) eliminate Jackson-Vanik or (2) invoke the "nonapplication principle" of the WTO. If a WTO member cannot comply with a WTO requirement toward a newly acceding country, it can opt out of its WTO commitments with respect to that country by invoking the nonapplication principle. If the United States were to invoke the nonapplication principle against Russia, it would mean that the United States would refuse to honor its WTO obligations toward Russia. But nonapplication is reciprocal. So the United States would not have any assurance that US exporters to or investors in Russia would be treated according to Russia's WTO commitments.

In practice, the United States has dropped Jackson-Vanik from all countries that have acceded to the WTO with one exception (Moldova). In the cases of Albania, Bulgaria, Cambodia, Estonia, Latvia, and Lithuania, Jackson-Vanik was repealed prior to accession. In the cases of Mongolia, Armenia, Georgia, and the Kyrgyz Republic it was repealed within a year or two after accession, so the nonapplication principle was invoked for a period of time. (In the case of Georgia, nonapplication was never invoked since Jackson-Vanik was removed soon after accession.)

Former US Trade Representative Rob Portman testified before Congress in 2006 that the United States will have to lift Jackson-Vanik against Russia, Ukraine, and Kazakhstan in order for US exporters and investors to gain the advantages of these countries' WTO commitments. The same year, Jackson-Vanik was dropped against Ukraine.

Foreign Direct Investment

In the first ten years of transition, FDI inflows to Russia were very low compared with Eastern European countries and the other so-called BRICs (Brazil, India, and China). This trend was reversed, however, around 2002–03. As fuel prices rose, FDI flows into Russia increased tenfold over time, and Russia became one of the top FDI recipients in the world (table 10.1). By 2006, FDI inflows to Russia surpassed even those to China in per capita terms. Russian outward FDI also has some unusual features: Outflows are more significant than in other emerging-market economies and started very early in the postcommunist transition.

Table 10.1   Foreign direct investment (FDI) inflows to Russia, 2000–2008

Year	Net FDI inflows (current billions of dollars)	FDI Percent of GDP	FDI Percent of gross capital formation
2000	2.7	1.0	5.5
2001	2.7	0.9	4.1
2002	3.4	1.0	5.0
2003	7.9	1.8	8.7
2004	15.4	2.6	12.4
2005	12.8	1.6	8.4
2006	29.7	2.9	14.2
2007	55.1	4.2	17.1
2008	72.8	4.5	18.1

Sources: World Bank, *World Development Indicators*, 2009; Central Bank of Russia.

Nevertheless, starting from such a low base, the stock of FDI in Russia remains substantially less than in some important comparator countries. The accumulated stock of FDI as a share of GDP was 9.5 percent in 2006. This compares with 26 percent in China and 20 percent in Brazil and is only slightly more than in India (7.5 percent).

The sectoral composition of inward FDI is dominated by mining and quarrying (49 percent in 2007) followed by manufacturing (17 percent) and real estate and business services (11 percent). Increased FDI in the last decade was predominantly channeled into oil and gas extraction, further improving this sector's already dominant position in FDI stock. Geographically, FDI flows are very concentrated: Moscow city got 38 percent in 2006, the Sakhalin region 15 percent, and the Moscow region 10 percent.

The two major source countries for FDI are Cyprus (around 35 percent in 2006) and the Netherlands (about the same). The latter enjoys a special position in managing cross-border transactions in the fuel and gas sectors, while the former is home to capital-rich Russian nationals, who have made substantial investments in Russia.[33] The next most important source country for FDI is Germany, which provided 4.4 percent of the inflow to Russia in 2006. China has also now emerged as a major FDI partner. FDI inflow in the first half of 2009 was cut in half compared with that in 2008 due mainly to the global financial crisis.

The significant increase in FDI inflows to Russia in the past seven years can be explained to some degree by its macroeconomic stability,

---

33. Organization for Economic Cooperation and Development (OECD), "Russian Federation: Strengthening the Policy Framework for Investment," *OECD Investment Policy Reviews* (Paris, 2008), 16.

sound fiscal policy, efficient external debt management, and accumulation of foreign reserves. Infrastructure projects initiated by the state may also have indirectly attracted FDI flows. But the major factor behind the increase in FDI was the increase in the price of oil, which made investments in the Russian oil and gas sectors more profitable.

While the large and expanding Russian domestic market can be attractive for foreign investors, several very clear risks are associated with the Russian economy. The first is the high share of output and exports in the energy sectors. Such heavy dependence on a small number of commodities with volatile prices makes the whole economy relatively volatile. Investors may need to be compensated for this volatility with higher returns, which could reduce FDI inflows. To fight the potential risks of macroeconomic instability associated with volatile oil prices, the government launched the Stabilization Fund of the Russian Federation in 2001.

On the other hand, in the past decade, increased government control over the economy and slow regulatory and administrative reforms have impeded FDI. Government control of the economy increased with Putin's first administration. He became progressively more open in establishing a dominant role for the Russian state in key sectors, including scrutiny of foreign investors in these sectors. The key piece of legislation on this was the Law on Foreign Investment in Strategic Sectors, approved in May 2008. It defines the conditions under which foreign investment can operate in 42 strategic sectors. A foreign investor requires prior authorization to be able to control any business entity in these industries. Most of the industries on the strategic list can be aggregated in broad categories such as military and defense industries, nuclear and radioactive hazardous materials, space and aviation-related sectors, subsoil exploration and exploitation, and fisheries. The list also includes industries covered by the Law on Natural Monopolies, large-scale communications companies, TV and radio broadcasting, and printing services.

The first obvious critique of this law is the extension of strategic status to sectors that are not deemed strategic in many economies. Some services sectors such as TV and radio broadcasting and printing are on the list so the state can control the major media outlets in Russia. Inclusion of industries covered by the Law on Natural Monopolies is aimed at widening state control over the Russian economy.[34]

While the procedures required for prior clearance of foreign investments are meticulously specified in the law, the time it takes an official to approve or declare the transaction a security threat is quite long and varies from case to case: from four to seven months. In this respect the law differs from the practice of similar legislation in many OECD countries.[35]

Overall, some experts point out the positive role this law might play

---

34. These industries include pipeline delivery of oil, petroleum products or natural gas, power-station operations, railway transportation, ports, and airports.

35. OECD, "Russian Federation: Strengthening the Policy Framework for Investment," 27.

in attracting FDI into the economy because the conditions the investor must take into account while planning business transactions are explicitly defined.[36] Nevertheless, by limiting foreign control in too many sectors and allowing officials too much time to reach decisions, the law can discourage a substantial amount of potential FDI inflows. It remains to be seen if foreign investors will see these determinations as ad hoc.

Another potential negative effect of the law could derive from the excessive controls on subsoil exploration and exploitation. It limits the degree of risk sharing related to subsoil exploration. Given volatile oil and gas prices, risks involved in the very substantial investments in the energy field are often shared. As foreign shares of these investments will be limited, greater risks will be borne by the Russian economy.

The Russian government has also substantially expanded its role through state strategic corporations in energy, aircraft, shipbuilding, car manufacturing, forestry, and banking. State enterprises absorbed many incumbent firms in these sectors and now are often the dominant firm in the sector; these enterprises may have access to budgetary support.[37]

In many of these markets, private firms may find it difficult to compete with state enterprises that are subsidized, leading to less competition in many domestic markets, an inevitable decline in efficiency, higher prices, and lower quality of domestic production.

Over the past two years, the government has changed its public stance, arguing for modernization of the economy via FDI. However, the increase in state control of productive assets, limitations on FDI in several questionable areas, and increased use of import-substitution industrialization all work against achievement of this objective. These tendencies emphasize internal conflicts in the current government regarding its economic policy in general and FDI in particular.

To increase Russia's attractiveness as a destination for FDI, the government should work in several important directions. First, it needs to improve domestic institutions to make Russia a better place for doing business. Russia's rankings in the Doing Business Survey and Enterprise Surveys are below the mean in almost all respects and have worsened in recent years.[38] In 2009, 50 percent of the surveyed firms in Russia mentioned corruption as a major constraint. Enormous efforts, involving legislation and court reform, should be made to curb corruption (see chapter 4).

Second, important steps should be taken toward making Russia a bet-

---

36. Toby T. Gati, "Russia's New Law on Foreign Investment in Strategic Sectors and the Role of State Corporations in the Russian Economy" (Akin Gump Strauss Hauer & Feld, October 1, 2008), 22. www.usrbc.org.

37. Ibid., 17, for a similar view.

38. World Bank, *Doing Business 2010*, www.doingbusiness.org; and *Enterprise Surveys 2009*, www.enterprisesurveys.org.

ter location for some part of the production process. Trade flows in the 21st century are highly linked with FDI flows. Much of FDI is "vertical" investment designed to achieve international production sharing in a vertical production chain. But to make Russia an attractive country for investment in the production of components in a production chain, Russia will have to significantly improve its business climate, including transparency of its laws, and improve trade facilitation at its national borders. Russia currently falls behind its major competitors for FDI on the Logistic Performance Index, ranked only 99th out of 150 countries.[39] The situation with customs is especially dreadful, with Russia ranking only 137th out of 150. Customs reform was not on the list of priorities for modernizing the Russian economy that President Medvedev highlighted in his annual address to the Federal Assembly on November 12, 2009.

Improving Customs: Uniform Tariffs or Preshipment Inspection?

Given the problems in Russia's customs performance, some experts have recommended uniform tariffs and preshipment inspection services. In our view, there is enormous merit in uniform tariffs, but preshipment inspection services are likely to produce only marginal benefits at best.

One of us has analyzed the advantages and disadvantages of a uniform tariff for Russia,[40] finding that the arguments against a uniform tariff are not persuasive.[41] That is, there is little merit in the argument for diverse tariffs for strategic trade policy, for optimum revenue, for exploitation of optimal power on imports, for negotiation leverage at the WTO, or for balance of payments purposes. A uniform tariff reduces the incentive to smuggle or to misclassify goods at customs by eliminating tariff peaks. But by far the biggest advantage of a uniform tariff is the political economy incentive. As the experience of Chile has shown, since the uniform tariff eliminates gains to individual sectors, it removes the incentive for industrialists to lobby for higher tariffs. So the country gets a more liberal tariff regime.

Even if under a uniform tariff there is no incentive to misclassify goods, an incentive to falsify the valuation of goods remains, which provides opportunities to customs officials to extract bribes. Preshipment inspection

---

39. World Bank, Logistics Performance Index, http://info.worldbank.org.

40. David Tarr, "Design of Tariff Policy for Russia," in *Russian Trade Policy Reform for WTO Accession*, ed. H. G. Broadman (Washington: World Bank, 1999). These ideas were developed further in David Tarr, "On the Design of Tariff Policy: Arguments for and Against Uniform Tariffs," *Development, Trade and the WTO: A Handbook*, eds. B. Hoekman, A. Mattoo, and P. English (Washington: World Bank, 2002).

41. Tarr, "Design of Tariff Policy for Russia" and "On the Design of Tariff Policy."

(PSI) is designed to deal with that problem (among others). PSI delegates valuation and some other functions to a foreign private firm for a fee (about 1 percent of the value of the imports). However, customs revenue from PSI is not impressive, and importers often complain that they have to incur extra expenses to undergo a PSI and are again put through customs inspections. This raises the costs of delivering the goods and further erodes any benefits to the home country. Crucially, PSI does nothing for building the capacity of the home country to effectively implement a customs regime (including customs valuation), which is the real long-run goal.

Is Russia's Accession to the WTO Crucial to the International Community or to Russia?

Small Economic Gains to the International Community

We are skeptical that Russian WTO accession will convey significant benefits to the international trading community. Multiregional trade models have shown that it is own-country liberalization that is important: Countries that make substantial commitments in multilateral negotiations gain more, and those that don't make commitments gain very little from the liberalization in the rest of the world. Numerous assessments of the Uruguay Round have found this result.[42] Harrison, Rutherford, and Tarr also found this result in multiregional trade models of regional arrangements.[43] Rutherford, Tarr, and Shepotylo showed that Russia has dramatically more to gain from its own liberalization in WTO accession than from liberalization in the rest of the world such as through a very successful Doha Development Agenda.[44] Adapting the well-known computer acronym, Alan Winters has summarized these results with the acronym "WYDIWYG—what you do is what you get." The bottom line is, notwithstanding the growing importance of Russia in world markets and the fact that some Western firms will find profits selling or investing in Russia, it is difficult to argue

42. Glenn Harrison, Thomas Rutherford, and David Tarr, "Quantifying the Uruguay Round," *Economic Journal* 107, no. 444 (1997): 1405–30; and Will Martin and L. Alan Winters, eds., *The Uruguay Round and the Developing Countries* (Cambridge University Press, 1996).

43. Glenn Harrison, Thomas Rutherford, and David Tarr, "Trade Policy Options for Chile: The Importance of Market Access," *World Bank Economic Review* 16, no. 1 (2002); Harrison, Rutherford, and Tarr, "Trade Policy and Poverty Reduction in Brazil," *World Bank Economic Review* 18 (2004): 289–317.

44. Thomas Rutherford, David Tarr, and Oleksandr Shepotylo, "The Impact on Russia of WTO Accession and The Doha Agenda: The Importance of Liberalization of Barriers against Foreign Direct Investment in Services for Growth and Poverty Reduction," in *Putting Development Back into the Doha Agenda: Poverty Impacts of a WTO Agreement*, eds. Thomas Hertel and L. Alan Winters (New York: Palgrave McMillan and World Bank, 2005).

that the United States or the rest of the world will significantly gain economically from Russia's accession.

We believe that the United States and the rest of the world would like to see Russia as a cooperative partner in dealing with international problems. And they would like to see Russia in the WTO, trading by the same rules, as part of that process. But this is more a geopolitical argument than an economic one.

Unique Historical Opportunity for Reform in Russia

We have shown estimates that suggest Russia will reap large gains from WTO accession and that the largest gains from WTO accession will derive from its own liberalization commitments. Some will argue that if virtually all the gains come from own liberalization, why bother going through the long, painful, contentious process of WTO accession when the country can independently liberalize and achieve virtually all the benefits of accession? We argue that WTO accession is a unique historical opportunity to dramatically move the country toward an open economy model of economic development. In a business as usual scenario, forces that want protection in their sectors are concentrated and will lobby to defeat liberalization, while those who gain from liberalization are diverse and due to a free-rider problem often do not lobby. Uneven lobbying therefore often leads to excessive protection.

WTO accession involves foreign business interests and foreign governments in the negotiations on the level of protection at home. WTO accession compels policymakers at the highest levels of government to engage in the process, and they often impose liberalization on slow-moving ministries and sectors. Moreover, commitments at the WTO "lock in" reform in a manner that is not easily reversed by future governments who may be less reform-minded.

Import-Substitution Industrialization or Open Economy Development with Institutional Reform?

Throughout the first decade of the 21st century, Russia has had large trade surpluses, which have exceeded $100 billion annually since 2005, giving Russia the largest trade surplus in the world in some of those years. Despite these large trade surpluses, which amounted to between 9 and 14 percent of Russian GDP since 2005 (table 10.2), Russia has become increasingly concerned about the mineral (mainly energy) dependence of its production structure and exports, as mineral exports alone constituted 65 percent of exports in 2007. In response, Russia has increasingly employed import-substitution industrialization and industrial policy for diversification of its economy or for political purposes. These measures include very high export taxes on timber to develop the wood-processing industry; in-

Table 10.2   Russia's trade balance, 2000–2008 (billions of current US dollars)

Year	Exports	Imports	Trade balance Billions of current US dollars	Percent share of GDP
2000	114.6	61.1	53.5	20.6
2001	112.7	73.0	39.7	12.9
2002	120.9	84.5	36.4	10.5
2003	152.1	103.2	48.9	11.3
2004	203.8	130.7	73.1	12.4
2005	268.8	164.2	104.6	13.7
2006	334.6	209.0	125.6	12.7
2007	393.8	282.5	111.3	8.6
2008	522.9	368.2	154.7	9.6

Sources: Rosstat; World Bank, *World Development Indicators*, 2009.

creased import tariffs on food processing, light industry, and automotive sectors; sanitary and phytosanitary measures for protection against meat imports from the United States and as a political tool against Georgia, Moldova (briefly), and allegedly Belarus in June 2009; increased agricultural production subsidies; restrictions on foreign investment in the Russian economy through the introduction in 2008 of the Law on Foreign Investment in Strategic Sectors; and creation of a grain marketing board with unclear objectives. Many of these actions would be constrained by WTO rules or commitments. Thus, Russian leaders may wish to more actively use industrial policy and import-substitution industrialization and could see the WTO rules as counterproductive to Russia's development.[45]

Diversification of the Russian economy is a worthy goal. However, as emphasized in chapter 1, institutional reform to improve the business climate is necessary. Russia rates badly on measures of institutional development. As noted earlier, it ranks 120th out of 183 countries on the Doing Business ranking; 99th out of 150 on the Logistics Performance Index; and 147th out of 180th on Transparency International's Corruption Perceptions Index. Small and medium enterprises depend crucially on the institutional environment for doing business. The incredible improvement of Georgia in the past eight years (now ranked 11th in the world on ease of doing business) has shown that rapid progress in institutional performance is possible when a concerted effort is made starting from the highest levels of government.

45. Anders Åslund, "Russia's Policy on Accession to the World Trade Organization," *Eurasian Economics and Geography* 48, no. 3 (May–June 2007), elaborated on the stiffening of political will in Russia on WTO accession.

11

The Post-Soviet Space: An Obituary

ANDERS ÅSLUND

Russia's relations with its post-Soviet neighbors reached an all-time low with the Russian-Georgian war in August 2008. How did Russia end up in this undesirable situation and what should it do to foster more constructive relations with its neighbors? In fact, the neighbors with which Russia has the best relations never belonged to the Soviet Union: China, Finland, and Norway.

Each former Soviet country has its own complaints, but the four dominant issues are Russia's lacking respect for territorial integrity, gas policy, trade policy, and finance. The Kremlin needs to fix each of these four policies to restore its reputation in the region. At the same time, foreign direct investment of private Russian corporations is proceeding with success and little concern. The big as yet untold story is the rapid advance of China into Central Asia, and in the west the European Union is showing new interest.

The best illustration of the current state of relations was the October 9, 2009 annual summit of the Commonwealth of Independent States (CIS) in Kishinev. The headline in *Nezavisimaya gazeta* said it all: "Summit in 30 Minutes. The CIS leaders…had nothing to tell one another."[1] The CIS had 12 members until Georgia left on August 18. From the remaining 11 members

Anders Åslund is a senior fellow at the Peterson Institute for International Economics. He gratefully acknowledges all the excellent comments he received at a workshop in Moscow on November 17, 2009, and in particular the detailed critique by Sergei Guriev. Anna Borshchevskaya provided valuable research assistance.

1. "Sammit na 30 minut. Liderami SNG, sobiravshimsya v Kishineve, nechego bylo skazat' drug drugu ["Summit in 30 Minutes. The CIS Leaders, Who Had Gathered in Kishinev, Had Nothing to Tell One Another"], *Nezavisimaya gazeta*, October 12, 2009.

only six presidents arrived—of Russia, Belarus, Ukraine, Armenia, Azerbaijan, and Kyrgyzstan—while the host Moldova temporarily had no president. Only one of five Central Asian presidents bothered to come. Needless to say, nothing was accomplished. To aggravate things further, President Dmitri Medvedev refused to meet Ukrainian President Viktor Yushchenko or Belarusian President Aleksandr Lukashenko. Everybody left quickly after their half-hour meeting. The CIS is Russia's baby and failure.

Arguably, Russia's relations with CIS countries are not better than they were in 1992. If the CIS does not have any positive contribution to make, why maintain it? All actual problem solving is done bilaterally in any case. The CIS stands out as a potential threat of Russian neoimperialism. Since Russia has neither apparent neoimperialist intentions nor the necessary resources to carry them out successfully, it should be in Russia's interest to close down the CIS and the suborganizations and establish normal bilateral relations with all the former Soviet republics. After all, the CIS was conceived as a vehicle for civilized divorce. As Yegor Gaidar, the author of the Belovezhskaya Pushcha agreements, wrote in his memoirs, this agreement was "the dissolution of the USSR by the three governments that had in 1922 been its founders."[2] By dissolving it, the CIS countries would recognize that they have achieved their aim.

Dissolution of the Soviet Union

The collapse of the Soviet Union in 1991 was as sudden as it was dramatic. The implosion was multiple and overdetermined. It was fiscal, monetary, national, systemic, and political but not military or religious. Its grace was that no great empire disappeared as swiftly or peacefully: "By the standards of other collapsing empires the bloodshed has been remarkably small…. In the post-Soviet case almost no Russian civilians were killed or ethnically cleansed from any of the fourteen republics of the former USSR."[3]

Its very peacefulness and speed left many with the impression that the dissolution was not necessary. Today it is difficult to imagine how close Moscow was to war with some republics in 1990 and 1991. Not without reason, Boris Yeltsin accused Soviet President Mikhail Gorbachev of "a deceptive compromise that had the country a hair's breadth away from an inevitable bloodbath and war between the center in Moscow and the republics."[4]

---

2. Yegor T. Gaidar, *Days of Defeat and Victory* (Seattle, WA: University of Washington Press, 1999), 124.

3. Dominic Lieven, *Empire: The Russian Empire and Its Rivals* (New Haven: Yale University Press, 2000), 379–80.

4. Boris Yeltsin, *The Struggle for Russia* (New York: Crown, 1994), 115.

After the August 1991 coup, the USSR ceased to function as a political entity in most regards. The three Baltic republics, Estonia, Latvia, and Lithuania, claimed their independence, and Yeltsin recognized them on August 24. Georgia, Armenia, Moldova, and Azerbaijan were well on their way toward national independence. The other republics were more hesitant, leaving Ukraine pivotal as the eighth of 15 union republics.

President Yeltsin thought strategically and moved radically on three issues. First, he secured power. Second, he dissolved the Soviet Union, thus easing the national tensions. Third, he focused on the rampant economic crisis, which demanded instant deregulation and financial stabilization.[5]

He understood that the Soviet Union could no longer survive and it had to be dissolved before he could proceed with other policies. Yeltsin presented union dissolution as a positive choice: "I was convinced that Russia needed to rid itself of its imperial mission."[6] On December 1, 1991, Ukraine voted with 90 percent majority for independence. Yeltsin acted instantly. In complete secrecy, he organized a meeting one week later in Belarus with the heads of state of Ukraine and Belarus. Together these three men dissolved the Soviet Union. As Yeltsin saw it: "In signing this agreement, Russia was choosing a different path, a path of internal development rather than an imperial one." He insisted that this was "a lawful alteration of the existing order," because it "was a revision of the Union Treaty among [the] three major republics of that Union."[7]

As a replacement for the USSR, they set up the loose Commonwealth of Independent States, which appeared most inspired by the British Commonwealth. Yeltsin wanted a minimal organization without supernational power: "There will be no coordinating organs.... If there is coordination, it will be between the heads of state of commonwealth members. They will have some kind of a working group to resolve certain questions, and that's it."[8]

Most of the other Soviet republics wanted to join the CIS. Yeltsin accommodated them. On December 21 in Kazakhstan's capital Almaty, the CIS was expanded to include 11 republics, while Georgia and the already-independent Baltic states stayed outside. The treaty of 1922 on the formation of the Soviet Union was formally abrogated. In 1993, Georgia also joined the CIS, increasing the membership to 12, though not all of them ratified the CIS charter, leaving the organization legally indeterminate.

---

5. I discuss this is detail in my book *Russia's Capitalist Revolution: Why Market Reform Succeeded and Democracy Failed* (Washington: Peterson Institute for International Economics, 2007).

6. Yeltsin, *The Struggle for Russia*, 115.

7. Ibid., 113. That some people still embrace the idea that the Soviet Union could have remained viable just shows the success of Yeltsin's sudden dissolution of it.

8. "'We Are Taking Over,'" interview with Yeltsin, *Newsweek*, January 6, 1992, 13.

Yeltsin refrained from making any claims on behalf of Russia on territories of other former Soviet republics. By respecting existing borders, Yeltsin left a valuable, peaceful legacy. The integrity of the existing borders between the union republics was enshrined in the CIS treaty and bilateral friendship treaties between Russia and most CIS members.

On December 25, 1991, the Soviet Union was formally dissolved. Surprisingly few problems remained unresolved. One was the four so-called frozen conflicts—unregulated, separatist territories outside the control of the national government, the Moldovan province of Transnistria, the Georgian territories of Abkhazia and South Ossetia, and the Azerbaijani autonomous territory of Nagorny Karabakh, which was controlled by ethnic Armenians. The leaders of the first three territories were pro-Russian, and the Kremlin supported them with troops.[9]

Military issues were resolved with impressive ease, as military assets were divided as other property. The biggest issue was the ample nuclear arms. In 1992 Ukraine was actually the third largest nuclear power in the world. By June 1996, even Ukraine had transferred all its nuclear arms to Russia, as had the others. This was an amazing achievement in containing the proliferation of nuclear arms. In these multiple multilateral and bilateral agreements, Russia made strong commitments to the national sovereignty and territorial integrity of the other former Soviet republics.[10]

One of the worst remaining problems was the common currency zone. A competitive issue of ruble credits had erupted between 15 newly formed republic central banks. The more ruble credits one republic issued, the larger share of the common GDP it extracted, but the higher overall inflation became. Everybody had a strong incentive to pursue a more expansionary monetary policy than others, but as a consequence all were worse off. In 1993 the Central Bank of Russia finally terminated the ruble zone by declaring old Soviet banknotes null and void. This action caused panic and compelled all remaining members of the ruble zone to establish their national currencies within the next few months.[11] As the dysfunctional ruble zone lingered for so long, 10 of the CIS countries experienced hyperinflation. The end of the ruble zone made monetary stabilization possible and completed the separation of the CIS countries. Contrary to popular views, there was no other solution. No preconditions for an orderly currency union were present. Any comparison with the European monetary union, which was then being formed, is misplaced.[12]

---

9. Nagorny Karabakh did not involve ethnic Russians or Russian forces.

10. James M. Goldgeier and Michael McFaul, *Power and Purpose: U.S. Policy Toward Russia after the Cold War* (Washington: Brookings Institution, 2003).

11. Brigitte Granville, *The Success of Russian Economic Reforms* (London: Royal Institute for International Affairs, 1995).

12. Anders Åslund, *How Russia Became a Market Economy* (Washington: Brookings Institution, 1995).

CIS: A Patchwork of Trial and Error

After the Soviet Union had been dissolved, the newly independent states had to establish new relations.[13] The CIS evolved in fits and starts. Almost every year, an attempt was made to set up a new organization with some CIS countries, but none of these organizations has proven successful. They have fallen by the wayside and been neglected. Instead of resolving the problems with the failed organization, Russia has instigated setting up a new suborganization to the CIS.

In Russia, two approaches have existed. Yeltsin wanted the CIS to be like the British Commonwealth, but his view was shared by only a small liberal minority. The dominant Russian view was that the Soviet demise was a tragedy and that as much as possible of this great power should be maintained and restored. These two lines of thought found an uncomfortable compromise in the idea that the CIS should become like the European Union. But Russia contained half of the former Soviet population, and most of its economy, so Russia would naturally constitute a majority, which was unacceptable to the other CIS countries.

The attitude of the other CIS states varied with their view of Russia. Essentially, they were divided into a group of five close friends to Russia and six that preferred to keep Russia at arm's length.

Among Russia's five friends, Belarus wanted the tightest links to Russia. For geographical and ethnic reasons, Kazakhstan was compelled to be close to Russia. The three small and poor nations of Kyrgyzstan, Tajikistan, and Armenia, none of which borders on Russia, desired Russian protection and economic support. With its allies, Russia has formed a customs union, the Eurasian Economic Community (EurAsEc), and a military pact, the Collective Security Treaty Organization (CSTO). Another group of six CIS countries kept greater distance from Russia. Ukraine, Moldova, Georgia, and Azerbaijan desired to be quite independent from Russia but favored trade cooperation with Russia. Together, they set up the alternative organization GUAM (stands for Georgia, Ukraine, Azerbaijan, and Moldova) in 1997. Georgia waited to join the CIS for more than a year and formally departed from the CIS on August 18, 2009. Uzbekistan tended to keep a distance from Russia but joined both the EurAsEc and CSTO briefly from 2006 and 2008, when their bilateral relationship temporarily improved. Turkmenistan has been outright isolationist. Ukraine and Turkmenistan never ratified the CIS statutes and do not consider themselves members, only participants.

As a consequence, the CIS became paradoxical in many ways. It was important in protocol terms, holding annual summits with heads of state

---

13. Martha Brill Olcott, Anders Åslund, and Sherman Garnett have elaborated on the evolution of the CIS in *Getting It Wrong* (Washington: Carnegie Endowment for International Peace, 1999).

and annual prime ministerial meetings. But little of significance was accomplished multilaterally, while bilateral meetings were vital. When a multilateral agreement was concluded, about half the CIS countries closest to Russia usually signed on, but hardly any ratified an agreement, so few came into force. Even ratified agreements were not necessarily complied with because there were no mechanisms for surveillance, arbitration, or penalty. Only 4 percent of CIS decisions actually resulted in national legislation.[14]

By and large, multilateral attempts at cooperation failed, because Russia aspired to closer cooperation than any other state. In reality, relations between Russia and the former Soviet republics have been predominantly bilateral.

Territorial Integrity or the "Biggest Geopolitical Disaster of the Century"

For the newly born CIS states, the most fundamental issue was security: Russia's respect for their national sovereignty and territorial integrity was sine qua non for their cooperation with Russia. They knew only too well that Yeltsin's view of the demise of the Soviet Union was a minority Russian view.

Unlike Yeltsin, President Vladimir Putin had all along expressed nostalgia about the Soviet Union. In his interview book *First Person* Putin stated: "We would have avoided a lot of problems if the Soviets had not made such a hasty exit from Eastern Europe." He expressed sympathy with the putschists in August 1991: "In principle, their goal—preserving the Soviet Union from collapse—was noble...."[15]

As president, Putin took some time to develop his policy on the former Soviet republics, and in his first term it was passive. In his second term, Russia's policy toward the CIS was dominated by the so-called colored revolutions in Georgia, Ukraine, and Kyrgyzstan, and gas trade. In his annual address in April 2005, Putin went all out: "the collapse of the Soviet Union was the biggest geopolitical disaster of the century.... Tens of millions of our co-citizens and compatriots found themselves outside Russian territory...old ideals [were] destroyed."[16] He presented himself as a neoimperialist.

The Moldovan government has persistently wanted to restore its national integrity over Transnistria, and so has the Georgian government

---

14. "Yushchenko ne ponravilsya sammit SNG" ["Yushchenko Did Not Like the CIS Summit"], www.rosbalt.ru, October 9, 2009.

15. Vladimir V. Putin, *First Person* (New York: Public Affairs, 2000), 81, 93.

16. Vladimir V. Putin, Annual Address to the Federal Assembly of the Russian Federation, April 25, 2005, www.kremlin.ru.

over Abkhazia and South Ossetia, whereas Moscow seems to have appreciated the complication. In 2006 these conflicts escalated, and Russia suddenly embargoed Georgia's and Moldova's large exports of wine and fruits to Russia. It also blocked most transportation to and from Georgia and even bank transactions. Georgia played hardball, revoking its bilateral protocol on Russia's accession to the World Trade Organization (WTO), thus blocking Russia's entry into that organization, of which Georgia was already a member.

In January 2008 the United States started campaigning for a Membership Action Plan to the North Atlantic Treaty Organization (NATO) for Ukraine and Georgia, but most of the European NATO members were surprised and some opposed. The issue came to a crunch at the NATO summit in Bucharest in April 2008. The summit did not offer a Membership Action Plan to Ukraine, but its communiqué stated boldly: "NATO welcomes Ukraine's and Georgia's Euro-Atlantic aspirations for membership in NATO. We agreed today that these countries will become members of NATO."[17]

President Putin also attended that NATO summit. In a closed meeting on April 4, 2008, he intimidated Ukraine. He disqualified Ukraine's claim to sovereign statehood and territorial integrity, reversing Yeltsin's policy and contradicting the 1997 Russian-Ukrainian Treaty on Friendship, Cooperation, and Partnership. He suggested that Ukraine's composition was artificial, its borders arbitrary, and the transfer of Crimea to Ukraine illegal.[18] More nationalist Russian politicians, notably Moscow Mayor Yuri Luzhkov, went much further, claiming that Sevastopol and Crimea belonged to Russia. In June 2008 Luzhkov stated: "Sevastopol was never given to Ukraine. I have studied all basic documents carefully, and I can make such a declaration."[19]

As president, Putin routinely confirmed Russia's commitment to Georgia's territorial integrity, but from 2006 Georgia became the focal point of Russia's CIS policy. From April 2008, Russia stepped up its engagement in Abkhazia and South Ossetia contrary to various international agreements.[20] In early August 2008 military action escalated in the secessionist Georgian territory of South Ossetia. On August 7, Georgian troops entered South Ossetia but were immediately rebuffed by well-prepared

---

17. Bucharest Summit Declaration, issued by the Heads of State and Government participating in the meeting of the North Atlantic Council, Bucharest, April 3, 2008, www.nato.int.

18. "What Precisely Vladimir Putin Said at Bucharest," *Zerkalo nedeli*, April 19, 2008.

19. "Luzhkov izuchil vopros Sevastpoloya i reshil, chto ego ne peredali" ["Luzhkov Studied the Sevastopol Question and Decided that They Had not Transferred It"], *Ukrainskaya pravda*, June 24, 2008.

20. Andrei Illarionov, "The Russian Leadership's Preparation for War, 1999-2008," in *The Guns of August 2008: Russia's War in Georgia*, ed. Svante E. Cornell and S. Frederick Starr (Armonk, NY: M. E. Sharpe), 68–72.

and overwhelming Russian troops, which secured South Ossetia and Abkhazia and occupied some other parts of Georgia. The Russia-Georgian war lasted only five days, August 8 to 12.

On August 26, 2008, the Kremlin dealt the most devastating blow to its own standing in the post-Soviet space by recognizing the sovereignty of Abkhazia and South Ossetia. Russia broke with its long-standing principles of respect for national sovereignty and territorial integrity inscribed in the Organization for Security and Cooperation in Europe (Helsinki) convention (OSCE), the CIS convention, and multiple bilateral friendship treaties with CIS countries. Its excuse was that Kosovo had declared independence from Russia's friend Serbia, but in the process Russia abandoned its broadly shared principle not to recognize secession. Many countries had considered Kosovo an extreme case, but few reckoned that South Ossetia or Abkahzia belonged to this category. South Ossetia was just too small with only a few tens of thousands of people, and in Abkhazia the Abkhaz had not been more than the third largest ethnic group for decades. In spite of considerable Russian pressure, no CIS state recognized them because ultimately it concerned their own sovereignty. Russia scared even its closest allies, Belarus and Kazakhstan, which harbor large Russian ethnic populations. After the war in Georgia, President Medvedev stated that Russia had "regions with privileged interests," referring to "close neighbors."[21]

Russia's actions confirmed that it had become a revisionist power in the region, preoccupying all the other CIS countries with their national integrity vis-à-vis Russia. Needless to say, they all rushed to the exits as fast as they could. If Russia is their main national threat, they have no need for the CSTO, which presupposes that these countries face common external threats. The Kremlin needs to restore its respect for its neighbors' territorial integrity to be able to improve its relations with them.

Gas Policy: More Aggressive than Successful

In its gas policy Russia has shown little respect for its neighbors.[22] As the former Soviet Ministry of Gas Industry, Gazprom lives in symbiosis with the Russian government and plays a unique political role outside Russia's borders. Its actions comprise an uneasy mixture of commerce, politics, and apparent conflicts of interest.

Since 2005, Gazprom has hiked prices, which had remained artificially low since the Soviet era. It has claimed to depoliticize prices but has boosted them in big steps, which have varied greatly between countries. Prices were raised faster for weak and not very friendly countries, such as

---

21. "Dmitri Medvedev's Interview with the television channels 'Rossiya', the First Channel, and NTV," www.kremlin.ru, August 31, 2008.

22. Russia's gas policy in general is discussed in chapter 7.

Georgia and Moldova, than for Russia's close ally Belarus. Neither the old nor new prices have been set by any objective standard. No world market prices exist for piped natural gas, as all prices depend on local demand and supply through one or few pipes, but Gazprom has long solved that problem in Europe through an agreed pricing formula.

In recent years, Gazprom has repeatedly cut gas supplies to many countries. Georgia, Azerbaijan, Moldova, Ukraine, and Belarus have experienced several such cuts. In January 2006 Gazprom turned off gas to and through Ukraine, which transits 80 percent of Gazprom's exports to the European Union. In January 2007 it meted out the same treatment to Belarus, the Kremlin's closest ally, through which the remaining 20 percent of Russia's gas deliveries go to the European Union. The worst disruption occurred in January 2009, when Gazprom cut off all gas deliveries through Ukraine. Few disagree with the principle of gradual transition to market prices, but the transition needs to be transparent and founded on agreed principles; frequent supply disruptions are unacceptable.

For years, Gazprom has tried to exchange gas arrears for gas pipelines in debt-equity swaps in customer countries. It has succeeded in doing so in several countries, notably Belarus and Moldova, but these countries have not found it any easier to reach agreements with Gazprom. Instead, Russia is attempting to resolve its persistent problems with gas transit through Ukraine and Belarus by building alternative gas pipelines that bypass these two countries, Nord Stream through the Baltic Sea and South Stream through the Black Sea and the Balkans.

Another Gazprom strategy is to extend monopolistic control over transportation, production, sales, and purchases in all directions through long-term contracts, trying to monopolize gas supplies from Central Asia. But when European gas demand and prices dropped, Turkmenistan's gas pipeline to Russia blew up as did two gas pipelines to Georgia in January 2005.[23] After the pipeline was repaired, Gazprom refused to accept the contracted volumes or pay the agreed price. Not surprisingly, the Turkmens instead turned to the Chinese, who have just built a large gas pipeline to Turkmenistan and are now preparing to buy most of Turkmenistan's gas exports, as is already the case with Kazakhstan. Turkmenistan has also shown interest in a Transcaspian gas pipeline to Europe.

Well-Intentioned but Unsuccessful Trade Policy

In trade, Russia has proven good intentions but has not been very successful. The CIS has long tried but persistently failed to establish a well-functioning free trade area.[24] The fundamental problem is that Russia has been

---

23. "Russia Blamed for 'Gas Sabotage'," BBC News, January 22, 2006, news.bbc.co.uk.

24. An excellent overview of CIS trade policy is Sherzod Shadikhodjaev, "Trade Integration

trying to reinvent the wheel with its own free trade agreements (FTAs) in an area where Russia has neither knowledge nor body of conventions. When it should have leaned on the established trade framework of the WTO. Having tried all the alternatives, it is now time for Russia to turn to the WTO (see chapter 10).

In the aftermath of the Soviet collapse, trade between the former Soviet republics dwindled from 1991 to 1994. One of the chief goals of the CIS was to facilitate mutual trade. In September 1993 CIS countries signed a treaty on an economic union. It was highly ambitious, supposed to lead to a free trade area, a customs union, a common market, and a currency union, but it was concluded just as the ruble zone was falling apart. It was declarative rather than operative and was never taken seriously.[25]

In April 1994, all the CIS countries, except Turkmenistan, signed a multilateral FTA. However, some countries, including Russia, never ratified it, so it has never come into force. An attempt was made to revive it in April 1999 through an additional protocol, but Russia never ratified that either. Still, the CIS FTA functions as a model agreement.

Instead, most CIS countries have concluded bilateral FTAs, which have been ratified but lack legal teeth. Whenever one country wants to undertake protectionist measures against another, it does so with impunity because detailed rules, arbitration, and penalty mechanisms are missing. For example, in 2006 Ukrainian vodka producers seized one-quarter of the Russian vodka market, which led to prohibition of their imports. Two years later, a Kyrgyz cement factory made headway into the Kazakh market but suddenly faced a prohibitive 100 percent import tariff and was forced to stop production until it was sold to a Kazakh businessman. Examples of prohibitions, quotas, and high tariffs abound. As a consequence, trade within the CIS is often disrupted, as successful exporters are blocked through quotas, tariffs, or outright prohibitions.

Because FTAs malfunctioned, Russia and its closest allies aimed at a customs union. In January 1995, Russia and Belarus signed an agreement on a customs union, which Kazakhstan joined. Kyrgyzstan and Turkmenistan signed on in 1996 and 1999, respectively. But the parties neither knew how to form a customs union nor could agree on it. Instead of giving up, they decided to form EurAsEc in 2000. It was designed to be a customs union and a common economic space, inspired by the European Union, but in reality little happened. Uzbekistan joined in 2006 for foreign policy reasons but suspended its membership in 2008. EurAsEc persists as a bureaucratic structure of little significance.

---

in the CIS Region: A Thorny Path towards a Customs Union," *Journal of International Economic Law* 12, no. 3 (2009), 555–78.

25. Constantine Michalopoulos and David G. Tarr, "The Economics of Customs Union in the Commonwealth of Independent States," *Post-Soviet Geography and Economics* 38, no. 3 (1997): 125–43.

True to its habit, Russia initiated a new, even more ambitious, pact rather than mending the old, failed one. In March 2003 it launched the Common Economic Space (CES) for Russia, Ukraine, Kazakhstan, and Belarus. The CES was supposed to start as a free trade area, become a customs union, and eventually a currency union, again modeled on the European Union. But it was an evident ploy to tie Ukraine closer to Russia before the presidential elections in late 2004. When Moscow's candidate lost, the CES lost meaning, but its structures linger.

In all these endeavors, no attempt was made to find a mechanism to reinforce the desired free trade. The resolution is evident: WTO accession for all. The WTO has the requisite rule book, arbitration, and penalties. Many WTO members use these WTO instruments to give teeth to their FTAs. Five CIS countries—Kyrgyzstan, Georgia, Moldova, Armenia, and Ukraine—have become members of the WTO, but Russia has failed to do so. It should be in Russia's interest to join the WTO as soon as possible and bring in the other CIS countries as well.

In June 2009, when Russia was close to WTO accession, Prime Minister Putin surprised everybody, including his own cabinet, by stating that Russia, Belarus, and Kazakhstan would enter the WTO as a customs union. WTO Secretary General Pascal Lamy declared that this was impossible. Putin also declared that the customs union was as important as the WTO to Russia, which is rather surprising as Russia's attempts to form a customs union with these two countries have yielded no success since 1995.

Russia, Kazakhstan, and Belarus are no natural partners for a customs union because their economic interests and structures vary greatly. Kazakhstan is largely a raw material exporter, and Belarus an exporter of the best Soviet-manufactured goods. Russia, with its large but substandard manufacturing, is inclined to impose high import tariffs, but Kazakhstan and Belarus want none of it. In early 2010, Kazakhstan insisted that 409 items be excluded from Russia's higher import tariffs; the list includes major import items such as cars, which Kazakhstan barely produces. Another conflict concerns Russia's low energy prices because of price regulation and export tariffs. Belarus has persistently demanded that Russia's low domestic energy prices also apply to it and has refused to accept export tariffs because of the purported customs union, which has led to severe supply disruptions. The benefits of this customs union remain doubtful.

In spite of persistent trade disputes, trade of and between the CIS countries has skyrocketed. From 2002 until 2008, total CIS trade rose by an average of 26 percent a year (figure 11.1), and the unweighted average of their mutual trade is about 40 percent of their total trade (table 11.1). The country that trades the least with the CIS is actually Russia, which has only about 15 percent of its trade with the region, so the weighted average is only about 20 percent. Yet this is natural for a big country and does not say anything about Russia's policy intention, rather a lot about how captive the others are because of geography and infrastructure.

Figure 11.1   Average annual increase in intra-CIS trade, 1996–2008
(percent)

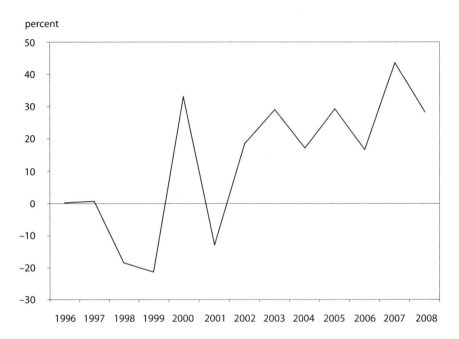

CIS = Commonwealth of Independent States

Note: Figure includes trade with Mongolia, but this amount is insignificant. The average annual increase is an unweighted average of the sum of exports and imports.

Sources: IMF, *Direction of Trade Statistics*, October 2009; author's calculations.

At first sight, the persistence of CIS trade might appear surprising, but a cursory look at the map explains it. Many CIS countries are land-locked, and distances over land are enormous. Poor transportation and barriers to trade limit their choices of trade partners. Often, disruption of trade does not mean diversion of trade but no trade or production at all.

Russia's persistent failures to build a customs union and a currency union are not haphazard but based on fundamental theoretical flaws, so there is no reason to believe in success in the foreseeable future (see chapter 10).[26] Even so, Russian leaders persistently advocate a customs union and a currency union, which only hurts Russia's national interests. In the early 1990s, Russia lacked trade expertise, but a decade later such expertise had evolved and a rational trade policy should have been possible. Even so, the Russian government has insisted on reinventing the wheel again rather than opting for free trade before a customs union and adopting the nearly universally accepted WTO rules.

26. Anders Åslund, "The Ruble as a Global Reserve Currency? No!", *Moscow Times*, September 23, 2009.

Table 11.1   Intra-CIS trade, 2000-08 (percent of total trade, unweighted average)

Country	2000	2001	2002	2003	2004	2005	2006	2007	2008
Armenia	21	25	27	25	25	26	29	32	30
Azerbaijan	21	18	23	23	25	28	26	26	7
Belarus	66	65	62	63	63	56	55	57	56
Georgia	35	37	40	37	40	42	39	36	32
Kazakhstan	34	38	32	32	31	29	30	31	31
Kyrgyzstan	48	45	46	47	52	56	55	59	52
Moldova	43	47	45	46	46	44	45	35	37
Russia	19	13	17	18	13	15	12	15	14
Tajikistan	65	56	50	44	44	47	41	46	44
Turkmenistan	46	48	44	45	50	54	55	55	48
Ukraine	44	42	38	36	39	40	39	40	38
Uzbekistan	45	44	41	40	43	45	43	45	50
Total Intra-CIS trade	41	40	39	38	39	40	39	40	37

Sources: IMF, *Direction of Trade Statistics*, October 2009; author's calculations.

Foreign Direct Investment: Quite Fortuitous

Russian foreign direct investment has skyrocketed since 2000 and has not been too controversial. In September 2003 Anatoly Chubais, then CEO of Russia's Unified Energy Systems, aroused an outcry when he pronounced the concept of "liberal imperialism," effectively saying that Russia would regain its influence in the former Soviet Union through corporate investment.[27]

Yet, Russia's private corporations have mainly been driven by commercial interests. They have invested grandly in other post-Soviet states, most of all in Ukraine. Their rights as investors have become a major issue of Russian policy. These investments have rarely been political but comply with the textbook of foreign direct investment. They have been initiated by Russian corporations, private or state-owned, and the Russian state has supported its companies abroad as any other state would. First, Russian oil companies undertook downstream investment in oil refineries and chains of gas stations, pursuing vertical integration. Second, Russia's metallurgical companies and retail chains went ahead with horizontal integration, that is, doing on a larger scale what they already did so well at home. Third, Russian consumer and mobile phone companies extended their successful business model abroad.

Russian foreign direct investment in the post-Soviet region has been huge.[28] Political reaction to it has been very limited because it has been so obviously commercial. Another reason is that Russian companies have competed with local companies on a fairly level playing field. The most controversial Russian investments in the CIS have been the biggest ones relative to the national economy (Rusal wanting to purchase the dominant Tajik aluminum company) and all state corporation purchases of infrastructure, notably Gazprom's debt-equity swaps to acquire pipelines.

Russian Financial Assistance to Counter the Global Financial Crisis

The global financial crisis offered Russia new possibilities of playing a major, helpful role in the CIS. The Russian government assumed this challenge. It provided mainly cofinancing to International Monetary Fund (IMF) agreements to Armenia ($500 million), Belarus ($2 billion), Kyrgyzstan (more than $2 billion), and Moldova ($500 million). It also initiated

27. Igor Torbakov, "Russian Policymakers Air Notion of 'Liberal Empire' in Caucasus, Central Asia," EurasiaNet.org, October 27, 2003.

28. Keith Crane, D. J. Peterson, and Olga Oliker, "Russian Investment in the Commonwealth of Independent States," *Eurasian Geography and Economics* 46, no. 6 (September 2005): 405–44.

a EurAsEc financial assistance fund of $10 billion, of which Russia would contribute $7.5 billion and Kazakhstan $1 billion.[29] With its $598 billion of international currency reserves in early August 2008, Russia seemed eminently equipped to relieve its poorer neighbors.

Yet the financial assistance has caused considerable chagrin. Not very surprisingly, Russia and Ukraine never succeeded in agreeing on tentative stabilization credit of $5 billion. Belarus, Kyrgyzstan, and Moldova all complained about not getting all the money promised. Belarusian President Aleksandr Lukashenko stated publicly about the Russian leaders: "It came to the point that they came and said: You recognize Ossetia and Abkhazia and you receive $500 million."[30]

EurAsEc's financial assistance fund seems to have stayed on paper. The reasons for Russia's partial fulfillment were real disagreements, which differed in each case. Its neighbors were not very appreciative of Russia's assistance, because only about half of the promised assistance was actually disbursed.

As Vladimir Ryzhkov concluded:

> The Kremlin was not able to exploit its huge reserves that it accumulated after eight years of an oil boom by turning its economic power into political clout in the global arena. On the contrary, Russia's global standing has worsened across the board. Russia's leaders have managed to alienate even its strongest allies.[31]

China's New Expansive Role

Nature abhors vacuum, but Russia has taken this vacuum as a given. That is no longer true. The big new factor in the region is China. For a long time, China seemed exceedingly cautious and constrained. Credibly, Chinese officials claimed that their interests in the former Soviet Union were limited to political stability in Central Asia.

As the Chinese economy has surged and trade liberalization proceeded, trade has exploded between China and most of the region. Relations between China and the post-Soviet region reached new heights with the formation of the Shanghai Cooperation Organization (SCO) in 2001. It has six members: China, Russia, and four Central Asian countries, Kazakhstan, Uzbekistan, Kyrgyzstan, and Tajikistan. The SCO maintains both security and economic aspirations and has brought Central Asia much closer to China.

---

29. "Central Asia: Eurasian Economic Community to Set up Financial Crisis Fund," EurasiaNet.org, February 4, 2009.

30. "Belarus-Russia—Mutual Accusations, Trade War Cause New Crisis," Open Source Center, June 25, 2009.

31. Vladimir Ryzhkov, "Kremlin Burning Bridges with Every Neighbor," *Moscow Times*, August 4, 2009.

The significance of the SCO became evident at its summit immediately after the Russian-Georgian war of August 2008. Russia appealed for support, but nobody complied, as China offered the Central Asian states the opportunity to hide behind its back. For the first time since the war over the Ussuri River in 1969, China openly challenged Russia in its own backyard and won.

China has already built pipelines to Kazakhstan and Turkmenistan, and it is likely to seize market control in the region from Gazprom. The global financial crisis offered China—with the world's largest international currency reserves—new opportunities in the region. It has bailed out not only Central Asia but also Belarus and Moldova with larger amounts than Russia, admittedly in bilateral loans in yuan.

Thus, while the Kremlin is spoiling its relations with its neighbors in a seemingly mindless fashion contradicting Russia's national interests, China is swiftly establishing itself as the major customer for Central Asia's gas exports and other products, while it provides tens of billions of dollars of finance.[32]

The European Union's Eastern Partnership

The European Union started taking a greater interest in the former Soviet Union when its big eastern enlargement was concluded in 2004. In 2003 it launched its European Neighborhood Policy, and in 2008 it presented its Eastern Partnership, which included six CIS countries—Ukraine, Belarus, Moldova, Georgia, Azerbaijan, and Armenia.

For the time being, the European Union has accomplished little in the region, but with Ukraine it is negotiating a European Association Agreement on deep and comprehensive free trade, which will also be offered to other members of the Eastern Partnership. These agreements will offer much more than greater market access. They will also involve harmonization of rules and institutions, bringing about a potentially far-reaching integration of these six countries with the European Union. So far, Russia has chosen to stay aloof from this cooperation.

As a consequence, at least Ukraine, Georgia, Belarus, and Moldova are now increasingly being attracted to the European Union for the sake of trade and institutional convergence, though unlike Russia and China the European Union has not offered any bilateral financial support.

Russia has chosen to stand outside all this multilateral cooperation with the European Union. In 2003, when the European Union proposed its European Neighborhood Policy for both North Africa and western CIS,

32. Bobo Lo, *Axis of Convenience: Moscow, Beijing, and the New Geopolitics* (Washington: Brookings Institution, 2008); Louis O'Neill, "China Is Gaining a Foothold in Russia's Backyard," *Financial Times*, July 29, 2009.

Russia turned down the offer. Instead it wanted to negotiate a new version of the rather empty ten-year Partnership and Cooperation Agreement concluded in 1994, while the three Caucasian states insisted on becoming part of the European Neighborhood Policy. In May 2009, when the European Union adopted its Eastern Partnership Policy, Russia was never part of it, having excluded itself in advance.

Conclusion: Dissolve the CIS as a Goodwill Gesture!

In sum, Russia's policy in the former Soviet space is strikingly ineffective. The only Russian activity that has really worked has been foreign direct investment of private corporations, which has not been part of government policy. The country has failed to develop good relations with its neighbors, but the Kremlin does not seem to care. Its policy in the former Soviet space cannot be characterized as neoimperialism but as disinterest and disrespect. Russia is increasingly behaving as if it can force the CIS countries to obey, without considering their national interests, but it does not have the strength nor is it prepared to devote the resources to do so. Deterred, its neighbors turn their backs on Russia.

Russia's recognition of Abkhazia and South Ossetia left the whole region worrying about territorial integrity. Although mutual trade remains plentiful, no Russian free trade initiative can work without a mechanism for conflict resolution; only the WTO can offer the necessary institutional framework. Russia has cut lingering gas subsidies to its poorer neighbors, who are trying to reduce their dependence on Russia because it no longer offers any benefits and has proven highly unreliable through many sudden disruptions of Russian gas deliveries and embargoes on successful exports.

In the last few years, Russia has solidified its reputation as an unreliable and unpredictable partner among its neighbors, who run for the exits, leaving Russia increasingly lonely. For the time being, Russia seems to have decent relations with only Armenia and Azerbaijan, which represents an all-time low. Russia has an obvious interest in improving its tarnished international reputation. For many years, many of its neighbors have been its captive customers and suppliers because of the existing infrastructure, but that situation can change with new pipelines and roads, especially given the new interests of China and the European Union. Russia's monopoly position in the region can suddenly be lost in the same way as Britain and France lost out in their former colonies.

Therefore, Russia urgently needs a new, constructive policy toward its post-Soviet neighbors so that it does not lose out altogether. As Dmitri Trenin writes: "Russia's foreign policy needs more than a reset: it requires a new strategy and new policy instruments and mechanisms to implement it."[33] This concerns most of all Russia's policy toward its neighbors. "Russia needs to focus on overcoming its economic, social, and political backwardness—and use foreign policy as a resource to meet this supreme national interest."[34] Russia can no longer afford to pursue policies that only aggravate its relations with the whole post-Soviet space. It needs to think anew.

In fact, the many failures of Russia's policies show that the opposite needs to be done. The CIS summit in Kishinev in October 2009 should be the last summit. As a goodwill gesture to its neighbors, Russia should take the initiative to dissolve the CIS, clarifying that it does not pursue any neoimperialist designs. While dissolving the CIS, Russia should also dissolve its suborganizations, EurAsEc, the CSTO, and the CES, none of which adds value but only costs to all parties concerned.

Russia does not benefit from alienating all its post-Soviet neighbors. Its interest should be to develop as good relations, including trade, finance, and investment, as have proven possible with other neighbors. Therefore, it must convince all countries in the region that it has no territorial claims. In one way or the other, the Kremlin should play down its recognition of Abkhazia and South Ossetia in its own interest.

With regard to trade policy, the obvious solution is the WTO, which Russia should join as soon as possible. It should encourage its neighbors to do so as well to facilitate trade with them. If Russia is to stay a major gas trader in the region, it will need to undertake market-oriented gas reforms at home and reach an agreement with the broader region on a framework of gas trade, be it the Energy Charter or some new agreement. Russia needs to restore its credibility as a reliable gas supplier.

The Ukrainian presidential elections in January and February 2010 did represent a substantial improvement in Russian-Ukrainian relations. In the last presidential elections in 2004, President Putin campaigned actively in Ukraine for then presidential candidate Viktor Yanukovych, who eventually lost. This time, the Kremlin revealed its preference for Yanukovych through the official television channel but not more, and Yanukovych actually won. Former president Viktor Yushchenko's contentious bid for a NATO Membership Action Plan for Ukraine has been set aside. Prime Minister Yulia Tymoshenko's gas agreement with Prime Minister Putin in January 2009 disarmed the gas conflict. Ukraine is still pursuing a European Association Agreement and is unwilling to join the Russia-sponsored customs union, but Russian-Ukrainian relations have been dedramatized. This improvement has entirely been based on bilateral actions, without any CIS institution playing any role.

33. Dmitri Trenin, "Reimagining Moscow's Foreign Policy," *Foreign Affairs* 88, no. 6 (November/December 2009), 65.

34. Ibid., 74.

12

US-Russia Relations: Constraints of Mismatched Strategic Outlooks

ANDREW C. KUCHINS

Policy toward Russia has been one of the greatest and most controversial challenges for four administrations in Washington since the end of the Cold War. Presidents Bill Clinton and George W. Bush, whose administrations were responsible for US Russia policy for most of the period from 1993 to 2009, each devoted a great deal of time and energy toward improving ties with Moscow. Yet each left office frustrated and disappointed and with a bilateral relationship worse than at the beginning of their administrations. Given the deep acrimony and near absence of trust between Washington and Moscow when President Barack Obama entered office, one can only hope that analysts will not be drawing similar conclusions at the end of his tenure.

Given that Russia was undertaking the monumental tasks of simultaneously democratizing, developing a market economy, and changing from being an empire to a nation-state—the virtually unprecedented "triple transformation" of a great power—it should not be surprising that Russia would present a massive challenge requiring a lot of "strategic patience," as Deputy Secretary of State Strobe Talbott put it near the end of the Clinton administration. The precipitous decline in Russia's status virtually overnight from superpower to recipient of international humanitarian assistance in 1991–92 and the radical restructuring of the international system from one of bipolar confrontation to unipolar US dominance

Andrew C. Kuchins is a senior fellow and director of the Russia and Eurasia Program at the Center for Strategic and International Studies (CSIS). He is grateful for very insightful comments on an earlier draft from Anders Aslund, Thomas Graham, and Steadman Hinckley, as well as the participants at a CSIS seminar to discuss the draft in March 2010. He also acknowledges the superb research assistance provided by Heidi Hoogerbeets, Olga Blyumin, and Travis Mills.

presented enormous challenges demanding inordinate wisdom and empathy, qualities that Washington policymaking—to be fair, Washington is hardly alone—is not renowned for.

Like his predecessors, President Obama has also made improvement of relations with Moscow one of his higher foreign policy priorities, and his administration has made considerable efforts in its first year to achieve this goal. I have argued elsewhere that as long as the Obama administration keeps its expectations modest, the less likelihood there will be of disappointment.[1] My argument for low expectations is based on the view that Moscow's interests in the three key issues for the Obama administration—Iran, Afghanistan, and nuclear security—are conflicted and not fully aligned with those of the United States. Perhaps just as significantly, rightly or wrongly, the leadership in Moscow feels "burned" by previous disappointments with Washington, especially the short-lived honeymoon with the George W. Bush administration in the wake of 9/11 and collaboration to defeat the Taliban. The residue of distrust is palpable.

Despite this troubled inheritance, as this book goes to press in the spring of 2010, there is no question that the Obama administration has been considerably successful in substantially improving US-Russia relations. President Obama's policy toward Russia, in addition to addressing the three issues noted earlier, has focused on promoting the sovereignty of Russia's near neighbors after the shock of the Georgia war as well as broadening the bilateral relationship and giving it new organizational structure through the establishment of 16 working groups under the leadership of a commission led by Secretary of State Hillary Clinton and Russian Foreign Minister Sergei Lavrov.[2] The most tangible "deliverable" so far has been the successful conclusion of the negotiations over the Strategic Arms Reduction Treaty (START I) replacement treaty signed by Presidents Obama and Dmitri Medvedev in Prague on April 8. The reversal of trajectory of the bilateral relationship is a significant achievement for which Moscow and Washington should be commended. However, major constraints remain in the relationship.

Most fundamentally, for now, Moscow and Washington hold incompatible strategic outlooks and threat assessments. US strategic interests and concerns have moved considerably beyond the eurocentric focus of the Cold War to instability in the Islamic world, how to manage the rapid development of Chinese power and global challenges of nonproliferation, terrorism, climate change, and others. Even though Russia, which tenu-

---

1. Andrew Kuchins, "The Obama Administration's 'Reset Button' for Russia," in *The Obama Moment: European and American Perspectives,* ed. Alvaro de Vasconcelos and M. Zaborowski (Paris: European Union Institute for Security Studies),187–99.

2. President Obama articulated his Russia policy in an impressive speech delivered at the New Economic School in Moscow on July 7, 2009; see Remarks by the President at the New Economic School Graduation, July 7, 2009, www.whitehouse.gov.

ously clings to great power status and privileges, is more vulnerable to many of these persisting and emerging global challenges, its security policy remains burdened by its enduring fixation on the United States and the West more broadly as the source of greatest threat. Until there is greater congruity in their strategic outlooks, cooperation between Moscow and Washington will remain painstakingly labor intensive. Given the plethora of major domestic and foreign policy challenges for the Obama administration, it is not clear how much political capital the US president will be ready to invest in a fairly intransigent and declining power in Moscow.

The Obama Administration's "Reset Button" for Russia: Back to Pragmatic Engagement and Multilateralism

In the last year of the George W. Bush administration, US-Russia relations reached their lowest point since the 1980s. The relationship was fraught with major cleavages over Kosovo's independence, NATO enlargement, and plans for deployment of missile defense "third site" components in the Czech Republic and Poland. Communication between Washington and Moscow virtually ceased after the war in Georgia in August 2008. But the breakdown in relations in the second half of 2008 was years in the making. The brief honeymoon in the fall of 2001 after 9/11 rapidly eroded with a series of conflicting issues highlighting both different interests and absence of trust despite the allegedly close personal relationship between presidents Bush and Putin. Perhaps fortunately for the beleaguered US-Russia relationship after the Georgia war, US and world attention was quickly overwhelmed in September 2008 by the global economic crisis, the repercussions of which contributed to the election of Barack Obama as president of the United States.

Obama assumed the presidency in January 2009 facing the greatest challenges of any US president since Franklin Delano Roosevelt during the Great Depression in the 1930s. The global economic system was still in free fall from a financial crisis catalyzed in the United States—a dramatic difference from the last global crisis that began in Asia in 1997 and resulted in the Russian default of 1998. The United States was also mired in two very difficult wars in Afghanistan and Iraq, with security in the former deteriorating rapidly. Putin's view that the unipolar moment was over found many supporters around the world, including in the United States. Obama promised a return to multilateralism in US foreign policy and assumed the demeanor of a pragmatic and deliberate problem solver facing some daunting challenges—a striking turn away from his neoconservative predecessor.

Whatever one thought about the origins of the Georgia war, a growing consensus in the moderate or pragmatic middle of the US political spectrum on both sides of the aisle viewed this if not as evidence of failure of US policy toward Russia and Eurasia, then at least as evidence that something had gone badly awry and needed to be corrected. Regime transformation looked far from imminent in Russia, and the growing centrist consensus in Washington argued for a more constructive relationship with Russia to deal more effectively with growing regional and global challenges.

Three compelling factors principally drive the interests of the Obama administration in improving ties with Russia, a policy metaphorically first described by Vice President Joe Biden in February 2009 as "pressing the reset button": (1) the heightened urgency of resolving the Iranian nuclear question; (2) the need for additional transport routes into Afghanistan to support larger US military presence; and (3) a return to a more multilateral approach to ensuring nuclear security and strengthening the nonprolif- eration regime. Broader global policy goals of the administration, includ- ing addressing the climate change challenge, energy security, health, and others, also require heightened cooperation with Russia, but urgency is not as intense as with the three main issues.

Critics on the left and the right in Washington argued that Russia was either too weak for or fundamentally antagonistic toward Obama's an- ticipated efforts to woo the Russians. The deeper concern has been that the Obama administration might be willing to compromise core values and interests to secure Russian support on the above issues. Russia's near neighbors are particularly sensitive to Washington's possibly compromis- ing their interests.[3]

The Washington policy community in the winter and spring of 2009 issued a plethora of reports and analyses calling for improved relations with Russia.[4] Critics of one of the most noteworthy of the reports, the

---

3. For example, see the policy brief issued by the German Marshall Fund just after the Obama trip to Moscow in July 2009: Pavol Demes, Istvan Gyarmati, Ivan Krastev, Kadri Liik, Adam Rotfel, and Alexandr Vondra, "Why the Obama Administration Should Not Take Central and Eastern Europe for Granted," Policy Brief (Washington: German Marshall Fund, July 13, 2009), www.gmfus.org.

4. See *The Right Direction on U.S. Policy toward Russia*, commonly known as the Hart-Hagel Report (Commission on US Policy toward Russia, Washington: Belfer Center for Science and International Affairs and Nixon Center, March 2009). Reports calling for improved relations with Russia and consulted in Anders Åslund and Andrew Kuchins, "Pressing the Reset Button," in *The Russia Balance Sheet* (Washington: Peterson Institute for International Economics and Center for Strategic and International Studies, 2009) include Steven Pifer, "Reversing the Decline: An Agenda for U.S.-Russian Relations in 2009," Brookings Policy Paper 10 (Washington: Brookings Institution, January 2009); Stephen Sestanovich, "What Has Moscow Done? Rebuilding U.S.-Russian Relations," *Foreign Affairs* 87, no. 6 (November/ December 2008), 12–28; Henry A. Kissinger and George P. Shultz, "Building on Common Ground With Russia," *Washington Post*, October 8, 2008; Michael McFaul's testimony to the House Committee on Foreign Affairs, US-Russia Relations in the Aftermath of the Georgia Crisis, 110th Congress, 2nd session, 2008, 50–58; Rose Gottemoeller, "Russian-American Security Relations After Georgia," Carnegie Endowment for International Peace Policy Brief no. 67 (Washington: Carnegie Endowment for International Peace, October 2008); and Dmitri

Hart-Hagel Commission, categorized many of the recommendations for improved ties with Russia as "realist" compromises of American values of liberty and democracy.[5] This critique, however, misses the crux of the reason why Eastern and Central European neighbors are especially nervous. The problem, as captured in the recent German Marshall Fund brief,[6] is that Russia is mostly a status quo power globally, but in its neighborhood it is a revisionist power. No American administration can give Russia what it wants without committing political suicide: an acknowledgement of "privileged relations" or a "sphere of influence" in its neighborhood. If that circle cannot be squared, the future of US-Russia relations is bleak.

Unfortunately for US policymakers, however, the core problem in US-Russia relations today is deeper than US differences over the post-Soviet space, although Moscow's obsession with geopolitical competition with Washington there is symptomatic. The root of the problem is Moscow's failure to accurately identify threats to Russian interests in a rapidly changing international environment. Without accurate assessment of the threats, the current Russian leadership cannot develop policies that facilitate rather than retard Russia's reemergence as a great power in a multipower world—the leadership's repeatedly stated core foreign policy goal.

Russia's Relative Strategic Decline and Core Miscalculation

The demise of the Soviet Union is the most decisive setback for Russian control over territory in modern history. Explaining why gets to the crux of the challenges in Moscow's current strategic environment. For the first time since its emergence from the dark forests of Muscovy, Russia finds itself surrounded by states and political groupings that are economically, demographically, and politically more dynamic than itself.[7]

The most obvious case is the rapid growth of China in the East. China's rise and Russia's fall over the past 30 years are the starkest in a short period during peacetime for any two neighboring great powers in modern history. To its South, India has sprinted by Russia to try to keep pace

Trenin, "Thinking Strategically About Russia," Carnegie Endowment for International Peace Policy Brief no. 71 (Washington: Carnegie Endowment for International Peace, December 2008).

5. See, for example, Lev Gudkov, Igor Klyamkin, Georgy Satarov, and Lilia Shevtsova, "False Choices for Russia," *Washington Post*, June 9, 2009, www.washingtonpost.com.

6. Demes et al., "Why the Obama Administration Should Not Take Central and Eastern Europe for Granted."

7. For an excellent articulation of this phenomenon, see Thomas Graham, "The Sources of Russian Insecurity," *Survival* 52, no. 1 (February-March 2010): 55–74.

with its main peer competitor, China. While the Muslim world remains deeply cleaved, the power of political Islam is also exposing vulnerabilities of Russia. The European economic and political union, a process that through ebbs and flows has moved forward, has proven far more attractive to Russia's neighbors. Finally, while the Kremlin gleefully documents and seemingly encourages the erosion of America's unipolar moment in spasmodic fits of schadenfreude, Russia's strategic decline has been continuing for nearly three decades.

While Russia's strategic decline is bad news, the good news is that, unlike during the Soviet period, none of the great powers against which Moscow's power has relatively declined find promotion of Russian weakness, let alone disintegration, remotely in their interests. However, the Russian government not only seems willfully blind to this but in fact promotes a contrary view based on the alleged threat of the United States and the West. The thorniest problem for US-Russia relations remains the totally anachronistic assumption that US power, especially as manifest via NATO enlargement and missile defense deployments in Europe, constitutes the greatest threat to Russian security. This assumption is the unmistakable core thrust of the "new" Russian military doctrine released by the Kremlin in February 2010.[8] The conceptual framework for this document seems more apt for the strategic environment of the Soviet Union in 1970 than the Russian Federation in 2010. Not only is threat identification misplaced but so is the identification of the key international institutions supposedly most useful for advancing Russian interests in the world: the Commonwealth of Independent States (CIS), the Collective Security Treaty Organization (CSTO), and the Shanghai Cooperation Organization (SCO). It is almost as if the Russian National Security Council exists in some strategic virtual world with Alice in Wonderland. NATO General Secretary Anders Fogh Rasmussen was absolutely right in describing Russia's military doctrine as not reflecting the real world and based on "a very outdated notion of the nature and role of NATO...." But he was further correct in pointing out that "we can't let this hold the whole relationship with Russia to ransom."[9]

Obama's Three Core Motivations for the "Reset Button"

In the latter section of this chapter I examine more closely the progress made in the past year in improving US-Russia relations, with close attention to cooperation on preventing Iran from acquiring nuclear weapons

---

8. Dmitri Medvedev, "Ukaz Prezidenta Rossiiskoi Federatsii ot 5 Fevralya 2010 g. N 146 'O Voennoi doktrine Rossiiskoi Federatsii'" ["Presidential decree N 146 of the 5 February 2010 on the war doctrine of the Russian Federation"], February 5, 2010, www.mil.ru.

9. "Russia's New Military Doctrine Is Outdated, NATO Chief Says," *Moscow Times*, March 15, 2010, www.themoscowtimes.com.

capability, stabilizing Afghanistan, and reenergizing bilateral and global nuclear security and nonproliferation cooperation. In each area, progress has been achieved, but I argue that it has been slower and more painstaking because of powerful forces in the Russian political system that continue to view the United States as the principal threat.

Iran

The Iranian nuclear and ballistic missile programs have been, along with differences over their shared neighborhood, the most persistent bones of contention between Russia and its Western partners since the collapse of the Soviet Union. In an effort to avert near-term challenges posed by Iran's nuclear program, Russian and European governments continue to urge Tehran to comply with UN Security Council resolutions to suspend its enrichment and reprocessing activities. While Russia joined with other UN Security Council members in supporting sanctions in 2006 and 2007, it remains an unenthusiastic backer of punitive measures, and Russian diplomats often work to weaken proposed sanctions.

The urgency for Washington to resolve the challenge of the Iranian nuclear program is great as Tehran has already demonstrated the capability to enrich uranium, and the capacity to weaponize this material is not far off. Russian efforts in recent years to serve as an intermediary with Tehran—e.g., a proposal to take back spent fuel to Russian territory—were tacitly supported by the Bush administration, but ultimately they were unsuccessful. Moscow's leverage with Tehran is very limited, and the Russians have shown signs of being nearly as frustrated with Iran's intransigence on the nuclear question as the Americans and Europeans. The Obama administration promised a new approach to engage Tehran in direct negotiations, but this has not been possible since the disputed Iranian presidential elections in June 2009.

While there has always been a link between missile defense plans and Iran, the Obama administration made this linkage more explicit to Moscow since taking office in January 2009. This topic was reportedly in a not-so-secret letter from newly inaugurated President Obama to Russian President Medvedev in February: the less of a threat Iran poses, the less theaterwide missile defense capabilities in Europe will be needed, thus giving greater incentive for Moscow to exercise more leverage on Tehran.[10] In the second half of September 2009, there was dramatic movement on issues tied to missile defense and the Iranian threat.

First, on September 17 the Obama administration abruptly announced plans to scrap the Bush administration's proposed antiballistic missile shield consisting of a missile-tracking radar facility in the Czech Republic

10. See Peter Baker, "In Secret Letter, Obama Offered Deal to Russia," *New York Times*, March 3, 2009, www.nytimes.com.

and 10 ground-based interceptors in Poland in favor of smaller Standard Missile-3 (SM-3) interceptors deployed on land and aboard warships using the sea-based Aegis system to shoot down short- and medium-range Iranian missiles. The administration justified this new, reconfigured system citing more rapid development of Iranian short- and medium-range ballistic missiles; lack of evidence of significant progress in its long-range missiles (ICBMs), which the Bush administration's system was more suited for; technical developments in alternative missile defense components; timeliness of system deployment; and cost factors. The administration emphasized this decision was not made because of Russian objections to the Bush administration's proposal but understood the Russians would receive it positively.

The second development concerns the dramatic revelation on September 24 by President Obama, announced with French President Nicolas Sarkozy and British Prime Minister Gordon Brown, that US intelligence sources confirmed that Iran had built another uranium enrichment facility near the city of Qom, which had not been revealed to the International Atomic Energy Agency (IAEA) in a timely manner, thus constituting a clear violation of its obligations to the Non-Proliferation Treaty. It is widely believed that the Russian government and its intelligence services were unaware of this facility and only learned about it from Washington.

While the Bush administration may or may not have overestimated how much Moscow could do to support the United States on Iran, the consensus in the Obama administration is that Moscow has very little leverage over Tehran. Principally, Obama wants Moscow's support on any UN Security Council decision for much tougher sanctions on Iran; Washington also hopes the support from Moscow may help China reconsider its position on sanctions so as not to be isolated from the five permanent members of the Security Council.

The United States has defined the possibility of Iran acquiring nuclear weapons capabilities an "existential threat," and Iran has been the most problematic issue in US-Russia relations for more than a decade. For Russia, a nuclear-armed Iran is clearly not an existential threat. It is not Moscow's preferred outcome, but the Russians are not prepared to sacrifice significant treasure, let alone blood, to try to prevent the Iran "threat." The Russians often justify their position by their belief that Tehran would never target Russia, and since it is mainly a threat to the United States and Israel, they should take the responsibility for preventing it.

A modified perception of its interests should make Moscow more concerned about the Iranian nuclear weapons program and thus more active in preventing it rather than persistently hedging. First, the assumption that Iranian nuclear missiles would never be targeted toward Moscow is dubious and likely wishful thinking. One would think Moscow would be more concerned by Turkey, Saudi Arabia, Egypt, and even other states and actors near Iran's borders possibly developing nuclear weapons capabilities in response to Iran. Russia's core security vulnerability is the volatile and mostly Islamic Northern Caucasus. Given Russia's own internal security vulnerabilities, Moscow might have even more incentive than the United States and its European allies to prevent further proliferation in the Islamic world. Russia's struggle with preventing terrorist attacks on its own territory over the past decade suggests that a catastrophic terrorist attack would be easier to carry out in Russia than in Europe or the United States.

If history is a guide, however, the Russians will seek to create the impression they are supporting the Obama administration while making every effort to water down efforts of the United Nations to take a tougher and more unified stance. The Russians have been successful in the past in "working with" the international community while maintaining their interests with Tehran. Such a strategy may not be possible this time, and finally Moscow may be forced to make a clearer decision to support the United States and the West to isolate Iran.

It would be especially interesting to see what China would do if Russia were to make a clear-cut decision to support tough sanctions on Iran. While Beijing has been perfectly happy to stand behind Moscow's vocal opposition on this and a number of other issues promoted by Washington, over the past year China has become far more confident and more willing to independently oppose US interests and policies. Some US officials have privately told me that Iran is the litmus test for the success or failure of the US-Russia relationship, but that is not the case for the US-China relationship. This is a stark indication of China's growing leverage in ties with the United States and declining importance of Russia in Washington.

Afghanistan and the Northern Distribution Network

Many Russian government officials as well as nongovernmental experts believe that Afghanistan is the most promising area for US-Russia cooperation.[11] Indeed, it was on Afghanistan in the fall of 2001 that US-Russian security and intelligence cooperation probably reached its high point in the post-Soviet period. US attention to Afghanistan has renewed in the context of the deteriorating security environment there as well as the reduction of violence in Iraq.

As a presidential candidate in 2008, Obama promised to deploy more US forces in Afghanistan. Because of increasing problems on the Afghani-

---

11. I travelled to Moscow four times in 2009 (February, April, June, and July) to consult with government officials as well as nongovernment experts on Afghanistan and broader US-Russia relations. There was a strong consensus that it is on Afghanistan that US and Russian security interests most coincide.

stan-Pakistan border, in the second half of 2008, US Central Command (CentCom) began to explore the possibility of opening a transit corridor from the north into Afghanistan, which came to be called the Northern Distribution Network (NDN).[12] Even if US force presence remained stable, opening the NDN would likely be required, but with increased troop presence, the required goods and materiel for the troops are estimated to grow by up to three times in 2010.[13]

The opening of the NDN increased the attention of US policymakers to Central Asia and the Caspian as well as Russia. As initially conceived, the NDN will be composed of two transit corridors. NDN North starts in the port of Riga, where goods are loaded into rail cars for shipment through Russia, Kazakhstan, and down to Heraton on the Uzbek-Kazakh border. NDN South would come in through the Caspian to either Kazakhstan or Turkmenistan then to Uzbekistan. The NDN rail route from Riga to Afghanistan became operational in the spring of 2009. Trains were making the trip to the Uzbek-Afghan border in only nine days with full support from Russia and Kazakhstan. Privately, US government officials laud Russian cooperation to expedite the trains.

Russian intentions, however, have been far more questionable on the issue of US access to Manas, the air base in Kyrgyzstan from which the US military had been transiting troops and goods into that country since 2001. In early February 2009, Kyrgyz President Kurmanbek Bakiev announced that the United States would lose access to Manas at virtually the same time as the Russians and Kyrgyz reached agreement on an economic assistance package of $2.25 billion.[14] While the Russian government denied any link between the base decision and the loan package, there was widespread speculation that the loan was contingent on Bishkek closing the base to the Americans.

Negotiations with Kyrgyzstan continued into June 2009 until Washington and Bishkek finally reached agreement to allow the United States to use Manas as a "transit center," paying more than three times the previous rent. The agreement was reached shortly before Obama's trip to Moscow in early July, but questions remained about the extent to which Moscow supported this decision.[15]

---

12. I met with CentCom planners to discuss NDN in May 2009.

13. Ibid. See Andrew Kuchins, Thomas Sanderson, David A. Gordon, and contributor S. Frederick Starr, *The Northern Distribution Network and the Modern Silk Road: Planning for Afghanistan's Future* (Washington: Center for Strategic and International Studies, December 2009).

14. See Clifford Levy, "Kyrgyzstan: At the Crossroad of Empires, a Mouse Struts," *New York Times*, July 25, 2009, www.nytimes.com.

15. See Oleg Schedrov, "Kyrgyzstan Agreed to US Base Deal with Russia-Source," Reuters, June 24, 2009, www.reuters.com.

In the run-up to the Moscow summit, US government officials were pleasantly surprised when the Russian government raised the idea of reaching agreement on transportation of lethal materials over Russian airspace.[16] Although not a high priority of the Pentagon at the time, the agreement on transit of lethal materials over Russian airspace was acclaimed in both Washington and Moscow as the most significant achievement of the July meetings in Moscow between Obama and Medvedev.

For US policymakers, Moscow's influence on Kyrgyzstan's decision about Manas highlights the question whether Moscow views supporting allied efforts in Afghanistan as a higher priority than maintaining and extending its own military influence on Central Asian neighbors. Later in the summer of 2009 Moscow lobbied for the CSTO to agree to establish a military base in Osh located in the volatile Ferghana Valley in Kyrgyzstan. Uzbekistan adamantly opposed it, so the agreement for the base was reached on a bilateral basis between Bishkek and Moscow. Tashkent views the establishment of this base as a security threat to Uzbekistan, and policymakers there are very skeptical about Russian policy in the region and even whether Moscow would like to see Afghanistan stabilized.[17]

Moscow's focus on the United States as the principal threat to its security interests is jeopardizing advancement of its power and influence in Afghanistan and more so in the Central Asian states between Russia and Afghanistan. Moscow seems overly concerned about the temporary US military presence in the region. It should be more concerned about the dramatically changing geoeconomic balance of power in Central Asia, where it is rapidly losing ground to China. Two events in 2009 highlight Russia's strategic miscalculation. First was the failed effort to buy off Kyrgyzstan with loans and credit in return for Bishkek denying Washington access to the military air base in Manas. Second was the Russians' loss of near monopoly control of Turkmen gas exports with the opening of the China-Turkmenistan gas pipeline. Russia's soft power comparative advantages of language, culture, and personal relationships are virtually nullified by its clumsy, intimidating, and ultimately self-defeating policies, and the principal beneficiary is China.

---

16. That this agreement was Moscow's initiative has been confirmed in the author's private discussions with US officials in Washington and Moscow. The NDN is designed to facilitate the transit of nonlethal goods, which constitute more than 80 percent of what the US forces require, and all of the goods are shipped on a commercial basis.

17. In private discussions with very high-level government officials in Tashkent in July 2009, the view was expressed that Moscow prefers to see Afghanistan unstable so as both to justify Russian military presence in Central Asia and to prevent Central Asian states from accessing global markets through southern transit corridors. See Andrew C. Kuchins and Thomas Sanderson, "Northern Exposure in Central Asia," *New York Times*, August 4, 2009, www.nytimes.com.

Nuclear Security and Nonproliferation: The Return of Arms Control

Many policy experts in Washington before and after the Obama administration assumed office argued that nuclear security and nonproliferation are areas where the Obama and Medvedev administrations should be able to "press the reset button."[18] Even though Russia has become more reliant on its nuclear arsenal due to deteriorating conventional forces in the 1990s, the continued aging of its nuclear arsenal leads Moscow to be interested in deeper cuts in strategic weapons.

In his speech in Prague in April 2009, President Obama announced that his administration would be committed to making significant progress toward "zero" nuclear weapons in the world. President Medvedev endorsed this goal in his speech in Helsinki in the spring of 2009, and the two presidents agreed in London in April that their negotiating teams would convene discussions for a replacement to START I, which was due to expire in December 2009.

Given the pressing time constraints to negotiate, the START replacement treaty called for a fairly modest reduction in offensive arms and launchers while maintaining many of the monitoring and verification measures of the original START. The Russians indicated that to get to deeper cuts, there would have to be some agreement about the limitations of ballistic missile defenses as Moscow was concerned that the combination of deep cuts, US developments in missile defenses, and powerful conventional weapons with near-nuclear capabilities would upset the strategic balance. Both Moscow and Washington also agreed that in order to make greater strategic reductions below a certain level, bilateral negotiations would have to become multilateral to include the other nuclear weapons states.

Progress in negotiations over the past year on the new START treaty was initially quite brisk, and on March 26, 2010 President Obama could announce that he and President Medvedev had reached a new agreement. The limits of strategic offensive arms are 800 launchers and 1,550 deployed warheads seven years after entry into force of the treaty and thereafter.[19] Differences over verification measures, sharing of missile telemetry, and role of missile defenses in the treaty were the last issues to be settled. During the negotiations, Obama administration officials expressed frustration that when the two presidents met or talked, conclusion seemed imminent, but when negotiators sat down, the Russian position had toughened, as if the Russian government was not singing from the same song sheet and/

---

18. For example, see Anders Åslund and Andrew Kuchins, "Pressing the Reset Button in US-Russia Relations," in *The Russia Balance Sheet* (Washington: Peterson Institute for International Economics and Center for Strategic and International Studies, 2009), 139–63.

19. For details on the treaty, see Key Facts about the New START Treaty, March 26, 2010, www.whitehouse.gov.

or they believed they had more leverage in the negotiations because of the perception that the Obama administration "needed" it more.

Another lingering nuclear arms control problem is intermediate-range weapons, those with ranges of 500 to 5,000 kilometers. The 1987 Intermediate-Range Nuclear Forces (INF) Treaty bans the two countries from developing, manufacturing, or deploying ground-launched ballistic and cruise missiles with these ranges. Russian dissatisfaction with the INF Treaty stems in part from how this bilateral agreement uniquely discriminates against Russia and the United States. In October 2007, Putin warned that Moscow would find it difficult to continue complying with the INF Treaty unless other countries ratified the agreement as well. Washington and Moscow subsequently agreed jointly to encourage other countries to join the INF Treaty, but their efforts have fallen on deaf ears. The most serious concern for Moscow in this regard is China, and privately Russian officials express frustration with the lack of transparency in their "strategic partner."

Russia's strategic miscalculation about the United States being its principal threat has prevented Moscow from developing a more enlightened and self-interested policy on nuclear security. The recently published Russian military doctrine categorically states that maintaining nuclear parity with the United States is imperative, yet the entire document says nothing about China, including its nuclear program. Given China's geographic proximity and hundreds of intermediate-range missiles, which could reach Russian territory, one can argue that Moscow should be just as concerned about being vulnerable to Beijing as to the United States. The best way this vulnerability can be mitigated is if US-Russia bilateral nuclear reductions progress rapidly so that international multilateral negotiations can start and hopefully reveal Chinese strategic nuclear plans and developments.

While the interests of Washington and Moscow may not be as closely aligned on the three issues as one would like, I strongly argue that on all three major security priorities for the Obama administration, Moscow's interests and policies are closer to the United States than to Beijing. Perhaps more overt recognition of this situation on the part of Washington and Moscow may facilitate more US-Russia cooperation. By no means am I advocating a China containment policy, but certainly Moscow could advance its interests with a more balanced and accurate assessment of its strategic challenges and potential threats.

Conclusion

Despite the tumultuous, nearly two-decade post–Cold War history in US-Russia relations, one dramatic conclusion is that Russia does not matter nearly as much for Washington's strategic goals today; the same can be said of the United States for Russia. The United States no longer considers Russia a strategic adversary, and Washington's 20th century eurocentric focus is rapidly shifting to East Asia and the Greater Middle East as well as to global challenges such as climate change and infectious diseases. Unfortunately, however, as I argue in the first part of this chapter, Russia continues to view the United States more as a strategic adversary than partner, and its strategic focus remains highly eurocentric. While in principle Washington and Moscow share some common concerns about the threat of radical Islam and terrorism in the Greater Middle East and the implications of the rise of China in the East, their security paradigms are far from being in sync.

The ongoing shift in the global balance of power to a genuinely multipolar structure contrasts the relative strategic decline of Russia, the United States, Europe, and Japan with the dramatic rise of China and to a lesser extent India. Russia's strategic decline dates back nearly three decades and is by far the most precipitous despite the boom years of Putin's presidency. The peak of US power may well have been at some point during the first term of George W. Bush. Fighting wars in Afghanistan and Iraq has proven far more challenging after initial successes, but the most worrisome development for US power in the world is economic in nature; specifically, fiscal irresponsibility on a massive scale. If the US political system does not soon muster the will to decisively address what looks now to be long-term unsustainable deficits, US power may erode more quickly and add considerable stress to the stability of an already fragile global order. Russia, meanwhile, will face gargantuan tasks of modernization to stem its own strategic decline. Perhaps this new environment will encourage Moscow and Washington to find a more constructive *modus operandi* in the challenging years ahead.

Ultimately, when Russia genuinely takes its own economic modernization goals seriously, the unsustainability of a security policy based on the West as the primary threat will be exposed and the policy adjusted. Russia's most important partner in achieving its best case "innovation scenario"—as articulated in the core economic goals to 2020—is the West, first and foremost Europe, but the United States and Japan have key roles to play as well.[20] That Moscow continues to promote a foreign policy strategy in which its most important economic partners by far are simultaneously members of a security alliance—NATO—that is supposedly its greatest security threat borders on the absurd. NATO General Secretary Rasmussen is absolutely correct in asserting that security ties between the West and Russia cannot be allowed to remain hostage to Moscow's obsolete view of its threat environment, but one also must be realistic and

---

20. See Andrew Kuchins, Amy Beavin, and Anna Bryndza, *Russia's 2020 Strategic Economic Goals and the Role of International Integration* (Washington: Center for Strategic and International Studies, 2008).

understand that until the Russian leadership clearly discards this view, efforts to work together, particularly in the US-Russia bilateral context, will remain quite limited.

The Obama administration has been successful in improving ties with Moscow and can point to several areas of tangible progress and cooperation. It can also point to things that did not happen, such as another war in Georgia in 2009 as some feared. In addition, the administration has made some progress in broadening the bilateral dialogue with the establishment of a range of working groups on health, counternarcotics, and others. But the administration must at the same time be prepared to ratchet down prioritization of the relationship in the event of Russian intransigence. The current Russian leadership appears to be operating under the illusion that Washington "needs" Moscow more than the other way around. The logic of my argument leads to the opposite conclusion if Moscow were to adjust its strategic outlook to be more consistent with its goals of modernization and prosperity. The Obama administration should also be more vocal in rebutting the false assumptions of Russia's strategic outlook that identify the United States and the West as its greatest threat. Such assumptions on the part of Russia not only are detrimental to the bilateral relationship but also support a deeply corrupt, dysfunctional domestic political system.

13

Russia's Course: Viable in the Short Term but Unsustainable in the Long Term

ANDERS ÅSLUND, SERGEI GURIEV, AND ANDREW C. KUCHINS

The Russia Balance Sheet series assesses Russia's major assets and liabilities. In this second book we take the reader through a discussion of Russia's economy, political system, innovation system, energy sector, military, and foreign policies and relations. Unlike the first book, which was written during the global economic crisis of 2008–09, we completed this book when it was clear that the crisis was over. This is a good time to check the pulse, as Russia and the rest of the world have just faced a huge shock, allowing us to assess the real state of affairs. This is also a good time to take a long-term view, which is the purpose of compiling any balance sheet—be it for a company or a country.

This book concludes that Russia is doing well in the short run. It is highly unlikely that Russia will run out of cash, both literally and figuratively. Russia faces no public finance crisis, and its current account surplus remains impressive. Russia's international currency reserves peaked at $598 billion in August 2008 and were at $436 billion in mid-March 2010, still the third largest in the world. With all its deficiencies, the system has come out of crisis virtually unscathed and has shown that it can function under extreme stress. Russia has weathered a perfect storm of oil price decrease, reversal of capital flows, and political isolation following the war with Georgia. Nor has the Russian political system fallen apart. As the oil price is rising ever higher, the next couple of years will certainly be much easier than the fall of 2008. Although the Russia-Georgia conflict remains,

Anders Åslund has been a senior fellow at the Peterson Institute for International Economics since 2006. Sergei Guriev is rector of and Morgan Stanley Professor of Economics at the New Economic School. Andrew C. Kuchins is a senior fellow and director of the Russia and Eurasia Program at the Center for Strategic and International Studies (CSIS).

little new drama has been added, and other global events have overshadowed Russia's recognition of Abkhazia and South Ossetia. Russia's short-term prospects appear neither dramatic nor problematic.

Yet, the other major lesson that a reader can draw from the book is that Russia is facing huge structural challenges in the long run. The analysis in this book shows that the current system has exhausted its potential. Some authors argue that the system has been successful and has solved many problems while others suggest it was flawed to start with. In some aspects, the system has evolved and is completely different from what it used to be, while in others it has come full circle. Yet, all conclude that the current system is no longer suitable for the challenges ahead and is facing a dead end; it is not sustainable in the long run and must change. This conclusion is for the economy, politics, rule of law, the gas behemoth Gazprom, the Commonwealth of Independent States (CIS), foreign relations in general, foreign economic relations, and military reform.

The discussion in this book is reminiscent of the one in the 1970s about how the Soviet Union would transition from "extensive" growth based on the mobilization of resources to "intensive" growth founded on increased efficiency and productivity. The big difference is while reform of the Soviet economic system was not possible, reform of current state capitalism is. The chapters lay out specific agendas for change. In some cases reform has already started. In particular, military reform is under way, and efforts to deregulate business and promote innovation are also being undertaken. If Russia is to succeed in the long run, however, it needs comprehensive change and needs it urgently.

Are the changes sufficient for Russia's prosperity? The good news is that Russia still has substantial assets—natural resources and human capital—and huge potential for further change: The economy is ridden with inefficiencies, energy is continued to be wasted, and Gazprom remains an inept behemoth. These changes are not going to be easy but if they happen, Russia will still be able to realize the true value of its assets, which will bring enormous benefits both for Russians and for the rest of the world.

An issue that this book touches upon only tangentially is political stability. Daniel Treisman's thorough study of presidential popularity in Russia over the last two decades reveals that economic performance is its dominant driver. Although the two political leaders' popularity has declined slightly during the last one and a half years of crisis, the decrease has been remarkably small. This can be interpreted in several ways. Perhaps the Kremlin has been successful in managing its image through controlled state television programming and extensive social transfers. An alternative interpretation is that popular dissatisfaction is growing but has not yet been fully expressed. Admittedly, new instances of social unrest have come to the surface, but so far they have been marginal.

One of the several serious structural problems that this book identifies is the nature of Russia's federalism, as Ekaterina Zhuravskaya illuminates in her chapter. It is one of the fundamental barriers to social development that has to be broken in line with modernization theory. In terms of economic development, Russia is at the upper bound from where, as Samuel Huntington indicated, a country would transition to full democracy. Indeed, all countries that are richer than Russia in terms of per capita GDP are democracies or small oil states, with tiny Singapore being the only exception.

Another broad area of structural concern is corruption, rule of law, state regulation of enterprise, and innovation. Timothy Frye shows that corruption has not abated after 2000 but become somewhat worse. The economic consequences of the poor business environment and corruption are severe. Big companies are given an unfair advantage over small firms, hampering the latter's development, whereas in the West, small businesses are the innovators. The fact that the total length of Russia's paved roads was slightly shorter in 2008 than in 1997 best illustrates the costs of poor governance. This long-promised development of infrastructure has failed spectacularly because of corruption.

Keith Crane and Artur Usanov provide similar evidence from Russian high-technology sectors. Apart from the software industry, high technology is concentrated in large state corporations, which—judging by Western experience—are unlikely to generate innovation. President Dmitri Medvedev has spelled out this dilemma: "Centuries of corruption have debilitated Russia from time immemorial. Until today this corrosion has been due to the excessive government presence in many significant aspects of economic and other social activities."[1]

One of Russia's great problems is its demography, which we discussed in the first book, *The Russia Balance Sheet*. President Medvedev has said it all: "Every year there are fewer and fewer Russians. Alcoholism, smoking, traffic accidents, the lack of availability of many medical technologies, and environmental problems take millions of lives. And the emerging rise in births has not compensated for our declining population."[2] The need for improvement on all these fronts remains.

In recent years, much of the public discussion in Russia has concerned the country's energy curse. The classic contribution on this topic is late Yegor Gaidar's book *Collapse of an Empire: Lessons for Modern Russia*.[3] In effect, Gaidar warned that the Putin regime could end as the Brezhnev

---

1. Dmitri Medvedev, "Go Russia," September 10, 2009, www.kremlin.ru (accessed on March 19, 2010).

2. Ibid.

3. Yegor Gaidar, *Collapse of an Empire: Lessons for Modern Russia* (Washington: Brookings Institution, 2007).

regime did, because the apparent achievements relied to a great extent on energy rents. This theme is the main thread in the lead chapter by Sergei Guriev and Aleh Tsyvinski. Their argument is that with an oil price of $70 to $80 per barrel, Russia will be like it was in the 1970s and 1980s. President Medvedev has warned against excessive dependence on energy rents: "Achieving leadership by relying on oil and gas markets is impossible."[4]

At present, the predominantly private oil industry in Russia is in splendid shape. For the first time, Russia is both the biggest producer and exporter of oil in the world. The state-dominated gas industry, by contrast, is in serious crisis, as Anders Åslund discusses in his chapter on Gazprom. Because of the gas glut in Europe, gas prices are likely to stay depressed. Also, Russia has great potential for energy saving, which Samuel Charap and Georgi Safonov explore in their chapter. As a consequence, Russia's gas rents, and energy rents in general, are likely to be much lower for a long time. This development would be advantageous for the country's future. It is true that energy accounts for two-thirds of Russia's exports at present, but not more than one-fifth of its GDP, so Russia is not an extreme petrostate.

The most curious element in the current Russian society is its military reform. This reform is truly radical, which Minister of Defense Anatoly Serdyukov is pursuing against furious resistance from the officer corps. Although this topic is subject to substantial public debate, as Pavel Baev shows in his chapter, it is still surprisingly low key in Russia. The problems of military reform are multiple and complex—insufficient financing, inconsistencies, military resistance, and poor armaments industry—but whatever the outcome, the Russian military will change for the better.

Four chapters in this book are devoted to foreign policy, two of them to pure foreign policy and two to foreign economic policy. All these chapters conclude that the current Russian foreign policy does not make much sense. Dmitri Trenin puts the current Russian dilemma starkly in his chapter's title: modernization or marginalization. The essence of his argument is that Russia should not oppose the West. Instead, Russia should aspire to emulate and join the West. Russia does not have the resources to pursue a separate course, nor would it make much sense.

David Tarr and Natalya Volchkova show that Russia has much to gain from accession to the World Trade Organization, which would spur Russia's modernization, while Russia has little to gain from the development of a customs union with Kazakhstan and Belarus, which would instead represent Russia's marginalization. In his obituary on the post-Soviet space, Åslund shows that Russia is not succeeding in building any new alliance with even close post-Soviet partners, who instead prefer to keep a distance from Russia's overbearing presence. He argues that Russia would benefit from winding up the CIS and all its suborganizations,

---

4. Medvedev, "Go Russia."

which increasingly are being perceived as a threat to the sovereignty of these newly independent states. Russia's relations would be better and more beneficial with a different policy.

The bottom-line for the Russia Balance Sheet project is its implications for US-Russia relations, which Andrew Kuchins discusses in the last chapter. Current strategic outlooks for Russia and the United States vary greatly, arguably much more than they should. President Barack Obama has gone out of his way to reset US-Russia relations. The key line in his big Russia speech at the New Economic School on July 7, 2009, was, "America wants a strong, peaceful, and prosperous Russia."[5] The US-Russia relationship has considerably improved since its low point during the Russia-Georgia war in August 2008, but its potential remains unfulfilled. Kuchins puts the main blame on the Kremlin for incorrectly believing that Washington needs Moscow more than the other way around and persisting in its belief that the United States is the greatest threat to Russia.

The Russian leadership has a great opportunity to change things for the better. On the one hand, it is evident that the current economic model cannot deliver sufficient growth in the next several years and the main problems are obvious. On the other hand, the Russian regime does not face any apparent immediate internal or external threat. Therefore, the Russian government can launch reforms if it so desires. Yet reforms always involve costs, not least to the insiders. The big question for the next couple of years is whether the stark analysis of Russia's shortcomings, which have been expressed by none other than the president of Russia himself, will prompt adequate reforms.

5. Remarks by the President at the New Economic School Graduation, July 7, 2009, www. whitehouse.gov (accessed on March 19, 2010).

About the Contributors

Anders Åslund is a leading specialist on Russia and postcommunist economic transformation with more than 30 years of experience in the field. In the mid-1980s, he worked as a Swedish diplomat in Moscow, which led him to boldly predict the fall of the Soviet communist system in his book *Gorbachev's Struggle for Economic Reform* (1989). He was one of the chief economic advisers to President Boris Yeltsin's reform government (1991–94) and concluded in *How Russia Became a Market Economy* (1995) that Russia had made its market choice. In *Russia's Capitalist Revolution* (2007) he explained why Russia's market reform succeeded and democracy failed. He has written a total of nine books, including *The Russia Balance Sheet* (with Andrew C. Kuchins, 2009), *How Capitalism Was Built: The Transformation of Central and Eastern Europe, Russia, and Central Asia* (2007) and *How Ukraine Became a Market Economy and Democracy* (2009). He is the editor or coeditor of 15 books.

Åslund joined the Peterson Institute for International Economics as senior fellow in 2006. He also teaches at Georgetown University. He was the director of the Russian and Eurasian Program at the Carnegie Endowment for International Peace (2003–05) and codirector of the Carnegie Moscow Center's project on Post-Soviet Economies. He was founding director of the Stockholm Institute of Transition Economics and professor at the Stockholm School of Economics (1989–94). He earned his doctorate from the University of Oxford.

Pavel K. Baev is a research professor at the International Peace Research Institute, Oslo (PRIO). He is also affiliated with the Centre for the Study of Civil War at PRIO. He served at a research institute in the USSR Defense Ministry, which he left in August 1988 to join the Institute of Europe, Moscow. He joined PRIO in October 1992. In 1995–2001, he was the editor of PRIO's quarterly journal *Security Dialogue*, and in 1998–2004, he was a member of the PRIO Board. His research on the transformation of the Russian military is supported by the Norwegian Defence Ministry; other research interests include the energy and security dimensions of the Russian-European relations and post-Soviet conflict management in the Caucasus and the greater Caspian area. His latest book is *Russian Energy Policy and Military Power* (London: Routledge, 2008). He received an MA degree in political geography from Moscow State University in 1979 and a PhD in international relations from the Institute of USA and Canada, USSR Academy of Sciences, in May 1988.

Samuel Charap is a fellow in the National Security and International Policy Program at the Center for American Progress. He focuses on the domestic politics, political economy, and foreign policies of the former Soviet states and US policy in the region. His work has been published in the *Washington Quarterly, International Herald Tribune, Current History, Moscow Times,* and several other journals and newspapers. His commentary has appeared in numerous news outlets, including the *Washington Post*, BBC Television, and NPR. He has provided advice on regional affairs to political risk advisory firms, US government officials, and congressional staff. He was a visiting scholar at the Carnegie Moscow Center and the International Center for Policy Studies (Kyiv) and a Fulbright Scholar at the Moscow State Institute of International Relations. Charap holds a doctorate in political science and a master's degree in Russian and East European studies from the University of Oxford, where he was a Marshall Scholar. He received his BA from Amherst College.

Keith Crane is director of the RAND Corporation's Environment, Energy, and Economic Development Program. He served on the Energy and Political and Economic Working Groups of US-EU Partnership Committee for Ukraine chaired by Zbigniew Brzezinski and Volker Rühe and on the Economy and Reconstruction Working Group for the Baker-Hamilton Iraq Study Group (2006). In fall 2003, he was an economic policy advisor to the Coalition Provisional Authority in Baghdad.

Before rejoining RAND in February 2002, Crane was chief operating officer and director of research at PlanEcon, Inc., a Washington-based research and consulting firm focusing on Central and Eastern Europe and the former Soviet republics. He was an adjunct professor in the Department of Economics at Georgetown University in 2001–02 and in the George Mason University public policy program between 1998 and 2000. He has served as a faculty member of the RAND-UCLA Center for the Study of Soviet International Behavior and as a Fulbright Professor at the Central School of Planning and Statistics in Warsaw, Poland. He writes extensively on transition issues and international economics in policy and academic journals. Crane received his PhD in economics from Indiana University in 1983.

Timothy Frye is Marshall D. Shulman Professor of Post-Soviet Foreign Policy at Columbia University and director of the Harriman Institute. His research and teaching interests are in comparative politics and political economy with a focus on the former Soviet Union and Eastern Europe. He is the author of *Brokers and Bureaucrats: Building Markets in Russia* (Michigan Press 2000), which won the 2001 Hewett Prize from the American Association for the Advancement of Slavic Studies, and *Incredible Transformation: Building States and Markets after Communism* (forthcoming, Cambridge University Press). He is currently working on a book manuscript, *Property Rights and Property Wrongs: What Russia Teaches Us About the Rule of Law.* He was a consultant for the World Bank, the European Bank for Reconstruction and Development, and the US Agency for International Development. He received a BA in Russian language and literature from Middlebury College, an MIA from the School of International and Public Affairs at Columbia University, and a PhD also from Columbia University in 1997.

Sergei Guriev is the Morgan Stanley Professor of Economics at and rector of the New Economic School in Moscow. He is also the president of the Center for Economic and Financial Research at the New Economic School. He teaches graduate courses in microeconomic theory, contract theory, and economics of strategy. His research interests include contract theory, corporate governance, and labor mobility.

In 2006, the World Economic Forum named Guriev a Young Global Leader. He has published in international refereed journals including *American Economic Review, Journal of European Economic Association, Journal of Economic Perspectives*, and *American Political Science Review*. Since 2007, he has been contributing a monthly column to *Forbes Russia*. He is also a biweekly columnist for the leading Russian business daily *Vedomosti*. He obtained his PhD in 1994 from the Russian Academy of Sciences.

Andrew C. Kuchins, an expert on Russian foreign and domestic policies, is a senior fellow and director of the Russia and Eurasia Program at the Center for Strategic and International Studies (CSIS). From 2000 to 2006, he was a senior associate at the Carnegie Endowment for International Peace, where he was director of its Russian and Eurasian Program 2000 to 2003 and again in 2006, and director of the Carnegie Moscow Center in Russia from 2003 to 2005. He has also held senior management and research positions at the John D. and Catherine T. MacArthur Foundation, Stanford University, and the University of California at Berkeley.

Kuchins teaches at Johns Hopkins School of Advanced International Studies (SAIS) and has also taught at Georgetown and Stanford Universities. Recently published books, articles, and reports include *Economic Whiplash in Russia: An Opportunity to Bolster U.S.-Russia Commercial Ties?* (CSIS, 2009) and *Alternative Futures for Russia to 2017* (CSIS, 2007). His latest book (coauthored with Anders Åslund), *The Russia Balance Sheet*, was published in April 2009. He holds a BA from Amherst College and an MA and PhD from Johns Hopkins SAIS.

Georgi V. Safonov is the director of the Center for Environmental and Natural Resource Economics at the State University–Higher School of Economics in Moscow. He has been a member of the official Russian delegation and observer organizations at the conferences and meetings of the United Nations Framework Convention on Climate Change since 1999. He is the author of over 80 scientific and analytical publications on the environmental economics, international and Russian climate policy, and carbon market development. He graduated from the Higher School of Economics in Moscow in 1996. His PhD thesis was on modeling of carbon emissions and climate change mitigation policy in Russia.

David G. Tarr is a consultant and former lead economist with the World Bank and adjunct professor of international economics at the New Economic School, Moscow. He has worked in more than 20 countries providing trade policy advice. His research interests include the link between liberalization of barriers in services and growth and poverty reduction (with applications in Tanzania and Kenya), World Trade Organization accession (with applications in Russia, Kazakhstan, and Ukraine), assessing the impact of diverse interrelated regional integration agreements (with applications in Chile, Brazil, Ukraine, Russia, Tanzania, and Kenya), and assessing the impact of trade liberalization with heterogeneous firms. He has authored more than 60 refereed journal articles and written or edited 11 books or monographs and over 100 other professional papers.

Daniel Treisman is a professor of political science at the University of California, Los Angeles, His research focuses on Russian politics and economics and comparative political economy. His articles have appeared in leading political science and economics journals, including the *American Political Science Review, World Politics, American Economic Review,* and *Journal of Economic Perspectives,* as well as the public affairs journals *Foreign Affairs* and *Foreign Policy.* He has published two books about Russian politics, one coauthored by Andrei Shleifer. His latest book, *The Return: Russia's Journey from Gorbachev to Medvedev,* will be published by the Free Press in November 2010. In 2007–08, he served as lead editor of the *American Political Science Review* and is currently a coeditor of the journal.

Treisman was educated at Oxford University (BA Hons, 1986) and Harvard University (PhD, 1995) and has received fellowships from the Guggenheim Foundation, the Hoover Institution (Stanford), the German Marshall Fund of the United States, and the Smith Richardson Foundation.

Dmitri Trenin, director of the Carnegie Moscow Center, has been with the center since its inception. From 1993 to 1997, Trenin held posts as a senior research fellow at the NATO Defense College in Rome and a senior research fellow at the Institute of Europe in Moscow. He served in the Soviet and Russian armed forces from 1972 to 1993, including working as a liaison officer in the External Relations Branch of the Group of Soviet Forces (stationed in Potsdam) and as a staff member of the delegation to the US-Soviet nuclear arms talks in Geneva from 1985 to 1991. He also taught at the war studies department of the Military Institute from 1986 to 1993. Trenin received his PhD from the Institute of the USA and Canada in 1984.

Aleh Tsyvinski, one of the youngest tenured full professors in the history of Yale University, is a professor of economics there and codirector of the Macroeconomics Research Program at the Cowles Foundation. He is also a professor by courtesy at the New Economic School in Moscow and a research fellow at the National Bureau of Economic Research. He was an associate professor at Harvard University's Department of Economics. He is a visiting scholar at the Einaudi Institute for Economics and Finance, a research and policy institute of Banca d'Italia, and was a regular visiting scholar at the Federal Reserve Bank of Minneapolis.

In 2009, the World Economic Forum selected Tsyvinski as a Young Global Leader. His research has been recognized by numerous awards, including a five-year CAREER award from the National Science Foundation. He is also the recipient of the Alfred P. Sloan Research Fellowship. He has published widely in all the top economics journals. He contributes a bi-weekly column, "Ratio Economica," to the editorial page of *Vedomosti*, a Russian business and political daily, and to economic policy debates, with recent editorials appearing in *Il Sole 24 Ore*, Project Syndicate, and *New Times*. He received a PhD in economics from the University of Minnesota.

Artur Usanov is completing his doctoral studies in policy analysis at the Pardee RAND Graduate School. He was chief executive of the Regional Economic Development Agency, a policy research institution in Kaliningrad, Russia, and project manager at the East West Institute. He also taught at the Kaliningrad State Technical University and the Kaliningrad International Business School. He received an MBA with distinction from the London Business School and an MS in engineering with distinction from the Kaliningrad Technical University.

Natalya Volchkova has been an assistant professor of economics at the New Economic School since 2007. She is also a core member of the Centre for Economic and Financial Research at New Economic School, which she joined when it was founded in 2000, and serves as its policy director. In this capacity, she conducts applied research for various Russian ministries and agencies, the Central Bank of Russia, and the World Bank. In 2008,

Volchkova was awarded the Fulbright scholarship and was a visiting scholar at Harvard University in 2008–09. She was a visiting researcher at the Massachusetts Institute of Technology in 2001–02. She has published articles in the *Journal of Finance* and Russian economic journals and coauthored chapters in books on the Russian economy. She earned her PhD from the Central Economic and Mathematic Institute of Russian Academy of Science in 2000.

Ekaterina Zhuravskaya is the Hans Rausing Professor of Economics at the New Economic School. She is also the academic director of the Center for Economic and Financial Research in Moscow, conducting research in political economics, public economics, development economics, and economics of transition. Her academic work has been published in several refereed journals. Zhuravskaya won the Young Economists Competition of the fifth Nobel Symposium in Economics, "The Economics of Transition," in 1999. She was named a Global Leader for Tomorrow by the World Economic Forum in Davos in 2001 and received the Best Economist prize by the President of the Russian Academy of Science in 2002 and 2003. She is an associate editor of the *Journal of Public Economics* and *Journal of Comparative Economics* and served as panel member in the *Economic Policy*. She received her PhD in economics from Harvard University in 1999.

About the Organizations

Center for Strategic and International Studies

At a time of new global opportunities and challenges, the Center for Strategic and International Studies (CSIS) provides strategic insights and policy solutions to decision makers in government, international institutions, the private sector, and civil society. A bipartisan, nonprofit organization headquartered in Washington, DC, CSIS conducts research and analysis and develops policy initiatives that look into the future and anticipate change. **www.csis.org**

Peter G. Peterson Institute for International Economics

The Peter G. Peterson Institute for International Economics is a private, nonprofit, nonpartisan research institution devoted to the study of international economic policy. Since 1981 the Institute has provided timely and objective analysis of, and concrete solutions to, a wide range of international economic problems. It is one of the very few economics think tanks that are widely regarded as "nonpartisan" by the press and "neutral" by the US Congress, it is cited by the quality media more than any other such institution, and it was selected as Top Think Tank in the World for 2008 in the first comprehensive survey of over 5,000 such institutions.

The Institute, which has been directed by C. Fred Bergsten throughout its existence, attempts to anticipate emerging issues and to be ready with practical ideas, presented in user-friendly formats, to inform and shape public debate. Its audience includes government officials and legislators, business and labor leaders, management and staff at international organizations, university-based scholars and their students, other research institutions and nongovernmental organizations, the media, and the public at large. It addresses these groups both in the United States and around the world.

The Institute's staff of about 50 includes more than two dozen senior fellows, who are widely viewed as one of the top groups of economists at any research center. Its agenda emphasizes global macroeconomic topics, international money and finance, trade and related social issues, energy and the environment, investment, and domestic adjustment policies. Current priority is attached to the global financial and economic crisis, globalization (including its financial aspects) and the backlash against it, international trade imbalances and currency relationships, the creation of an international regime to address global warming and especially its trade dimension, the competitiveness of the United States and other major countries, reform of the international economic and financial architecture, sovereign wealth funds, and trade negotiations at the multilateral, regional, and bilateral levels. Institute staff and research cover all key regions—especially Asia, Europe, Latin America, and the Middle East, as well as the United States itself and with special reference to China, India, and Russia.

Institute studies have helped provide the intellectual foundation for many of the major international financial initiatives of the past two decades: reforms of the International Monetary Fund (IMF), including those initiated by the G-20 in 2009; adoption of international banking standards and broader financial regulatory reforms; exchange systems in the G-7 and emerging-market economies; policies toward the dollar, the euro, the Chinese renminbi, and other important currencies; and responses to debt and currency crises (including the crisis of 2008–09). The Institute has made important contributions to key trade policy decisions including the Doha Round, the restoration and then extension of trade promotion authority in the United States, the Uruguay Round and development of the World Trade Organization, the North American Free Trade Agreement (NAFTA) and other US free trade agreements (notably including Korea), the Asia Pacific Economic Cooperation (APEC) Forum and East Asian regionalism, initiation of the Strategic Economic Dialogue between the United States and China, a series of United States–Japan negotiations, reform of sanctions policy, liberalization of US export controls and export credits, and specific issues such as permanent normal trade relations (PNTR) for China in 2000, import protection for steel, and Buy American legislation in 2009.

Other influential analyses have addressed economic reform in Europe, Japan, the former communist countries, and Latin America (including the Washington Consensus), the economic and social impact of globalization and policy responses to it, outsourcing, electronic commerce, corruption, foreign direct investment both into and out of the United States, global warming and international environmental policy, and key sectors such as agriculture, financial services, steel, telecommunications, and textiles.

The Institute celebrated its 25th anniversary in 2006 and adopted its new name at that time, having previously been the Institute for International Economics. It moved into its new building in 2001, which was given an Award of Excellence for Extraordinary Achievement in Architecture by the American Institute of Architecture and a Best Architecture in Washington Award by the *Washington Business Journal*. **www.piie.com**

New Economic School

The New Economic School (NES), an independent graduate school of economics in Moscow, was established in 1992 to introduce modern economics into Russia as a critical part of the transition to a market economy. The mission of NES is to benefit Russia's private and public sectors through excellence in economics education and research. The School offers two-year graduate level programs in economics and finance, similar to programs in top Western institutions. Most NES faculty have received their PhDs in the leading US and European universities and published in top international academic journals. NES is consistently ranked as the top economics institution in postcommunist countries and is among the top five in non-OECD countries. **www.nes.ru**

The Russia Balance Sheet
Advisory Committee

Leon Aron, American Enterprise Institute
Anders Åslund, Peterson Institute for International Economics
David Bailey, ExxonMobil
William Beddow, Caterpillar
C. Fred Bergsten, Peterson Institute for International Economics
Steve Biegun, Ford Motor Company
Zbigniew Brzezinski, Center for Strategic and International Studies
Michael Calvey, Baring Vostok Capital Partners
Sarah Carey, Squire, Sanders & Dempsey
Edward Chow, Center for Strategic and International Studies
Ariel Cohen, Heritage Foundation
Keith Crane, Rand Corporation
Dorothy Dwoskin, Microsoft Corporation
Thomas Graham, Kissinger Associates
Michael Green, Center for Strategic and International Studies
John Hamre, Center for Strategic and International Studies
Fiona Hill, Brookings Institution
Carla Hills, Hills & Company
Gary Clyde Hufbauer, Peterson Institute for International Economics
Andrei Illarionov, Cato Institute
Neville Isdell, formerly Coca-Cola
Bruce Jackson, Project on Transitional Democracies
Oakley Johnson, AIG
Steven Kehoe, PepsiCo
Henry Kissinger, Center for Strategic and International Studies
Andrew C. Kuchins, Center for Strategic and International Studies

Cliff Kupchan, Eurasia Group
Eugene Lawson, APCO Worldwide
Randi Levinas, US-Russia Business Council
Jack F. Matlock, Jr., Princeton University
Michael Mandelbaum, Johns Hopkins University, School of Advanced
  International Studies
Sarah Mendelson, Center for Strategic and International Studies
Scott Miller, Procter & Gamble
Sam Nunn, US Senate (ret.) and Nuclear Threat Initiative
Thomas Pickering, Hills & Company
Steven Pifer, Brookings Institution
Charles Ryan, UFG Asset Management
Diana Sedney, Chevron
Stephen Sestanovich, Council on Foreign Relations
Andrew Somers, American Chamber of Commerce in Moscow
Angela Stent, Georgetown University
John Sullivan, Center for International Private Enterprise (CIPE)
Dmitri Trenin, Carnegie Moscow Center
Judyth Twigg, Virginia Commonwealth University
Edward Verona, US-Russia Business Council

Index

Information and Communications
Technology Development Index
(International Telecommunications
Unions), 104, 104*t*
information technology–business process
outsourcing (IT-BPO) market, 101.
See also software and information
technology services
infrastructure
lack of, 25
modernization of, 142, 196
INF (Intermediate-Range Nuclear Forces)
Treaty, 253
Ingushetia, 192
institutional reforms, 30
during postcommunist period, 50
WTO accession and, 221–22
Institutional Revolutionary Party (PRI)
[Mexico], 71, 77
insurance, 208
Intel, 103
intellectual property rights, 101, 120, 213
Interior Ministry, 92–93
Intermediate-Range Nuclear Forces (INF)
Treaty, 253
International Atomic Energy Agency
(IAEA), 248
international climate policy, 130–34, 149–50,
199
international community, WTO accession
impact, 220–22
International Energy Agency, 160
internationalization of Russian firms, 12
International Monetary Fund (IMF), 28,
236–37
International Telecommunications Unions,
Information and Communications
Technology Development Index, 104,
104*t*
International Uranium Enrichment Center,
108
investment, foreign. *See* foreign direct
investment
investment decisions, rule of law and,
88–89, 89*t*
Iran
arms exports to, 118
US-Russia relations and, 244, 247–49
Iraq War, 254
IT. *See* software and information technology
services
IT-BPO (information technology–business
process outsourcing) market, 101

Ivanov, Sergei, 170, 175, 182

Jackson-Vanik Amendment, 202, 214–15
Japan
foreign policy, 198
gas supplies, 156
"lost decade," 22, 23*b*–24*b*, 38
Journal of Nano and Microsystem Techniques,
106
judicial reform, 82–83, 94

Kalmykia, Republic of, 75–76
Kazakhstan, 194
agricultural subsidies, 211
attitude toward Russia, 227
Chinese influence in, 237–38
CIS membership, 225
customs union, 191, 194, 202, 213–14,
232–33
Jackson-Vanik Amendment, 215
Northern Distribution Network, 250–51
Khodorkovsky, Mikhail, 92, 191
Khrushchev, Nikita, 82, 172
KIT Finance, 16
Korea, 198
Kovykta gas field, 165
Kyoto Protocol, 130–32, 136
Kyrgyzstan, 190, 191
attitude toward Russia, 227
Chinese influence in, 237–38
colored revolution, 228–29
financial assistance, 236–37

labor, 101, 203
Lamy, Pascal, 233
language, 196
large companies, privatization of, 34
Latvia, 225
law enforcement. *See also* corruption; police
force; rule of law
energy efficiency policy, 146
Law on Energy Efficiency, 144–45, 145*b*
Law on Foreign Investment in Strategic
Sectors, 217–18, 222
Law on Natural Monopolies, 217
legal disputes
with federal government, 88–89, 89*t*
with regional government, 86–89
political connections and, 90–91, 91*t*
legal institutions, 86–89
legal reforms, 79–83, 92–94
Levada Center, 42, 83
life satisfaction, 13

Other Publications from the Peterson Institute for International Economics

Japan in the World Economy*
Bela Balassa and Marcus Noland
1988   ISBN 0-88132-041-2
America in the World Economy: A Strategy
for the 1990s*   C. Fred Bergsten
1988   ISBN 0-88132-089-7
Managing the Dollar: From the Plaza to the
Louvre*   Yoichi Funabashi
1988, 2d. ed. 1989   ISBN 0-88132-097-8
United States External Adjustment and the
World Economy*   William R. Cline
May 1989   ISBN 0-88132-048-X
Free Trade Areas and U.S. Trade Policy*
Jeffrey J. Schott, editor
May 1989   ISBN 0-88132-094-3
Dollar Politics: Exchange Rate Policymaking
in the United States*
I. M. Destler and C. Randall Henning
September 1989   ISBN 0-88132-079-X
Latin American Adjustment: How Much Has
Happened?*   John Williamson, editor
April 1990   ISBN 0-88132-125-7
The Future of World Trade in Textiles and
Apparel*   William R. Cline
1987, 2d ed. June 1999   ISBN 0-88132-110-9
Completing the Uruguay Round: A Results-
Oriented Approach to the GATT Trade
Negotiations*   Jeffrey J. Schott, editor
September 1990   ISBN 0-88132-130-3
Economic Sanctions Reconsidered (2
volumes) Economic Sanctions Reconsidered:
Supplemental Case Histories
Gary Clyde Hufbauer, Jeffrey J. Schott, and
Kimberly Ann Elliott
1985, 2d ed. Dec. 1990   ISBN cloth 0-88132-115-X
                         ISBN paper 0-88132-105-2
Economic Sanctions Reconsidered: History
and Current Policy   Gary Clyde Hufbauer,
Jeffrey J. Schott, and Kimberly Ann Elliott
December 1990   ISBN cloth 0-88132-140-0
                         ISBN paper 0-88132-136-2
Pacific Basin Developing Countries: Prospects
for Economic Sanctions Reconsidered: History
and Current Policy   Gary Clyde Hufbauer,
Jeffrey J. Schott, and Kimberly Ann Elliott
December 1990   ISBN cloth 0-88132-140-0
                         ISBN paper 0-88132-136-2
Pacific Basin Developing Countries: Prospects
for the Future*   Marcus Noland
January 1991   ISBN cloth 0-88132-141-9
                         ISBN paper 0-88132-081-1
Currency Convertibility in Eastern Europe*
John Williamson, editor
October 1991   ISBN 0-88132-128-1
International Adjustment and Financing: The
Lessons of 1985-1991*   C. Fred Bergsten, editor
January 1992   ISBN 0-88132-112-5
North American Free Trade: Issues and
Recommendations*   Gary Clyde Hufbauer and
Jeffrey J. Schott
April 1992   ISBN 0-88132-120-6
Narrowing the U.S. Current Account Deficit*
Alan J. Lenz
June 1992   ISBN 0-88132-103-6

The Economics of Global Warming
William R. Cline
June 1992   ISBN 0-88132-132-X
US Taxation of International Income:
Blueprint for Reform   Gary Clyde Hufbauer,
assisted by Joanna M. van Rooij
October 1992   ISBN 0-88132-134-6
Who's Bashing Whom? Trade Conflict in High-
Technology Industries   Laura D'Andrea Tyson
November 1992   ISBN 0-88132-106-0
Korea in the World Economy*   Il SaKong
January 1993   ISBN 0-88132-183-4
Pacific Dynamism and the International Eco-
nomic System*   C. Fred Bergsten and
Marcus Noland, editors
May 1993   ISBN 0-88132-196-6
Economic Consequences of Soviet
Disintegration*   John Williamson, editor
May 1993   ISBN 0-88132-190-7
Reconcilable Differences? United States-Japan
Economic Conflict*   C. Fred Bergsten and
Marcus Noland
June 1993   ISBN 0-88132-129-X
Does Foreign Exchange Intervention Work?
Kathryn M. Dominguez and Jeffrey A. Frankel
September 1993   ISBN 0-88132-104-4
Sizing Up U.S. Export Disincentives*
J. David Richardson
September 1993   ISBN 0-88132-107-9
NAFTA: An Assessment   Gary C. Hufbauer and
Jeffrey J. Schott/rev. ed.
October 1993   ISBN 0-88132-199-0
Adjusting to Volatile Energy Prices
Philip K. Verleger, Jr.
November 1993   ISBN 0-88132-069-2
The Political Economy of Policy Reform
John Williamson, editor
January 1994   ISBN 0-88132-195-8
Measuring the Costs of Protection in the
United States   Gary Clyde Hufbauer and
Kimberly Ann Elliott
January 1994   ISBN 0-88132-108-7
The Dynamics of Korean Economic
Development*   Cho Soon
March 1994   ISBN 0-88132-162-1
Reviving the European Union*
C. Randall Henning, Eduard Hochreiter, and
Gary Clyde Hufbauer, editors
April 1994   ISBN 0-88132-208-3
China in the World Economy   Nicholas R. Lardy
April 1994   ISBN 0-88132-200-8
Greening the GATT: Trade, Environment,
and the Future   Daniel C. Esty
July 1994   ISBN 0-88132-205-9
Western Hemisphere Economic Integration*
Gary Clyde Hufbauer and Jeffrey J. Schott
July 1994   ISBN 0-88132-159-1
Currencies and Politics in the United States,
Germany, and Japan   C. Randall Henning
September 1994   ISBN 0-88132-127-3
Estimating Equilibrium Exchange Rates
John Williamson, editor
September 1994   ISBN 0-88132-076-5

Managing the World Economy: Fifty Years after Bretton Woods   Peter B. Kenen, editor
September 1994   ISBN 0-88132-212-1
Reciprocity and Retaliation in U.S. Trade Policy   Thomas O. Bayard and Kimberly Ann Elliott
September 1994   ISBN 0-88132-084-6
The Uruguay Round: An Assessment*
Jeffrey J. Schott, assisted by Johanna Buurman
November 1994   ISBN 0-88132-206-7
Measuring the Costs of Protection in Japan*
Yoko Sazanami, Shujiro Urata, and Hiroki Kawai
January 1995   ISBN 0-88132-211-3
Foreign Direct Investment in the United States, 3d ed.,   Edward M. Graham and Paul R. Krugman
January 1995   ISBN 0-88132-204-0
The Political Economy of Korea-United States Cooperation*   C. Fred Bergsten and Il SaKong, editors
February 1995   ISBN 0-88132-213-X
International Debt Reexamined*
William R. Cline
February 1995   ISBN 0-88132-083-8
American Trade Politics, 3d ed.   I. M. Destler
April 1995   ISBN 0-88132-215-6
Managing Official Export Credits: The Quest for a Global Regime*   John E. Ray
July 1995   ISBN 0-88132-207-5
Asia Pacific Fusion: Japan's Role in APEC*
Yoichi Funabashi
October 1995   ISBN 0-88132-224-5
Korea-United States Cooperation in the New World Order*   C. Fred Bergsten/Il SaKong, eds.
February 1996   ISBN 0-88132-226-1
Why Exports Really Matter!*   ISBN 0-88132-221-0
Why Exports Matter More!*   ISBN 0-88132-229-6
J. David Richardson and Karin Rindal
July 1995; February 1996
Global Corporations and National Governments   Edward M. Graham
May 1996   ISBN 0-88132-111-7
Global Economic Leadership and the Group of Seven   C. Fred Bergsten and C. Randall Henning
May 1996   ISBN 0-88132-218-0
The Trading System after the Uruguay Round*
John Whalley and Colleen Hamilton
July 1996   ISBN 0-88132-131-1
Private Capital Flows to Emerging Markets after the Mexican Crisis*   Guillermo A. Calvo, Morris Goldstein, and Eduard Hochreiter
September 1996   ISBN 0-88132-232-6
The Crawling Band as an Exchange Rate Regime: Lessons from Chile, Colombia, and Israel   John Williamson
September 1996   ISBN 0-88132-231-8
Flying High: Liberalizing Civil Aviation in the Asia Pacific*   Gary Clyde Hufbauer and Christopher Findlay
November 1996   ISBN 0-88132-227-X
Measuring the Costs of Visible Protection in Korea*   Namdoo Kim
November 1996   ISBN 0-88132-236-9

The World Trading System: Challenges Ahead
Jeffrey J. Schott
December 1996   ISBN 0-88132-235-0
Has Globalization Gone Too Far?   Dani Rodrik
March 1997   ISBN paper 0-88132-241-5
Korea-United States Economic Relationship*
C. Fred Bergsten and Il SaKong, editors
March 1997   ISBN 0-88132-240-7
Summitry in the Americas: A Progress Report
Richard E. Feinberg
April 1997   ISBN 0-88132-242-3
Corruption and the Global Economy
Kimberly Ann Elliott
June 1997   ISBN 0-88132-233-4
Regional Trading Blocs in the World Economic System   Jeffrey A. Frankel
October 1997   ISBN 0-88132-202-4
Sustaining the Asia Pacific Miracle: Environmental Protection and Economic Integration   Andre Dua and Daniel C. Esty
October 1997   ISBN 0-88132-250-4
Trade and Income Distribution
William R. Cline
November 1997   ISBN 0-88132-216-4
Global Competition Policy
Edward M. Graham and J. David Richardson
December 1997   ISBN 0-88132-166-4
Unfinished Business: Telecommunications after the Uruguay Round
Gary Clyde Hufbauer and Erika Wada
December 1997   ISBN 0-88132-257-1
Financial Services Liberalization in the WTO
Wendy Dobson and Pierre Jacquet
June 1998   ISBN 0-88132-254-7
Restoring Japan's Economic Growth
Adam S. Posen
September 1998   ISBN 0-88132-262-8
Measuring the Costs of Protection in China
Zhang Shuguang, Zhang Yansheng, and Wan Zhongxin
November 1998   ISBN 0-88132-247-4
Foreign Direct Investment and Development: The New Policy Agenda for Developing Countries and Economies in Transition
Theodore H. Moran
December 1998   ISBN 0-88132-258-X
Behind the Open Door: Foreign Enterprises in the Chinese Marketplace   Daniel H. Rosen
January 1999   ISBN 0-88132-263-6
Toward A New International Financial Architecture: A Practical Post-Asia Agenda
Barry Eichengreen
February 1999   ISBN 0-88132-270-9
Is the U.S. Trade Deficit Sustainable?
Catherine L. Mann
September 1999   ISBN 0-88132-265-2
Safeguarding Prosperity in a Global Financial System: The Future International Financial Architecture, Independent Task Force Report Sponsored by the Council on Foreign Relations
Morris Goldstein, Project Director
October 1999   ISBN 0-88132-287-3
Avoiding the Apocalypse: The Future of the Two Koreas   Marcus Noland
June 2000   ISBN 0-88132-278-4

The United States and the World Economy:
Foreign Economic Policy for the Next Decade
C. Fred Bergsten
January 2005   ISBN 0-88132-380-2
Does Foreign Direct Investment Promote
Development?   Theodore Moran,
Edward M. Graham, and Magnus Blomström,
editors
April 2005   ISBN 0-88132-381-0
American Trade Politics, 4th ed.   I. M. Destler
June 2005   ISBN 0-88132-382-9
Why Does Immigration Divide America?
Public Finance and Political Opposition to
Open Borders   Gordon Hanson
August 2005   ISBN 0-88132-400-0
Reforming the US Corporate Tax
Gary Clyde Hufbauer and Paul L. E. Grieco
September 2005   ISBN 0-88132-384-5
The United States as a Debtor Nation
William R. Cline
September 2005   ISBN 0-88132-399-3
NAFTA Revisited: Achievements and
Challenges   Gary Clyde Hufbauer
and Jeffrey J. Schott, assisted by Paul L. E. Grieco
and Yee Wong
October 2005   ISBN 0-88132-334-9
US National Security and Foreign Direct
Investment   Edward M. Graham and
David M. Marchick
May 2006   ISBN 978-0-88132-391-7
Accelerating the Globalization of America: The
Role for Information Technology
Catherine L. Mann, assisted by Jacob Kirkegaard
June 2006   ISBN 978-0-88132-390-0
Delivering on Doha: Farm Trade and the Poor
Kimberly Ann Elliott
July 2006   ISBN 978-0-88132-392-4
Case Studies in US Trade Negotiation, Vol. 1:
Making the Rules   Charan Devereaux, Robert
Z. Lawrence, and Michael Watkins
September 2006   ISBN 978-0-88132-362-7
Case Studies in US Trade Negotiation, Vol. 2:
Resolving Disputes   Charan Devereaux, Robert
Z. Lawrence, and Michael Watkins
September 2006   ISBN 978-0-88132-363-2
C. Fred Bergsten and the World Economy
Michael Mussa, editor
December 2006   ISBN 978-0-88132-397-9
Working Papers, Volume I   Peterson Institute
December 2006   ISBN 978-0-88132-388-7
The Arab Economies in a Changing World
Marcus Noland and Howard Pack
April 2007   ISBN 978-0-88132-393-1
Working Papers, Volume II   Peterson Institute
April 2007   ISBN 978-0-88132-404-4
Global Warming and Agriculture: Impact
Estimates by Country   William R. Cline
July 2007   ISBN 978-0-88132-403-7
US Taxation of Foreign Income
Gary Clyde Hufbauer and Ariel Assa
October 2007   ISBN 978-0-88132-405-1

Russia's Capitalist Revolution: Why Market
Reform Succeeded and Democracy Failed
Anders Åslund
October 2007   ISBN 978-0-88132-409-9
Economic Sanctions Reconsidered, 3d. ed.
Gary C. Hufbauer, Jeffrey J. Schott, Kimberly
Ann Elliott, and Barbara Oegg
November 2007
          ISBN hardcover 978-0-88132-407-5
    ISBN hardcover/CD-ROM 978-0-88132-408-2
Debating China's Exchange Rate Policy
Morris Goldstein and Nicholas R. Lardy, eds.
April 2008   ISBN 978-0-88132-415-0
Leveling the Carbon Playing Field:
International Competition and US Climate
Policy Design   Trevor Houser, Rob Bradley,
Britt Childs, Jacob Werksman, and Robert
Heilmayr
May 2008   ISBN 978-0-88132-420-4
Accountability and Oversight of US Exchange
Rate Policy   C. Randall Henning
June 2008   ISBN 978-0-88132-419-8
Challenges of Globalization: Imbalances and
Growth   Anders Åslund and
Marek Dabrowski, eds.
July 2008   ISBN 978-0-88132-418-1
China's Rise: Challenges and Opportunities
C. Fred Bergsten, Charles Freeman, Nicholas R.
Lardy, and Derek J. Mitchell
September 2008   ISBN 978-0-88132-417-4
Banking on Basel: The Future of International
Financial Regulation   Daniel K. Tarullo
September 2008   ISBN 978-0-88132-423-5
US Pension Reform: Lessons from Other
Countries   Martin N. Baily/Jacob Kirkegaard
February 2009   ISBN 978-0-88132-425-9
How Ukraine Became a Market Economy and
Democracy   Anders Åslund
March 2009   ISBN 978-0-88132-427-3
Global Warming and the World Trading
System   Gary Clyde Hufbauer,
Steve Charnovitz, and Jisun Kim
March 2009   ISBN 978-0-88132-428-0
The Russia Balance Sheet   Anders Åslund and
Andrew Kuchins
March 2009   ISBN 978-0-88132-424-2
The Euro at Ten: The Next Global Currency?
Jean Pisani-Ferry and Adam S. Posen, eds.
July 2009   ISBN 978-0-88132-430-3
Financial Globalization, Economic Growth, and
the Crisis of 2007–09   William R. Cline
May 2010   ISBN 978-0-88132-4990-0
Russia after the Global Economic Crisis
Anders Åslund, Sergei Guriev, and Andrew
Kuchins, eds.
June 2010   ISBN 978-0-88132-497-6

SPECIAL REPORTS

1   Promoting World Recovery: A Statement
     on Global Economic Strategy*
     by 26 Economists from Fourteen Countries
     December 1982   ISBN 0-88132-013-7

WORKS IN PROGRESS

DISTRIBUTORS OUTSIDE THE UNITED STATES

**Australia, New Zealand,
and Papua New Guinea**
D. A. Information Services
648 Whitehorse Road
Mitcham, Victoria 3132, Australia
Tel: 61-3-9210-7777
Fax: 61-3-9210-7788
Email: service@dadirect.com.au
www.dadirect.com.au

India, Bangladesh, Nepal, and Sri Lanka
Viva Books Private Limited
Mr. Vinod Vasishtha
4737/23 Ansari Road
Daryaganj, New Delhi 110002
India
Tel: 91-11-4224-2200
Fax: 91-11-4224-2240
Email: viva@vivagroupindia.net
www.vivagroupindia.com

**Mexico, Central America, South America,
and Puerto Rico**
US PubRep, Inc.
311 Dean Drive
Rockville, MD 20851
Tel: 301-838-9276
Fax: 301-838-9278
Email: c.falk@ieee.org

Asia (*Brunei, Burma, Cambodia, China,
Hong Kong, Indonesia, Korea, Laos, Malaysia,
Philippines, Singapore, Taiwan, Thailand,
and Vietnam*)
East-West Export Books (EWEB)
University of Hawaii Press
2840 Kolowalu Street
Honolulu, Hawaii 96822-1888
Tel: 808-956-8830
Fax: 808-988-6052
Email: eweb@hawaii.edu

Canada
Renouf Bookstore
5369 Canotek Road, Unit 1
Ottawa, Ontario KlJ 9J3, Canada
Tel: 613-745-2665
Fax: 613-745-7660
www.renoufbooks.com

Japan
United Publishers Services Ltd.
1-32-5, Higashi-shinagawa
Shinagawa-ku, Tokyo 140-0002
Japan
Tel: 81-3-5479-7251
Fax: 81-3-5479-7307
Email: purchasing@ups.co.jp
*For trade accounts only. Individuals will find
Institute books in leading Tokyo bookstores.*

Middle East
MERIC
2 Bahgat Ali Street, El Masry Towers
Tower D, Apt. 24
Zamalek, Cairo
Egypt
Tel. 20-2-7633824
Fax: 20-2-7369355
Email: mahmoud_fouda@mericonline.com
www.mericonline.com

United Kingdom, Europe
(*including Russia and Turkey*)**, Africa,
and Israel**
The Eurospan Group
c/o Turpin Distribution
Pegasus Drive
Stratton Business Park
Biggleswade, Bedfordshire
SG18 8TQ
United Kingdom
Tel: 44 (0) 1767-604972
Fax: 44 (0) 1767-601640
Email: eurospan@turpin-distribution.com
www.eurospangroup.com/bookstore

**Visit our website at:
www.piie.com
E-mail orders to:
petersonmail@presswarehouse.com**